THE RESISTIBLE RISE OF ANTISEMITISM

THE *Resistible Rise*

THE MENAHEM STERN JERUSALEM LECTURES

Brandeis University Press

Historical Society of Israel

of Antisemitism

Exemplary Cases from Russia, Ukraine, and Poland

LAURA ENGELSTEIN

Brandeis University Press ⁂ Waltham, Massachusetts

Historical Society of Israel
BRANDEIS UNIVERSITY PRESS

Manufactured in the United States of America
Designed by Scott Cahoon
Typeset in Garamond Premier Pro
by Passumpsic Publishing

Library of Congress Cataloging-in Publication Data
available upon request
Hardcover ISBN: 978-1-68458-008-8
Paperback ISBN: 978-1-68458-009-5
Ebook ISBN: 978-1-68458-010-1

5 4 3 2 1

For Michael

CONTENTS

FOREWORD

Eli Lederhendler

The book that follows grew out of a series of lectures presented by Laura Engelstein, the Henry S. McNeil Professor Emerita of Russian History at Yale University, as the 2016 Jerusalem Lectures in History in Memory of Menahem Stern. The Historical Society of Israel, which sponsors this distinguished series of lectures, has made it its practice to seek out innovative scholars who are at the cutting edge of historical research. Often, lecturers and their chosen topics have been related to issues that were at the heart of Professor Stern's own scholarship. In this case, Professor Engelstein's thought-provoking foray into non-Jewish opinion on Jews and Judaism in the early to mid-twentieth century fits well within the broad conceptual range of Menahem Stern's own explorations of Jewish-non-Jewish relations and their representations in large cultural systems, as exemplified in his classic collection of *Greek and Latin Authors on Jews and Judaism*. The Historical Society of Israel is honored to present here the expanded version of Laura Engelstein's lectures, which deals with distinctive cases of non-Jews' relations to Jews in the Eastern European milieu. The book focuses on individuals who may be said to straddle and to complicate the issue, and they adumbrate what may be called "anti-antisemitism."

Laura Engelstein's seminal, bold, and provocative contributions to Russian political and cultural history are well known to anyone familiar with the field. She has delved deeply and innovatively into the history of late Imperial Russia, cultural politics, and the theoretical understanding of sexuality in history, religion, and the history of European liberal and illiberal thought from the late nineteenth through the twentieth centuries.

Engelstein, a member of the American Academy of Arts and Sciences and a corresponding fellow of the British Academy, has taught at Cornell University and at Princeton and has held distinguished fellowships at the Woodrow Wilson International Center for Scholars, the John Simon Guggenheim Foundation, the Rockefeller Foundation's Center at Bellagio, and the New York Public Library's Dorothy and Lewis B. Cullman Center for Scholars and Writers, before joining the Yale faculty in 2002. Her landmark works include *Moscow, 1905: Working-Class Organization and Political Conflict*; *The Keys to Happiness: Sex and the Search for Modernity in Fin-de-Siècle Russia*; a further exploration of sexuality, in relation to Russian popular religion, *Castration and the Heavenly Kingdom: A Russian Folktale*; as well as numerous essays and other works that span both the imperial and the post-revolutionary periods in Russian history. Some of her memorable studies in Russian intellectual and political history have appeared in her collection entitled: *Slavophile Empire: Imperial Russia's Illiberal Path*.

In particular, her most recently published book, *Russia in Flames: War, Revolution, and Civil War, 1914–1921* (Oxford University Press, 2018), is a definitive contribution to our understanding of that crucial era, now a century behind us, but still reverberating in so many ways. Indeed, it is in that book that Engelstein develops the argument that violent antisemitism—culminating in mass-scale murder and rape during the Civil War—was not simply a coincidental by-product of the chaos and struggles of wartime and revolutionary Russia. She argues, rather, that it permeated the era and was a key to understanding the general violence that doomed the imperial regime and indelibly marked the contours of the Revolution.

The present study of historical images and episodes follows naturally upon those other insightful works. In reexamining the question of "the Jews" as a political problem in twentieth-century Eastern Europe, she poses the counter-intuitive problem: How not to be an antisemite, in a social and political milieu infused with Jew-hatred? What, she asks, are we to make of public figures who, if they are to be taken at their word, sought to disavow or at least distance themselves from the worst that modern antisemitism represented and foreshadowed? How much historical credence should be given to such disavowals? How did organized Jewish mobilization against political antisemitism foment a wider discrediting of anti-Jewish ideology that, in one way or another, dialectically influenced the web of antisemitic discourse? When did the political fallout of antisemitic populism motivate Jews and non-Jews to modulate their strategies, and when, on the other hand, did liberal and pro-Jewish points of view retain the upper hand and even impose a defensive posture on those who took antagonistic positions?

The question of the shifting rhetoric and motives of her chosen public figures and intellectuals, and the way they maneuvered in a fraught political landscape, requires subtle parsing. The range of statements and actions under examination spans the principled and the expedient, alike. These are people who, in retrospect, seemed to "have it both ways" (to borrow a phrase from one of Engelstein's own works), and their ambiguity or their ability to compartmentalize their own sentiments was not entirely disingenuous.[1] The cases at hand, she argues, exemplify how antisemitism pervaded the socio-political and mental space of twentieth-century Eastern Europe. It was nonetheless also seen by many as a morally reprehensible posture, or at least a political liability from which one needed to disengage. Above all, its taint was inescapable — so much so, that even liberals and even some Jews amongst them proved unable to avoid its pitfalls.

This book exemplifies new conceptual approaches to the study of modern antisemitism. That is, beyond contemplating antisemitism and its fruits as examples par excellence of the modern era's most virulent forms of ethno-racial persecution, historians and social scientists alike are likely to benefit from taking antisemitism seriously as a complex problem in the history of human relations, and not just as an inglorious epitaph to the scourge of destruction and murder.

Moreover, while antisemitism in Russia and its successor states is familiar to all students of that history mostly from research stemming from Jewish sources and stressing the victims' perspective, it is less conventional and entirely more thought provoking to consider the entire subject as a Russian question and, indeed, also a Polish and a Ukrainian question: a question that not only perturbed the Jews and their various opponents, but also a fair number of writers and public figures whose perspectives spanned a gamut of positions — all of them imperfect, and few of them very familiar to non-specialist readers.

By parsing the limits of Russian philosemitism and its opposite, she returns to a method that has figured so prominently in much of her research, which is intriguingly calculated to upset the proverbial applecart of conventional ideas. We have grown to expect her to bring us up short, which is her way of warning us to take care the next time we are tempted to expostulate in over-generalizations. In probing the most sensitive historical issues with a delicate instrument, pointing a beam of light at the under-explored, the rare, and the unexpected, Engelstein pits specific case histories against a broad canvas of ideas and events.

Note

1. Laura Engelstein, "Having it Both Ways: Rozanov, Modernity, and the Skopcy," *Slavica Lundensia* 21 (2001): 1–15.

PREFACE & ACKNOWLEDGMENTS

Let me begin by thanking the Historical Society of Israel for inviting me to present the Menahem Stern Jerusalem Lectures in spring 2016. In particular, I am grateful to Maayan Avineri-Rebhun for her hospitality and for her patience in awaiting the final version of the talks. Miriam Eliav-Feldon has followed in her footsteps, with equal efficiency and warmth. While working on the revisions, I was fortunate to have access to the Joseph Regenstein Library at the University of Chicago, which has a magnificent collection of primary material and up-to-date sources, on the shelf and online (thanks to the Hathi Trust). The staff at Yale University's Sterling Memorial Library and in the Yale IT office (Richard Walser, in particular) supplied instant and essential backup. It is also a pleasure to acknowledge the presence of YIVO in this book —as a subject of history, a source of documentary material, and the manuscript repository of the memoir by Morris Greenfield that marks my personal connection to the subject.

When it came to revising the manuscript of the expanded lectures, my dear friend and long-time colleague, Barbara Engel, provided, heroically and meticulously, what every writer dreams of—a thoroughgoing interrogation of the draft for language, logic, organization, and ideas. If there are any weeds left in this garden, I'm the one who left them there. Irina Paperno, another old friend and colleague, applied her literary skills to the structure of the argument and demonstrated an interest in the "*pol'skii vopros*." In Jerusalem, Eli Lederhendler reviewed the almost final draft, noted some soft spots, and made useful suggestions. Sylvia Fuks Fried was of enormous support during the process of production.

The image of the tiger on our dust jacket deserves special mention. It belongs to a children's book published in Kiev and Petrograd in 1919, in the midst of the Russian Civil War, called *Di hon vos gevolt hobn a kam* (The Hen Who Wanted a Comb), illustrated by El Lissitzky (1890–1941), a prominent member of the Russian-Soviet artistic avant-garde. The image appears over a caption that reads: "*kumt aroys fun vald a tigr*" (out of the woods comes a tiger). The book and its illustrations belong to a time in which East European Jews not only suffered, but engaged as active participants in the political and aesthetic transformation in which they were caught up. Lissitzky himself evolved from an interpreter of Yiddish themes to an iconographer of the Russian Revolution. His famous Civil War poster, "Beat the Whites" (*Bei belykh*), can be read as a direct response to the White slogan: "Beat the Jews" (*Bei zhidov*). Here, the tiger is meant to symbolize the ferocity of Jewish resistance in the face of danger; the charms of traditional East European Yiddish culture; and the burst of creativity that affected Jewish artists and intellectuals as part of the modernist moment. Thanks to Jessica Seet, in Special Collections at Regenstein Library, who located a copy of the book, which was found, fittingly enough, at Princeton University. Andrea Immel, curator of Princeton's Cotsen Children's Library, graciously provided a scan.[1]

The book owes the most, however, to the influence and encouragement of my husband, Michael Geyer. He joined me in Mishkenot Sha'ananim when I gave the original lectures and continued to press me on my ideas. He remains my essential intellectual companion—and my essential companion in everything else. Michael is, in addition, the source of the book's title, courtesy of Bertolt Brecht, whose 1941 play, *Der aufhaltsame Aufstieg des Arturo Ui* (*The Resistible Rise of Arturo Ui*),[2] satirizes the rise of Adolf Hitler, deemed by many at the time and in retrospect "unstoppable." This book presents cases of resistance to supposedly "unstoppable" forces. The efforts to counteract antisemitism as a political tool, as described here, were surprisingly effective in the short term, and even the relatively longer term, though incapable of preventing the ultimate consequences of its twentieth-century rise. "Resistible" raises the question of what could have been, should have been, and was actually done.

For Jews living in the era of antisemitic mobilization a century ago, there was no "Jewish Question," merely the challenge of being Jewish, as the story of the young Morris Greenfield shows. The lectures indeed connect me to what my grandparents on both sides, my parents along with them, lived through and what they were spared.

Notes

1. Bentsiyon Raskin, *Di hon vos gevolt hobn a kam* (Kiev-Petersburg: Yidisher folks-farlag, 1919). Cotsen Children's Library, Department of Rare Books and Special Collections, Princeton University Library.

2. Bertolt Brecht, *The Resistible Rise of Arturo Ui*, trans. Ralph Manheim (London: Bloomsbury, 2014).

THE RESISTIBLE RISE OF ANTISEMITISM

INTRODUCTION

Morris Greenfield Encounters Some "Very Fine People"

MY GRANDFATHER, Morris (Moyshe) Greenfield, was born in 1886 in the village of Kopanka (today, Copanca), about twenty miles south of Bendery (Bender, Tighina), west of the Dniester River, in the imperial Russian province of Bessarabia.[1] He died in Brooklyn in 1961, leaving a short memoir recounting his early life. The manuscript was translated from the Yiddish by my mother, Phima Engelstein, his eldest child. Phima was born in 1920 in the town of Tiraspol, across the Dniester from Bendery, on the Soviet side of what had become, in March 1918, the border with Romania.[2] I spent many of my early childhood years in the company of my maternal grandparents, listening to the sound of their Yiddish, grasping intuitively much of what they said, yet never learning Hebrew or Yiddish myself and waiting to read my grandfather's story (in translation) until I was almost the age he had reached when he wrote it. By then, I had devoted much of my adult life to studying the country he had come from and the events that caused him to leave it behind.

Morris Greenfield's story describes how, by hook or by crook, he survived the First World War, the Russian Revolution, and the Russian Civil War, making it finally to the United States in 1930, in time to avoid future disasters. It depicts a world in which antisemitism was an ever-present constraint and menace, but one that offered many opportunities to maneuver around it. My grandfather did not rebel; he put his mind and talents to adapting. He was a Jewish "little man," young, clean-shaven, enterprising, and energetic. His Jewishness was a fact of life; so was antisemitism, but surprisingly often it failed to appear or failed to deter him.

Morris himself embodied a number of Jewish stereotypes, but he defied a number of others. He appreciated good treatment when it came his way and did everything, short of denying or masking his Jewishness, to make a good impression, choosing the traditional Jewish strategy of appeasing rather than confronting authority. Indifferent to politics, when faced with physical danger he fought back. His experience provides a reflection on the role of antisemitism in the life of an ordinary Jewish man through two decades of war and social turmoil, but antisemitism is far from his central concern. His is not a lachrymose tale.[3]

Despite its upbeat tone, it is a story in which Morris encounters obstacles at every step, a story that unfolded in a world of contingency, in which the authorities represented a threat, not a promise of safety. It was a world in which mobility, improvisation, and ingenuity were key to survival, not to mention success; a world in which cultural and linguistic dexterity were essential tools. Hostility to the Jews was an institutionalized feature of everyday life; goodwill depended on the personal disposition of gentiles able to dispense or withhold favor. It was the old imperial world both of intermingled cultures and elaborate barriers to integration, governed not by the rule of law, but at the ground level by communal practices and local conventions that circumvented official regulations. In moments of crisis, contenders for political power activated popular antagonisms, particularly those aimed at the Jews, undermining the informal systems of accommodation on which the imperial regime normally relied, leaving its vulnerable subjects more vulnerable even than before. It was one such moment of crisis — the fall of the autocracy — that propelled Morris Greenfield and his young family across the ocean into a world of different rules.

My grandfather's story offers a fitting introduction to the essays in this book, which consider three cases in which antisemitism constituted a challenge, not only for the Jews, but for gentiles confronted with its extreme consequences: the physical threat to an entire population embedded in their own social landscape. In each case, gentiles were compelled to take a stand; in each case the Jews themselves featured not merely as victims but as advocates for their own cause. Morris, for his part, was neither warrior nor victim, though he stood up for himself when necessary and often escaped calamity by a hair. He pressed against the limits of the possible under circumstances, both commonplace and catastrophic, on both sides of the revolutionary divide, that he could not control.

The memoir is, of course, designed for its readership — his children and grandchildren. It does not paint the Old World in dark colors or present the author's young self in a heroic light, and it resolutely avoids political issues. It fails to mention the two most egregious examples of antisemitism in this era, of which Morris could not have been unaware — the 1903 pogrom in Kishinev (Chişinău), a scant sixty miles away, constituting a local and international cause célèbre; and the scandalous Beilis Case of 1911–1913, reported in all the Russian and Yiddish newspapers. There is no moral to his story, no indictments are leveled. The mere act of writing reflected his life-long goal of acquiring the instruments of culture, becoming a person who could do more than keep the books, who could participate in the wider world on an equal footing, as a modern Jew.

This goal remained beyond his reach, attainable only by the following generations in a different place and time, but he had taken the first steps. Growing up in a small village, one of sixteen children, of whom eleven survived into adulthood, he obtained what he called his "Jewish education" from teachers who visited each year from Poland. But this was not enough. "I wanted to teach myself to write and to calculate," he explains. "Otherwise, one could not engage in commerce." Here was the first obstacle to his ambitions. Jewish children were excluded from the only Russian school in Kopanka, which was held in the church. "Not because the priest was an antisemite — on the contrary. The teachers were also fine people. We knew each other very well. They often came to our home to pass the time. It was the government that was very strict about it and frequently sent inspectors, whom the teachers feared. But both the teachers and the priest had pity on me and sneaked me in." This Orthodox priest was "a friend of the Jews. For instance, if a Jew wanted to buy a house, he could only do so under a Christian name and the priest was trusted to arrange the matter." Thanks to these village ties, the Jewish boy acquired the rudiments of the Russian language and a fine Russian script that later stood him in good stead.

The question of antisemitism thus arises early in the story, but in the form of an exception. Again and again, in the course of his adventures, often where you would most expect it, antisemitism does not show up. The army was the next testing ground. In 1907, at the age of twenty-one, Morris was drafted. His contingent was shipped by train to Vladivostok, a journey of forty-two days, he tells us. There, he remarks, "it didn't take long for us to discover there is such a thing as antisemitism." This could not have been a revelation. Perhaps he means that in Kopanka antisemitism had been easier to circumvent or ignore. Perhaps the intimate relationships of village life caused gentiles and Jews to forge neighborly attachments.

If antisemitism was attenuated in his experience of everyday life, in the army it was heightened. The military authorities were convinced that Jews were unfit for combat; also, somewhat contradictorily, they believed that Jews did not appear in sufficient numbers, evading the uniform at a greater rate than any other group. Some high-ranking officials drew the logical conclusion that Jews should be excluded altogether from the service, as they were already barred from the officer ranks. This view did not prevail, but invidious attitudes and policies were firmly in place before the Great War, when antisemitic propaganda inside and outside the armed forces only intensified.[4]

There was plenty for Morris to resent, but goodwill emerged from surprising quarters. His company commander noticed his quick answers to questions, his command of Russian, and his "beautiful handwriting," and engaged him as a bookkeeper. Once in Vladivostok, though again enjoying his commander's confidence, he was angered by regulations penalizing Jewish soldiers. He recalls feeling "as if scalded with hot water, full of shame and pain." His captain apparently shared his indignation. As Morris remembers it, this encounter with official antisemitism prompted his decision to desert. "Now I understood why Jewish sons did themselves all kinds of damage to avoid service. . . . I decided to go to America." His oldest brother had settled in New York before the Russo-Japanese War. Following his example, Morris confirmed the charge routinely leveled by antisemitic ideologues and military bureaucrats that emigration was one of numerous Jewish ploys to evade the draft.[5]

His was thus a well-trodden path, if not the standard itinerary. As Austrian writer Joseph Roth (1894–1939) observed in 1927, "America signifies distance. America signifies freedom. There is always some relative or other living in America. . . . Somebody emigrated, twenty years ago, say. He fled the draft. Or he received his call-up papers and deserted."[6] En route to this remote destination, Morris takes the Chinese Eastern Railroad from Vladivostok to Harbin, where he depends on the kindness of (Jewish) strangers. The Chinese Eastern Railroad, completed in 1905 with Russian and foreign financing, traversed Manchuria, linking two points on the Trans-Siberian Railroad. Harbin was a Russian-built and Russian-administered city on Chinese territory, where Jews were welcomed as part of state-sponsored economic development. It was a circumscribed local exception to the attitudes governing policy within the empire itself.[7]

Here, in this foreign outpost, Yiddish and the domestic diaspora of far-flung Jews provided a safety net. At the station, Morris noticed a cab driver who seemed to be Jewish, whom he asked to take him to a Jewish home. The head of the house, it turned out, was acquainted with a Greenfield family friend now living in Vladivostok. This connection led to offers of assistance — money and arrangements — to get him from Harbin, across the border of territory now controlled by the Japanese, then to Dalny (Dalian), still within the Japanese sphere, and then on to Shanghai.[8] In both cities, he had the names of Jewish innkeepers originally from Odessa, who took him under their wing. Jews were not his only helpers, however. A stranger speaking "broken Russian" guides him to the railway station, where the station master treats him well, which is to say, treats him like a normal traveler.

At Dalny he boards a Japanese ship and after a rough three-day crossing arrives in Shanghai. An international treaty port, in the 1920s Shanghai became a destination for Russians, Jewish and non-Jewish, fleeing the Civil War. When Morris arrived, there was only a small Sephardic colony and a few Russian Jews, mostly engaged in business.[9] While he waits for money to arrive from his brother in New York, a Jewish innkeeper allows him to earn his keep by dealing with suppliers. His fluent Russian is his calling card. He befriends a Russian journalist and his wife, also at the hotel, who lend him the cost of wiring his brother. Morris is at pains to note that he returned the loan as soon as the funds arrived, repaying not only the money but the trust these "very fine people" had shown him. He is grateful for the helping hand but does not want to feel indebted, even for their respect. There is a fine line to be drawn on the Jewish side between gratitude and resentment, dependency and dignity, when normal treatment (the absence of antisemitism) cannot be taken for granted.

At this point, Morris is twenty-one or twenty-two, describing himself as clean-shaven, smartly dressed, well-spoken in Russian. In Shanghai he boarded a German ship, on which he was to travel third-class to Naples. "I was sent off by the innkeeper and his wife, the journalist and his wife, a runaway soldier, and an anarchist who was leaving for

Australia in a few weeks. I was very pleased to be sent off by them." A handful of characters out of context: an Odessan Jew installed in Shanghai, gentile Russians who were not antisemites, an army deserter (like Morris himself), and a revolutionary. Morris was following the well-worn Jewish path of emigration, by an unusually circuitous route.[10]

In Naples Morris would board another ship for the voyage to New York. With the reluctant support of his brother, he spent three years and seven months in that city, trying to make a living in the garment trade, and meanwhile acquiring some English. In 1911 he decided to return to visit his widowed mother, knowing he would have to answer for having deserted. The passage from New York to Rotterdam took eleven days. Arriving by train at the border between Germany and Russian Poland, he was reluctant to linger without a passport and looked for a way to steal across.

For once, Jewish networks failed him. A man he describes as "a Jew in a caftan" took him to a house occupied by "Polish Hasidim" in the business of smuggling people across the border. Finding them busy at cards, he decides he "did not want to place myself in their hands."[11] Instead, he wandered around town until he encountered "a Pole carrying a Bible under his arm," whom he paid to be his guide. The German border guard took a bribe and let them pass. On the other side, a couple of local peasants helped them avoid the patrols and led them through the forest. The Pole lived nearby and the two stopped to share a meal at his table. Having trusted this "Pole with a Bible" more than the Hasidim lost in their cards and having given him money for their lunch, Morris nevertheless does not trust him with the price of a train ticket to Odessa and has to risk buying it himself. These monetary transactions, which Morris recalls in strict detail, are an index of human relations: selfless good deeds or good deeds for a price, trust demonstrated and returned, trust risked or withheld, a lifeline or a threat to one's existence.

At the railway station in this Polish border town, Morris recalls, he was "dressed in a nice suit, a white hat, with a cigar in my mouth." This was the appearance he believed would inspire respect. When the train pulled in and the gates were opened, the gendarmes searched the luggage for concealed weapons, but fortunately did not ask for passports. In Odessa, the Greenfield family converged on his sister's house to welcome him back, but someone had reported his presence to the military authorities. Hoping to lighten the penalty by turning himself in, he presented himself to officials in Bendery.

Unexpectedly, he was not at first arrested but "put under surveillance." Penmanship once again intervened. For six months, because "he was lucky to have beautiful handwriting," he was employed as a clerk, waiting for his regiment in Vladivostok to confirm that he had absconded with nothing beyond his own clothes and part of his gun. At his court-martial, Morris remembers surveying the audience in the courtroom, thinking their faces showed "they were mean people and no doubt antisemites as well." The opposite of "very fine people." There is no reason to suppose that the terms or the circumstances of his sentence — eighteen months in a disciplinary battalion — had anything to do with his identity as a Jew. He nevertheless comments, with reference to what came next, that "no friend of Israel should know about such a thing."

He might have expected Jewish soldiers to be treated more harshly than the rest, but that is not what he observed. The men in the large Kherson prison were equally subject to military discipline and corporal punishment — flogging on the bare behind — for the slightest offense. "Two soldiers would administer the blows while four soldiers would hold the victim down. The officer kept count." When the contingent from Bendery arrived, they felt they "had fallen into a real Hell. You can imagine how all this affected me. It was barely seven months since I had left America, the freest land in the world, where I had spent almost four years and became accustomed to an American way of life."

The contrast between the streets of New York and a Russian military prison could not have been starker. Yet even in this "hell," not all options were foreclosed. Discipline was harsh, but the food was good. Though it was obviously not kosher, Morris ate with everyone else. Many Jewish soldiers did the same, either because they had no choice or because they didn't care.[12] He objects only that Jews were not exempt from instruction in "Russian hymns and some prayers." Minor infractions — smoking, in particular — resulted in confinement to the internal prison, an ordeal some men did not survive. Morris is careful to behave properly. Shaving was not permitted. Concerned to maintain a respectable appearance, he trimmed his beard with scissors. His performance in prison is thus a magnified version of his self-presentation in the outside world: designed to maximize good treatment.

Rewarded for good behavior, he was included among the inmates transferred to a barracks with a less onerous regime, where they were employed as guards and permitted to carry guns. They were also allowed to receive packages and money from home. "The commander," Morris comments, "was a very intelligent person. He had also been sentenced for something." As in the case of the "very fine" couple in Shanghai, the "very intelligent" or "refined" person is also somehow marginalized, but retains the status—money, rank, culture—from which toleration can be dispensed. None are, of course, antisemites. That is the acid test.

At this point, Morris got to know another Jew "who had also escaped to America to avoid service" and now worked in the prison hospital, which was staffed by physicians from the nearby town and two nurses, "both refined young men." Morris managed to get transferred there as well. At first put to washing floors, he was soon allowed, thanks to his "nice handwriting," to complete the patients' charts. Even more propitiously, he attracted the attention of the captain in charge of supplies and became his secretary. "This made the time go quickly and I felt much, much freer. I could smoke a cigarette without fear of punishment; I could buy the things I wanted."

After a year thus employed, he was granted six months' amnesty for good behavior and returned to his battalion in Vladivostok. There, his former captain, whom Morris praises as "one of the finest people among the Russian officers, especially of that rank," regretfully informed him that Jews were not allowed to serve on the fortified island where the unit was stationed.[13] Morris was therefore transferred to a battalion fifty miles to the north, where he was to complete another eight months of service and face the experience of army life without his patron's protection.[14]

What was it like in the army for this Jewish young man? Not so bad, in his portrayal. "Soon Passover came. Jewish soldiers were given passes for the first and second days of the holiday. We rented four rooms with a kitchen in the nearby town. We obtained kosher matzos, kosher goose fat, and everything required for the cooking. It was customary for the Jewish soldiers to invite the battalion commander for a meal and they were never refused." The other Jews in the battalion were all from Warsaw. Morris, with better Russian, composed the invitation. The captain got drunk on kosher schnapps. Morris was soon providing him with a regular supply. The connection established, he advanced from giving the officer a shave, to the role of personal secretary. As Morris explains, soldiers "versed in Russian" were rare. Jewish subordinates were useful and a symbiosis was established. It depended, of course, on the superior's personal disposition and could at any moment dissolve.

This was a battalion in which the abusive sergeant major was eventually shot dead by his own men. The culprit was identified and arrested, but Morris managed to keep his head down. The commander was transferred and replaced by a Georgian, "a very fine person who liked Jews. But he liked gambling, drink, and women as well. So he was very busy." Morris receives his superior's mail and writes his reports. In summer 1914, the officer confides that war is looming. Morris is asked to compile lists of necessary supplies—"meat, potatoes, onions, fats, oil, cabbage, and so forth." Soon preparations begin—"new clothing, new underwear, new boots. Everything was changed in a hurry." His new battalion commander, a Captain Mosnev, promises to protect him. "Thank the Lord first and then the captain. He fulfilled everything he promised me." Another "very fine person."

It took the battalion thirty-five days to travel from Vladivostok to Warsaw. Its first engagement was at the town of Piaseczno, south of the Polish capital, where a battle raged in September and October, 1914. Morris was not involved, but many of the soldiers simply ran away and his special captain was wounded. One Saturday, he decided to head for town and find a Jewish home where he could "enjoy a good cholent"—the traditional Sabbath midday meal. His attention was caught by a man in a yarmulke, apparently returning from synagogue, who invited him to join his family. "The table was set for the Sabbath." Blessings were said; dinner was served. It had been a Jewish custom to invite Jewish soldiers quartered nearby to share a family meal, but the custom was not always observed, as many communities could not afford it.[15]

Back in the regiment, Morris continued his clerical duties, making lists of dead, wounded, missing, or captured. The majority of battalion secretaries, he comments, were Jews. Most Jewish recruits, though literate, did not have the command of Russian needed for this role. Only a small percentage in fact served as clerks and artisans, but their visibility strengthened the authorities in their conviction that Jews were prone to avoid combat.[16] Morris was among the minority that confirmed the canard. As part of his job, he also helped the quartermaster fix the books. "The front changed frequently. Sometimes we defeated the Germans, sometimes they defeated us. So it was impossible to determine where we had purchased our provisions." He was instructed to record fictitious payments.

Morris was not apparently bothered by this chronic finagling, nor by his role in serving his officers' needs, providing the kinds of favors and performing the numerous private tasks that bolstered the system of patronage and privilege on which the tsarist army relied and on which his own security depended. Yet, there was a breaking point. When the sergeant major insisted he procure personal luxuries — a silk shirt, schnapps — Morris balked and the officer decided, as Morris understood it, to teach the uppity Jew a lesson. The wounded captain was no longer there to protect him and his replacement agreed to have Morris sent to the front.

For the eleven months until his trusty patron returned, Morris endured the perils of the battlefield. At one point, a bullet penetrated his knapsack but failed to wound him. Salvation came in the form once again of his protector, Captain Mosnev, now stationed in a town not far from Łódź. Morris boldly sends him a letter asking to be rescued and is restored to his former role. When the captain dispatches him to Odessa on personal errands, he now willingly buys oranges, wine, and smoked sardines and visits with his family. Back at the front, the regiment was billeted in a town in western Ukraine, likely Kozyatyn,[17] where the rabbi's wife provided Morris with lodgings. Hungry, dirty, and tired, the troops spend five weeks in a forest under heavy German bombardment. When they lose the battle, Morris notes his pleasure in "the defeat of the tsar." A rare political remark.

The war was not yet over, however. Captain Mosnev was now a colonel and Morris continued in his service. Aware, as before, of the privileges officers enjoyed, the luxuries he himself helped them acquire, even in the midst of carnage and deprivation, he offers no comment. Indeed, he welcomed the chance to improve his own situation. "All officers," he recalls, "had a separate kitchen and a bakery and a little shop especially for them. About twelve soldiers tended to all this, a cook, a baker, and a man in charge who procured everything that the officers needed." Soon Morris became Mosnev's right-hand man, traveling to Moscow, Petrograd, Kiev, or Poltava to purchase delicacies such as smoked pork and sausages. It was a role he clearly relished.

The common soldiers who resented their superiors might well end up resenting someone like him, performing the function of provisioner and intermediary not untypical for Jews in everyday life. This future was not long in coming. His job as Colonel Mosnev's steward continued, he says laconically, "until revolution came and Kerensky took over the regime for a short while and the circumstances seemed to change —a sweet illusion. . . . All sorts of soviets sprang up, the front was neglected. German soldiers and Russian soldiers fraternized in each other's trenches and drank schnapps. It felt like something was about to happen. Once, Kerensky appeared at our front and actually asked the soldiers to continue guarding the front and be ready to attack the enemy. But it didn't help. The officers were ignored, discipline ran out, they were not saluted. The officers lost courage."

Morris's sympathies are with the higher-ups who employed and protected him. If a private were to call him "comrade and asks for a cigarette," Mosnev announced, he would throw in the towel. The officers were being threatened with more than disrespect. "As the revolution spread," Morris observes, "the commissariat refused to supply meat and flour and some other products for the officers. Everything was diverted for the soldiers. The officers went hungry and their situation became critical." Morris to the rescue. He was dispatched to Yekaterinoslav Province, in southeast Ukraine, where he managed to purchase a quantity of flour. The soldiers guarding the station were reluctant to permit the transport of food destined for the officers' table, but with a bit of subterfuge Morris prevailed. Reaching his unit after some delay, he discovered the army in a state of collapse. His friends thought him foolish not to have sold the flour and pocketed the cash, but Morris dutifully delivered the goods. He had witnessed soldiers on the Romanian front deserting, pillaging, and heading for home. Ever the obedient servitor, he requested (or so he says) and obtained permission to leave for home himself. This time he did not return.

Thus did the Jewish "little man," proud of his good grooming, his knowledge of Russian, his beautiful handwriting, and his honesty, grateful for the protection of authority figures who did not despise Jews, repay them with loyalty and appreciation. Not lining his own pocket, not shirking responsibility, foiling some antisemitic expectations—though confirming others. His account of the war includes few interactions with common soldiers, apart from the occasional escapade with fellow Jews. Morris recalls no hostility directed at himself, or else wishes not to remember. His focus is to ensure his own survival by making himself useful to the men in command. He objects to the brutal treatment of inmates in the military prison, he is glad when the tsar is swept away, he cannot avoid observing the effects of the revolution, but he seems entirely deaf to the political issues — the parties, the rhetoric, the conflicts — swirling around him.

Even as the Civil War unfolded and the Bolsheviks made their presence known, the main challenge was to survive. In the business of survival, being Jewish provided him with contacts and partners, opportunities rather than vulnerabilities. Again, antisemitism rarely intervenes in his story, even though Morris now incarnated some of the classic Bolshevik stereotypes — speculator, petty trader, gold and currency hoarder, draft resister, and army deserter — that conformed to antisemitic tropes, as well. These attributes got him into trouble, not as a Jew, but as the vestige of a doomed social order.

Back home in Bessarabia, he encountered deserters from the nearby front who were roaming the region, marauding, pillaging, stealing horses, and also robbing Jews. He recalls having been "greeted enthusiastically by both Jews and non-Jews. I was healthy" — he was now about thirty years old — "and dressed in the Tsar's uniform. As I always had a loaded revolver on me, they looked upon me as their defender." The threat he and his neighbors confronted was not at this point directed specifically at the Jews, who were engulfed in the violence like everyone else. A landed estate and vineyard near Kopanka was the scene of pillaging and destruction by local peasants. Having witnessed the attack, in which the lives of the landowner's family were endangered, Morris warned his village "that we too would not escape that fate. We immediately organized a self-defense group. We obtained guns and ammunition" — though he doesn't say how. "Every night a few young men stood guard. And in this way we saved ourselves for the moment."[18]

In January 1918, in the wake of the Bolshevik armistice with the Central Powers and the disintegration of the Russian army on the Romanian front, the Allies backed a plan for Romanian troops to invade Bessarabia, as part of a campaign to support the armed opponents of Bolshevik power gathering in the south.[19] When the Romanians bombarded Bendery, Morris fled across the partly frozen Dniester to Odessa. He soon settled in Tiraspol, nine miles east, directly across the river in Kherson Province. Tiraspol was home to his childhood sweetheart, Riva Rosenfeld, who soon became his wife and eventually my grandmother.

Tiraspol was on Soviet territory, but the Soviet regime was not yet in control. Ukrainian nationalists were also fighting for this corner of the old empire. "Bands of all kinds roamed through the town," Morris recalls. "It goes without saying, no commerce was allowed. Travel from the city by train was not allowed. A pass was required. And there was no one to appeal to. The bands changed frequently. . . . Everything became expensive and unavailable." This was a good description of the situation throughout the Ukrainian region following the Germans' departure at the end of 1918.

Despite the prohibitions, Morris took advantage of the trade in currency that sprang up across the border. It was a risky business. Jewish networks still existed, but the rules of the game had changed. One day he went to see his contact in Odessa and knocked on the door with the agreed signal. This time, "out came two sturdy Bolsheviks, armed to the teeth." When he attempted to leave, he recalls, "they grabbed me by the arm and dragged me into the room." There he confronted "a commissar, blind in one eye, with disheveled hair. At one end of the table lay a revolver, at the other end a bomb. The table was covered with all kinds of money and a gold watch and chain." The Bolsheviks demanded his passport (in all this chaos, he actually had one), searched his bags, and took his money. He feared for his life, but suddenly the commissar returned his papers and told him to make himself scarce.

Undeterred, Morris kept looking for ways to earn a living, trading in cotton thread, among other things, hiding the goods, fearing arrest, evading the secret police, the Cheka. Caught yet again, interrogated by Cheka agents and threatened with a gun, he told them "the truth from A to Z," as he puts it. He is a law-breaker with a tendency to respect authority, a young fellow with a family to support trying to get by and stay out of trouble. All these activities, however, are just what the new regime, the Cheka in particular, is trying to suppress. Morris had transitioned from an antisemitic bête noire to a Soviet one.

But all is not lost. Other networks now go into play. My grandmother and her sisters mobilized to get him out, making the rounds of local notables who had joined the Bolshevik camp. Bribes and contacts—the lubricants of old regime life—were still effective. He was released on condition he provide his captors with benzene for their motorcycles, a scarce commodity, he explains, because shopkeepers were hiding their stores. Set a thief to catch a thief, a hoarder to catch a hoarder. To his surprise, they reimbursed him, as promised.

This episode seems to be a new version of what he had encountered in the imperial army: supplying the authorities with their personal needs in return for protection. Bribing and placating those in power were venerable strategies employed in tsarist times by Jewish communities obliged to circumvent onerous legal restrictions.[20] The opportunity provided by corruption had not disappeared. The local Cheka was soon taken in hand, however, by men from Moscow, who were made of sterner stuff. Morris was again interrogated about the money he had earned in the business with the cotton thread. After surrendering the proceeds, he was left with an assortment of largely worthless paper bills.

Soon, "a worse time arrived," as Morris puts it. "The White Guards and the Petlyurovtsy tried to stop the march of the Bolsheviks. There was a regular war in our town."[21] Soon the Bolsheviks "began to conscript all the young men from all the surrounding villages, myself among them." Supplied with guns and ammunition, the recruits were loaded onto trains. At a key railroad junction in central Ukraine, Morris abandons his gun and makes for the station. Once again, a deserter. Local Jews help him get a ticket and a pass from the Cheka. Not far from the station, however, the train, which he had barely managed to board, comes to a stop. "Soldiers surrounded the train immediately and asked for tickets and passes, and at the same time they were looking for contrabandists. Many people jumped off and ran toward the fields," Morris remembers. "They were shot at and many were arrested with their bags." This is a classic Civil War scene—the campaign against the so-called bag-people. He could have been one of them, but not this time.

Back in Tiraspol, the men were ordered to appear for labor duty, but again, the family managed to pull strings. It was easy enough to forge or alter papers. "The comrades did not as yet have any books where things could be recorded," he notes. But soon, unfortunately from his perspective, controls improved. "The real comrades began to arrive from Moscow. They began to requisition everything in the apartment. We were practically barefoot and naked. Food was scarce." "This is the end," he remembers telling my grandmother. "We must flee across the Dniester." The river was by then the Romanian border. The Romanian claim to Bessarabia had been endorsed by the Supreme Council at Versailles in 1919 and again in October 1920 by the Allied Powers in the Treaty of Trianon, against the objections of Soviet Russia. Morris was therefore able to change countries simply by returning to his home town.

He goes on ahead, smuggled across the frozen river with the help of a peasant girl and a Romanian soldier. Kind strangers, for a fee, since Morris is not short of cash. Later, Riva and their first child—my mother Phima—also made the perilous crossing over the ice. On the Romanian side they were all initially quarantined. Riva was quickly released, but Morris was held for seven weeks, then brought before a military court. "I had no difficulty in obtaining my papers," he comments, "because I was Bessarabian born and knew the Romanian language well." He thinks of settling in Kopanka, but he can no longer tolerate village life and there was no doctor for pregnant Riva. Instead, they set up house in Bendery.

Again, as on the Russian side, the Jews engage in activities that attract the attention of authorities eager to enforce the newly established borders. This is the world described so eloquently by the Yiddish writer David Bergelson (1884–1952), Morris's exact contemporary, in his 1929 novel, *Judgment*, invoking similar circumstances on the Soviet-Polish border.[22] Relying on traditional community ties, ordinary small-town Jews take advantage of new opportunities to improve their lives, but the fabric of this communal culture will soon be torn apart, as the new regime establishes control. Bergelson, who threw in his lot with the Communists in the end, still viewed this doomed world with gentle irony and affection. It was a world of ritual and tradition, but also ingenuity and adaptation. There was nevertheless a limit to how far this accommodation could go, even as official antisemitism was disappearing.

On the Romanian side, Morris ran afoul of the local police, who were trying to disrupt the network of Jews smuggling people and things across the border.[23] For a time he ended up in prison, while Riva made the rounds of influential people, both Jews and Romanians, trying to get him out. He was tortured to reveal names he insisted he did not know but was soon released and recovered his passport. Meanwhile the money the couple had brought along was now worthless. A second child was born. On the proceeds of a diamond ring, they opened a grocery store and managed to get by, counting themselves lucky they had not drowned in the river or been murdered on the way across. In 1941, Morris's sister Pesya and most of her family were slaughtered by Romanian neighbors who envied their solid country house. This was something he must have known when gathering his recollections but doesn't mention. It belonged to a different time.

Riva had sisters in Chicago who sent affidavits and tickets, but the papers were not quite right and the process had to be repeated. When the proper documents finally arrived, Morris was not ready. This was 1923 and by the time he changed his mind, the Johnson-Reed Immigration Act of 1924 had severely limited quotas. It was not clear how long they would have to wait this time. Now, to supplement the grocery store, Morris joined a local Romanian in a fishing business. He describes his partner as "a very refined person . . . not antisemitic." Here was another of the many exceptions that stand out against a potentially menacing background and defy his anxious expectations.

The dangers had intensified under the emergency conditions of civil war and the attendant disruptions of everyday life. The pogroms that swept across the western and southern provinces in 1919 and 1920 took tens of thousands of Jewish lives. The worst perpetrators were associated with the anti-Bolshevik White forces and those attached to the uncertain leadership of an unstable Ukraine. In some cases, Red Army units or pro-Red irregulars were also to blame, but the sheer scale of the violence on the other side caused numerous Jewish intellectuals to overcome their reservations and join the Communist regime.[24] Soviet policies proved destructive in other ways, however, both for Jewish cultural aspirations and for ordinary Jews. The commercial roles into which Jews had traditionally been thrust and their enforced concentration in the politically sensitive frontier zones reinforced the animus against them, on both sides of the border.

The same networks and cultural intelligence that enabled Morris to survive thus also threatened his existence. He defied regulations, and he understood how to deploy the survival tactics that Jews as a community had evolved over the years. In that sense, he conformed to the stereotypes denounced by both Communists and antisemites, for different reasons. But he frustrated stereotypes, as well. Much as he relied on Jewish networks, he was open to the world. Yiddish was indispensable, but Russian was his salvation.[25] In Marxist terms, he was securely "petty bourgeois." With access to education he might have made his way into the Russian intellectual or professional classes, like many Jews of his generation.

Fundamentally, Morris aspired to be an educated man, both Jewish and worldly. In that sense, he reflected the spirit of the Yiddish cultural revival occurring at the time.[26] He mentions in his youth walking eight miles to a library, perhaps a product of this very Yiddishist movement, but otherwise he seems not to have been affected by its work. He distrusted the Hasidim; he sought out observant but not overly pious Jews; he was willing to eat nonkosher meat in the army but relished a Sabbath meal; when necessary he trusted and joined forces with gentiles. The ascent of the Bolsheviks is what pushed him to leave the Old World behind. The dangers entailed in being Jewish had acquired new names.

The organization that was finally to help Morris and his family make it to New York was the Hebrew Immigrant Aid Society (HIAS), which had been established in the wake of the 1881 pogroms.[27] It is the only Jewish organization he ever mentions, but he is not particularly grateful for its assistance. The office manager in Bucharest was in love with the red-headed bookkeeper, it turned out, and needed money to keep her in style. He obtained it by selling "Nexts." Morris had to find a way around him. Dressed in his best suit, he appealed directly to the shipping company, where a sympathetic clerk found the Greenfields a berth on a passenger ship leaving from Le Havre. Once again, the kindness of gentile strangers. They were on their way.

Morris Greenfield's personal experience, as he cared to remember it many years later, from the safe haven of Brooklyn, New York, illustrates the degree to which antisemitism permeated the lives of ordinary Jewish people in the last years of the Russian Empire. Official regulations restricted their mobility, their access to education, their ability to find a place in gentile society, to occupy positions of authority or power. His story reflects the constant anxiety not to be treated badly — by bureaucrats, army officers, station masters, and hostile strangers. Yet the memories are upbeat, even jaunty. Here is a young man who took risks, put his best foot forward — carefully clothed and groomed, who nursed ambitions, however modest, and acknowledged a variety of "very fine people" whom he trusted and who repaid his trust. In other words, he testified to the many occasions on which antisemitism failed to appear or impede his progress.

Luck was part of it. Morris had many a close shave and many a fortunate chance encounter. Even as war, revolution, and civil war intensified the dangers, his decisions worked to his advantage, with the near-fatal exception of the delay in 1923 and 1924. But, overall, the failures of antisemitism provided loopholes through which he could save himself from destruction. The creation, on a broader scale, of interstitial spaces in which antisemitism failed to operate or became a liability even when it remained the dominant cultural mode was the work of politically engaged members of the Jewish and non-Jewish Russian intelligentsia.

The term antisemitism describes a way of thinking that endows "the Jews"—a symbolic construct—with a set of contradictory attributes. They are at the same time denigrated and accorded enormous power in organizing the world. Described as insular, narrow-minded, fanatical, money-grubbing, materialistic, cowardly, and passive, they are feared as hyper-intelligent, conniving, exploitative, aggressive, and well organized in their own defense. But antisemitism, as it emerged in the period covered by this book, was also—and above all—an instrument of political mobilization. It was deployed by official institutions to bolster state power; it was used by threatened elites to channel popular unrest in directions they thought would serve their interests. Antisemitism therefore became an issue for Jewish leaders, who mobilized in political terms to counteract it.

It was in this period—the early decades of the twentieth century, as the authority of the Russian autocracy faltered, and war, revolution, and civil war tore the social fabric apart—that the physical consequences of antisemitism became apparent in their extreme form. The expropriation and murder of hundreds, then thousands of ordinary Jews, which began before the war as an indirect consequence of state policy, escalated during the war as its direct result. The intensification of violence after the war was a product both of regime collapse and of the emergence of fledgling nation-states on the ruins of empire, whose leaders adopted antisemitism as a key component of popular mobilization. This was a period, at the same time, that saw the systematic efforts of the transnational Jewish diaspora to mitigate the unfolding disaster. These campaigns did not save the Jews from the growing threat to their existence, but they put antisemites—even proud ones—on the defensive. It is the morally compromised status of antisemitism that is the subject of this book. In the aftermath of the Holocaust, we in the Western democracies may think that antisemitism as a political platform can only be transgressive, an insult to accepted ethical norms, but that assumption had to be fought for and has not always prevailed.

Jewish advocacy across the twentieth century has always been embedded in issues that transcended the fate of the Jews as a particular community, but the terms of this advocacy have shifted with the changing context. From the turn of the century through the First World War (and, in Russia, through the postrevolutionary civil wars), Jewish spokesmen and their gentile allies argued the Jewish case as exemplary of the principle of civil rights and legal equality. This strategy existed in tension with the need to promote and protect the collective right to cultural and communal identity, the Jews constituting a nation without a state within a state made up of nations.[28] The double thrust of Jewish activism reflected the composite nature of the autocratic regime, which denied the principle of civil rights across the board and classified its subjects in terms of ethnic and religious distinctions.

The war caused the breakup of the Romanov, Hapsburg, and Ottoman empires along these very ethnic lines, generating an ethnically intolerant nationalism that moved the question of so-called minority rights to center stage. The Jewish case was only the most dramatic demonstration of the problem of embedded minority populations in an environment of nationalist self-assertion. The victorious Allied powers feared the potential of ethnic conflict to destabilize the redrawn map of postwar Europe.[29]

The democratic nations that in this broader context backed the Jewish cause were not themselves, of course, free of the antisemitism they were perceived—by both Jews and antisemites—as opposing on the international stage. Yet the standards introduced by the international community after the war imposed constraints on the domestic politics of weaker or defeated nations. The standards were resented, they were violated, more honored in the breach than in the observance, but Jewish leaders who aligned their cause with the defining values of the Western democracies achieved at least a temporary advantage. Other Jewish activists took the nationalist route—the fight to establish a Jewish state, on the grounds that political sovereignty alone could guarantee Jewish survival. Still others, acting not as Jews and not on behalf of the Jews, opted for revolutionary ideals of social transformation, which they expected to save the Jews along with everyone else.

The positive interlude of the 1920s, though it managed to secure the reprobate status of antisemitic rhetoric and anti-Jewish violence, did not, however, banish antisemitism from the public or political arena. The democratic and republican values with which Jewish advocacy was allied were on the defensive in Europe. The resentment of minority rights became a rallying point for right-wing mobilization, stoking fear of the alleged Judeo-Bolshevik menace.[30] And indeed, the 1920s were followed in the 1930s by a resurgence of political antisemitism across Europe, culminating in the 1940s in the full force of exterminationist National Socialism in Germany, its enablers in various occupied countries, and the collaborationist Vichy regime in France. In the wake of the war, Stalin launched his murderous "anticosmopolitanism" campaign, directed against Soviet intellectuals identified as Jews. The establishment of the state of Israel in 1948 prompted the emergence of anti-Zionism as an ideologically charged weapon in the Cold War, while antisemitism as an officially sponsored campaign resurfaced, though thinly disguised, in Communist Poland in the 1960s and in the Soviet Union of the 1970s. Belated awareness of the Holocaust revived the taboo in the West, but Israel's own policies and the contentious politics of the Middle East have complicated the role of the diaspora. The current crisis of liberal democracy has occasioned the revival of classically anti-Jewish rhetoric even in mainstream public discourse, as part of a transnational populist mobilization.

The fluctuations in the status and function of antisemitism across the twentieth century reflect the contours of an ongoing political struggle, in which many players were involved. The governments of empires and nation-states, the leaders of mass-based political movements, and the spokesmen of various ethnic diasporas—all engaged the issue of Jewish rights and Jewish survival across two world wars and the rise and fall of ideologically driven imperial powers. The essays in this book examine three moments in this contest, at three different crisis points, in three national contexts. In each case, antisemitism was a key component of nationalist insurgency, but also an impediment to its political success.

The first essay illustrates the model in which the Jewish cause is couched in terms of political principles shared by the broader public. It focuses on the role of early twentieth-century Russian intellectuals and public figures who rejected the prejudices of their own social milieux and took a stand against official discrimination. In partnership with leaders of the Jewish community and Jewish professionals, these writers, lawyers, and political activists used the law courts, the press, and other public institutions—including, after 1905, the newly created State Duma—to press for Jewish rights. Located to the left-of-middle of the ideological spectrum, from conservative liberals to moderate socialists, they understood the fight against antisemitism as a component of the larger campaign to establish a modern Russian political sphere, based on the rule of law and equality of citizenship.

The increasing weakness of the monarchy, even before 1905, had generated a demagogic radical Right, which employed antisemitism as an instrument of popular mobilization, a response to the threat of popular revolution — or even of moderate reforms that challenged the basis of autocratic authority. The united front for Jewish rights pressed against this growing menace, which increased in virulence after 1905, and again during the First World War, and which laid the groundwork for the massive anti-Jewish violence that followed. With the collapse of the state structures against which it had directed its reforming zeal, liberalism itself lost its footing. Faced with authoritarian choices, liberals — both gentiles and Jews — made compromises on the issue of Jewish rights that violated their basic principles. They had no alternative to the demagogic appeals of the competing parties. Despite the failure of the liberal project to survive the impact of revolution and civil war, the goal of Jewish rights was not relinquished by the spokesmen of Eastern European Jewry who continued in emigration and across the diaspora to pursue what was intrinsically a transnational project. Its purpose was to leverage the influence of the democratic powers in mitigating the dangers faced by the Jewish population still caught at the intersection of warring ideologies and nations.

Proponents of this ongoing campaign of Jewish advocacy played a role in the dramatic scenario explored in the second essay. Operating on the stage provided by the legal institutions of the French Republic, the quintessential symbol of citizens' rights and republican values, they confronted the issue of responsibility for the wave of pogroms that in 1918, 1919, and 1920 had engulfed the territory claimed by Ukrainian nationalist leaders in the struggle for independence. This opportunity was afforded by the 1927 trial in a Paris courtroom of Russian-born Sholem (Solomon) Schwarzbard (1888–1938), a survivor of the civil war violence, who, in broad daylight on a Parisian street, had shot and killed the exiled Ukrainian leader, Symon Petlyura (1879–1926), to avenge the Jewish victims of his erstwhile regime.

The trial did not focus on the question of Schwarzbard's guilt, which he did not deny. It focused on the validity of the charge that Petlyura, as leader of the fledgling Ukrainian nation, was responsible for the fate of the Jews murdered in his name, thus justifying Schwarzbard's desire for revenge. Petlyura's record, in fact, echoes aspects of the dilemma faced by the Russian liberals. It demonstrates once again that a principled opposition to antisemitism depends on certain enabling conditions to have more than rhetorical force. As a socialist, Petlyura abjured antisemitism, and his official pronouncements reflected these views. Yet his followers were responsible for some of the worst pogroms of the Civil War. Forces acting on Petlyura's behalf are mentioned by Morris Greenfield among the armed bands that plagued the region east of the Dniester River.

Bolshevik leaders fighting for control of Ukraine faced a similar conflict between abstract principles and the reality of civil conflict. Pogroms were also perpetrated, though to a lesser degree, by Red Army troops and by irregulars fighting on their side, despite warnings issued by the Soviet command. This contradiction derived from the array of cultural and social complexities Morris knew only too well and to some extent embodied. The bitter civil war stories of Isaac Babel (1894–1940), collected under the title *Konarmiia* (*Red Cavalry*, 1926), as well as the diary he kept at the time, reflect the painful tension between revolutionary ideals and the persistence of anti-Jewish violence among the foot soldiers of the revolution.[31] The problem was one of authority, which neither the Ukrainian nationalists nor the Bolsheviks were able to secure in conditions of endemic violence and social disintegration.

Ultimately, Soviet forces prevailed. The leaders of the defeated Ukrainian Republic retreated to Poland and finally to France. At the trial, Petlyura's reputation was upheld by representatives of the Ukrainian emigration, who insisted the leader had not been antisemitic and could not be held responsible for events beyond his control. The charge of antisemitism in itself, they asserted, defamed the Ukrainian nation in the eyes of the world, thus damaging its future prospects. The Jewish press and Jewish public opinion, for their part, denounced Petlyura's champions for exemplifying the very prejudices they claimed to disavow. Schwarzbard's acquittal, in the end, seemed to demonstrate, yet again, the importance of democratic institutions—in this case, the Paris tribunal—to the success of Jewish efforts to set the tone and impose moral standards on the international stage. The moral claims were articulated in universal terms on behalf of a particular people with no political power to call its own.

The third essay, which jumps ahead to the aftermath of the Second World War, presents another case in which the accusation of antisemitism inflicts a moral injury. This story revolves around Andrzej Bobkowski (1913–1961), a Polish writer of a later generation, who spent the years 1940 to 1944 in occupied France. His observations of everyday life and his reflections on culture, history, and politics, recorded in a series of copybooks at the time, were published in 1957, after a decade of revision, by a Polish émigré press of liberal views established near Paris after the war. Unavailable in domestic editions until 1989, the work was then embraced with enthusiasm in Poland. The notebooks present a conundrum, however. The original manuscripts, it was later revealed, contain aggressively antisemitic views omitted from the published version.[32] Styling himself a rebel and nonconformist, the young writer, it turned out, had echoed the same antisemitic assumptions and crude rhetoric that pervaded interwar Polish society and persisted among exiled Polish leaders and in occupied Poland.

After the war, Bobkowski distanced himself from his former life and seems to have adjusted his perspective as well. He did not return to Poland, but left Europe altogether and settled in Guatemala. There, in revising his handwritten notes, he not only eliminated the most offensive passages, but introduced new passages that give the impression he had repudiated antisemitism even at the time. In response to queries concerning fragments published in advance of the 1957 edition, he insisted he had made no substantial alterations to the original text. In fact, however, he had modified his position on a number of issues, in relation not only to the Jews, but to politics, culture, and the future of postwar Europe, for reasons he did not explain.

The unconventional and vividly portrayed record of the young writer's wartime experience, his quirky, irreverent, yet moralistic temper, had led his new Polish readers to believe he had avoided the prejudices of his day. They were dismayed to learn that he had not in fact escaped them. Bobkowski was not, of course, responsible for violence of any kind and had even—though reluctantly—come to the aid of a Jewish woman stranded in occupied Paris. But the repetition of antisemitic clichés, tinged with personal revulsion, contrasted with the image of moral rectitude attached to the narrator of his youthful notes.

Overt antisemitism has recently made a comeback on the public stage, and not just in Poland.[33] The agitated response to Bobkowski's damaged reputation—whether to denounce him for his past or credit him with having renounced it—shows that charges of antisemitism are nevertheless not taken lightly in the political culture of Poland today.

Indeed, the controversy over Bobkowski comes in the wake of much soul-searching among the post-Communist Polish intelligentsia. In 2000, Jan Tomasz Gross (b. 1947), a native of Warsaw, now professor emeritus at Princeton University, published a study of the murder of the Jewish population of the town of Jedwabne by its Polish inhabitants in 1941.[34] *Neighbors*, in its original Polish version as *Sąsiedzi*, provoked outrage and indignation, but also new research and widespread discussion. In 2004, Warsaw-based journalist Anna Bikont (b. 1954) published *My z Jedwabnego* (in English, as *The Crime and the Silence*, 2015), a follow-up to Gross's study, in which she delved more deeply into the historical documentation and interviewed current residents of Jedwabne and the nearby area. Bikont observes that antisemitism was so much the norm in such Polish towns during and after the war that no one felt the need to apologize for it, no one was embarrassed. It was absolutely taken for granted. "In this region," she writes, using the present tense, "antisemitism is the default position, nothing to be ashamed of."[35]

And yet, as these three cases show, the default mode was not always accepted. Standing up to antisemitism could sometimes exact a price, but sometimes there was a price to pay for acquiescence. Petlyura's apologists were correct in thinking that Jews across the Western world had mobilized on their own behalf, publicizing the worst consequences of antisemitism and pressuring the international community of nations to stigmatize prejudice against Jews and the violence it fosters.[36] The Jews in villages under assault may not always have defended themselves with gun in hand, though they often did (see Morris). This failure troubled Jewish intellectuals at the time, but the worldwide Jewish diaspora had modern means of self-defense at its disposal. Clearly, its campaigns were not always successful, but they managed to shift the moral terrain, with clear political consequences, at least at certain moments.

None of these debates, none of these tactical dilemmas, no echo of these setbacks and successes on the world stage, or even in the Russian public sphere, make an appearance in Morris Greenfield's memoir of his youthful adventures. The only Jewish organization he mentions is HIAS, where the charms of the red-headed bookkeeper obstructed his plans. Always in the picaresque mode, he is dry-eyed and ironic. Jews are not saints, gentiles are not villains. He reserves his sentiment for the Bessarabian countryside, where, in May "all the fruit trees and acacias that ringed each garden burst into bloom, perfuming the air." Where "the winter-hungry bees descended on the blossoms to sate themselves on God's gift and busy themselves producing the most aromatic honey." Where his family harvested grapes that were shipped to Odessa and to Warsaw and by train to Germany and France.

World politics, which Morris seems to have ignored, was nevertheless what forced him out of this bucolic paradise. He was twenty-one in 1907, escaping the draft, when he first made it to New York and experienced another way of life, an entirely different universe from the corner of Bessarabia he had grown up in. This awareness expanded his horizons, but he was still most comfortable in his own oyster; he understood how his home culture worked. Attuned to the dangers it presented, he exercised his talents in the arts of negotiation and survival. He managed to ride the tides of war and revolution, taking antisemitism in stride, until the dangers became more than he could handle. The escape as late as 1930 was something of a miracle, because the United States by then had virtually closed its doors to new arrivals. The ongoing fight against antisemitism sustained by the organized Jewish diaspora was supposed to make it possible for ordinary Jews, like the Greenfields, to live where they wanted to live, in the Old World or the New, pursuing whatever private ambitions they may have harbored, without fear of persecution or extinction.

CHAPTER ONE

Against the Grain

Russians in Defense of the Jews

At the end of the nineteenth century, the population of the Russian Empire included 5.2 million Jews, a total half again as numerous as all the Jews in Europe, of whom most were concentrated in Austria-Hungary. Jews constituted only 4 percent of the imperial population overall, but 12 percent in the so-called Pale of Settlement, the fifteen western provinces plus the Russian-ruled sector of Poland, where most of them were obliged by law to reside. Some cities in this region were over a third Jewish. By 1910 the figure for Warsaw was almost 40 percent.[1]

The origins of the Pale of Settlement date back to the late eighteenth century, when by joining in the tripartite division of the Polish-Lithuanian Commonwealth, the Russian Empire first acquired a significant concentration of Jews. Over the following long century, the autocracy persisted in policies that narrowed Jewish access to the broader society and culture. Limits were imposed not only on residency but on admission to educational institutions at all levels, on access to certain professions, state service, and the military ranks. At moments of political crisis, notably after the assassination of Tsar Alexander II in 1881 and in connection with the 1905 Revolution, Jews were targets of deadly mob violence, the so-called pogroms, a term that entered the international lexicon. The 1907 edition of Murray's *New English Dictionary* defined "pogrom" as: "An organized massacre in Russia for the destruction or annihilation of any body or class; chiefly applied to those directed against the Jews."[2]

Despite these impediments, many Russian Jews nevertheless benefited from exemptions and opportunities.[3] A considerable minority managed to leave the Pale and acquire residency in the big cities. A number made it into the universities and contributed to professional and cultural life. Jewish intellectuals and public figures, fluent in Russian and Polish, engaged in the common civic discourse that emerged in the monarchy's closing years. Others used Hebrew and Yiddish to shape a public sphere oriented toward the communities of the Pale, which helped bring their distinctive traditions into the orbit of modern life.[4] Within the Jewish fold, intellectuals and activists debated the question of the Jewish place in Russian imperial society, articulating positions and attitudes expressed in a range of political parties and ideologies.

In short, the Jews of the Russian Empire were both integrated and segregated. Antisemitism was enshrined in official policies and permeated the general culture at many levels: as a common attribute of village life, though only occasionally translated into violence; taken for granted in upper-class society and the bureaucracy; as an unabashed posture at court; as a guiding principle in the higher military administration. Jews who entered the civic mainstream used the public platform to challenge these attitudes and advocate for equal rights. This challenge was embedded in the larger initiatives on the part of liberal society to promote the rule of law even within the framework of the monarchy. It involved a collaboration, or symbiosis, between Jewish spokesmen for the Jewish cause and gentile proponents of liberal modernity.[5]

The broad push for constitutional reform began to coalesce at the turn of the twentieth century in the so-called Liberation Movement, a loose association of professionals and public figures. Revolution broke out in January 1905, when the long-simmering political discontent of educated society joined with the growing unrest in factories, villages, and the armed forces, a mood exacerbated by the pressure of the Russo-Japanese War, to generate a massive, empirewide challenge to the autocratic regime. In the broad spectrum of revolutionary grievances and demands, the cause of Jewish rights found its place alongside calls for ethnic, religious, and women's equality, social justice, and the rule of law.

By conceding the revolution's least radical demands, the autocracy survived the upheaval. The crisis forced Nicholas to issue a manifesto in October 1905, establishing a parliament—the State Duma, with actual, though limited powers—and promising the extension of civil rights. The subsequent legalization of political parties and the loosening of restrictions on the press established a public stage on which Jewish leaders could address issues of common, as well as specifically Jewish concern. But the revolution also generated an emboldened and militant antisemitic Right, enjoying the tsar's endorsement. Two dozen monarchist organizations emerged after the October Manifesto, which they interpreted as an assault on the basic Christian values of Orthodox Russia. Their followers called themselves the "true Russian people" (*istinno-russkie liudi*)—as distinct from ethnic minorities, political subversives, and in particular, the Jews. Their enemies derided them as Black Hundreds (*chernosotentsy*) and *pogromshchiki*.[6]

The outbreak of war in 1914, a mere seven years after the revolutionary disturbances had subsided, intensified the xenophobia associated with Great Russian patriotism. Increasingly repressive policies directed at potentially hostile groups, in particular, Poles, domestic Germans, and Jews, justified on grounds of wartime security, only magnified the disruptive impact of the war. Meanwhile, failures of provisioning and materiel, blamed for Russia's shocking military defeats, emboldened civil society to shoulder responsibilities the administration seemed unable to handle and sharpened public criticism of the regime. Punitive treatment of the Jews was rightly perceived by many, even in conservative spheres, as impeding Russia's prospects for victory. Influential public figures who already, before 1914, had recognized the political importance of the so-called Jewish Question now joined with Jewish spokesmen in opposing official policies and propaganda targeting the Jews.[7] They encountered strenuous resistance. Long taken for granted, hostility to the Jews had recently acquired a new lease on life, but its destructive consequences, long decried by Jewish and liberal spokesmen, had become even more damaging and more obvious.

Jewish participation in Russian political life not surprisingly followed the general contours of the broader mobilization of imperial society. Though far from a majority, Jews were prominent among the young people attracted to the revolutionary movement of the 1870s. The Jewish activists were dedicated not to the emancipation of the Jews, but to the cause of social justice.[8] In 1881 a handful of populist radicals succeeded in assassinating Alexander II, the monarch who had liberated the serfs twenty years before. The populists had condemned the results of his reforms as ineffective and took aim at the pinnacle of power. Among those arrested for the deed, only one, Gesia Gelfman

(1855–1882), had a Jewish surname, but the assassination was widely blamed on the Jews and gave rise to a massive wave of pogroms.[9] In the 1890s, the populist impulses of preceding decades took the form of clandestine political parties attuned to the problems of the growing modern sector — industry, an emerging working class, increasing urban poverty. These included, most notably, the Marxist-oriented Russian Social Democratic Labor Party, along with a number of groups competing for a specifically Jewish constituency within the framework of the Left: the socialist Bund, the Zionists, and the socialist-Zionists of Poalei Zion.[10]

The Jewish presence on the revolutionary Left was the focus of official attention and provoked an antisemitic response. The primary thrust of Jewish public activity was not, however, to destroy the imperial system, but to improve the place of Jews within it. This took the form of community-oriented philanthropy, but also of participation in the movement for political reform that emerged at the turn of the century. In the context of an increasingly articulate imperial public sphere, politically moderate Jews with successful professional careers began to organize in defense of Jewish interests.[11] The wealthy Baron Horace Günzburg (in Russian, Gintsburg, 1833–1909), an active philanthropist and the most influential Russian Jewish figure at the time, had financed the establishment of Jewish welfare organizations; a Russian-language Jewish press had emerged in the capitals.[12] These developments were part of a broader sweep of Jewish civic activism that spread across Europe and the United States in the second half of the nineteenth century.[13] In Russia, they were part of the general struggle for equal rights that engaged the liberal opposition to autocracy.

While the revolutionary parties focused on social and economic justice, the Liberation Movement pressed for political reform. In the years leading up to the Great War, the demand for Jewish rights remained integral to this struggle. Indeed, a series of landmark events affecting the Jews punctuated the opening years of the new century, prompting intensified organization and outreach, engaging the participation of Jewish leaders, gentile allies, and the transnational Jewish community.[14] A sense of outrage and emergency was generated by an initial group of closely spaced incidents: the Blondes Case of 1900–1902, in which a Jewish resident of Vilna (Vilnius in today's Lithuania) was accused by his housemaid of attempting to kill her and extract her blood for ritual purposes; the Kishinev pogrom of 1903, in which

49 Jews were murdered, a shocking number at the time, followed by another, though less murderous pogrom in Gomel (now in Belarus) four months later; climaxing in the surge of pogroms unleashed by the 1905 Revolution, most in the Ukrainian provinces and Bessarabia. Those fatalities counted in the hundreds. After a brief pause, two additional episodes in 1911 again turned the public spotlight on the Jewish Question. In February, a vigorous debate on the Duma floor concerning the Pale of Settlement attracted considerable attention. In July an ordinary Jewish employee of a Kiev brick factory, one Mendel Beilis (1874–1934), was arrested and charged with the murder of an adolescent Christian boy for ritual purposes, the so-called Blood Libel accusation. The trial that ensued in 1913 became an international sensation, amply covered in the domestic and foreign press.

The Jewish population responded to accusations, insults, and physical aggression in a variety of ways. When it came to the immediate impact of the pogroms, the mainstream Jewish press and the socialist Bund called on the inhabitants of the Jewish towns to organize in armed self-defense. The various trials of pogrom perpetrators—and, more prominently, the Beilis Case—provided the chance to publicize the issue of violence and injustice and demand official redress. The court transcripts appeared in the Russian and Russian Jewish press and as separate books and pamphlets,[15] while reports on the pogroms were disseminated by Jewish organizations abroad.[16] Jewish spokesmen used the courtrooms, beyond the immediate criminal charges, to highlight the broader question of Jewish rights and expose the fatal consequences of official policy and official antisemitism.

Around 1901, a group of lawyers established a so-called Defense Bureau (Biuro zashchity), with the financial backing of Baron Günzburg. Its purpose was to provide assistance to individual Jews in surmounting bureaucratic obstacles, but also to address the question of discrimination in political terms. In response to the pogroms, the bureau not only represented the victims in court, but used the legal forum to educate the public about the plight of the Jews.[17] Its central figures were Maxim Vinaver (1862–1926); Oskar Gruzenberg (1866–1940), and Genrikh Sliozberg (1863–1937), all of whom had entered adulthood in the wake of the 1881–1882 pogroms.[18] Born in the ethnic outposts of the empire—respectively, Polish Warsaw, Ukrainian Dniepropetrovsk, and Byelorussian Minsk Province—they were highly educated, Russian-speaking professionals, who shared a common mission.

As Vinaver put it two decades later, in emigration, when reflecting back on his activist cohort: "Though fighting for equal rights for the Jews, aspiring to union with other Russian citizens and European education, they did not break the ties binding them to the Jews as a people in the cultural and historical sense of the word."[19]

The attorneys in the St. Petersburg Defense Bureau were the animating force behind a broad program of domestic activism, focusing on three primary targets — the courts, the Duma, and public outreach, through cultural partnerships and the press.[20] In this endeavor, they enlisted the participation of well-known Russian personalities — fellow lawyers, popular writers, and cultural celebrities — in support of their campaigns.[21] In the wake of the Kishinev events, the bureau delegated the lawyer Alexander Zarudny (1863–1934) to investigate.[22] Zarudny's father had been among the authors of Alexander II's 1864 judicial reforms; he himself later served as minister of justice in the Provisional Government. Another scion of the reformist imperial elite who supported the Jewish cause was the lawyer Vladimir Nabokov (1870–1922), son of Alexander II's enlightened minister of justice and the future novelist's father.

The trial following the 1903 Gomel pogrom — opening on October 11, 1904, concluding on January 29, 1905, three weeks after the outbreak of revolution — in which Vinaver, Sliozberg, and Zarudny were all involved, was a staging ground for patterns that persisted into the post-1917 Civil War. It showcased the mixed messages of denial and complicity along the official chain of command and the limits of legal remedies absent the rule of law or lawfulness altogether. Among the defendants this time were thirty-six Jews, arrested for having in any way attempted to defend themselves against attack. In taking their case, the lawyers saw themselves as defending "the interests of the whole Jewish people," which they understood as the true target of the trial.[23] They faced off against an opposing team that included the virulent antisemitic attorney and Moscow city council member Aleksey Shmakov (1852–1916), who would later make an appearance in the Beilis trial. An "implacable battle" ensued, in which the prosecution actively intervened to impede the work of the Jewish defense and discredit the Jewish witnesses.[24]

So abusive and prejudicial were the actions of the court that two months into the proceedings the Jewish lawyers announced their refusal to proceed and demonstratively withdrew. The trial had nevertheless revealed the brutality of the violence visited on the Jews, the involvement of the authorities, and the impossibility of justice being served. The court concluded that the damage to Jewish lives and property had resulted from "the brazen and provocative behavior of the Jews themselves," having allegedly started the ruckus that set the riots in motion. The verdict declared that "the Jews of Gomel had resorted to violence against the Christians in revenge for the sufferings of their fellow tribesmen and co-religionists in Kishinev and to demonstrate their solidarity and power."[25]

The trial had turned the case against the pogromists into an indictment of the Jews. As the Jewish editor of the unofficial published transcript put it: "Until the time that we have freedom and civil equality, the authorities will flout the law with impunity. Until then there can be no true citizenship nor a truly impartial court."[26] The Jewish problem could only be solved in that larger framework, but meanwhile the legal strategy was not enough. Reaching beyond the court and beyond the domestic audience, the Defense Bureau engaged with Jewish philanthropic and advocacy organizations across the diaspora, for whom the fate of the East European communities was of special concern. After the Kishinev pogrom, the bureau invited the support of the newly established Berlin-based Hilfsverein der deutschen Juden (Relief Organization of German Jews),[27] which mediated between the long-standing Alliance israélite universelle in France,[28] and the Conjoint Foreign Committee in Britain.[29] The Defense Bureau also established its own branch in Berlin, directed by the mathematician Leo Motzkin (1867–1933).[30] In Paris the bureau established ties with Lucian Wolf (1857–1930), editor of the British *Jewish Chronicle* and a leading proponent of extraterritorial Jewish diplomacy.[31] In the United States, the post-1905 violence prompted the formation in 1906 of the American Jewish Committee, led by the German-born banker Jacob Schiff (1847–1920) and the lawyer Louis Marshall (1856–1929).[32] The American Joint Distribution Committee was constituted in November 1914, in response to the outbreak of war.[33] Both organizations were deeply involved in advocacy and relief with special focus on Russia.

Each crisis point in Russian Jewish life thus resonated abroad and elicited outside intervention. News of the Kishinev pogrom led to the formation of local relief committees in New York, Paris, and Berlin, and protests were held in many cities.[34] Jacob Schiff pressured Washington to remonstrate with the tsarist government.[35] During the

Russo-Japanese War, he had considerable success convincing other Jewish bankers to join him in refusing loans to Russia and lending support to Japan, though some European banks resisted his appeal.[36] During the Revolution of 1905, Jewish newspapers in the United States reported extensively on the post-October pogroms and gathered funds for relief.[37] In 1911, coinciding with the Duma debate on the Pale, Schiff became the driving force behind the American Jewish Committee's campaign to block the renewal of an 1832 trade treaty with Russia. The treaty had allowed for reciprocal visa rights for U.S. and Russian travelers, but Russia had begun to restrict entry for American Jews, providing an occasion to intervene on behalf of Jewish American rights and by extension to protest the treatment of Russian Jews at home. The highly publicized pressure campaign convinced Congress in 1912 to vote for abrogation.[38] Such actions earned the banker a reputation among Russian antisemites as a "fierce enemy of Russia," who had "dedicated his life to her destruction."[39]

In the years leading up to 1905, the Jewish leadership had drawn its strength from its place within the Russian professional intelligentsia. The revolution drew its initiatives more directly into the mainstream political opposition. In parallel with other politicized professional associations formed at the time, the Defense Bureau reconstituted itself in March 1905 as a "union," in this case, the Union for the Attainment of Equal Rights for the Jewish People in Russia (Soiuz dostizheniia polnopraviia evreiskogo naroda v Rossii), its awkward title reflecting a compromise among the diverse viewpoints of its founding members.[40] The Union for Jewish Equality became part of the broad social movement (*obshchestvennoe dvizhenie*) pushing for political reform, which laid the basis for the liberal Kadet (Constitutional Democratic) Party that emerged in 1906, with a platform demanding equal rights for ethnic and religious minorities, among them the Jews.[41] The tsar and his advisers had briefly thought of excluding the Jews from the Duma franchise, but a widely publicized protest by Jewish leaders had apparently dissuaded them. Jewish historian Simon Dubnow (1860–1941) noted the paradoxical result that "the Jews, still without civil rights, obtained the political right to vote and be elected to parliament."[42]

But if the revolution provided a new arena for initiatives on behalf of Jewish rights, perhaps for that very reason it also inspired a surge in antisemitic mobilization. The upheaval had all along been accompanied by an uptick in anti-Jewish violence. Jews—or persons perceived as Jewish—were targeted not only by self-professed defenders of the autocracy, but sometimes by workers in the socialist camp.[43] The level of aggression and invective escalated, however, after the October Manifesto. The most powerful expression of this right-wing backlash was the Union of the Russian People (Soiuz russkogo naroda), founded in 1906 and hailed by Nicholas as a "faithful support, serving for everyone and in all ways as a model of law and order."[44] Denouncing "the persistent hostility of the Jewish people not only to Christianity, but to non-Jewish peoples, and the Jews' thirst for world domination,"[45] the Union was active in disseminating the notorious *Protocols of the Elders of Zion*, from which these notions derived.[46]

The Jews, despite the obvious disabilities imposed on them by the imperial regime, were imagined by their enemies to constitute a mighty political force, not just as revolutionaries, but as infiltrators of Russian public life. Efforts were therefore made to limit their access. Combining hostility to the Duma as an infringement on the monarch's power with hostility to the Jews, a conference of radical right-wing parties meeting in Kiev in October 1906 proposed that Jews, including converts to other religions, be limited in their representation in the Duma.[47] A less extreme version of the same sentiment came from more respectable quarters. Soon after taking office, Prime Minister Count Sergey Witte (1849–1915) was approached by Baron Günzburg and a delegation of Vinaver and other lawyers. In his former role as minister of finance Witte had recognized the importance of the Jewish role in the imperial economy, but he now believed the Jews were harming their own cause by supporting the political opposition. Equal rights should result from the gradual extension of the rights of all imperial subjects, he informed his visitors. Meanwhile, the Jews should leave politics to the Russians and mind their own business. This was precisely the view repudiated by Vinaver and his activist colleagues, as Vinaver told the minister to his face.[48]

Confirming the liberals' association of Jewish rights with the prospect of constitutional reform, the Union of Russian People considered the Kadets a more serious threat to the autocracy than the revolutionary parties, whose chances of success appeared slim.[49] On July 18, 1906, Kadet Duma deputy Mikhail Gertsenshtein (1869–1906) was murdered at his dacha in Terioki, Finland. A specialist in land reform who had converted to Orthodoxy, he was featured in the right-wing press as an icon of Jewish manipulation and rapaciousness.[50] A fellow Kadet praised him, in a defensive spirit, as a Jew who had never suggested "that Russian Jews had their own specific interests, separate from those of the Russian people," to whose welfare he had dedicated his life.[51] From the point of view of the Right, the distinction was meaningless —the liberal cause was the Jewish cause.[52] As Count Witte had put it, the Jews "had no business" telling the Russians what to do.[53]

Two months before his assassination, Gertsenshtein's speech in the Duma advocating the alleviation of peasant land hunger had aroused the fury of the benches on the right. In March 1907 another Kadet deputy, Grigory Iollos (1859–1907), a prominent Jewish journalist and Gertsenshtein's close friend, was murdered in Moscow.[54] The culprits were never caught. Vasily Shulgin (1878–1976), editor of the influential antisemitic newspaper, *Kievlianin* (The Kievan), interpreted the agrarian program promoted by the two murdered men as an incitement to the destruction of manorial estates then occurring in the countryside. These "political Jews," Shulgin charged, were instigating a "pogrom"—he used that word—directed against traditional Russian culture and society. The murders had aroused a "hysterical hue and cry" (*istericheskii vopl'*), Shulgin recalled, but, he was pleased to say, they were effective—the "political Jews" took fright.[55]

The murders of the Duma deputies, which dramatized the extreme Right's conflation of liberal reform with alleged Jewish plans to seize control of Russia, occurred against the backdrop of the post-October wave of anti-Jewish pogroms, which right-wing leaders considered a "defensive reaction" to that other "pogrom"—against Russia.[56] The most dramatic of the actual pogroms began in Białystok on June 1, 1906, a month after the convocation of the First Duma, six weeks before Gertsenshtein's murder. Białystok was a city in northeastern Poland, which by the end of the nineteenth century had a population of about 63,000, three-quarters Jewish. Jews played a dominant role, both as entrepreneurs and workers, in the local textile industry. The pogrom, which lasted three days, took more than 200 Jewish lives, left 700 wounded, and caused extensive damage to Jewish property and dwellings.[57] A mere three years after Kishinev, the toll was exponentially more dramatic.

A week later, on June 8, the shocking events inspired an impassioned debate on the Duma floor, which continued on June 26.[58] The starting point for discussion was the discovery that a secret printing press in the Ministry of Internal Affairs had been issuing pamphlets promoting attacks on the Jews. The first session's most arresting moment was the speech delivered by Prince Sergey Urusov (1862–1937), lately governor of Bessarabia Province, now representing Kaluga Province.[59] The descendant of an ancient princely clan, Urusov was the only deputy in the First Duma who had been a government official.[60] Arriving at his new post in the aftermath of the Kishinev pogrom, he had managed to quiet the unsettled mood by firm application of existing laws. Mob violence was a punishable offense in the criminal code, he reminded his fellow deputies, as was the incitement of hatred between ethnic and religious communities. Officials doing their duty had a legal obligation to prevent and punish attacks on the Jews.[61]

Contrary to the widespread belief in Jewish towns and villages, the tsar and his ministers did not encourage the pogroms, but discriminatory laws and policies targeting the Jews, reinforced by reactionary public opinion, created a sense down the line—among lowly policemen and crowds in the street—that the government welcomed the violence. Denouncing the "dark forces" at work behind the scenes, Urusov warned against "the influence of people with the habits of policemen and the hearts of *pogromshchiki*." Despite the complacency or cooperation of local officials, the real impetus behind the violence came from mobilized right-wing groups pursuing an ideological agenda. Ultimately, the higher authorities were nevertheless responsible for encouraging a disregard for the law that undermined the very principle of legality.

The speech made a powerful impression, Maxim Vinaver recalled, not only in Russia but in Europe.[62] The banker Jacob Schiff financed its publication in English.[63] The prince's account of his experience in Kishinev, on which the speech relied, was published in 1907 by a Russian-language press in Berlin, and shortly thereafter in English, French, and German translation.[64] Before arriving in the region, Urusov recalled, the Jews and their problems had not interested him at all; rumors of official involvement in the pogrom had seemed to him "either stupid or malicious."[65] His attitude once he arrived, however, soon turned to sympathy for the victims and disgust with the instigators and promulgators of anti-Jewish violence and slander. He was accused, as a result, of having been bought by the Yids. In 1912 a minor local official by the name of Georgy Pronin (b. 1861, thus Urusov's own generation), who had actively supported the perpetrators and their ideological backers, sued Urusov for defamation. In December 1913 the prince was sentenced to four months in jail.[66]

Urusov's 1906 Duma speech encapsulated the essence of the liberal position. On the other side, the rhetorical devices favored by pogrom apologists and committed antisemites were displayed in the comments by a deputy from Vilna Province, the Catholic bishop Baron Eduard von der Ropp (1851–1939). This offshoot of the German-speaking Latvian nobility began by acknowledging that pogroms could be averted if officials took resolute steps to prevent them, since he was convinced they were planned in advance. He nevertheless blamed the outbursts of violence on tensions created by the provocative behavior of the Jews themselves.[67] This was the typical right-wing accusation. Thus, in October 1903, the most influential and most respectable of Russia's antisemitic newspapers, *Novoe vremia* (Modern Times), had accused the Jewish inhabitants of Kishinev of setting off the confrontation that escalated into the pogrom. Only Christians, the paper complained, had subsequently been brought to trial, while the true instigators went scot-free.[68] An article by Urusov's future accuser Georgy Pronin, titled "Who Is To Blame?" published in the more rabidly antisemitic *Znamia* (The Banner), accused the Jews of inventing "fanciful stories" about the "horrors of Kishinev" supposedly visited upon "innocent" victims, stories they circulated around the globe, generating a sympathy that earned them huge sums of money from gullible donors.[69]

In this same spirit, von der Ropp pursued the familiar claim that Jews should be considered perpetrators, not victims. The Jewish people had many virtues, he began, among them a powerful organization, which other ethnic groups indeed might envy, since their solidarity allowed the Jews to dominate everyone around them. This organization, at once revolutionary and liberal, sometimes armed, was responsible, he claimed, for "tactless" behavior that aroused the anxiety and fear of the non-Jewish population and even of the police. Normally of peaceful disposition, the locals were all as a result ready, under current unstable conditions, to strike back. This was the view promoted at the Gomel trial by the prosecution and its "true-Russian" patriotic supporters, who considered the pogrom "an inevitable and necessary act of retribution for the sins committed by all Russian Jews."[70]

Incoherent, as well as offensive, von der Ropp's speech provoked a rejoinder from the deputy representing the city of Vilna, the center of von der Ropp's own district. This was an intimate confrontation.

Unlike the baron, Shmarya Levin (1867–1935) was a native of Vilna Province. A Zionist member of the Union for Jewish Equality and the Kadet Party, he had studied philosophy in Königsberg, attended the Hochschule für die Wissenschaft des Judentums in Berlin, then served as the state-appointed rabbi, an administrative position, in Grodno and Yekaterinoslav.[71] Von der Ropp appeared in the Duma in his clerical garb, Levin with a neatly trimmed beard, in a well-tailored suit. "Baron Ropp," Levin remarked, "inadvertently commits the same error that our government commits on purpose—holding all Jewry responsible for the actions of a single organization, referring to this organization not by its proper name, but calling it a Jewish organization."[72] The baron, he warned, should avoid "the slippery slope of omnibus accusations." Not all Jews were revolutionaries; self-defense was not revolution. The Jews took up arms because the authorities failed to protect them. After Kishinev, Levin himself had purchased a gun with which to protect his eleven-year-old daughter, not only from murder but from "dishonor." He, too, had taken to the streets to ward off the "hooligans." But though these issues touched him personally, Levin concluded with a statement of general principle: "Everything leads from the individual through the national to the universally human."[73] By "national" (*natsional'noe*) here, he meant the Jewish nation.

Echoing Urusov's indictment of the higher authorities, Maxim Vinaver, speaking as a deputy from the city of St. Petersburg, explained the pogroms as a sign of the government's weakness, its helplessness in dealing with the actual revolutionaries, its inability in fact to fight the revolution. Revolutionaries were hard to distinguish by their appearance. The Jews, by contrast, were easily identifiable—"by their dress, their accents, their lingo"—and thus easier to attack, on the pretext that "the revolutionaries are upsetting the population." Meanwhile, the government says to the Jews: "Give us your revolutionaries and we'll leave you alone."[74]

"There was in fact no pogrom in Białystok," Vinaver charged. "There was a military-police expedition meant to intimidate the revolutionaries by murdering the innocent."[75] The fault, he concluded, lay not in the Russian people—"imbued with the spirit of true humanity."[76] It lay in "the clique" that set the people against the Jews. "Criminally blind, they do not notice they are undermining not only the Jews, but the healthy body of the great mass of the Russian population, undermining the entire organism of state."[77] Condemning antisemitism as a political tool of the regime, to be opposed by political means in the service of an overarching political goal, had been the guiding strategy of the Defense Bureau and the Union for Jewish Equality. It was the approach endorsed by the Kadet Party and the position taken by the establishment liberal press.[78]

Described by his colleagues as a natural political leader, Vinaver had become something of a celebrity in Jewish circles after an indignant speech and his demonstrative exit in December 1904 at the Gomel pogrom trial.[79] After graduating from Warsaw University, he had moved to St. Petersburg, where he practiced as an assistant attorney, the highest level open to Jews, and was regarded as an expert in civil law. A central figure in the Defense Bureau, the Union for Jewish Equality, the Kadet Party, and the Jewish National Group (Evreiskaia narodnaia gruppa), created in 1907 to pursue the fight against antisemitism,[80] he considered his devotion to Jewish causes an aspect not only of his commitment to the principle of civic equality, but a feature of his imperial Russian patriotism, a loyalty that transcended ethnic and cultural divides.

Vinaver belonged, as he put it, in a riposte to attacks from the xenophobic Right, to the "true Great Russia" (*istinnaia Velikaia Rossiia*). In a volume of reminiscences published in Petrograd in early 1917, just before the February collapse, he profiled fifteen members of that "truly Russian" intelligentsia. Included, by his own definitions, were six Russians, three Poles, two Ukrainians, two Jews, a Baltic German, and the son of a German colonist. All, aside from the "Russians," were suspect categories after August 1914, when ethnic non-Russians across the board, though some more than others, were accused in official propaganda and in the patriotic press of disloyalty to the imperial cause.[81]

When the Kadet deputies in the Duma took the lead on the issue of Jewish equality, Vinaver insisted, they did so not merely from sympathy with the plight of the Jews, but as part of the wider concern for legal guarantees and equality before the law. "The Kadets raised the Jewish question," he explained, "from the legal perspective and in the context of challenges to the government."[82] It was not necessary to be Jewish to grasp the broader implications of Jewish rights for Russia's political future.[83] As the British activist Lucien Wolf wrote in a letter to the London *Times* à propos the 1905 Revolution: "The Jewish question at the present moment cannot be separated from the general political question. . . . Russian Jews are fighting solely for the liberation of the whole Russian people and in harmonious and zealous concert with them. Properly speaking there are no Jews in this great struggle."[84]

To say there were "no Jews in this struggle" was also to protect the cause from the animosity of conservative or reactionary opponents, who used their hostility to the Jews to discredit its underlying goals. Jewish activists like Wolf and Vinaver were well aware that the association of Jewish rights with the larger endeavor threatened both objectives. The connection between constitutional reform, the cause of legal rights, and the specifics of the Jewish Question was the cornerstone of extreme Right thinking. If Wolf attempted to cleanse the Jewish activists' political goals of the Jewish stain, their enemies reversed the equation, staining the revolution with the Jews. Thus, Foreign Minister Count Vladimir Lamsdorf (1845–1907) insisted, in a 1906 memo that Nicholas endorsed, that the Jews "have figured and still figure as a specially active and aggressive element of the revolution, whether as individuals, or as leaders of the movement, or in the shape of entire organizations. . . . There is . . . no room for doubt as to the close connexion of the Russian revolution with the Jewish question in general, and with the foreign Jewish organisations in particular."[85]

Among liberals dedicated to the cause of Jewish rights in this larger framework, the most ingenious in confronting this strategic dilemma was Vasily Maklakov (1869–1957). A progressive-minded establishment figure of aristocratic background, part of the same generation and social milieu as Vladimir Nabokov, Maklakov took the path of political reformism. Already a successful trial lawyer by 1905, after the revolution he joined the Kadet Party and later served as deputy in three State Dumas. Under the Provisional Government he was appointed ambassador to France, which is where the Bolshevik coup found him.[86] Devoted to the principle of civic equality, he displayed both the strengths and weaknesses of liberalism. He championed the rights of Jews, but his desire to accommodate existing institutions, if only to change them from within, led him to compromise on pragmatic grounds in situations where political choices had narrowed.

The odd couple, Maklakov and Vinaver, both lawyers, represented two contrasting cultural, social, and temperamental types. The Russified Polish Jew was pugnacious, the Russian aristocrat calculating, ironic, and far removed in personal terms from the realities of Jewish life. Years later, he confessed to finding stereotypically Jewish Jews distasteful.[87] Yet the two men shared a common dedication to the Jewish cause and a common understanding of why it mattered. Looking back over Vinaver's career, ten years after his death in Paris in 1926, Maklakov praised in his colleague the political style he himself preferred: attention to particular cases with the aim of achieving concrete results in defense of general principles. Vinaver, he recalled, saw Jewish inequality as a symptom of the autocracy's general disregard for legality. "The introduction of the rule of law, for which Vinaver the jurist stubbornly fought for so long, resolved both questions—the general and the particular." When arguing in the First Duma, Maklakov observed, "Vinaver felt both joy and pride, not as a representative of the Jews, but as the deputy from St. Petersburg; when he could link the fate of the Jews in Russia with a victory needed not only by them but by the legal principle itself."[88]

This approach seemed to make sense in the years leading up to the Great War, when the prospect of change from within the old regime had not yet been exhausted. True, the First Duma was unceremoniously dissolved on July 8, 1906, in violation of the promises of the October Manifesto. Vinaver had drafted a protest, signed by 120 deputies (about a quarter of the total) in the Finnish town of Vyborg. As a result of the Vyborg Manifesto, most were sentenced to three months in prison and deprived of the right to stand for election. Among them was Prince Urusov, who in addition forfeited his eligibility for government service.[89] Vinaver was angered when Maklakov, with typical caution, declined to sign. Appearing only reluctantly at his colleagues' ensuing trial, Maklakov nevertheless gave a courtroom speech that moved Vinaver to embrace him.[90] Just as discouraging, on June 3, 1907, the Second Duma, which had lasted only three months, was summarily dismissed and the electoral laws adjusted to ensure a more conservative profile for the next one.

The Białystok pogrom was another ominous sign, yet, in the subsequent trial, which lasted from May 26 to June 8, 1908, the perpetrators were nevertheless called to account.[91] And, despite the relatively conservative profile of the Third Duma, which opened on November 7, 1907, it still provided an opportunity to press for Jewish rights. In May 1910, a proposal calling for the abolition of residence restrictions on the Jews was submitted by 166 deputies, over a third of the total number. Debate on the question, which began on February 9, 1911, centered not on the merits of the proposal, but on the question of whether it should be forwarded for consideration to a commission formed in

November 1909 to review a bill on the principle of personal inviolability (*neprikosnovennost' lichnosti*).[92] Equality on the basis of national or religious affiliation was at the same time an issue of individual rights.

In the more conservative Third Duma, the terms of discourse shifted. The monarchist parties had moved from the street, where, as one spokesman put it, their own crowds had countered the throngs waving "red rags," to sit on the Duma benches.[93] The Right was now more numerous and less inhibited in its verbal assaults on the institution it was determined to subvert from within. The cards were on the table. In the course of the debate on February 9, 1911, Maklakov engaged the opposition on its own ground. Recognizing that antisemitism, as a cultural habit, could not be eliminated or discounted but had to be addressed, he insisted on the distinction between personal prejudice and its public consequences. Removing legal restrictions on the Jews, he asserted with his characteristic irony, would give those who hated them "the moral right to be antisemites," because antisemitism would revert from a question of public policy to one of private opinion.[94]

Maklakov appeared to be engaging the psychology of his opponents, but it was not an argument to which deputies across the aisle would in fact respond. The ideological antisemites in the Duma directed their animosity not merely against the Jews, but against the very model of legal equality and rule of law that Maklakov promoted. They considered morality to be on their side already. The Duma was a tribune, however, whose voice reached beyond the capital into the far-flung corners of imperial civil society. Its proceedings were published in the newspapers, its leading figures were widely known. Speeches were an opportunity to make a resounding public statement and Maklakov's verbal skills stood him in good stead.

Mimicking the perspective of antisemites faced with the inconvenience of modern political life, he assured them that formal equality would not endanger their right to express their opinions; it might even lend those opinions greater weight in the marketplace of ideas by removing the link to injustice and oppression. "Anyone can be an antisemite and express his antisemitism, but he can do so only in the sphere of personal and social relations. This is a very wide sphere. Let the enemies of the Jews avoid them and boycott Jews in business affairs, refuse to buy from them or sell to them. . . . They can even take their Puritanism much farther: outside the economic domain, they can turn away from Antokolsky's statues and close their ears to the music of Rubinshtein. Everyone has that right, but if everyone has the right to be an antisemite, the state does not have this right. . . . The state can only be a legal institution [*pravovoe iavlenie*]. This is why official justice [*spravedlivost'*] and legal equality are compatible with the most stubborn and unsightly personal and social antisemitism."[95]

The fact that antisemitism was untenable as the basis for official policy, Maklakov observed, was reflected in its obvious contradictions. The authorities and their ideological proxies, he taunted, lacked the courage of their convictions. "I understand that the state might recognize, as some say, that the Jews are an evil that must be extirpated [*iskorenenie*]. The state might say, as is suggested here, that the goal of Jewish policy should be the elimination [*istreblenie*] of the Jews, and whatever means you choose—resettlement in Palestine, expulsion across the border, or drowning them in the Black Sea, this elimination is the state's goal." If so, they should tell the Jews their place is not here, that they must leave. "This will be cruel, it will perhaps be surprising, but in the end not much crueler than certain aspects of the law on the Pale and those everyday events called pogroms." Reluctant to demand the elimination of the Jews, the authorities nevertheless denied them the benefits guaranteed in the Fundamental Laws: equality of rights and protection for all religious faiths.[96]

The Jews' loyalty to each other might arouse suspicion; their tendency to stand apart might arouse distrust. But, Maklakov insisted, the so-called Jewish problem lay not in the Jews, but in the misguided policy that shaped their lives. "This policy has managed to unite the Jews into a separate nation [*natsiia*]. It has turned the Jewish Question in Russia from a social or confessional question, to one of national identity." "As objects of government injustice," the Jews had come collectively to hate the authorities. The government "then uses this hatred, incited by itself, as justification for its antisemitism." The vicious circle also applied to economic relations. Concentrated in the Pale, Jews suffered from crowding and limited opportunities. When they competed with their Russian neighbors, the government denounced them as exploiters, yet this competition was itself the product of official rules.[97] Accusing the government of having "ceded to the social prejudice called racial antisemitism,"[98] Maklakov warned the Duma to resist this temptation. "If the State Duma, which represents the people, cannot be just, then it will show that it cannot be free. And for this reason the

Jewish Question is our question, a legal question. The Jewish Question is the general question of the triumph of legality in Russia."[99]

Maklakov knew better than to expect his eloquence to affect the outcome of the session. "Lies!" shouted the benches on the right. The debates on the Pale did not result in changes to the existing laws. He spoke for the record. The Pale ended de facto after 1914, partly as a result of the same antisemitic policies that had for so long sustained it but during the war led to the uprooting of the population of the western provinces. These policies reflected the failing autocracy's weakened hold on power, which left the highest offices, both military and civilian, in the hands of men who had lost touch with reality. The Pale ended de jure only after the regime had collapsed, a decision of the Provisional Government that replaced it, for whose liberal members this had been a persistent goal.

The failure of the autocracy's anti-Jewish policies to bolster its authority was clearly demonstrated during the war. This danger was already evident in the notorious Beilis Case, which had played out in Kiev, a hotbed of antisemitic agitation, not long before the war began. Like the debates on the Białystok pogrom and on the abolition of the Pale, the trial drew prominent members of the Russian professional intelligentsia into public engagement with the Jewish Question. Lasting from September 25 to October 28, 1913, the proceedings came under intense public scrutiny.[100] The initiative both in framing the charge and finding a suitable culprit was taken by the powerful Ukrainian branch of the Union of the Russian People, which also supplied lawyers for the prosecution and actively propagandized in the right-wing press.[101] Beilis's defense was financed by the fabulously wealthy Jewish industrialist and banker, Grigory Benenson (1860–1939), a Minsk native who made his fortune in Baku oil and the Siberian Lena Goldfields. His Catholic-convert grandson, Peter Solomon Benenson (1921–2005) was the founder of Amnesty International.[102]

The trial was a face-off between the progressive and the proudly reactionary positions already at loggerheads in the Duma. The case was prosecuted by the minister of justice, Ivan Shcheglovitov (1861–1918), with the support of Vasily Maklakov's reactionary younger brother, Nikolay Maklakov (1871–1918), then minister of internal affairs. Both former officials were shot by the Bolsheviks in 1918, along with other leaders of the antisemitic Right.[103] The split that ran through the Maklakov family testified to the intimate character of antisemitism in the experience of the imperial elite and the reason it could not easily be countered in purely institutional terms.

The Beilis Case was widely interpreted, at home and abroad, as the government's attempt, by defaming the Jewish people, to subvert the moves in the Duma to abolish the Pale.[104] The uproar it created caused Shcheglovitov to complain, however, that the affair had "attracted such publicity and taken such a turn that not to bring it to trial is impossible or it will be said that I and the entire government have been bought by the Yids."[105] The minister was indeed caught between competing needs, not easy to reconcile. As the proceedings were drawing to a close, the U.S. State Department received an official Russian communication indicating that Beilis was likely to be acquitted. On this basis, the American Jewish Committee decided the whole business must have been "prearranged." The jurors had clearly been instructed to find Beilis not guilty, the committee inferred, in order "to satisfy the public opinion of the civilized world." While at the same time, "to satisfy the Black Hundreds" they were "ordered to leave the ritual charge unsettled."[106]

Overall, the affair was a public relations disaster for the regime. It aroused indignation in Jewish circles across the world and fortified liberal sentiment at home.[107] The Russian ambassador to the United States, Georgy Bakhmetev (1847–1928)—not to be confused with Boris Bakhmetyev (1880–1951), who represented the Provisional Government in the same post—complained that the "American *Zhidi* [*sic*] have not failed to take advantage of an opportunity, and have used the Kiev case to foment a new agitation against Russia."[108]

A campaign is precisely what ensued, but it took some maneuvering to make sure it did not backfire. The Berlin Hilfsverein, eager to avoid the appearance of an exclusively Jewish effort, gathered the signatures of leading German personalities in protest.[109] In the delicate context of diplomatic alliances, Lucien Wolf in London took care not to question the Anglo-Russian entente, and feared that "any protest meetings or other Jewish agitation on the Blood Accusation just now"—in September 1913—"will only play into the hand of the anti-Semites."[110] Yet protests were held and prominent British names appeared on petitions.[111] In a stunning coup, Lord Nathaniel Rothschild (1840–1915) induced the Vatican to confirm the authenticity of an eighteenth-century statement by the future Pope Clement XIV, while still a cardinal, condemning the Blood Libel accusation.[112] In retrospect, Wolf confessed he had "never expected much from the verdict. All that was necessary for us was to obtain the utmost publicity for the trial so as to enlighten public opinion outside Russia as to what is going on in that country. There, I think, we have succeeded."[113]

Publicity—or rather, public enlightenment—was also a key goal of the domestic initiative, which, as in the earlier Blondes Case, likewise entailing a charge of ritual murder, did not restrict itself to legal defense and involved the participation of prominent non-Jewish figures. In 1902, the Jewish lawyer Oskar Gruzenberg had been joined in the defense by the Russified Pole Vladimir Spasovich (Spasowicz, 1829–1906). Now, Gruzenberg was joined by four other lawyers, including Vasily Maklakov. The prominent psychiatrist Vladimir Bekhterev (1857–1927) testified on Beilis's behalf as a medical expert.[114] Vladimir Nabokov attended the trial.[115] The affair gripped the Russian public; intellectuals felt they had to take a stand; routine expressions of anti-Jewish feeling which had earlier seemed benign now raised hackles in cultured circles. This, for example, was the case of the habitually antisemitic philosopher Vasily Rozanov (1856–1919), long tolerated, despite his extreme views, as a brilliant eccentric, who was now finally censured by his friends.[116]

Indeed, the trial showcased the full spectrum of public discourse on the subject of the Jews, from the arch-reactionary Black Hundreds, funded by the minister of internal affairs, to the cream of the liberal establishment.[117] Two points were at issue: the fate of the accused and the defamation of the Jewish religion constituted by the terms of the accusation. Gruzenberg defined his task as the defense of Beilis, not the vindication of the Jewish religion, which the Union of the Russian People had chosen for its target. Accusations of ritual murder were insulting, he declared; Jews must not stoop to refute them.[118] In his address to the jury Gruzenberg nevertheless did not limit himself to challenging the evidence, but spoke as a Jew defending the honor of his faith.[119]

This was a posture Maklakov obviously could not adopt. While recognizing that the case was directed not against the particular Jewish defendant but against the Jewish people as a whole, he insisted on keeping to a narrow defense, focused on the seemingly technical, but fundamental, issue—the absence of evidence implicating Beilis in the murder. As he had in the Duma debate on the Pale, Maklakov did not try to undermine the basis of antisemitic beliefs or, in this case, challenge the prejudices likely harbored by the jury. It was acceptable, he allowed, for jurymen, in their private capacity, to dislike the Jews or harbor fantasies about the Jewish religion. In their formal capacity, however, they must observe the demands of the law.

Outside the courtroom, in the pages of the Russian press, prominent cultural figures weighed in on Beilis's behalf. In 1902, moral support had been solicited from a handful of well-known figures: the left-leaning journalist and well-known writer Maxim Gorky (1868–1936), the world-renowned author and spiritual guru Leo Tolstoy (1828–1910), and the popular writer of mixed Polish and Ukrainian parentage, Vladimir Korolenko (1853–1921).[120] Now, ten years later, Gorky and Korolenko again responded. Active in progressive causes and the author of a vivid depiction of the aftermath of the Kishinev pogrom, Korolenko issued "A Call to Russian Society," which declared: "In the name of justice, in the name of reason and the love of humanity, we raise our voices against the new outburst of fanaticism and ignorant untruth."[121]

In the end, the jury of ordinary Russians accepted the plausibility of the original charge, acceding to the existence of the blood ritual, but judged the evidence inadequate to convict the accused of murder. As in the less widely followed Blondes Case, the defendant was thus acquitted.[122] In an article written after the Beilis trial, Maklakov described the entire affair as a test not of antisemitism or of a particular man's guilt, but of the Russian legal system. The case discredited the regime, but the acquittal vindicated the institutions of justice.[123] If, as the American Jewish Committee had supposed, the scenario had been orchestrated with the purpose of satisfying the wolves and the sheep, the strategy had failed. The outcome was understood as a double defeat. The jury's decision was derided as a "judicial Tsushima," with reference to the monarchy's humiliating loss to the Japanese in 1905.[124] Only the February Revolution, the regime's political Tsushima, prevented Maklakov from serving the three-month prison term to which he was sentenced for publishing his views on the trial.[125]

The Beilis verdict was rendered in October 1913. Nine months later, Russia was at war. The patriotic xenophobia encouraged by official propaganda provided new justification for antisemitic policies already in place well before 1914. In the 1890s, the Army High Command had begun distributing antisemitic propaganda in the ranks, a move with ominous consequences.[126] Accusations against the Jews as an entire people reflected the conviction, harbored by many in positions of power and disseminated in the right-wing press, that the Jews, as civilians and in uniform, were traitors to the Russian cause.[127]

The demands of wartime patriotism complicated the position of Jewish leaders everywhere. As the case of Lucien Wolf demonstrates, the question of antisemitism had become a factor in Britain's relationship to Russia well before the war. In 1914, the Anglo-Jewish press protested the Russian alliance, but the Conjoint Foreign Committee, representing the Jewish community leadership, realized it had no choice but to come around.[128] It nevertheless continued to gather information on the treatment of Jews in the eastern war zone.[129] On the American side, representatives of the Joint Distribution Committee, newly created in November 1914 to raise money in support of victims of expulsion, dispossession, and violence, toured the region and sent back damning reports.[130] Funding for the Joint Distribution Committee was raised with the help of Jacob Schiff, the same financier-philanthropist who had tried to shift the balance in the Russo-Japanese War and had sponsored the publication of Prince Urusov's 1906 Duma speech.[131] American Jews were perceived to have political clout and the belligerent nations were concerned to influence America's role in the war.[132]

Jews without borders had a certain leverage for a while. Despite the delicacy of Britain's diplomatic position, the point of Wolf's diplomacy was to pressure the Great Powers into exerting influence on the countries that most glaringly mistreated their Jewish minorities. Jewish financial prowess provided muscle. As Lord Robert Cecil (1864–1958) in the Foreign Office remarked in 1916: "It might be pointed out to the Russian Minister of Finance that antisemitism makes Jewish financial assistance to the Allies very difficult to obtain and this war may well turn on finance."[133] The Russian minister of finance was all too aware of this dilemma.

During the war Jewish organizations abroad maintained contact with progressive leaders in the Russian State Duma. Wolf let Russian officials know that outside support for the war effort, Jewish money in particular, depended on the introduction of Jewish rights.[134] Yet the Foreign Office was reluctant to campaign against their ally's mistreatment of the Jews, when German atrocities were the focus of Entente propaganda. British diplomats preferred to accept the charges of Jewish treason at face value. Leading figures such as Sir George Buchanan (1854–1924), the British ambassador in Petrograd, and the Russia expert Bernard Pares (1867–1949) echoed the official Russian line, despite the barrage of information emanating in particular from American Jewish sources.[135] At the American end, Jewish leaders were pressuring Washington to impose conditions on U.S. trade with Russia.[136]

The Jewish diaspora thus mobilized a campaign to influence the fate of the Jews on the eastern front, partly through the agency of foreign governments, partly in concert with Jewish leaders inside Russia. The latter also continued to rely on their domestic allies, a contingent of gentile intellectuals and public figures who, against the backdrop of sometimes ideological, but often routine prejudice, continued to speak out in defense of the Jews. They did so in the face of an amplified crusade in the right-wing press against Jewish treachery and the army's assault on the inhabitants of the Pale. This involved mass expulsions, hostage-taking, and incitement to pogrom violence, which even the Council of Ministers decried as a mistake.[137] In addition to the cost in lives and suffering of those who fled or were expelled, the policies contributed to the flood of refugees into the interior, damaging the areas left behind, as well as the places forced to absorb them. The result was a humanitarian crisis of serious proportions.[138] Exacerbated xenophobia at the same time deepened ethnic divisions within the empire, weakening the sense of common resolve and loyalty.

Jews responded to the threat in practical terms. On the local level, communities organized armed self-defense. In Petrograd, a group including Maxim Vinaver and Genrikh Sliozberg, Defense Bureau veterans, established the Jewish Committee for the Relief of War Victims (Evreiskii komitet pomoshchi zhertvam voiny). The committee not only provided material assistance but also sent agents into the field to gather information on pogrom violence. Among them was the ethnographer S. An-sky (Solomon Rappoport, 1863–1920), later known as the author of the play *The Dybbuk*.[139] Meanwhile, the Russian-language Jewish press worked to counter the stereotypes of Jews as shirkers or cowards, though whether its message reached the general public is hard to tell. An illustrated magazine published in Moscow, called *Evrei na voine* (Jews in the War), celebrated Jewish courage on the battlefield. Featuring portraits of decorated Jewish soldiers and Jewish medics, it noted examples of Jewish valor recognized even in the right-wing press.[140] In a similar spirit, the Petrograd weekly, *Novyi voskhod* (A New Dawn), published lists of Jewish wounded, fallen, and decorated.[141] On the Duma floor, Jewish deputies denounced official policy, while pledging the loyalty of their people.[142] A speech in August 1914 by Naftali Fridman (1863–1921), from Kovno Province, circulated widely.[143]

The war changed the context for liberal politics. The question of rights—in general and for the Jews, in particular—was off the table. The regime, for all its deficiencies, could not be challenged in wartime. The Kadet Party nevertheless continued to provide an important forum for Jewish advocacy, even if its efforts seemed increasingly inadequate.[144] At the Kadet Party congress in June 1915, Vinaver began by stressing the Jews' patriotic support for the war, despite their status as second-class subjects.[145] They were imperial patriots, he affirmed, not only from loyalty to their homeland, but also from self-interest. The war must be won, not to preserve the monarchy, but to guarantee the integrity of empire, on which the Jews relied for their economic livelihood. "Russian Jews understand that Russia, as a living organism, cannot be diced up or have one or another organ sliced off, because Russia, as an organism, is an indivisible unit." A Polish-born Russian subject of the Jewish faith, Vinaver lauded the framework in which multiple identities could survive and flourish. "From the purely Jewish national point of view," he concluded, reassuring his audience and admonishing his fellow Jews, "it would be a great misfortune for the core of Russia to be torn to pieces."[146] Aside from the economic motive, the Jews in Russian Poland had other reasons to prefer imperial rule, despite the hardships it imposed, to the prospect of an independent Poland. Polish nationalists, Vinaver observed, advocated "if not the elimination [*istreblenie*] of the Jews, then their economic ruin [*razorenie*] or at least the restriction of their rights" in the envisioned postwar nation.[147]

If the campaign for civil and political equality was on hold, the humanitarian crisis facing the Jews demanded other strategies. The problem for Jewish advocates was to refute the noxious stereotypes that flooded the right-wing press, "the slippery slope of omnibus accusations" encouraged by official policies and propaganda. At first the antisemites had depicted the declarations of Jewish patriotism in the Duma and the press as a ruse to extract legal equality, but they soon accused the Jews collectively of treason.[148] Jews were not a myth, however, but a complex reality. Most, like Morris Greenfield, did their patriotic duty, though he, like many others, also did his best to avoid it. Some might indeed have engaged in espionage, Vinaver conceded, for a number of reasons—better or worse, but the wartime disregard for due process made it impossible to distinguish fact from fantasy. The government had political reasons for wanting to blame the Jews—perhaps to deflect attention from cases of actual treason—but its appeals to widespread prejudice built on circumstances peculiar to the war.[149] Russian soldiers, Vinaver observed, were disturbed by the strange appearance of the Polish Jews, who did not resemble the Russian type and spoke a language the enemy understood but Russians in uniform did not. Wartime anxieties thus amplified long-held myths, which became dangerous, however, only when the military authorities encouraged or failed to counteract them.

Following Vinaver's presentation, the Kadet congress drafted a resolution that emphasized Jewish patriotism, denounced the principle of "collective responsibility" (*krugovaia otvetstvennost'*), and called for active opposition to antisemitic propaganda.[150] During the discussion, Maklakov reported his own observations of the Galician front, where antisemitism had reached "colossal" proportions. The problem, as he saw it, was how to correct the attitudes of the fighting men, without discrediting the same authorities that led them into battle and encouraged them to believe in Jewish treachery.[151] In short, how to sustain the existing regime (of which he was an outspoken critic) when engaged in war, despite the antisemitism that was harmful to its own existence.

Under the circumstances, Maklakov admitted in a provocative phrase, he would not blame the Russian Jews, whom he believed to be patriotic, if they indeed welcomed the invaders. "The Austrian Jews have a civic duty to support their army," he noted, "and the Russian Jews have the moral right . . . ," he began, but was interrupted by cries of "enough." He had not said he believed in Jewish treason, he objected, adding that in any case "no factual evidence of Jewish spying would justify the way they are being treated." Some might be offended by his choice of words, but he doubted the party's resolution as it stood would be taken seriously in the army.[152] The objective, as in the Beilis trial, was to influence minds saturated with harmful misconceptions—if one's goal was to influence them at all.

To all this, Kadet leader Pavel Miliukov (1859–1943) replied that the resolution in fact accepted the possibility of individual cases of Jewish treason, as did Vinaver's report, but he objected to Maklakov's seeming to implicate the Jews en masse. No one, Maklakov retorted, believes all Jews are spies, but the army thinks all spies are Jews. The Kadets must fight that conviction, and the only way to do so was with facts. Insisting on equal rights for Jews would not address the problem. Maklakov recommended the resolution be less "one-sided." Miliukov defended Maklakov's right to state his own opinion, but a delegate insisted the congress repudiate the idea that the Jews "have the moral right to be spies."[153] Missing the intended irony, Maklakov's listeners seem to have misinterpreted the meaning of his clever phrase, but they did not misconstrue his position: in violating its part of the social contract the state had liberated the Jews from the obligation to uphold theirs. More important, if the party wanted to have a political impact, it must work within the realm of the possible.

Inflammatory rhetoric aside, the delegates debated how best to combat the "scourge of antisemitism."[154] How could the party speak with authority, given that it was already considered prejudiced in favor of the Jews—"Yidified." Better to act in consort with other parties, through the medium of the Duma, to arouse society as a whole.[155] Two months later, in August 1915, in response to the crisis set off by the imperial army's Great Retreat eastward into the interior, such a coalition emerged. The majority in the Fourth Duma, which sat with interruptions from November 15, 1912, until February 1917, established the so-called Progressive Bloc. Its program included a demand for gradual progress toward the goal of Jewish rights, a watered-down version of the basic Kadet position.[156] The Bloc surprisingly enough attracted the support of the Kiev journalist Vasily Shulgin, who agreed that persecuting the Jews in the context of the war was counterproductive.[157] Shulgin had broken ranks with fellow antisemites during the Beilis affair, denouncing the entire campaign as an embarrassment.[158] He now again defined himself as a moderate in comparison with the extreme Right, which, in response to the formation of the Progressive Bloc, had stepped up its campaign of obstruction.[159]

The official campaign against the Jews also intensified as the crisis deepened. In early 1916 it came to the attention of the Duma that the ministries of finance and of internal affairs had issued secret circulars that accused the Jews of sabotaging the war effort by various underhanded economic maneuvers and ordered the police to take action against them. The government insisted the instructions were not intended to encourage violence.[160] In February and March, the Jewish deputies, with Kadet support, demanded the Duma interpellate the minister on the status of the circulars and the charge of fomenting hostility to the Jews. In another of his provocative moves, Maklakov refused to sign the demand for interpellation. He seems to have wished to avoid a split in the Progressive Bloc on this issue, but his posture made a bad impression on the Jewish public.[161]

Maklakov seemed again to betray the cause on a related occasion. When the ardent antisemite Georgy Zamyslovsky (1872–1920), a member of the Right Fraction, who had supported the government's case against Beilis, rose to denounce the "Yids," a Social Democratic delegate called him a hooligan and was expelled from the chamber.[162] Maklakov approved the expulsion. It was the Kadet deputy Andrey Shingarev (1869–1918), not himself Jewish, who denounced Zamyslovsky, in a speech that circulated widely.[163] Ultimately, Miliukov convinced the Jewish deputies to withdraw their demand to confront the minister, who was certain to turn the case against them. The Jewish press was deeply disappointed in this concession. The well-known writer Leonid Andreev (1871–1919), prominent among the gentile intellectuals earlier enlisted by Vinaver's Defense Bureau to support the Jewish cause, for his part, took Maklakov personally to task.[164]

Maklakov's brand of political realism was in evidence again in June 1916, when the Progressive Bloc decided to put on the Duma agenda consideration of a 1907 bill on civic equality for peasants. The bill affirmed provisions instituted by the late Prime Minister Pyotr Stolypin (1862–1911) in October 1906 in the interval between Duma sittings. The Kadets wished to attach the demand for Jewish equality to the bill's provisions, but Maklakov feared this step would doom it. Its defeat would deprive the peasants of rights they already in fact enjoyed and invite them to blame the Jews for the damage. In violation of party discipline, he altered the draft, angering some Jewish members. The Kadet deputy Fridman, whose speech in 1914 affirming Jewish dedication to the war had made such a vivid impression, now quit the Progressive Bloc.[165] The entire issue of Jewish rights was soon rendered moot, however, when the Provisional Government decreed legal equality for all citizens of the still politically undefined successor to the defunct autocratic regime.[166]

Before arriving at the achievement of legal equality after February 1917, an event that did nothing to stem the incidence of anti-Jewish violence, we must return to the context of the war and the dilemma posed, perhaps awkwardly, by Maklakov in his response to Vinaver's draft resolution. How indeed to alter hostile preconceptions about the Jews? Such perceptions, as Vinaver had explained in his remarks, did not derive from the actual facts of occasional Jewish espionage, but from stereotypes nourished by official and unofficial propaganda. Wars increased the friction among domestic populations with habits of suspicion to draw upon. They also, however, provided occasions for solidarity and patriotic display. Advocates for Jewish rights must use the chance to alter images and prejudices, as well as laws.

The task of countering stereotypes belonged to the empire's cosmopolitan literary intelligentsia. Visiting Kishinev two months after the 1903 pogrom, Vladimir Korolenko had composed a description of the massacre based on the testimony of witnesses, which deplored the atmosphere of "savage enmity and hatred" that still pervaded the site where "a crowd had murdered defenseless people, murdered them slowly and deliberately, in the midst of a populated town, as though in the depths of a dark forest."[167] The account was first published in Russian by the Jewish Bund in London, in English translation again in London in 1904, in Russia after 1905. Leo Tolstoy, for his part, wrote a letter deploring the "horrible Kishinev events," which was widely circulated abroad.[168] He also contributed three sketches to a volume organized by the Yiddish writer Sholem-Aleichem (Solomon Rabinovich, 1859–1916) to raise money for pogrom victims.[169]

In response to the next major crisis, the post-1905 pogroms, the prominent journalist Vasily Nemirovich-Danchenko (1845–1936) used the press as his pulpit. Citing the Jews' valiant contribution to the Russo-Japanese War, he denounced the Odessa Black Hundreds as "a frenzied mob of murderers and plunderers." They were no less savage than the "Bashi-Bazouks" vilified during the Russo-Turkish War as symbols of infidel brutality. Some of the innocent families murdered in the days after the October Manifesto, he observed, belonged to the Jewish soldiers who had been fighting in Manchuria. "They died side by side with our men. They lay side by side in field hospitals, they are buried together in common graves."[170] Most of the military physicians working tirelessly under terrible conditions were Jewish. "This is my revenge for Kishinev," the writer quoted one of them as saying. "We out here are fighting to win respect for the Jews, to gain equality and brotherhood with the Russians. As a result of our work, the returning soldiers will tell everyone about us and we will no longer hear the repulsive cry—beat the Jews. The 'Yid' will disappear into the realm of the past."[171]

The "Yid" was not ready for the history books, however. Positive images were still needed. After Kishinev, Korolenko had provided the Jewish victims with individual stories and faces. A similar focus on innocent victimhood characterized a short story by the Jewish writer David Aizman (1869–1922), published while the trial of the 1906 Białystok pogrom was unfolding. "Krovavyi razliv" (The Blood-Letting) depicted the fate of a Jewish family in which the invalid mother had died of shock and the daughter had been raped.[172] Abram, the father and husband, a simple shoemaker, is powerless to stop the assault. The story appeared in Maxim Gorky's literary quarterly, *Znanie* (Knowledge), where it was accompanied in the same issue by the penultimate installment of his novel *Mat'* (*Mother*), establishing a contrast between the two plots.[173] In one, the patriarch does not fight back; in the other, an elderly mother of simple peasant background—the least enlightened of all social character types—proceeds from passivity to action and implicitly from powerlessness to potential power, or at least to the dignity of self-assertion. Gorky's tale is a call to revolt. Equally unabashed and moralistic, Aizman's pogrom story lacks Gorky's triumphalism. He, too, suggests that revolution is the only solution, but revolution was a Russian problem; the Jewish male protagonist was not yet ready to act on his own or others' behalf.

Six years later, when the next war came along, the traitorous, cowardly "Yid" made another appearance, now accompanied by the Bestial Teuton and the Perfidious Pole, diaspora groups with whom the Jews were associated or intermingled. In the case of the Germans, the threat of the foreign invader activated resentment at the power that domestic Germans—ranging from Baltic noblemen, who had for generations played a major role in the imperial army and state administration, to factory owners and shopkeepers—were felt to exercise in Russian life (*nemetskoe zasil'e*).[174] The patriotic anger sometimes took the form of mob violence, as in the attack on the German embassy in Petrograd and the trashing of foreign-sounding businesses in May 1915.[175] These, too, were "pogroms."

The Poles, for their part, were regarded with suspicion for a number of reasons: because of their repeated attempts to achieve independence, because ethnic Poles fought also in the German and Austrian armies, and because the Polish and western provinces constituted a border with the enemy and a principal military battleground. The majority of the empire's Jewish population, speaking a Germanic tongue, as Vinaver had reminded his colleagues, occupied this same marginal terrain, increasing the already well-established tendency to view them as potential or actual internal enemies. Jews served as conduits between cultures and as economic middlemen, dangerous roles to play in times of war, when national differences were supposed to anchor the loyalty of the so-called masses. And the Jewish masses under Russian rule, as Maklakov dared to say out loud, had many reasons to resent the way they were treated. The expectation of disloyalty might have a basis in fact.

Striving to defuse the charges of collective responsibility (all Jews were traitors), writers responded with romanticized individual portraits. Typical efforts in this vein took the form of "impressions from the front" narrated by an officer-intellectual. A popular series of pamphlets on the war included one example in which we meet "Gershka" (diminutive for Hirsch), a shtetl musician. At the front, he becomes a signalist. Thoroughly civilian in outlook, with no concept of danger, "Gershka turned out to have courage."[176] From his outpost above the battlefield, he uses his bugle to relay the commander's orders. One day, surprised from behind, his head bloodied, his horn smashed, he rushes without thinking in the direction of the troops. Eager to convey his vital message, he forgets he has no weapon of his own, and is felled in his tracks. Gershka is naive, trustworthy, and sincere—inadvertently heroic.

The Jew thus has a form of courage that is honorable, but not aggressive. Whatever respect the Jewish figures can muster is typically mixed with condescension. Another story in the same collection centers on "Khrabryi Iashka" (Brave Jackie), described by his junior officer as a "small, dark-eyed little soldier," whose surname was Mendelevich, "as everybody knew." At first, this Yashka trembles at every noise—in short, "he was a coward." During one ferocious bombardment, Yashka is ordered to find out what is going on. Craven but subservient, off he goes, "with the speed of a hare." The minute he leaves, a powerful blast destroys the spot he had huddled in for safety and everyone else around it. He returns to find a crater filled with bloody flesh. Transformed, Yashka joins the next attack at full throttle—"his face distorted in the expression of wickedly inhuman ecstasy." Caught up in the clash, the junior officer vaguely discerns the naked bayonet of a German soldier advancing toward him. Just in time, the German is stopped in his tracks by "some sort of person in a drenched overcoat," who wrestles him to the ground. That evening the Russians manage to disentangle the German and his assailant from their mortal embrace. They bury "brave Yashka, who had selflessly and unexpectedly sacrificed his own life."[177]

The pattern repeats itself: the Jew in these tales is described as diminutive — in stature, in name, by items of clothing — in terms at once affectionate and patronizing, infantilizing and emasculating. In the course of the typical story the Jewish character rises to the occasion, displaying a childlike courage: fearful in a childish way, he plunges into danger with naive disregard for the risk. Or else he turns out to be selfless — compassionate and disinterested, never asking for money or any kind of reward on his own behalf.[178] Respectful, even self-abasing, the fictional Jew never appears, even on the battlefield, as a self-confident or aggressive male. The opposite of the scheming, devious Yid, he proves his loyalty again and again. In "Smert' soldata Branfmana" (The Death of Soldier Branfman), a sketch by Jakov Okunev (Okun', 1882–1932), appearing in *Evrei na voine*, the protagonist tells the Russian narrator that Jews must always prove themselves in the war; their deaths refute the slander against them.[179] In Okunev's idealized vision, all men in the Russian trenches are brothers — the skeptical intellectual (the author's persona), the peasant from Ryazan, and the Jewish drummer.[180]

Such sentimental counter-propaganda offended the philosopher Fyodor Stepun (1884–1965). Of mixed Russified German and Russian Orthodox background, he was now an artillery ensign serving in Galicia.[181] His published letters from the front took aim at the antisemites, who slandered the Jews as a species. They also took aim at fairy tales of harmony between Russians, Jews, and Poles, allegedly now reconciled by the war. Stepun preferred to describe what he himself had witnessed. In Galicia an ancient Jew, with terror-filled eyes, is led to the gallows by Russian soldiers who accuse him of reporting to the Austrians.[182] In another tableau, a Cossack rides a miserable sled pulled by a bony nag (ribs like the springs of an old mattress), driven by an aged, ragged "Yid" (Stepun's quotes) in side-locks, his face frozen in horror. The Cossack is whipping the Yid, who is whipping the horse. Stepun calls this "the specter of a pogrom — the pogrom that haunts us" (*etot pogromnyi prizrak*). And if not a pogrom, then humiliation. These are not occasional incidents, comments Stepun, but the "entire pattern of our recent history."[183]

The opposition to antisemitism among Russian intellectuals revolved around a handful of well-known writers. Maxim Gorky had originally been contacted by the St. Petersburg Defense Bureau after the 1903 Gomel pogrom.[184] In 1908 he published Aizman's "Blood-Letting"; in 1911 he was among the first to protest against the Beilis Case. In November 1914, Leonid Andreev published a wake-up call in a middle-class Moscow newspaper, which began: "Yes, we are still barbarians."[185] In 1915, Gorky and Andreev teamed with Symbolist poet and writer Fyodor Sologub (1863–1927) to disturb the "pattern of our recent history" once again. Together they formed the Russian Society for the Study of Jewish Life (Rossiiskoe obshchestvo izucheniia evreiskoi zhizni), a deceptively banal label. The Society arranged a series of public events and organized a volume of essays addressing the Jewish Question. Called *Shchit* (*The Shield*), it was a gesture on the part of the gentile intelligentsia, opposing antisemitism and in defense of the Jews.[186]

The project enjoyed the patronage of Petrograd mayor Count Ivan Tolstoy (1858–1916), the Society's president, who already had a reputation as a "Yid-lover."[187] A caricature in the May 1914 issue of *Novoe vremia* depicted him unflatteringly with an elongated nose, unruly whiskers, and a long black coat. His activism on behalf of Jewish rights was in fact the anomaly in a distinguished but conventional career. The scion of an old aristocratic family, he spent his life in scholarly pursuits and public service. By avocation a numismatist, he served as vice president of the Imperial Academy of Art and secretary of the Imperial Russian Archeological Society. From October 1905 to April 1906, despite his progressive views, he served as minister of education in Witte's cabinet, but when Witte stepped down he was not reappointed. In 1913 he was elected mayor of St. Petersburg (later Petrograd), which he remained until his death in 1916.[188]

Alongside these varied activities and obligations, in autumn 1905 Tolstoy organized a Circle for Equality and Brotherhood (Kruzhok ravnopraviia i bratstva), in which the Baron Günzburg and his son, David (1857–1910), played a leading role. The Circle was reconstituted in 1909 as the Society for the Brotherhood of Peoples Inhabiting Russia (Obshchestvo bratstva narodnostei, naseliaiushikh Rossiiu). Its title reflected Tolstoy's conviction, in the Kadet spirit, that resolution of the Jewish Question transcended the fate of the Jews. In a personal audience with Nicholas himself, he argued that equal rights would deprive the Jews of incentive to support the revolutionary movement.[189] But his objections to official policy went deeper. As he explained in an essay published in 1907: "A whole series of reforms, are, if not organically, then intimately connected" with the resolution of the Jewish Question. This resolution was part of the broader issue of equality before the law, a precondition for Russia's economic and political evolution.[190] Antisemitism could be found everywhere, Tolstoy noted, but only in Russia was it enshrined in law and only in Russia were there people "who in their hatred for the Jews are ready to bring the gravest charges against them, with the sole purpose of arousing the hatred of the crude, uneducated masses."[191]

Under increasing pressure during the war, Tolstoy maintained his public stance. He demonstratively appeared next to Baron Günzburg in the Petrograd Choral Synagogue, which the financier had funded, and he denounced the violent xenophobia of patriotic propaganda.[192] The Günzburg family indeed embodied the core antisemitic attributes: "profiteering," social climbing, and liberal views. They had made their wealth in two traditionally Jewish ways—distilling and purveying alcohol and provisioning the army. They later formed a private bank, which serviced the imperial government, and had invested in railroad construction. In short, while also enriching themselves, they had made a significant contribution to Russia's economic development. Yet, they were rewarded for their efforts not by the tsar, but by the Archduke of Hesse-Darmstadt, who provided them with titles of nobility for services rendered to him, titles that Alexander II had recognized as hereditary but Nicholas II did not. The Günzburgs were active in Jewish public life, promoting legal equality, engaging in philanthropy, and providing relief for the victims of pogroms. They lent their support to liberal parties in the Duma, whose position on civil rights was consonant with their own.[193]

Tolstoy's association with the family constituted a public endorsement of their positive role in Russian life. The mayor's patronage of *Shchit*, the natural extension of his own civic activism, relayed a similar message about the Jews in general. *Shchit* included essays on the political and moral dangers of antisemitism, as well as a selection of fables in the counter-stereotype mode. The authors included several Kadets, among them Pavel Miliukov, along with neo-Christian Orthodox progressives Anton Kartashev (1875–1960), a church historian, and philosopher Sergey Bulgakov (1871–1944). Dmitry Merezhkovsky (1865–1941) and Zinaida Gippius (1869–1945), stars of the Petrograd literary intelligentsia, also participated, as did psychiatrist Vladimir Bekhterev, who had testified for the defense in the Beilis trial.[194]

The contribution of the renowned Polish linguist Jan Niecisław Baudouin de Courtenay (1845–1929) deserves special attention. It reiterated the position he had expressed before the war, in opposition to the anti-Jewish boycott instituted in 1912 by the National Democratic Party (Narodowa Demokracja: Endecja or Endeks), under the leadership of Roman Dmowski (1864–1939), which made antisemitism central to its platform.[195] Baudouin de Courtenay was what the late historian Jerzy Jedlicki calls an "ethical individualist."[196] Then as now he challenged the basic premise of antisemitic rhetoric, which targeted Jews as a bloc, a collective entity constituting by its very existence a danger to the surrounding Christian society. With stinging irony and considerable civic courage, the linguist rejected what had become the dominant discourse in prewar Polish public life.[197]

Most of the fictional contributions to *Shchit* adopted the strategy employed by the Russian-language Jewish press of turning that discourse on its head. The Jewish protagonists here assume uniformly heroic postures. Mikhail Artsybashev (1878–1927) thus describes a battle in which the officers have somehow disappeared, but the abandoned peasant-soldiers are saved by the quick thinking of the single Jew in their ranks.[198] The sketch by Count Aleksey Tolstoy (1882–1945) compressed a number of common themes. A humble Jewish mill owner finds himself confronted by a party of Germans who insist he let them signal from the top of his mill. His educated son and daughter, home from Europe, disdain their father's traditional and apparently subservient ways. The next morning, when the father does not return, the daughter finds his body lying beside the mill. Guessing he has died resisting the Germans, who are still inside, she locks the door and runs to warn the nearby Russian forces. Struck in the back by a German bullet, she crumples to the snow. Amazed to find a Jewish woman dead at their feet, the Russians discover the trapped Germans and wipe them out.[199] The simple father is vindicated in his honor and dignity, the Europeanized youth in their loyalty to their Russian home.

The contribution by the former Orthodox priest, Sergey Gusev-Orenburgsky (1867–1963), bore the derisive, but here ironic title, "Evreichik" (Jew-boy). It features a selfless Jewish medic ("*evreichik-sanitar*") and the selfless Russian soldiers he cares for. At the climactic moment, the story's narrator takes cover in a Christian cemetery but is felled by shrapnel. Returning to consciousness, he finds the "Jew-boy" at his side, binding his wounds—a Jewish savior surrounded by crosses, white against the dark sky.[200]

Such tales all begin with the expectation of cowardice or weakness and turn on the surprise of bravery and inner strength. This strength, however, is not equated with power. The painter Leonid Pasternak (1862–1945), father of the poet Boris Pasternak (1890–1960), a secular Jew known for his patriotic war posters, provided a sketch for the volume's cover. It depicts a downcast Jewish father or husband, a simple tradesman or worker—like Aizman's protagonist in "Krovavyi razliv"—at the bedside of his injured young wife or daughter. He is despondent, not angry, mourning the injury but not prepared to strike back. The image underscores the point that Jews are dignified but not dangerous.

It is hard to imagine that any minds were changed by such maudlin attempts to refute antisemitic fantasies of Jewish power and subversion. Russian Jews knew very well that they were fighting in the army, participating in politics, and organizing on their own behalf; antisemites were unlikely to renounce their cherished myths and symbols. Efforts to mitigate the impact of the war indeed had little effect in this regard. In February 1915, the Jewish historian Simon Dubnow remarked: "The terrible news of the military pogroms and the prospect of a pogrom epidemic, as the crown of the war, have frozen our hearts."[201] An agent for the American Joint Distribution Committee reported in May 1916: "Everyone is generally convinced that at some point after the war pogroms will break out all over Russia with a force and ferocity the Jews have not experienced before. The attackers will not go after Jewish property, as is their custom. They will use the bloodbath as revenge for the Jews' crime of treason."[202]

The revolution, when it came in February 1917, only confirmed the Russian antisemites in their long-standing view of the Jews as agents of destruction. The Allied Powers, by contrast, were relieved to be fighting alongside a newly democratic Russia. They feared, however, that the moderate leaders, like the autocracy before them, would be unable to withstand the stress of the war. The British Foreign Office was disturbed by reports indicating that Jews were particularly active in the socialist opposition to the Provisional Government and to the alliance with Britain and France, promoting, if not a separate peace, then "peace without indemnities and annexations."[203]

Having long and strenuously repudiated the blanket accusations launched against the Jews from the Right, Vinaver and Sliozberg, too, for their own reasons, now more than ever deplored the tendency of Jewish youth to support the radical Left. As liberals, they feared for the future of the Provisional Government; as Jews they feared that Jewish radicalism would stoke the antisemitism already magnified by the war. Vinaver refused a position in the new cabinet, to avoid the presence of a Jew even in that moderate embodiment of the revolution.[204] Of course, as he might have learned by now, no adjustment to the behavior of actual Jews could affect the power of antisemitic mythmaking. The liberal Vinaver might stand aside; the Menshevik Julius Martov (1873–1923) might deplore Bolshevik excess and challenge his "Russian" comrade Vladimir Lenin (1870–1924), but Jews would continue to be associated with the plot to destroy Russia in which they were already assigned starring roles.

With the Bolshevik takeover in October, both wartime images of the Jew acquired new salience: the Jew as power-hungry agent of destruction; the Jew as defenseless victim of prejudice and assault.[205] The imperial regime had endangered Jewish existence during the war, but its collapse opened the door to a proliferation of threats from many directions. The charged conflicts that followed the coup unleashed a storm of uncontrolled violence across the former empire. The area of the Pale, which had dissolved de facto during the war and been abolished de jure by the Provisional Government, was the battlefield on which Poles and Ukrainian nationalists fought to free themselves from Russian domination. The remaining Jewish population became the object of prolonged pogrom-style attacks, which took tens of thousands of lives, and involved abuse, humiliation, and rape. Entire communities were destroyed.[206]

In this environment, Jewish advocacy reverted largely to philanthropic mode, striving to alleviate and at the same time publicize the humanitarian catastrophe unfolding. Jewish organizations continued to monitor the evolving disaster. Following the strategy earlier employed by the Defense Bureau and elaborated by the *Shchit* collective during the war, they gathered information and interviewed victims. The material provided the basis for a volume of documents and testimony covering the pogroms then raging in the Ukraine, which was assembled in 1921 by Gusev-Orenburgsky, a *Shchit* contributor. Edited by Gorky, the volume was published in Petrograd under the imprint of the Jewish graphic artist Zinovy Grzebin (1877–1929), now in Berlin, whom Gorky had initially approached in connection with the publication of *Shchit*.[207] In 1922, a longer edition of the same work was sponsored by the Far Eastern Jewish Civic Committee for Aid to Orphan-Victims of the Pogroms, located in Harbin, a refuge to which many Jews had fled.[208]

Given the political alternatives presented by the Civil War, the question of the pogroms and of antisemitism was not, however, straightforward, either for liberal Jews or their gentile supporters. The Kadets faced terrible choices. On the one side, the Bolsheviks condemned antisemitism and included many Jews at all levels of the state and party apparatus. Yet they repudiated what they derided as "bourgeois" concepts of citizenship and civil rights and the rule of law model at the heart of the liberal credo. And in the service of building a new state, they were dispensers of extraordinary violence. Nor were the Reds able to eliminate the antisemitism among their own supporters or the pogrom violence of their own troops. On the other side, the White leaders used antisemitism as a mobilizing ideology and often condoned, if they did not directly encourage, pogrom violence as a response to the Bolshevik threat, which they equated with Jewish power. The Whites also promised a return to the kind of society that had nurtured official antisemitism to begin with.

Few White leaders favored a revival of autocracy, however, and the prospect of their success offered liberals the possibility of restoring those aspects of capitalist society, if not the old regime, they deemed essential to a progressive future: private property, "bourgeois" legality, cultural freedom. The Whites in addition fought to maintain the territorial integrity of the old empire, a goal the Kadets also espoused, against the Bolshevik willingness (for ideological and tactical reasons) to condone the "self-determination" of formerly subordinate peoples. It turned out, of course, that Soviet Russia ended by retaining most of what had been Russian imperial terrain, in the form of a federal republic, at least in name. The repressive character of Soviet rule and its murderous methods did, by contrast, confirm the liberals in their worst expectations.

The most successful military leader of the anti-Bolshevik White forces was General Anton Denikin (1872–1947), whose biography illustrates some of the paradoxes of the old empire. Born in Russian-ruled Poland, the son of a former serf, who had achieved the rank of major in the imperial army, and a Polish mother, he spoke both languages but was raised in the Orthodox faith. A successful general in the Great War, Denikin became chief of staff after the February Revolution, but in August joined with General Lavr Kornilov (1870–1918) in trying to unseat the increasingly unstable government. After the October coup, he became a leading figure in the military opposition and eventually commander of the anti-Bolshevik Volunteer Army.

Despite—or because—of his own mixed background, Denikin stood for the integrity of empire and the dominance of the Russian-speaking Orthodox core. His slogan, "Russia—United, Great, and Indivisible" (*Rossiia edinaia, velikaia i nedelimaia*), a formula taken from the fundamental laws of the old empire, echoed the motto of the prerevolutionary extreme Right, which insisted on Russia "United and Indivisible" (*edinaia i nedelimaia*).[209] This was to be a "Russia for the Russians," as the popular author Ivan Nazhivin (1874–1940), a spokesman for Denikin's propaganda office, insisted. It was a vision that considered Jews a hostile foreign element. Nazhivin, for example, deplored "[t]he abundance of Jewish names among those who destroyed Russia . . . , or more precisely of the scum of the Jews, in the torture chambers of the various Extraordinary Commissions, their participation in all these monstrous murders, to begin with in the loathsome murder of the unfortunate Emperor and his family. All this," he declared, "revolts . . . the Russian people."[210]

The claim that Jews were responsible for the murder of the imperial family, under house arrest in Yekaterinburg, was particularly inflammatory. The slaughter of the deposed monarch and his defenseless children in July 1918 was not only shocking in its brutality, but it carried enormous symbolic weight. The accusation that Jews were to blame endorsed the myth of an anti-Russian, anti-Christian Jewish conspiracy. Its plausibility was enhanced when the charge was taken up by the former British military attaché to Russia, now head of the Allied military mission in Siberia, General Sir Alfred Knox (1870–1964), known for his antisemitic inclinations. Claude G. Montefiore (1858–1938), president of the Anglo-Jewish Association in London, demanded the *Times* publish a rebuttal of Knox's views.[211] In fact, the firing squad was composed of Russians and Hungarian prisoners of war. The Jewish origins of Filipp Goloshchekin (Isai Isaevich, 1876–1941), the military commissar of the Urals region who signed the order to proceed, were apparently unknown to either the champions or the impugners of Jewish honor. Later in charge of Kazakhstan during the genocidal famine of 1930–1933, Goloshchekin was arrested in 1939 and shot by the NKVD (The People's Commissariat of Internal Affairs), but not as punishment for his former zeal.

Despite the programmatic antisemitism of the Volunteer Army, the Kadets nevertheless persisted in seeing the Bolsheviks as the greatest threat to Russia's future and the Whites as the only hope of destroying Soviet power and reestablishing the Russian state on a constitutional foundation. The choice involved an obvious compromise with their basic principles, a compromise reflected in their response to the charged issue of Jewish support for the Bolshevik regime. The wave of brutal pogroms that swept the western provinces in 1919 was the work largely of Ukrainian and White armies, but instead of taking Denikin to task, the Kadet party congress of that year blamed the pogroms on the poisoned moral atmosphere created by Bolshevik rule, allegedly fostering the kind of brutality that easily turned against the Jews. The Kadets therefore urged "the healthy tendencies among Russian Jews," in their own interests, to "declare all-out war" against the Bolsheviks' Jewish supporters. White victory and the reestablishment of a strong government encompassing the former imperial lands were the only hope, the Kadets insisted, for the future of liberal values, among them equal rights for all.[212]

The Kadets did not accept the equation of Jews and Communism, but they seemed to credit the Jews as a community with the power to counteract it. This approach was later adopted by a group of émigré liberals that gathered in Paris around the ever-energetic Vinaver. Together with Miliukov and Alexander Konovalov (1875–1948), minister of trade and industry in the first Provisional Government, they joined in founding the weekly *Evreiskaia tribuna* (*The Jewish Tribune*, *La Tribune juive*).[213] In its pages, Vinaver continued to berate the misguided Jewish Bolsheviks who fed the prejudices of the antisemites.[214]

In exile, Vinaver continued to speak as an imperial Russian patriot, linking the future prospects of the Jewish people with the preservation of the integral Russian state. Although the Jews had not been well served by the empire in its old form, he predicted they would be still more vulnerable in the breakaway states of Ukraine, Latvia, Lithuania, and Estonia. He made an exception only for newly independent Poland, his original homeland, insisting, contrary to his position during the Great War, that Polish Jews had always favored the restoration of Polish statehood.[215] With Polish independence now a fait accompli and the National Democrats making antisemitism the keystone of their nationalist program, he may have been advocating on behalf of Polish Jews, as he had for Russian Jews with respect to the Russian Empire in 1914.

Vinaver was the animating spirit of *Evreiskaia tribuna*, but the journal was notable also for its roster of non-Jewish contributors. These included: Vladimir Nabokov; the long-serving Duma deputy and Progressive Bloc supporter Fyodor Rodichev (1854–1933); the Orthodox Church historian Anton Kartashev, a *Shchit* contributor; the international legal expert Baron Boris Nolde (1876–1948); and Count Anatoly Nesselrode (1850–1923), grandson of Nicholas I's foreign minister. All denounced antisemitism as an absolute evil, a defining feature of the unlamented old regime. They had trouble, however, fashioning a position that combined their commitment to Jewish rights (a consequence of their larger political vision) with the reality of the Civil War. Caught between the violence of class warfare unleashed by Bolshevik forces and the anti-Jewish violence perpetrated by the anti-Bolshevik Whites, and lacking any social constituency of their own, they seem to have lost their bearings.

The mere fact of appearing in *Evreiskaia tribuna*—accessible in English and French editions to an international readership—testified to the gentile liberals' continued devotion to the Jewish cause. Yet slippage occurred. An impeccable champion of Jewish rights such as Vladimir Nabokov, writing in its pages in 1920 at the height of the conflict, defended General Denikin against accusations voiced in the British Parliament that the general had countenanced the pogroms committed by his own troops. It was only the "ignorant dregs" (*temnye nizy*), Nabokov insisted, that were responsible for the horrors "staining the Volunteer Army's heroic record."[216] Fyodor Rodichev, also in *Evreiskaia tribuna*, again echoed the Kadet resolution of 1919, blaming the Bolsheviks for perverting the moral atmosphere, thus arousing the base instincts of the masses and fostering anti-Jewish violence.[217]

Nabokov, for his part, deplored the handful of Jewish Bolsheviks soiling the reputation of their entire people and exposing their innocent coreligionists to the anger of the mob. He urged the Jews to do their part in opposing Soviet power. The Jews in the Bolshevik leadership, he charged, "display some of the worst features typical of the worst representatives of their nationality, thus outraging and infuriating Russian people [*russkie liudi*]." The principle of collective responsibility was unacceptable in logical and moral terms, but it was an undeniable "psychological fact." Therefore the Jews as a nation must take a stand against the Bolshevik regime in which they were all implicated, even if unfairly.[218] "Jews as a nation"—the antisemitic shibboleth Vinaver and Maklakov had spent their careers debunking. "Outraging the Russian people"—the very phrase deployed by Baron von der Ropp in 1906 on the Duma floor, when Vinaver had energetically opposed him. Denikin's Kadet supporters thus seemed to share some of the assumptions—or at least the rhetoric—of the antisemites they deplored and whose influence did so much to damage the White cause.

The most notorious version of the argument blaming the Jews for their own suffering, and then again for complaining about it, was the work of Kievan journalist Vasily Shulgin, now editor of Denikin's flagship organ, *Velikaia Rossiia* (Great Russia). Appearing in October 1919 in Shulgin's own newspaper, *Kievlianin*, his article, "Pytka strakhom" (Torture by Fear), warned the Jews that they were faced with two paths. "The first, to confess and repent. The second, to deny and blame everyone except themselves. Which path they choose will determine their fate."[219] They must repent of promoting an evil regime and also of ensuring its success by weakening the forces arrayed against it. Their very presence in the ranks of the commissars provoked the kind of pogrom violence that gave the Whites a bad name among potential foreign backers. Similar accusations were leveled by Pyotr Struve (1870–1944), whose credentials dated to the origins of the pre-1905 Liberation Movement. Struve blamed the Jews for damaging Denikin's reputation by harping on the problem of pogroms.[220]

Writing in Berlin in 1923, the prominent Kadet Daniil Pasmanik (1869–1930) reflected back on the arguments and appeals marshalled while the struggle was still ongoing. In retrospect, he still blamed the Bolsheviks for the "descent into cultural barbarism [*kul'turnoe odichanie*],"[221] which had affected "the entire Russian populace," the

White Army included.[222] The ultimate responsibility for creating the environment that encouraged atrocities of all kinds thus lay with the Soviet regime. Yet, Pasmanik concluded, the "unrestrained antisemitism" of Denikin's armies "strongly affected the attitude of the Jewish people toward the White movement." Why should they join in the struggle against "Soviet tyranny," if the Whites promised to solve the Jewish Question by slaughtering all the Jews? Antisemitism as a sensibility was not going away—to expect as much was "utopian." "The Jews are not asking for love," Pasmanik observed wryly, but for the good of Russia, for the success of the anti-Bolshevik movement, Jews must have reason to support it. Antisemitism therefore "must disappear from the arena of positive law and political relations."[223] This was the tune that Maklakov had been singing since before the war. By 1923, it was an empty refrain.

The Bolsheviks rejected antisemitism, but they recognized violence as an important political tool. Their summons to ruthless class warfare, the Kadets charged, encouraged mob violence and rode roughshod over any concept of legal or civil rights. Bolshevik ascendancy was indeed a threat to the kind of society the liberals hoped would emerge from the revolution, but the Bolsheviks were not alone in fostering the climate of violence that characterized a civil war in which anti-Jewish pogroms became ever more numerous and vicious. In warning the Jews against supporting Soviet power, the liberals imagined they were warning them against the consequences—for the Jews, as well as everyone else—of encouraging a regime that did not respect the rights of citizens or the rule of law. Calling upon the Jews to exercise collective discipline thus seems to stand antisemitism on its head—endowing them with the special capacity as an ethnic community to influence the direction of political events.

Yet the Kadets had not abandoned their principled commitment to Jewish rights, which had always been tied to their political goals and basic values. To do so, as Maklakov realized, would be a tactical, as well as moral error. While the outcome of the struggle was still uncertain, he had pressed Denikin to take a stronger stand. It was also Maklakov, with his habit of calling a spade a spade, who refused to explain the pogroms as a reflex of the benighted soldier masses—the "populace" supposedly affected by moral degradation. The problem, as he saw it, originated at the level of political leadership. It stemmed from the virulent antisemitism of the officer corps on which Denikin relied. With an eye to placating Western public opinion and attracting support for the anti-Bolshevik cause, Maklakov repeatedly urged the general to investigate the charges leveled against him and publicize his condemnation of the pogroms.[224] Faced with the same kind of damage to their own reputation, the Ukrainians had done just that: "Even the *pogromshchik* Petlyura has made such a gesture," Maklakov observed. In response to the charge of fostering pogroms, Petlyura could therefore reply: "You see that we are not antisemites; antisemitism is only the expression of the base impulses of the dregs of society or perhaps only of certain particular milieux." The Whites, by contrast, "can claim no such thing." By expelling Jews from the Volunteer Army, Maklakov complained, the White leadership showed it had "capitulated to antisemitism. All this presents the Jewish cause in Russia in an offensive light and does our enemies a great service."[225]

Denikin was caught between the need to attract support from outside and the need to retain the loyalty of those closest around him. He objected that an explicit defense of the Jews would only increase the anger against them.[226] Maklakov, however, focused on the wider context. He had feared that Denikin's failure either to limit or condemn the overt antisemitism of his followers would hurt the White cause, particularly within the international Jewish community, which had the power to influence the policies of foreign states. In spring 1920, Denikin was succeeded at the head of the Volunteer Army by Baron Pyotr Wrangel (1878–1928), whose remaining forces held out on the Crimean Peninsula until the end of the year. Maklakov yet again stressed the need to take a decisive stand against antisemitism and the pogroms. The Russian Jews in emigration had demonstrated a commercial interest in the reestablishment of a strong Russian state. If Wrangel were only to advertise his favorable disposition, the Kadet advised, "we will have the entire Jewish people [*vse evreistvo*], that is, all its capital, on our side."[227]

In appealing, as he had before, to the psychology of the antisemites he was trying to deter from harming their shared political project, Maklakov was being pragmatic. His commitment to the ultimate goal had not wavered. On visiting the Crimea, he was appalled by the intensity of the antisemitism he found not only among the Orthodox clergy in Wrangel's entourage, but also among members of his own cultural milieu. The philosopher, now also priest, Sergey Bulgakov, erstwhile contributor to *Shchit*, was "too civilized" (*dostatochno kul'turen*), in

Maklakov's words, to countenance pogroms, yet believed the world was run by a Jewish cabal. "Such an abyss in points of departure" had opened between them, Maklakov felt, "that no kind of agreement was possible."[228] Maklakov had clung to his convictions; Bulgakov had switched sides.[229]

Maklakov had insisted to both Denikin and Wrangel that renouncing antisemitism was essential to the success of the anti-Bolshevik cause. Yet, as the Kadets had learned in the rough and tumble of Duma debates and in centers of ideological polarization such as Kiev (also the site of the Beilis trial), the liberal advocacy of Jewish rights strengthened the hand of their political opponents.[230] In the struggle for hegemony after the monarchy fell, antisemitism was an effective instrument of mass mobilization, able to compete for the same popular constituencies with the equally vociferous ideologies of the radical Left. White leaders, whatever their personal convictions, were caught between these two conflicting demands. The Kadets had brought themselves, for instrumental reasons, to tolerate the antisemitism promoted by the Whites, but antisemitism, whatever its popular appeal, had not saved the anti-Bolshevik movement. Abandoning antisemitic formulas for rhetoric acceptable to potential foreign backers would not have saved it, either. Both Whites and liberals were remote from the concrete interests and outlook of the vast majority of the former imperial population. By 1921 their political hopes had collapsed, for reasons that went beyond the Jewish Question.

Although a powerful symbolic tool, antisemitism was never the decisive factor in the confusing conflicts of the Civil War. Yet its power as the rallying cry of right-wing ideologues was only strengthened by Bolshevik victory. Its adoption or rejection continued to mark fundamentally opposing political values. These contrasting perspectives are vividly illustrated in the twenty-year exchange, beginning in 1919, between two mismatched correspondents, Vasily Maklakov, the dedicated advocate of Jewish rights, and Vasily Shulgin, once propaganda meister for General Denikin, in which they assessed the nature of the Russian Revolution and the question of the Jews.[231] For both, this had been a central concern and it continued to engage them in emigration.

The two controversial figures had lost their political context and their entire cultural habitus. In reflecting on what had been at stake in the fight they both had lost for different reasons, they refought old battles. Shulgin, for one, had not engaged in any rethinking. He had not needed the myth of the Judeo-Bolshevik conspiracy to identify the Jewish hand in the demise of Old Russia. He had already hated the Kadets in the First State Duma for their position on land reform. "Who, in the end," Shulgin had asked from the Duma floor in 1906, "rules Russia today? The Emperor Nicholas II or His Highness Vinaver I?" While meddling in Russian affairs, Vinaver had remained "the leader of the Jews." You could not be both a Jew and a Russian, Shulgin opined, à propos Vinaver's obituary in 1926, seeming to forget that Vinaver could just as well be thought of as Polish, not Russian.[232]

There was in fact an obvious parallel between himself and that most hated of "political Jews," as he called them.[233] Vinaver had abandoned Warsaw to join the Russian intelligentsia and enter imperial Russian political life. Shulgin was a Russian-speaking activist from Kiev, the center of burgeoning Ukrainian nationalism. The publisher of its leading Russian-language newspaper, he made a name for himself in Russian politics, opposed Ukrainian separatism, and considered himself an imperial Russian patriot.[234] Both men were elected to the State Duma. Neither believed their respective cultural communities could survive outside the larger Russian whole. Vinaver limited his Jewish nationalism to demands for full inclusion and equal treatment; Shulgin considered the Ukrainian nation a political fiction, a plaything of misguided elites.

Shulgin called himself and Maklakov the "black sheep" of their respective camps.[235] Shulgin's idiosyncrasy found them both on the same side of the line during the Beilis trial. On September 27, 1913, Shulgin ran an editorial in *Kievlianin*, in which he called the charges nonsense and the affair a disgrace to Russian justice. His opinions earned him a three-month prison sentence, which he evaded by enlisting in the army. At the same time, the radical antisemitic press attacked him as a Jew-lover.[236] During the war he joined the Progressive Bloc, again alongside Maklakov. In 1917, still a monarchist, he helped convince Nicholas to abdicate. At the start of the Civil War, he spoke out against pogroms, but in late 1919 he published the infamous article blaming the Jews for their own misfortunes. There was always a twist. Reflecting years later on the "idiotic" Beilis trial, Shulgin claimed it was the Jews themselves who had used the occasion to attract the attention of the worldwide press, in order to blacken Russia's reputation. The ability to cook up such a fuss reflected the "solidarity and enormous power of the Jews in all lands. One for all and all for one."[237]

Shulgin's political profile was not simple, and yet the core belief remained. Explaining his "zigzags" (*zigzagi*) on the Jewish question before 1917, he remarked: "When the Jews were against Russia, I was against them. When, in my view, they began to work 'for Russia,' I became reconciled to them."[238] In 1929, he was still convinced the Kadet Party had been led by Jews trying to revolutionize—and take over—Russia even before the Bolsheviks came along. In 1919, he nevertheless entered into dialogue with Maklakov. Maklakov belonged on the Kadet party's cautious right flank, but he had stood shoulder to shoulder with Vinaver on the question of Jewish rights and the unacceptability of antisemitism. Shulgin had agreed with Maklakov on various occasions, but the two represented opposing views of the world.

If Shulgin zigged and zagged, he remained an antisemite. Maklakov, for all his tactical maneuvers, consistently was not. At the end of 1924 he published a three-part essay on the origins of the Russian Revolution in *La Revue de Paris*.[239] In it he blamed the old regime and political moderates such as himself for paving the way for the Bolshevik disaster. "The Revolution was set off and sanctioned by moderate circles—this is no less symbolic than the old regime's docile capitulation. This capitulation of the moderates was a premonition of the funeral march of our Revolution."[240] Before the war the monarchy had crushed political life; when the monarchy collapsed the liberals had abandoned their commitment to legality. The Bolsheviks had inherited the old regime's disregard for individual rights and also its reliance on state power (*étatisme*).[241] In the end, in his opinion, the Bolsheviks' triumph had "dealt socialism the most devastating possible blow."[242] Abandoning Marxism, "they imagined they could achieve everything by force."[243]

In short, Maklakov provided a political analysis of the origins and unfolding of the revolution. On February 14, 1925, Shulgin, then in the Serbian town of Sremski Karlovtsi, in the Kingdom of Yugoslavia, wrote to Maklakov in Paris, enclosing the draft of a critique of the *Revue de Paris* essays, which he had decided not to publish but wanted Maklakov to see.[244] The draft reflected on the "enormous mistake" (*gromadnaia oshibka*) made by Maklakov and his ilk. "In his article," Shulgin complains, "Maklakov does not once mention the Jews." He fails to inform the French reader "that in Russia there are six million

Jews, who played an enormous role in the rise and consolidation of Bolshevik power." This reader would come away thinking all those Bolsheviks, Mensheviks, and Socialist Revolutionaries (SRs) were "pure-blooded Russians," not realizing that Russia (the Soviet Union) was now "completely in Jewish hands."[245]

In the atmosphere prevailing in Russia before the war, Shulgin observed, the (gentile) Russian intelligentsia had been terrorized by the Jewish-dominated press into avoiding any criticism of the Jews, for fear of being labeled antisemitic. "A person who dared write anything even approaching the truth was immediately declared a *pogromshchik*. And the Jews managed to make this word so terrible and so intolerable to the Russian intelligentsia" that the writer would do anything to avoid the charge.[246] By 1925, Shulgin was pleased to report, the Russian emigration had already shaken off these constraints. Maklakov had perhaps retained his outmoded inhibitions and been hindered, moreover, in addressing the French public by the norms governing journalism in France, where speaking ill of the Jews was taboo.[247] In fact, Shulgin was pleased to say, the truth could now be told. What was the real cause of the monarchy's undoing? "Inside Russia, the internal enemy watched and waited: compact—all for one, one for all, wielding enormous psychological power, perfected by a thousand years of psychological training, persistent and rapacious, bitterly enraged by its lack of rights."[248]

Maklakov replied, in a letter of March 1925, that the two of them indeed saw things differently. The comportment of Russian Jews was not inherent in their traditions or psychology, he observed, repeating a theme he had often evoked: their resentment was the justified response to the laws and circumstances that oppressed them. "I know," he wrote, "that Jews do not readily assimilate to other nationalities, but I observe the Jews in France, and there is nothing here of the psychology of Russian Jews. Even less so in England."[249] As for the revolution, "to understand how the revolution unfolded in Russia, I do not need to discuss the Jewish Question. The role of the Jews is so secondary that I am convinced that if you eliminated all the Jews, the revolution would have developed in its main contours in exactly the way it did."[250] Shulgin's reply, May 1925: "Someone has bewitched you, thrown murky water in your clear eyes."[251] Maklakov to Shulgin, June 1925: "You have become a monomaniac under the power of an idée fixe that excludes everything else."[252] "You have driven your thinking into a blind alley."[253]

This thinking had indeed not changed. In 1928, a Russian-Jewish journalist in France, known to Shulgin from before the war, asked him rhetorically if anyone among the émigrés had the courage to admit their antisemitism and engage in debate with the Jewish side. Shulgin took up the challenge in the form of a book published in Russian in Paris in 1929: *"What We Don't Like About Them . . .": On Antisemitism in Russia*.[254] He thought the time was right. "Once, if someone said he was an antisemite, in certain circles he was considered a scoundrel or a psychopath."[255] Now, in the Russian emigration, antisemitism had become respectable. "So—I'm an antisemite. 'I have the courage' to announce this to the world. However, for me personally at any rate no courage is required. I've made it clear 100,000 times in the past twenty-five years of my political life. . . . In this connection, please note: I'm no Johnny-come-lately antisemite. . . . I'm an antisemite from before the war."[256]

Having read Shulgin's screed, Maklakov accuses him of vulgarity and of "arbitrary and tendentious generalizations of flagrant injustice."[257] At this point, in 1929, after ten years of butting heads, he is nevertheless willing to concede that the Jews had indeed played a role in the revolution, but he insists they were only a "*quantité négligeable*," not its cause.[258] He confesses, moreover, that there were "two kinds of people with whom I cannot debate." The first were the rabid Jew-haters. "I cannot talk with them precisely because I understand them very well and moreover, unlike you, I share their attitude. Personally, I find the way Jews look unappealing and I think that's true of most of us. Not for nothing, when we want to praise a Jew, do we say he doesn't look like one."[259] A surprising admission for a life-long champion of Jewish rights, yet consistent with his approach to the issue—and its acid test. The problem was not private but public. Recalling his own speech in the Duma in which he insisted people had a right to their dislikes, including dislike of Jews, he warned yet again that such feelings must not get the better of "healthy and normal thinking."[260]

The second kind of person with whom he cannot engage in debate is the Jew who sees the slightest criticism as an insult to the entire people, the critic an antisemite, and the antisemite a *pogromshchik*.[261] Maklakov continues to debate with Shulgin, but rejects the suggestion that they make their conversation public. If they were to publish their exchange, Maklakov is sure, "our antisemites would consider I had sold out to the Jews, and the Jews that I was no better than a *pogromsh-*

chik."[262] Both were charges he wished to avoid. Despite the passage of the years and the decade of Soviet power, the fate of the Jews and their place in modern societies was still a sore point.

Shulamit Volkov has called antisemitism a "cultural code."[263] By this she means a complex of words, symbols, and slogans that provides a template for explaining the world. "Solving the Jewish problem," getting rid of the Jew, she explains, signaled opposition to modern politics (democracy, socialism, civic equality) in favor of conservative (but in fact equally modern) militant nationalism. In the Russian Empire, unlike the self-assertive nation-states of Germany or Poland, antisemitism did not function as an instrument of nationalist mobilization. It did, however, serve as a rear-guard defense of the old imperial regime, whose attitude toward social and economic modernization was contradictory, but whose symbolic arsenal was aggressively antimodern. By focusing anger on the Jews, official antisemitism was intended to cement the bond between the peasant masses and the traditional ruler, but the violence it unleashed was hard to control and could end by challenging the authority it seemed to endorse.

In Germany, as Volkov puts it, "opposition to antisemitism [came to] mean a stand for emancipation, not of Jews alone but of society at large."[264] The same was true in Russia, where the liberal elites who promoted the model of Western constitutionalism rejected antisemitism as a matter of principle. Whatever their tactical maneuvers, before and after 1917, they were firmly embedded in a political culture inimical to the posture of the counterrevolutionary Right, which perpetuated the old regime's symbolic order. The liberals shared the Whites' opposition to Bolshevism, but rejected their interpretation of what Bolshevism meant and the alternative to Soviet power they envisioned.

Yet antisemitism was a pliable code that explained or responded to a range of perceived ills. The mobs that descended on vulnerable Jewish towns viewed their inhabitants as threats to their own existence: agents of economic exploitation, quintessential city dwellers—literate, mobile, questioning. Even if their actual victims were themselves impoverished, they seemed to represent a larger power. When the Bolsheviks launched campaigns against "speculators" and "exploiters," the categories fit the antisemitic typology, as well.[265] The Bolsheviks did not consciously mobilize antisemitic stereotypes for their own purposes, but the new terms nevertheless suited familiar targets. The association

"Jew-speculator" was already in place. Nor were the old terms entirely abandoned. The "Yid" was an all-purpose vilification. When the Bolsheviks took charge of the state apparatus and began to extract grain and draft manpower, disillusioned peasants and workers denounced as "Yid-Commissars" the same leaders they had earlier hailed. As the history of interwar Europe demonstrates, antisemitism remained both a potent and a destabilizing force for any system of power.

CHAPTER TWO

"That Scoundrel Petlyura"

The 1927 Schwarzbard Trial

TWO INFAMOUS TRIALS flanked the start of the twentieth century in Europe, both hinging on charges leveled against the Jews: the Dreyfus Case, lasting from 1894 to 1906, and the Beilis Case, from 1911 to 1913. Alfred Dreyfus (1859–1935), a captain in the French army, was accused of treason for allegedly passing military information to the Germans. Mendel Beilis was tried for the murder of an adolescent Christian boy allegedly for ritual purposes. Both men were eventually acquitted; both cases became notorious as examples of official antisemitism, one on the part of the French military, the other on the part of the imperial Russian Ministry of Justice. A third case involving a Jewish defendant and accusations of antisemitism occurred in Paris in 1927. Unlike Dreyfus or Beilis, the defendant in this case was in fact guilty of the crime as charged—the assassination of a political figure, in which he was caught red-handed. Now, as commentators noted at the time, the roles were reversed: it was the victim, not the perpetrator, who was in the dock.[1] In this courtroom, antisemitism was not a weapon but a liability. The Jews were acting as "the accusers, not the accused," the role activist-historian Simon Dubnow had urged them to assume back in 1905.[2]

The circumstances of the case are well-known. On May 25, 1926, Sholem (Solomon) Schwarzbard, a Russian-born naturalized French citizen, shot and killed Symon Petlyura, president in exile of the short-lived Ukrainian National Republic (Ukraïns'ka narodna respublika, or UNR),[3] as he emerged from a restaurant on the corner of rue Racine and boulevard Saint-Michel in Paris. Schwarzbard claimed to be avenging the murder of tens of thousands of Jews by forces fighting for Ukrainian independence against Soviet Russia during the Russian

Civil War. He was said to have cried: "This is for the pogroms! This is for the massacres!"[4]

Schwarzbard was a native of a region plagued by anti-Jewish violence even before the Civil War. Born in 1888, two years after Morris Greenfield, in the Danube River town of Izmail in southern Bessarabia, he was raised near Odessa, where he learned the watchmaker's trade. During the pogroms of 1905 he joined a Jewish self-defense squad. Arriving in France in 1910, he practiced his craft, fought in the Foreign Legion during the Great War, was wounded and earned the Croix de Guerre. Back in Russia in 1917, he supported no political party, but did join the Odessa Red Guard. In 1920 he returned to Paris and gained French citizenship in 1925.[5]

The case was brought before the Cour d'Assises de la Seine, composed of three judges and a twelve-man jury. Schwarzbard faced the death penalty, but the court had a record of leniency.[6] Between 1914 and 1923 four cases of politically motivated assassination had ended in acquittal in French courts.[7] Schwarzbard's defense argued that on learning of the presence in Paris of the man he blamed for the anti-Jewish violence in Ukraine, Schwarzbard had been moved by powerful emotion to take this drastic step. After nine days of speechmaking on both sides, the display of documentary evidence, and the airing of personal testimony, the jury accepted the terms of the defense and Schwarzbard was acquitted, by a vote of eight to four.[8] The "cosmopolitan crowd" that filled the heavily guarded court and the adjacent corridors, along with journalists "from almost every nation," burst into cheers and cries of "Vive la France!" The *New York Times* concluded that the trial had become "a protest against the Ukrainian pogroms, in which thousands of Jews were victims." The American Jewish Congress declared it had served the intended purpose of informing the world of a hitherto unrecognized tragedy, indeed "a great crime against mankind."[9]

Such an outcome was not unprecedented. A similar trial had occurred in Berlin in 1921 with similar results. An Armenian student named Soghomon (Salomon) Tehlirian (1896–1960) had shot and killed Talaat Pasha (1874–1921), an exiled leader of the former Ottoman Empire during the Armenian massacre of 1915. Tehlirian had not acted on impulse, but as part of an organized campaign of revenge mounted by the Armenian Revolutionary Federation (Dashnaktsutyun). In court, however, he claimed to have acted alone, under the shock of encountering the official he blamed for his family's death. His acquittal on the charge of murder was seen by many as validating the justice of his cause.[10]

The Schwarzbard trial, which lasted from October 18 to 26, 1927 (ending almost exactly ten years after the Bolshevik seizure of power), likewise took for granted the fact of the crime. Arguments focused, rather, on the question of Schwarzbard's motivation. Was he correct in holding Petlyura responsible for the pogroms committed by forces acting in the name of the government he led? Was Petlyura an antisemite? Could this be proven or refuted in a court of law? "Personalities became symbols," it was noted at the time. "[T]he assassin had not killed a man; he had struck at Antisemitism. . . . Antisemitism was called . . . Petlyura."[11] As posed in the judicial setting, these questions were too blunt to accommodate the challenges facing Ukrainian leaders in the Civil War. Both sides in the back-and-forth resorted to caricature. Both sides wished to send a message to the world.

If the charge of antisemitism was the center of dispute, its moral implications were not contested. In the Dreyfus Case, the enlightened French public rallied on the defendant's behalf; in the Beilis Case the progressive Russian public (indeed, the cream of the Russian bar) sprang to the accused's defense. In Paris in 1927 the organized transnational Jewish community, supported by a number of figures on the French Left, faced off against the Ukrainian nationalist emigration. In the quarrel over Dreyfus, his enemies unabashedly denounced the perfidy of Jews; in Kiev the government called witnesses to testify to the threat constituted by the Jewish religion. Now, by contrast, the two sides seemed to share — or claimed to share — a common assumption: being an antisemite was not a good thing.

Petlyura's posthumous reputation therefore hung on demonstrating he had been free of the antisemitic taint. Schwarzbard's defense hung on demonstrating the leader's role in abetting or endorsing its most terrible consequences. The trial offered Jewish spokesmen the chance to remind the international public in more general terms of the dangers of antisemitism, not only for the Jews, but for the democratic values supposedly vindicated by the outcome of the Great War. Framing the Jewish cause in universal terms, as we have seen in the Russian case, was a strategy designed, not to divert attention from the harm inflicted on the Jews, but, by widening the scope for alliance, to enhance the demand for justice in relation to the institutions and societies that governed their fate. It was a strategy designed to neutralize the power of antisemitism to discredit the Jewish cause as a self-serving mission, thereby increasing its promoters' chances of success.[12]

Schwarzbard was acquitted, but the victory came at a moral cost. The confessed murderer of an erstwhile public figure deprived of all but symbolic power became the lynchpin of a campaign for moral reckoning. Success in legal terms came also at a practical cost. By defining themselves as the collective voice of Jewish interests in opposition to the symbolic head of Ukrainian nationhood, Schwarzbard's advocates seemed to endorse the deepest convictions of Ukrainian antisemites. In that sense, as some Jewish leaders warned, their efforts did not undermine, but encouraged antisemitic assumptions and worsened the relationship between the two camps. The dissenters favored a collaborative, not antagonistic posture in relation to the ideological champions of the Ukrainian nation—precisely to promote the welfare of Ukrainian Jews.

In fact, both sides in the Paris courtroom faced a similar problem. Neither Petlyura in his heyday, nor what remained of his associates after his fall, exercised any kind of real power. The existing Ukrainian state now belonged to the Soviet Union. The unofficial spokesmen of the Jewish diaspora, for their part, might struggle to publicize the costs of antisemitism in graphic terms, hoping to exercise moral leverage on the international stage, but they were unable to defend the Jews in their various political homelands and in the face of physical assault. In short, in 1927 two stateless, extraterritorial parties confronted each other in the court of world opinion.

The enormity of what had happened to the Jews of Eastern Europe during the Russian Civil War and the still impending threats to their status in the emerging postwar nations nevertheless fueled the urgency felt by leaders of the Jewish diaspora to assert themselves on the public stage. Despite the moral and tactical complexities involved and their own internal disagreements, the assassination offered them a dramatic opportunity to speak to the world. They began with a certain advantage. If the opprobrium attached to antisemitism, itself a product of long-term Jewish lobbying, was a given at the trial, the basic facts were also not in question: the horrors and extent of the recent pogroms, if not widely enough known, were well established.

The question at issue at the trial was whether Schwarzbard was justified in holding Petlyura responsible for what had occurred. In this respect, his defense need only have established a reasonable basis for that belief, even if unfounded. Whether or not Petlyura had endorsed or encouraged the pogroms, his position as head of state and commander in chief would have led the victims to blame him for actions taken in his name. Schwarzbard would naturally have shared this view, thus motivating his deed. The Jewish organizations that mounted Schwarzbard's defense took the occasion, however, not merely to demonstrate the force of Schwarzbard's belief in Petlyura's role, but to insist on the truth behind it. The trial became a forum for the dissemination of information about the pogroms and more generally about the plight of the Jews in Eastern Europe during and after the Great War. Eight years after the Paris Peace Conference, at which these same organizations had raised the issue of the pogroms and pressed for sanctions against future atrocities in the emerging nations, the issue of antisemitism and anti-Jewish violence was again in the public eye.

The UNR in exile, defending its own and Petlyura's honor, needed, for its part, to demonstrate—in a court of law, not merely of public opinion—that its cause deserved the world's respect. Its spokesmen needed to show that Schwarzbard's belief in Petlyura's responsibility for the pogroms, however sincere and widely shared, was mistaken. Among the figures testifying on Petlyura's behalf was Oleksander Shulhyn (Alexandre Choulguine, 1889–1960), UNR foreign minister in exile.[13] Oleksander's father was a cousin of Vasily Shulgin, the prominent Kiev antisemite and Russian patriot whom we have already encountered. In adulthood, the cousin broke with the family's Russophile tradition and joined the Ukrainophile camp. Vasily Shulgin considered him a "renegade" (*otstupnik*) from the cause of "Russianness" (*russkost'*) and viewed Oleksander, eleven years younger than himself, in the same light.[14] At the time of the Schwarzbard trial, Vasily Shulgin was proudly advertising his record as an antisemite—nothing to be ashamed of.[15] Oleksander, by contrast, was defending Petlyura against the charge of being one at all. "If the pogroms continued into 1919, it is because Petlyura did not have enough authority," the foreign minister testified. "He considered the Jews an asset to the Ukrainian nation. He was not antisemitic, I swear."[16] Of himself, he said: "No one can suspect the democrat that I am of having had the least sympathy for antisemitic propaganda."[17] He might indeed have mentioned his role in 1918, when he worked with Jewish leaders to establish the basis for Jewish communal self-rule in the framework of an independent Ukraine.[18]

Was Petlyura an antisemite? What in fact did the accusation entail? How should an antisemite be recognized? Vasily Shulgin, overtly hostile to the Jews, considered them alien to the Russian nation and wished to exclude them from public life, yet he deplored the use of lethal violence against them. It was possible, as in the case of Vladimir Nabokov, to repudiate all forms of antisemitism, yet in moments of political frustration use forms of expression and mimic ways of thinking that made him sound like one. If Petlyura had in fact rejected the use of antisemitism in his political appeals, as his defenders claimed, he would have distinguished himself both from the Russia-centered anti-Bolshevik movement and from the dominant voices in Polish nationalism. Yet the armed forces fighting on his behalf and in his name had been responsible for many of the most deadly pogroms of the Civil War.

Petlyura's champions would need to explain this disjunction and do so while avoiding the antisemitic rhetoric common to opponents of Soviet power. Even the Kadets, as we have seen, in assuming that Jews were playing an essential role in the nascent Soviet regime, seemed at times to evoke the pejorative symbol of the "Yid-Commissar," or, more generally, "Judeo-Bolshevism," a connection by now firmly implanted in European political discourse.[19] To maintain one's enlightened bona fides, it would be dangerous to explain the pogroms as a plausible response to Jewish behavior or to identify the Jews in some general way with Soviet rule. It would be questionable to describe the lawyers in the courtroom and the witnesses they summoned as a conspiracy directed against the Ukrainian nation. Such omnibus accusations were a danger for the Jewish side, as well. Schwarzbard's defenders needed to distinguish between Petlyura, the man; Petlyura, the political figure; Petlyura, the symbol of the Ukrainian nation; and the Ukrainian nation as a whole. Both sides had thus to step delicately through a minefield of well-established, mutually injurious assumptions and clichés.

For the Ukrainian leaders, the trial was not the first time they had distanced themselves from the kind of overt antisemitism displayed by the White movement. The Ukrainian National Government was already conscious during the Civil War of the need to persuade the foreign public of its good intentions with regard to the Jews. In citing the example of "that *pogromshchik* Petlyura," Maklakov had depicted the posture of denial and repudiation as a cynical ploy. Unable to stop the pogroms, or perhaps not wanting to, Petlyura, as a political strategist, knew he had to disavow them. The "gesture" Maklakov had urged on Denikin and Wrangel had been to denounce what they could not stop, thus presenting a morally acceptable face to the Western public.

Cynical or sincere, the Ukrainian publicity campaign began early. A pamphlet published in Washington, DC, in 1919, under the imprint of the Friends of Ukraine, included three Jewish contributors.[20] One was the historian Dr. Mark Wischnitzer (1882–1955), a native of Western Ukraine, with impeccable credentials. Before the war he had been an editor of the Russian-language *Evreiskaia entsiklopediia* (Jewish Encyclopedia) and a member of the group of Jewish lawyers and professionals who had gathered in St. Petersburg to organize in defense of Jewish rights. After 1921, in exile, he went on to serve as secretary general of the Hilfsverein der deutschen Juden in Berlin.[21]

In 1919 Wischnitzer assured the London *Jewish Chronicle* that the Ukrainian government was doing all it could to protect the Jews and punish their attackers.[22] A pamphlet issued by the Ukrainischer Pressedienst in Berlin in 1920 said it again: "The Ukrainian national movement . . . not only bears no responsibility for the persecution of the Jews, but has in its own interests made the greatest efforts to live in complete accord with the Jewish population."[23] The Jewish emigration was unimpressed. In 1920 the *Jewish Tribune* called Petlyura a militant antisemite, a "bloodthirsty hetman" responsible for the deaths of "several thousand Jews."[24]

The trial thus presented the Ukrainian nationalists with a familiar challenge. Now that the Civil War was over and Petlyura himself out of the way, it was possible to review the record. Yet the desire for national independence among Ukrainian émigré leaders had not abated with his death or with Soviet victory, and the record was still controversial. The fate of the Jews remained a key point of contention. The question in 1927 was how much of a gesture the UNR had in fact made at the time the pogroms were raging, how energetic its actions had been, and in what terms its position had been expressed. Petlyura's side needed to refute the charge that antisemitism and the pogroms were intrinsic to the Ukrainian political project. His defenders had to document his efforts to stem the violence, while confirming his inability to succeed, and at the same time affirming the role he had played as leader of an independent state, against Soviet claims to sovereignty on Ukrainian soil. These goals were sometimes in tension.

Both sides at the trial were thus, in a sense, saddled with the problem of Petlyura. He continued, even in death, to symbolize the aspiring Ukrainian nation for those who had lost the bid for independence, yet his personal profile alone could not adequately represent the complexity of the Ukrainian nationalist movement or the tumultuous circumstances of the Civil War, in which he did not call all the shots and in which Jews and Ukrainians were far from the only players. Now, in the courtroom, two parties—respectively, self-described "Ukrainians" and self-described "Jews"—stood face to face, but the pattern of Jewish-Ukrainian relations during the revolution had been one of constant negotiation and adjustment, not simple opposition.

Like the questions presented at the trial, the history of this relationship was more complex than the issue of Petlyura. The first organs of Ukrainian self-rule had emerged in 1917, after the collapse of the monarchy. The original Central Rada (Tsentral'na Rada, or council) had formed in March, under the joint leadership of Petlyura and Volodymyr Vynnychenko (1880–1951),[25] two Social Democrats, who initially conceived of Ukraine's future as an autonomous part of an emerging Russian federation. The Rada enlisted the support of local Jewish leaders, who welcomed its commitment to the rights of ethnic minorities. After the October coup, however, when the Bolsheviks embarked on peace negotiations with the Central Powers, the Rada concluded its own separate peace and announced Ukraine's break from what was nominally now Soviet Russia. It was a step not all Jewish parties welcomed.[26]

The separate peace allowed the Rada, ousted from Kiev by the Bolsheviks in December 1917, to return in January 1918, with German protection. Under the Rada's auspices, Jews, along with other minorities, enjoyed the right to establish their own communal institutions, including political representation and self-administration.[27] Yet the Rada's reappearance was accompanied by anti-Jewish violence, which its leaders condemned but did little to stop.[28] Jewish delegates were the target of curses hurled from the gallery during Rada sessions, their speeches interrupted by catcalls: "Go back to the synagogue!"[29] The Rada, for all its mixed profile, did not last long. In April 1918, the Germans replaced it with the puppet regime of Hetman Pavlo Skoropadsky (1873–1945), who revoked Jewish autonomy. The foreign occupiers did their part in spreading hostile rumors about the Jews, but they kept a lid on mob violence.[30]

Upon the German withdrawal and Skoropadsky's fall, Vynnychenko and Petlyura formed a new government, called the Directory. Petlyura led the troops that took Kiev on December 14, 1918, in the name of Ukrainian independence. By February 5, 1919, the Reds had expelled him yet again from Kiev and the Directory had moved to Vinnitsa. There, on February 10, 1919, Petlyura replaced Vynnychenko as its head, while also adopting the position of "ataman in chief" (*glavnyi ataman*, *holovnyi otaman*), thus combining military and civilian authority. This was the same archaic title adopted by the various local chieftains, whose support Petlyura enlisted and whom he allowed, given the weakness of his regular army, to exercise authority over military units that owed loyalty directly to them.[31]

As far as the Jews were concerned, the Directory, like the Rada before it, was a mixed blessing. On the one hand, weak central command over its armed forces and the explicit delegation of authority to the level of autonomous brigade or militia chiefs were invitations to violence, as Vynnychenko himself observed.[32] Indeed, the most persistent and destructive pogroms occurred while Petlyura's government claimed to represent the Ukrainian nation. On the other hand, this government had a Ministry of Jewish Affairs and invited Jewish leaders to staff it. It periodically issued statements denouncing pogroms and provided relief to their victims. It also created a mechanism by which perpetrators could be tried and punished.

The UNR, with Petlyura at its head, would seem to have made a good-faith effort to stem anti-Jewish violence. But Petlyura's pronouncements did not determine the behavior of his own institutions. Cases dealing with pogroms originated in the Ministry of Jewish Affairs, which forwarded the evidence to the Ministry of Justice. The Ministry of Justice, for its part, was reluctant to act and very few cases were investigated or tried.[33] The army, moreover, disseminated language that emphasized the Jewish role in promoting Communist power, while the Ministry of Jewish Affairs was itself regarded with suspicion. The Special Commission established to investigate pogroms accused it of "tak[ing] under its wing all Jews, even if they are Bolsheviks and even the Trotsky-Bronshteins."[34] To focus exclusively on Petlyura and his personal intentions was therefore to miss the daunting situation he himself faced.

Throughout 1919, the Directory fought for its life, against Soviet and White forces. When the Red Army finally established control of

Kiev in December, Petlyura and his troops withdrew to Poland. By the Treaty of Warsaw in April 1920, the UNR ceded Eastern Galicia (Western Ukraine) in exchange for Polish military support and diplomatic recognition. In the war between Poland and Soviet Russia, Petlyura fought on the Polish side, hoping to displace the Soviets from Ukrainian territory. After peace was concluded in March 1921, Petlyura formed a government in exile in Poland, but left in December 1923. He ended up in Paris in October 1924, where he edited the Ukrainian weekly, *Tryzub* (Trident), and remained head of state and commander in chief of a regime that no longer existed.[35]

This was the regime Schwarzbard's defenders accused of having actively perpetrated, or at the very least failed to prevent or impede, massive deadly violence against the Jewish population of the territory it claimed to govern during 1919 and on which its troops continued to fight in 1920. Their first task was to demonstrate the scope of the damage. For this they relied on a body of material, both testimonies and statistics, which had been gathered by Jewish philanthropic and relief organizations, continuing a pattern established during the Great War, when the Jewish population of the region had been the object of violence and dislocation. Interrupted by the Bolshevik coup, the project of documenting the plight of the Jews resumed in January 1919, with the creation of the Central Committee for Aid to Pogrom Victims (Tsentral'nyi komitet pomoshchi postradavshim ot pogromov), combining an array of Jewish political and cultural associations.[36]

The aid committee worked in collaboration with the Directory's organ of Jewish autonomy, the Jewish National Secretariat in Ukraine, headed by Elias Tcherikower (1881–1943), which established an editorial board to gather material on the pogroms.[37] A native of Poltava, in central Ukraine, Tcherikower had studied in St. Petersburg and been drawn into the events of 1905. After a stint in prison, he became a specialist in Jewish history and culture, writing for the *Evreiskaia entsiklopediia* and taking an active part in Jewish public life. Having spent the war years in the United States, he returned to Russia after February 1917 and settled in Kiev.[38]

In Kiev Tcherikower took charge of the data-collecting operation, creating an archive of testimony and information on the victims and the material damage caused by the pogroms. In 1921 he left for Berlin, where the material became the basis of the East European Jewish Historical Archive (Ostjüdisches historisches Archiv).[39] In 1923 he published a Yiddish-language volume on the pogroms of 1917 and 1918.[40] A second volume, on the year 1919, appeared in New York only in 1965, two decades after his death.[41] Another dozen volumes presenting statistical material on the pogroms, most published in Yiddish, appeared during the 1920s.[42] In 1925 Tcherikower helped found YIVO (Yidisher visnshaftlekher institut, Institute for Jewish Research) in Vilna/Vilnius. Now located in New York, YIVO is the repository of his archive, on which this chapter and much scholarly research draws.[43]

Like the data collectors, Schwarzbard's advocates were veteran campaigners for Jewish rights and welfare. Some of the same Russian Jewish lawyers involved in the landmark cases that preceded the revolution appeared now in emigration in a similar role: using the judicial setting as a platform from which to advertise the plight of the Jews and denounce the myths and prejudices that threatened their existence. In this case, however, the alleged perpetrator of anti-Jewish violence had already been punished and the Russian Jewish lawyers and activists were now themselves part of the diaspora, addressing an audience without borders. Maxim Vinaver, active in Paris as editor of the *Tribune juive* until his death in October 1926, did not make it to the trial.

The strategy displayed in 1927 was thus nothing new. The crisis caused by massive Jewish emigration from Eastern Europe after 1900 and the calamity of successive pogroms in 1903 and 1905, followed by the refugee crisis of the war, had laid the ground for the coordinated activities of Jewish philanthropic organizations on a transnational scale.[44] The Civil War pogroms increased the urgency; the anticipated peace settlement provided a goal. In March 1919 a group of Jewish associations from across Eastern Europe joined to form the Comité des délégations juives auprès de la Conférence de la paix, headed by the mathematician Leo Motzkin. Born in Brovary, a town not far from Kiev, he had collaborated with the original St. Petersburg Defense Bureau.[45] Under Motzkin's direction, the Comité, along with the Alliance israélite universelle, the Board of Deputies of British Jews, and the American Jewish Committee, focused their attention on the minority rights treaties and the role of the League of Nations and Permanent Court of International Justice.[46]

The aim of this mobilization was originally to secure cultural autonomy and legal equality for the Jewish minorities in the postwar nations and to influence public opinion in support of Jewish rights. Violence against the Jews was the most dramatic symptom of the absence of these rights. The Paris Peace Conference had concluded its deliberations in January 1920; the Civil War had ended in 1921; in December 1922 the Soviet Union had announced its formation, including within its borders the Ukrainian Soviet Socialist Republic. Jewish leaders in 1926 nevertheless had reason to fear that the attitudes behind the Civil War pogroms still had not lost their hold and their fatal consequences in human terms were still not widely acknowledged.[47] The trial, though focused on Schwarzbard's act and Petlyura's reputation, provided Jewish spokesmen with another chance to publicize the causes and consequences of the humanitarian crisis generated by the war and its aftermath. It was the Comité des délégations juives that assembled the dossier used in 1927, relying on material collected by Tcherikower. "An unexpected opportunity presented itself," Motzkin explained, "to disclose the horrible aspect of what the Jews had gone through and to arouse the indignation of the entire world."[48]

As part of the battle for public opinion waged between the two sides at the trial, the Comité issued a volume of documents, supported by historical background, dramatizing the trauma to which Schwarzbard claimed to be responding. A similar volume of material was issued by the opposing camp, as a rejoinder, documenting the efforts undertaken to prevent or mitigate the harm.[49] The compilers of the statistical reports on the Jewish side were aware of the inadequacy of their data, but thought of themselves as striving for "scientific objectivity."[50] Nor were they outsiders to the Ukrainian scene. Naum Gergel (d. 1931), the author of an extensive study still cited by historians as a reliable source, had initially been a supporter of Ukrainian independence. In 1918 he had taken a position in the Central Rada's Ministry of Jewish Affairs and remained in office under Skoropadsky. In 1919–1920 he worked for the committee for aid to pogrom victims sponsored by the Russian Red Cross and in this capacity participated in the collection of information that was disseminated to an international readership, even while the events were unfolding.[51] After emigrating to Germany, Gergel worked with Tcherikower in the East European Jewish Historical Archive. In 1926 he joined in Schwarzbard's defense.[52]

The data were indeed incomplete, but even so, impressive. Estimates of the overall death toll on Ukrainian territory in 1919 and 1920 range widely, from a minimum of 20,000 to 35,000 or perhaps 60,000, to a maximum of 125,000.[53] A sober assessment from the Jewish side proposed before the trial opted for 40,000 to 70,000 as a reasonable figure for the number killed, with a figure of 300,000 including all victims.[54] In terms of responsibility, the information presented at the trial demonstrated that in the context of chronic instability during the crucial years of 1919 and 1920 none of the contenders for political authority controlled the forces with which they fought; none were free from the problem of anti-Jewish violence.[55] The incidence of pogroms on Petlyura's watch had peaked in July 1919, then diminished in August. After Denikin entered Kiev at the end of August, pogroms became the work of the Volunteer Army.[56] They continued, though to a lesser extent, after December 16, 1919, when Kiev was retaken by the Red Army. Irregular forces fighting for the Reds, among them followers of the Ukrainian ataman Matvy Hryhoriïv (Mykola/Nikifor Grigoriev, 1885–1919), were the worst offenders. Overall, the data showed, forces associated with the UNR, as well as freelance irregulars fighting on its behalf, were responsible for the greatest number of pogroms and murders.[57]

Two of the most notorious incidents associated with Petlyura's forces occurred early in 1919, one in the city of Proskurov (Proskuriv), beginning on February 5 (1,650 dead), the other in the town of Felshtin (Fel'shtyn) on February 16 (487 dead).[58] The Proskurov pogrom was the work of a self-styled ataman called Ivan Semesenko (1894–1920). His "Order to the Zaporozhian Cossack Brigade of the Ukrainian Republican Army, bearing the name of the Ataman in Chief, Petlyura," was presented in evidence at the trial.[59] It warned the Jews: "Know that you are a people detested by all the nations. You cause trouble among the Christian people. Do you not want to live? Do you not have pity on your own nation? If you are left in peace, then remain peaceful. Unfortunate people, you do not cease to trouble the poor Ukrainian people."[60]

In Proskurov, the ataman invoked Petlyura's name, but he was essentially a free agent, like the other chieftains who offered their services to the various warring parties, not infrequently changing sides. The UNR subsequently investigated his role in the pogrom, decided he was responsible for the deaths of over 800 Jews, and had him arrested. He escaped from prison when the Whites captured the town and fled to Galicia, where, however, he again fought with the UNR. In 1920, he was arrested a second time and executed, not for his role in the Proskurov events but for corruption and insubordination.[61] The UNR leadership had repudiated his behavior and his message, but retained his services.

Semesenko's rhetoric conflicted with the face the UNR wished to present to the outside world. It also violated injunctions issued by Petlyura on a number of occasions in warnings to his own commanders, though perhaps intended as much for external as internal consumption. The first of these proclamations was timed to anticipate the opening of the Paris Peace Conference in January 1919, to which the UNR sent a delegation. The delegation was soon joined by Arnold Margolin (1877–1956), until recently a member of Petlyura's cabinet, whose profile encapsulates many of the tensions inherent in the Ukrainian situation. Margolin's father had been a wealthy Kiev-based industrialist and entrepreneur, the owner of sugar-beet processing plants, shipping lines, gas, water, electricity, and tram companies. A well-respected figure in Kiev society, active in the Jewish community and in philanthropy, he sent his son to Russian-language schools.

Arnold was educated in the law, first in Kiev, then in Germany and France. As a young attorney, he participated in the 1904 Gomel pogrom trial[62] and defended the victims of the 1905 Kiev pogroms, in which his own apartment had been trashed, acquiring a reputation as an antigovernment firebrand. His plans to serve as Beilis's defender were foiled, however, after he was accused of violating professional ethics and disbarred.[63] In 1914, facing threats from the Kiev Black Hundreds, he moved his family to St. Petersburg, where he remained until the declaration of Ukrainian independence in 1918. Active in the Union for Jewish Equality, he believed that Russian and Ukrainian Jews must create their intertwined future in the place he considered their home. After the Constituent Assembly in Petrograd was dispersed by the Bolsheviks in January 1918, he rejected the Kadet platform of a united Russia in favor of the Ukrainian national cause and rapidly learned Ukrainian.[64]

Elected by the Rada to a seat on the Supreme Court, Margolin continued in this position under Skoropadsky, was briefly arrested by the Directory when it took over, but was then appointed its assistant minister of foreign affairs. His commitment was to the nascent Ukrainian nation, which he saw both as his own homeland and as a parallel to the national aspirations of the Jews. However, on March 11, 1919, Margolin resigned his post. He recognized, he said, that Vynnychenko and Petlyura were doing their best to stop the pogroms, but they lacked the power to do so. As a member of their cabinet, he felt he shared responsibility for this failure and needed to step down.[65]

Margolin nevertheless agreed to join the Ukrainian delegation to the Paris Peace Conference. In statements to the foreign press, he insisted that Petlyura had made every effort to stop the pogroms, which, he told the London *Jewish Chronicle*, "were instigated by criminals, Black Hundreds, and Bolshevists, who wished to discredit the Ukrainian government."[66] His contribution to the propaganda pamphlet produced by the American Friends of the Ukraine took the same line.[67] In September, however, Margolin withdrew from the delegation. He had failed to secure Entente support for Ukrainian independence, without which, he explained, pogrom violence would inevitably continue. Two years later, Margolin published an account, written in Russian, published in Berlin, concerning the government to which he had belonged and, in particular, its response to the challenge of the pogroms.[68]

In 1922, Margolin moved to the United States, where he practiced as a journalist and lawyer. In 1926 he published a volume in English, in which he absolved "all Jews" of responsibility for those of them who supported the Bolsheviks, joined the Soviet apparatus, and abused their new-found power. It also absolved "all Ukrainians" of responsibility for the pogroms, which he continued to attribute to "the most undesirable Black Hundred type and even criminal and other dangerous characters."[69] He continued, in particular, to absolve Petlyura, like other "fine Ukrainian patriots," of moral responsibility. The leader's response to the pogroms was delayed, but as early as April 1919, Margolin claimed, the Directory had initiated an active campaign against them.[70] Beleaguered from all sides, the Ukrainian government, he contended, was simply not strong enough, despite its best intentions, to stop the outrages of later that year.[71]

Whatever his motivation, as head of the UNR Petlyura had indeed made the kind of public-relations "gesture" Maklakov had vainly urged on General Denikin. Despite the pervasiveness of antisemitism across Europe, antisemitism as an official posture had become a political liability in the international arena. Petlyura's posture was perhaps sincere, but it was also pragmatic. The Directory's message was not entirely clear, however. Over the course of 1919, it issued proclamations on a number of occasions forcefully condemning the pogroms occurring on the territory it aspired to govern. Yet these warnings were often ambiguous in themselves and contradicted by the language used in leaflets issued by the UNR army, which did not hesitate to refer to the enemy as "Communist-Jews" or the "Jewish Sovnarkom"—the Council of People's Commissars—or to accuse "the Jews Lenin and Trotsky" of being "the greatest enemy of Christ."[72]

Petlyura's own proclamations expressed his disapproval of the pogroms, but also his reluctance to confront the role of his own officials and followers in provoking the violence. Presented in evidence, for example, was a proclamation of January 11, 1919, which called for the arrest and trial of instigators, whom it described as "provocateurs from among followers of the Hetman [Skoropadsky], the Volunteer Army, and among those calling themselves Bolsheviks." These intruders were determined to "disgrace the Ukrainian Republican Army and sow hatred for Ukrainian Cossacks among the population."[73]

This will not be the only time that Bolsheviks—here "those calling themselves Bolsheviks"—will be accused of infiltrating Ukrainian forces with the purpose of fomenting pogroms, even though the Bolsheviks were routinely identified as Jews in UNR—and all overtly antisemitic—rhetoric. The association of Jews and Bolsheviks is indeed referenced directly in the January 11 appeal, which urged "all democratic Jews to fight energetically against the individual anarchist-Bolshevik members of the Jewish nation [*natsiia*], who cause harm to the Ukrainian state and the Ukrainian laboring people." These Jewish Bolsheviks caused harm not only as agents of the Soviet regime, which opposed Ukrainian independence. Their presence also gave credence to the claims of outright antisemites, thus providing "provocateurs with the basis for the demagogic and harmful agitation they direct against Jews as a whole, who have nothing to do with Bolshevism."[74] The solution to the problem of the pogroms into which the Ukrainian people had been inveigled was thus alleged to be in Jewish hands, though it was not clear what influence "democratic Jews" could possibly exert on Jews who had opted for Bolshevik internationalism.

Similar, equally implausible formulations characterized the appeal issued by the Kadet Party at its November 1919 congress, as we have seen. In neither case did this reproach reflect a conscious endorsement of antisemitic attitudes or an antisemitic political agenda. Yet some Jewish leaders in Ukraine were nevertheless offended by the passage in the Directory's January 11 statement and asked Vynnychenko to remove it. He insisted the language was necessary as a response to the charge of collective responsibility leveled by antisemites against Jews across the board.[75] In the eyes of antisemites, the role of Jews as

Communists might justify the pogroms, in the eyes of liberal anti-Bolsheviks, it might explain them, but the pogroms certainly turned many Jews into Communists — a seemingly endless cycle.[76]

A statement issued by the Ukrainian army a week later, on January 19, 1919, seemed to underscore the ambiguity of the Directory's stand: "In whose hands," the military asked rhetorically, "are Ukrainian lands, rivers, factories and so on? In the hands of wealthy Russians, Jews, and Poles. Who always argues against an independent Ukrainian National Republic? Russians, Jews, and Poles."[77] In February and March, while the violence persisted, the Directory remained silent. By this point it had forfeited the support of most Jewish political parties, while many Jewish activists had opted for the Communist side.[78] It was in March 1919 that Margolin resigned his cabinet position — on the issue of responsibility. This fierce champion of Ukrainian honor could well be viewed as one of those "wealthy Jews," Russian speaking to boot, who were allegedly exploiting Ukrainian riches.

The question of responsibility, of political authority, was key to the debates in the Schwarzbard trial. The issue had been central all along, as the UNR leadership attempted to assert control over its own forces and command the respect of foreign powers. The record was confusing. The decree of January 11, which called on Jews to dissuade their fellows from joining the Communists, had conceded that Ukrainian troops and even Cossacks had succumbed to provocation. A decree of April 12, 1919, again acknowledged that Ukrainian forces were among the perpetrators. "The government will root out brigands and *pogromshchiki* with the most severe measures," it warned. "The government, in particular, will not tolerate under any circumstances pogroms against the Jewish population . . . which dishonor the Ukrainian nation in the eyes of all civilized nations."[79]

This seemingly unequivocal injunction addressed to Petlyura's own forces was followed, a month later, however, by an official statement rejecting the possibility of any wrongdoing on their part. On May 19, 1919, the Ukrainian press office insisted that "Petlyura's troops have never harmed the Jews, but have protected them everywhere. . . . If pogroms have occurred and are the work of anarchists and Russian Bolsheviks, the responsibility in no way falls on Petlyura and his troops."[80] Denials aside, the UNR nevertheless established a special commission to investigate anti-Jewish pogroms. Those guilty of violence or incitement to violence would be penalized under the law. With some notable exceptions (civil and military legal personnel), government officials would be liable to prosecution for the same offenses.[81] Thus, even as the leadership insisted the incitement to violence came from outside, it seemed, at least sporadically, to accept responsibility for the results, while also at times seeming to reject it.

By early July 1919, the violence had still not abated. Petlyura wired his ministers and army commanders, urging them yet again to prevent the outbreak of pogroms and depicting the Jews as loyal allies.[82] The argument had a new twist. Instead of complaining that Jews, as Communists, opposed Ukrainian independence, thus arousing the wrath of Ukrainian patriots, Petlyura now blamed the Communists for punishing Jews who were loyal to the Ukrainian cause. Writing in the third person, as "ataman in chief," Petlyura cited cases "when representatives of the Jewish population who helped our troops, who loyally supported the legitimate republican authorities, were set upon by our enemies, the Communist-Bolsheviks, who shot them down, raped their women and children, perpetrated pogroms against the Jewish population, and plundered their last material means of existence." By contrast, he continued, "our Cossacks" were touched to the core by Jewish devotion. He reported having seen "Cossacks in our army" guarding Jewish shops, "protecting their property from looting." He insisted "that incitement to pogroms is often the work of Bolshevik provocateurs in the rear of our army, with the purpose of disorganizing our front and the entire state-building work of our government." In short, the ataman in chief denounced the pogroms, but wanted to believe his men had been led by clever manipulators to disregard their own better instincts. The Communists—Jews and Cossacks should both remember—were the true evil.

Pogroms were not only a stain on Ukraine's national honor, as Petlyura understood it. They constituted a threat to the morale and discipline of his armed forces and an obstacle to cooperation with representatives of the Jews on Ukrainian soil, who after all continued to live together with their Ukrainian neighbors. It was difficult, however, to draw a clear line between outsiders and insiders, to denounce provocateurs while absolving Cossacks, even for rhetorical effect. As the summer progressed and Petlyura's position weakened, the Council of Ministers increased the penalties for perpetrators.[83] Finally, on August 26, 1919, Petlyura issued his most important decree. Addressing "Commanders and Cossacks," he seemed to take responsibility for the continuing incidence of pogroms and acknowledged the vulnerability of his followers to the sinister appeal of antisemitic anti-Communism. The Jews, he reminded them, were suffering along with everyone else from the Bolshevik regime. The pogroms were not only a crime, but treason.[84]

The August 26 decree, with its strong language, was invoked at the trial on Petlyura's behalf, as evidence of his attempt to assert his authority in the matter of anti-Jewish violence. Presenting the pogroms as the work of Ukraine's bitterest enemies, it appealed to patriotic feeling. These were the "bandit-Bolsheviks," who had fled back to their "dark wilderness" but left behind the "stench of the dying enemy-beast." Not content with honorable battle, they now thirsted for "innocent blood." The "Black Hundreds and Red Hundreds (a single benighted pack)" were the ones who "instigate pogroms against the Jewish nation, and have sometimes incited certain unreliable elements of our army to commit these terrible deeds. They thus attempt to defile our struggle for liberty in the eyes of the entire honest world and discredit our national cause."[85] This devious campaign must be thwarted.

The "unreliable elements" were not imagined scapegoats. All the armies fighting the Civil War had their share of violent and undisciplined men, and all, to different degrees, were responsible for pogroms in areas dense with Jewish settlement. These "unreliable elements," the August 26 decree declared, were alien to the true spirit of the "brave Ukrainian army."[86] The Jews, by contrast, must be considered part of the Ukrainian nation. "It is now time to understand that the peaceful Jewish population—its women and children, have been subjugated and deprived of their national liberty just as we have been. They cannot escape from us; they have lived among us from ancient times, sharing our fate and our misfortunes. Our chivalrous army . . . must not contribute to the terrible fate of the Jews. Whoever abets this serious crime is a traitor and enemy of our country."[87]

Most important, the decree stressed the consequences of the pogroms for Ukraine's national aspirations. "Commanders and Cossacks," Petlyura admonished, "The whole world is watching and is amazed by our feats of liberation. Do not tarnish them, even if inadvertently, by this shameful business and do not dishonor our state in the eyes of the world. Our numerous external and internal enemies make use of the pogroms" to show that we are "incapable of independent statehood." Speaking as ataman in chief, Petlyura reminded his men that "the international tribunal is at this very moment deciding the question: whether or not our independent state will survive."[88] Pogroms were harmful to the Ukrainian state; perpetrators would be punished to the full extent of the law. The decree ended by calling on the population "to oppose all actions taken by our enemies to instigate pogroms against the Jewish population."[89] Seeking the support of outside powers against both Reds and Whites, in 1919 the Directory sent a delegation to Washington, but its reception was clouded by divisions within the American Ukrainian community and by accusations that Petlyura was responsible for the pogroms.[90]

Even in emigration, such accusations continued to dog him. Presiding over his surviving cabinet in the Polish city of Tarnów, Petlyura was disturbed in December 1920 by charges that Ukrainian troops fighting alongside the Poles on Ukrainian territory were guilty of pogroms. He asked his minister of Jewish affairs to "explain to Jewish circles abroad" the true situation in Ukraine. The campaign against the Ukrainian government, he assured his minister, was not actually a response to pogroms, "which in fact have not occurred," but was "led by persons wishing to discredit the Ukrainian cause." Since it was hard to maintain that pogroms "had not in fact occurred," it was useful again to blame outsiders. "Robber gangs" might still be at work. "Many are holdovers from the Bolshevik occupation and cannot instantly be destroyed. Of pogroms, mass pillage, and murders of the peaceful Jewish population I know nothing and cannot imagine that such a thing could be."[91] This was a less plausible assertion.

Petlyura had gone from blaming the susceptibility of "unreliable elements" to denying his forces were guilty of pogroms at all. From his outpost in Poland, he continued to issue pronouncements. On March 18, 1921, the very day of the treaty between Poland and Soviet Russia, he once more denied the rumors, spread, he claimed, by the Bolsheviks, that the Ukrainian people were "destroying the Jewish population." This was not true, he insisted. He felt obliged nevertheless to warn the Ukrainian peasants against associating the Jews with their Communist oppressors. As petty traders, artisans, and workers, he admonished, the Jews suffered under Communism no less than they. Jews who joined the Communists were as much traitors to their own people as Ukrainian Communists were to theirs. Still worrying about Ukraine's image in the eyes of the outside world, he insisted the Jewish population had welcomed the return of the Ukrainian army and grieved when it withdrew.[92]

Despite his good words on behalf of the Jews, Petlyura was still angry that "Jewish circles" abroad, by which he had in mind primarily the Délégations juives in Paris, continued to blame the Ukrainian government for the pogroms—which, in fact, despite his whimsical denial, were still occurring.[93] Petlyura's government had left Ukrainian territory and he could well have denied responsibility for what was happening there, yet he had not relinquished all claim to authority, as his pronouncements showed, and, as he complained, the Jewish press continued to hold him accountable. Jewish commentators continued to view him, as he viewed himself, as head of the Ukrainian nation.

Indeed, his denials met with sarcasm from Jewish quarters. "Wherever the Petlyura bands appear," reported the *Wiener Morgenzeitung* (November 7, 1920), "the Jewish masses in the small towns become their victims. . . . No Jewish house escapes plunder, and whoever has nothing to give is shot to death."[94] Did the Jewish population of Proskurov, the site of the earlier pogrom, welcome the army's return? When General Mykhailo Omelyanovych-Pavlenko (1878–1952), commander of the Ukrainian army and later defense minister in exile, announced that Polish troops would soon be retreating west beyond the Zbrucz River, the *Morgenzeitung* reported, "a mass exodus of the Jewish population in the direction of Poland began."[95]

Writing in the *Jewish Tribune*, the Kiev-born jurist Boris Mirsky (Mirkin-Getsevich, 1892–1955) described Petlyura's regime as "indissolubly linked with active antisemitism in its most monstrous form." Seeming to ignore the various pronouncements denouncing pogroms, Mirsky insisted that pogroms were its "motto . . . its list of commandments, its watch-word, the rallying call of bestial bandits devoid of any definite political tendencies in their yearning for pogroms." Europeans should not be fooled "by the unscrupulous interviews given by Ukrainian Counts and by the portraits of Petlioura which are so carefully placed before its eyes. European public opinion must realise that the whole of the Petlioura adventure, in its essence, its basis and its development, is an undisguised pretext for pogroms of the Jews devoid even of the pretence of any particular ideology."[96]

In the same vein, the Central Jewish Press Agency in Zurich reported in September 1920 that the UNR had blamed the pogroms in Eastern Galicia on erstwhile soldiers of Denikin's army. This, the agency commented acerbically, was to ignore the fact "that the atrocities had been the work of troops under the command of General Pawlenko, whose successes against the Bolsheviks had been praised to the skies by the Ukrainian as well as Polish press."[97] No less harsh, the Berlin *Jüdische Rundschau* (Jewish Observer) cited a communiqué in which Petlyura's government tried to blame its Polish allies for the pogroms it could not deny had happened. "The communiqué is a laughable document of a fictitious government," the editors declared.[98]

The Jewish press thus persisted in crediting Petlyura with more control than he actually possessed over the behavior of forces directly under his command or attached to his armies. Dismissing his refusal to acknowledge the involvement of his followers as "laughable," they wrongly conflated the behavior of these volatile forces with Petlyura's own political convictions or with the official attitude of his regime, but they were not wrong to be skeptical of his moralistic posturing. Their hostility was most fundamentally a response to the contradiction built into his own position: a commander in chief who did not command, an opponent of antisemitism operating in a culture imbued with antisemitic assumptions.

Not all Jewish leaders were equally unreceptive to Petlyura's appeals, however. In August 1921, Ze'ev (Vladimir) Jabotinsky (1880–1940), head of a militant faction of the Zionist movement, approached Petlyura with the idea of forming a Jewish legion to fight alongside Ukrainian forces then allied with the Poles against the Red Army. A native of Odessa, Jabotinsky was sympathetic to the drive for Ukrainian independence. The rationale of his proposal was allegedly to protect the Jewish population from the pogroms unleashed by the war. His approach to Petlyura was roundly condemned by fellow Zionists, however, and their reaction contributed to Jabotinsky's eventual break with the movement.[99]

The UNR welcomed Jabotinsky's friendly gesture. While talks with him were in the works, the head of the UNR mission in Prague, Maksym Slavynsky (1868–1945), addressed a letter to the Twelfth Zionist Congress then meeting in Karlsbad, at which Jabotinsky's proposal was the subject of contentious debate. The Ukrainian people, Slavynsky assured them, identified with the Jewish striving for national independence, and since so many Jews inhabited Ukrainian "ethnographic territory," as he put it, Ukrainians had a particular interest in

Zionist success. The Jews, he regretted to say, had "suffered terrible persecutions from various sides," but they were not the only casualties. "The excesses to which they have fallen victim have hit the Ukrainian people just as painfully as the mass of Jews. Not only can the enlightened part of the Ukrainian party not be held responsible, but it disapproves of and condemns the criminal attacks of which irresponsible elements have made themselves guilty."[100]

Slavynsky's statement encapsulated Petlyura's position: he personally deplored the pogroms, which the "unreliable elements" among his followers could be misled into committing, but the real responsibility lay elsewhere. There was a grain of truth on each count, but such denials were hard to credit, when any leader, no matter how bloodthirsty, with an interest in attracting outside support was eager to present himself in a good light. Take the example of Lieutenant Colonel Stanisław Bułak-Bałachowicz (1883–1940), an independent chieftain notorious for the brutality of his men. Bułak-Bałachowicz at times attached himself to the Socialist Revolutionary terrorist Boris Savinkov (1879–1925), a militant opponent of Bolshevik power during the Civil War, and at other times to Petlyura. In December 1920 Savinkov and Bułak-Bałachowicz visited Paris. When questioned by Jewish journalists about the vicious pogroms committed by their men, they insisted they had no "antisemitic inclinations." Interviewed by a Russian journalist, also in Paris, Bułak-Bałachowicz explained that he was fighting against the Communists, not the Jews. If, however, he clarified, "it turned out that among the Jews 80 percent were Communists, I would not hesitate to exterminate them, not as Jews, but as Communists."[101] Cold comfort for ordinary Jews indifferent to politics of any kind who might suffer from the equation of Communists and Jews motivating the anger of hotheads like Bułak and his men.

The relationship of the self-declared governments, whether Soviet or Ukrainian, to the question of responsibility was in fact not straightforward. In the Ukrainian case, the entire institution of the *atamanshchina* mitigated against responsibility.[102] The ataman in chief depended on this very system. The problem from the Ukrainian side in defending Petlyura's reputation at the trial was to insist on his stature as head of state, the leader of an existing nation—though now represented only abroad—while at the same time demonstrating the limits of his power. "The time came," wrote Oleksander Shulhyn, UNR foreign minister in exile, "*when he was no longer master of his troops*. The period of the 'atamanshchina,' to put it mildly, was extremely damaging to Symon Petlyura, even personally."[103]

Schwarzbard's defenders agreed. The kind of power Petlyura exercised during the Civil War fostered the kind of abuses he both denounced and attempted to disclaim. "That Petlyura is implicated in the pogroms [*povinen v pogromakh*] is clear to everyone," a Jewish leader from Galicia remarked. "It does not matter whether or not he himself was present during a pogrom in this or that city, or whether or not he was personally hostile to the Jewish delegations that appealed for his help. What is essential is that Petlyura's political line, his method, inevitably led to pogroms. . . . Petlyura was the slave of his own 'atamans,' 'generals,' and leaders."[104]

The fact that Petlyura was not in control was not meant here as exculpation, but similar arguments could be used to mitigate the assumption of his guilt. In June 1926, soon after the assassination became news, Jabotinsky, once again dissenting from the consensus of Jewish opinion, offered just such a defense. In an article for the New York Yiddish-language newspaper, the *Jewish Morning Journal*, included in Petlyura's portfolio at the trial, Jabotinsky insisted that "neither Petlyura nor Vynnychenko, nor the other members of the Ukrainian government, have ever been what one calls 'pogromists.' Although I have not known them personally, I am very familiar with this type of Ukrainian nationalist intellectual contaminated by socialism. . . . The danger resides, not in the subjective antisemitism of individual persons, but in the 'active antisemitism of circumstances.' In Ukraine the circumstances are against us. . . . Today . . . the air is infused with an antisemitic poison, and it's enough to disturb the air on the occasion of any excitement . . . for this poison to degenerate into a growing hatred."[105]

Such words led Oleksander Shulhyn to praise Jabotinsky as "the only one in the entire world Jewish press bravely to raise his voice against the slander directed at Petlyura."[106] In October 1927, however, with the trial under way, Shulhyn reported with regret that Jabotinsky had reversed himself and declared Petlyura, in his capacity as head of state, to be responsible for the actions committed in his name.[107] The two issues were, in fact, separate: Petlyura's personal reputation, on the one hand; the "actions committed in his name," on the other. Jabotinsky's analysis of the broader context for antisemitic violence was not enough to settle the question. Both sides in the trial agreed: someone must be held responsible.

While the trial was in progress, Oleksander Shulhyn published an extended defense of Petlyura's record on the Jewish Question. *L'Ukraine et le cauchemar rouge: Les massacres en Ukraine* echoed the statements issued by Petlyura at the time. "The calamities known as the Jewish 'pogroms,'" Shulhyn wrote, "are but particular instances of a much greater misfortune in which the victim has been an entire country, all of Ukraine."[108] The Jews and Ukrainians, in his view, were equal casualties of an offensive launched by an enemy dangerous to them both. As a consequence of the revolution, "[m]illions of Ukrainians are dead, and among all these deaths, Jews have also been massacred."[109] Who was to blame? "The instigators of anarchy in Ukraine, those who caused her ruin, devastated her countryside, *the men responsible for the pogroms*, the epidemics, the famine, these are *the criminals in Moscow*."[110]

Shulhyn, like Petlyura, had to admit that the actual perpetrators, the tools of this sinister campaign, had operated from within the Ukrainian army. They were "first of all common criminals, released from various Ukrainian and Russian prisons by the Bolshevik authorities and eager to pillage, who managed to join the Ukrainian army. Second, they were *agents provocateurs*, sent by the Soviets to cause trouble behind the Ukrainian lines. Third, they were ignorant creatures launched against the Jewish population by Red or reactionary agitators, looking to discredit the Ukrainian national movement in the eyes of the civilized world."[111]

Shulhyn's book was not a mere screed. It offered thoughtful reflections on the situation in Ukraine, on the difficulties confronting Petlyura, on popular psychology, on the undeniable excesses of Bolshevik policy. Yet it tends to slip into language that belies its good faith. The Bolsheviks, Shulhyn repeats at every turn, exacerbated the intensity of antisemitism in the Ukraine, but the perpetrators who translated resentment into murder end up blameless in his eyes. "Perhaps the little Jews of the townships who donned the uniforms of the Red Army or the Cheka commissars are most at fault? But these little traitors to their Ukrainian fatherland can say in their own excuse that they were trying to save the world. . . . Should one blame the Ukrainian masses, after terrible travails, horrified by plunder, arson, bombardments, the destruction of entire villages, who occasionally threw themselves on the men they considered their enemy's accomplices?"[112] The "little Jews" are traitors; the "Ukrainian masses" are victims—an unfortunate juxtaposition.

Blaming Moscow for the pogroms, as part of a Soviet strategy to undermine Ukrainian chances at independence, was not merely an attempt to avoid responsibility for atrocities that were clearly the work of Ukrainians, whether directly or indirectly under Petlyura's command. It might also be understood, paradoxically, as an attempt to avoid the antisemitic clichés that crept into the rhetoric of Petlyura's apologists and that seemed also to underlie the premises of Schwarzbard's defense. To frame the confrontation as Jew against Ukrainian, symbol against symbol, was to invite the kind of oppositions that gave rise to pogroms in the first place. It was safer to substitute a political interpretation of the assassination, in which Schwarzbard figured as a tool of Communist power.

In advance of the trial, the Ukrainian émigré weekly, *Tryzub*, accused the assassin of doing the Communists' dirty work. The Ukrainian Social Democratic Party endorsed this view: "The Moscow Communists . . . purposefully sent the Jew Schwarzbard to kill Petlyura, allegedly in revenge for the pogroms in Ukraine." Their purpose was "to smear the Ukrainian people's heroic struggle for independence as a struggle of robbers and pogromists."[113] Moscow, *Tryzub* asserted, had selected "for the commission of this terrorist act an agent of Jewish nationality." The editors then proceeded, however, to stumble into exactly the kind of rhetoric they seemed eager to avoid. Moscow had inspired and planned the deed, but, they complained, "practically all of Jewry" had immediately rallied around Schwarzbard and were using "all their material and moral resources to prove before the court and world public opinion that Petlyura was guilty of the pogroms."[114]

At the trial, Oleksander Shulhyn said of Schwarzbard: "He doesn't even need to be a Bolshevik to be an agent of the Cheka."[115] Such formulations were no doubt intended to blame the politics, not the person, but the figure of the Jew-Communist was recognizable as an antisemitic cliché that transcended the existence of actual Jewish communists. This entanglement was evident yet again when one of the attorneys for the Ukrainian side reversed the equation: it was not Moscow using the Jews, but the other way around. When conquering Ukraine, attorney Albert Willm (1868–1944) explained, the Bolsheviks were clever enough to staff the Cheka with Jews, who abused the Ukrainian population, which therefore blamed Communist atrocities on the Jews.[116] Now, Willm observed, the Jews were taking their revenge for the instances in which Ukrainian peasants had expressed their understandable anger at the violence inflicted upon them, a spontaneous reaction that did not involve Petlyura. The Jewish role in the present trial, by contrast, was anything but spontaneous. "For months and months, petitions and appeals for contributions have been circulated in all the Jewish communities of the world." This was a "frenetic," but organized, global campaign intended to make Schwarzbard "a national hero."[117]

Before the war, Willm had twice been elected to the Chambre des députés on a socialist ticket. This did not prevent him, however, from accepting the basic postulates of the antisemitic worldview.[118] The worldwide Jewish mobilization had as its goal, he explained, "to demonstrate yet one more time . . . that the moment one touches a single member of this great Jewish Nation, which . . . through the centuries and from country to country pursues its messianic dream of universal domination, all Israel instantly appears, hearing the debates and following them passionately!"[119] The Jews had virtues, Willm conceded: work ethic, intelligence, family values; they were tenacious and stuck together. But they also liked to complain. Of course, the massacres were terrible, but "on various occasions it was often the attitude of the Jews themselves that provoked the pogrom movement."[120]

The scripted nature of Willm's intervention was clear at the time. The Berlin *Jüdische Rundschau* commented immediately after the trial: "Mr. Willm perhaps intended to work upon the basest instincts of the jury and the public when he evoked the specter of a 'Jewish world conspiracy,' which, with the help of the Bolsheviks or in league with them, seeks out innocent victims. . . . It is unworthy in such a moment to use the kind of terminology that is the favorite instrument of pogrom instigators in every land."[121] Willm had refuted the charge of antisemitism in classic antisemitic terms. Nor did the argument die with the verdict. In the wake of the trial, the UNR in exile issued a statement again pointing the finger at Moscow. The trial, according to *Tryzub*, demonstrated the Jewish role in "Moscow imperialism."[122] The strategy had failed to persuade the jury, however, which found the evidence of Schwarzbard's collusion with Moscow unconvincing.[123]

As historian Christopher Gilley has pointed out, Petlyura's defenders "seemed to want to disavow pogroms in one breath and justify them in the next."[124] Spokesmen for the UNR, even when denying they were antisemites, Gilley observes, "resorted to the canard of Judeo-Bolshevism."[125] They explained the wrath of the people as a reaction not only to the Jewish commissars but also, as they put it, to the "Bolshevized parts of the Jewish population." The considerable number of Jews who welcomed Soviet power, even if they were not part of the apparatus, in this view, were nevertheless complicit in the harm suffered by "the Ukrainian population in general."[126] The victims of Soviet aggression, in this scenario, were said to have responded—understandably—in retaliation or self-defense.

Defending Petlyura on the basis of his personal convictions, though justified in its own terms, ended by whitewashing the nationalist movement as a whole. There was more to the UNR than a single charismatic personality at the top and the mass of freelance chieftains and desperate peasants who did the actual damage at the bottom. Official pronouncements that blamed the Jews for exploiting Ukraine or harped on the link between Jews and Communists were clearly at odds with the leader's injunctions. In the context of the trial, Petlyura's good name could only be salvaged by separating him from the government he claimed to have led and stressing his political impotence. Among the various causes of the pogroms cited by Shulhyn were "the temporary success of Bolshevik propaganda, the rapid retreat of the Ukrainian Army, the system of the *atamanshchina*." These factors, he argued, "diminished the authority of Petlyura and his government," making it difficult to combat the pogroms.[127] "The pogroms of 1919," he stated more emphatically still, "broke out despite that government, against it."[128] In order to defend Petlyura, to bolster his moral stature, his claim to authority thus had to be denied, but a leader without authority and a government without power do not constitute the basis for statehood. This was the dilemma faced by the champions of Petlyura's posthumous reputation, who still carried the torch for an independent, non-Soviet Ukraine.

Schwarzbard's side also faced difficult dilemmas. As Leo Motzkin explained to Louis Marshall, president of the American Jewish Committee in New York, the Comité des délégations juives was "endeavouring to obtain Schwarzbard's acquittal as it would signify not a justification of Schwarzbard's deed, but a condemnation of those who committed or connived at the pogroms."[129] The Comité had tried before, on the occasion of the Paris Peace Conference, while the pogroms in Ukraine were unfolding, to publicize the magnitude of the events. It had gathered the information available at the time, organized public protests, and appealed to governments for support, though little response was forthcoming.[130] That crisis was now in the past, but the Jews of Ukraine were still not out of danger, Motzkin explained, in presenting the Comité's current goals. Reviewing the past events was important "for the security of Ukrainian Jews, because all great political conflicts contain the potential for renewed pogroms." It is always possible, he observed, "that some unexpected upheaval may cause governments to make use of the antisemitic inclinations of their people for political ends."[131]

The defense committee was anxious to keep attention focused on the pogroms, but it was hard to curb the enthusiasm of the far-flung Jewish press, which hailed Schwarzbard as a national hero and savior.[132] "Petliura, May His Bones Be Ground to Dust!" screamed an American paper. Schwarzbard has "avenged our spilled blood. . . . There is noble tragedy and glorious devotion in his deed."[133] More effusively still, "Dear, precious Schwarzbard—the redeemer of our blood," wrote another.[134] Disentangling the threads was not easy, however. It was difficult at the trial to counter the perception of Schwarzbard as a symbol of the Jewish people, a sign that the Jews as a world community were at last standing up for themselves, just as it was difficult to see Petlyura as anything but a symbol of the Ukrainian nation.[135]

The trial bolstered both positions. Schwarzbard's defense, ironically, confirmed Petlyura's symbolic status by treating him as a sovereign head of state, responsible for his government's actions and reputation. And since this defense was indeed the product of a transnational network of Jewish organizations, it could easily be viewed by antisemites as a worldwide conspiracy. In a similar mirror effect, two plausible assumptions faced off against each other: the Ukrainians' belief in a Soviet plot—not entirely far-fetched given Bolshevik methods—against the Jewish insistence that Petlyura, given his position, was personally accountable for their suffering.

The defense strategy was not without its critics, however, from within the Jewish camp. Objections were raised on moral grounds, notably by Louis Marshall, to the justification of Schwarzbard's deed—the murder of a civilian for the alleged failure to prevent the past actions of alleged subordinates. Others argued on pragmatic grounds that a successful defense could only increase Ukrainian resentment of the Jews, to the detriment of the Jewish population still in Ukraine.[136] How the outcome of the Paris trial would affect the attitudes of

Ukrainian peasants and the lives of the Jews now under Soviet rule was unclear, but it was an argument advanced by Petlyura's defenders, who invoked the omnibus "Ukrainians" as freely as they invoked "the Jews." More cogently, it was argued on the Jewish side that focusing on Petlyura's personal culpability was unnecessary to a successful defense, if its goal was to disclose the damage inflicted on the Jews. "If the full story of the pogroms comes out—as it must," noted Marvin Lowenthal (1890–1969), a representative of the American Jewish Congress, "and if Petlura was really guilty beyond a doubt—whether the lawyer emphasizes his guilt or not, it will be revealed to the world."[137]

Among those who emphasized the risk of intensifying Ukrainian antisemitism and thus worsening the situation of the Jews in Ukraine was Arnold Margolin. Margolin had positioned himself as a spokesman for Ukrainian-Jewish understanding and cooperation long before the trial, though not without conflicted feelings. He now declined to join Shulhyn in Paris, but from his outpost in New York he pressed Schwarzbard's defense committee to modify its approach. In July 1926, Margolin wrote to Motzkin (in Russian, their common native language), complaining that "our Russian patriots"—meaning Russia-oriented members of the committee, such as Maxim Vinaver—were hostile to Ukrainian nationalism. He warned that "the more unnecessary harm we do to the reputation of the Ukrainian people and the Ukrainian movement in the eyes of the entire reading public, the deeper will be the feeling of resentment on their part—and the more difficult it will be subsequently to bring about the cohabitation of the two peoples in a single territory."[138]

Motzkin resisted. "We have the strongest desire," he assured Margolin, "to do everything so that this trial does not damage the mutual relations between Ukrainians and Jews."[139] The trial was a chance, however, to "bring to the attention of the entire world, and first of all to the Ukrainians themselves, the full horror of the martyrdom that the Jews have experienced. It seems to me that first of all the Ukrainians themselves need to recognize the reality of the facts and to cleanse themselves of them, not through all sorts of evasive tactics and statements such as can easily be put to the test at the trial but by establishing a definite boundary between themselves and such acts."[140] The defense committee saw the trial as a political opportunity. "All political parties and political leaders must be brought to understand," Motzkin explained, "that pogroms as a political weapon are not only despicable in themselves but must bring ruin on those who resort to them."[141] Exposing the horrors "ought to serve not only as a way to compensate the hundreds of thousands of victims but also as a prophylaxis in the future."[142]

Margolin was more successful with Louis Marshall, who objected to the defense of Schwarzbard's deed as a political statement. "There is no justification," Marshall insisted, "for making him a national Jewish hero, or for the Jewish people to assume the responsibility for his deed."[143] In a letter to the editor of the *Jewish Morning Journal* in New York, he warned of the consequences. "Shall we so associate ourselves with the assassination that the followers of Petlura and Ukrainians in general, who have looked upon Petlura as a national hero, shall make reprisals upon the Jews of the Ukraine, . . . shall develop an intense hatred against the Jews? Can we not let well enough alone?"[144] Marshall's views, the editor replied, contradicted "the opinion of hundreds of thousands of intelligent and law abiding Jews and Gentiles on both sides of the ocean that the fate of Petlura was well deserved even if [it] took so long a time until he was overtaken by retribution." If published, Marshall's statement "would arouse considerable resentment."[145] Motzkin, for his part, continued to insist that the accusations against Petlyura were not directed at the Ukrainian people as a whole, "because we Jews must in no case countenance generalizations regarding entire nations." He noted, however, that "even certain progressive Ukrainian leaders who emphasize regularly their negative attitude toward antisemitism have not done everything to avoid hostile propaganda about Jews surrounding the trial."[146]

The reproach was not unfair. After the trial, the UNR cabinet published a statement in *Tryzub*, repeating the opinion that "the Red occupiers of Ukraine employed a hired hand to kill . . . Petliura," in order to turn the Ukrainian people's anger at Soviet occupation against the Jews. By means of this "hideous crime," Moscow "shamefully slandered the pure memory of our national leader and the good name of our entire people by accusing them of pogroms." By defending Schwarzbard in the name of the Jews, Jewish leaders were thus unjustly charging the Ukrainian people and their leaders with the antisemitism they had not felt until the trial turned them in that direction. "Schwarzbard is actually a Judeophobe," a Ukrainian socialist remarked.[147] Many Jews "in émigré circles," *Tryzub* charged, had been taken in by "the Bolshevik provocations." In justifying the murder, they lent their support to

Soviet efforts "to destroy the very idea of an independent Ukrainian state. . . . thereby uniting all of the enemies of our statehood."[148] The Jewish organizations had thus adopted a "disgraceful, deplorable, and harmful position" that "has outraged the entire Ukrainian nation." Alas, "blinded by hatred," Jewish leaders did not realize the harm they had done in championing "the tool in the hands of Moscow."[149]

Motzkin, in justifying the opportunity to publicize the enormity of the Civil War pogroms, had wanted the Ukrainians to "recognize the reality of the facts and to cleanse themselves of them . . . by establishing a definite boundary between themselves and such acts." What kind of confession or recognition was he expecting? Petlyura's record showed that he had condemned the evil and made a number of efforts to contain it, under circumstances in which it would have been hard to succeed. Perhaps he could have done more. At the same time, the UNR had also issued statements fostering the connection between Communists and Jews that encouraged antisemitic assumptions. The Ukrainians at the trial had not justified the pogroms, but they had rejected the idea that Petlyura was in any way responsible for their occurrence, thus divorcing the leadership from the masses it claimed to represent or the armed forces it employed. They had, moreover, preferred to see themselves, not the Jews, as victims—both of Soviet aggression and of a Jewish campaign to defame Petlyura and with him the Ukrainian nation. Jews and Communists were linked yet again.

Motzin had not achieved his goal. The remaining UNR leaders had never acknowledged that anything about their own movement or the nature of its leadership had encouraged pogroms. They insisted Petlyura was not himself an antisemite, but they did not confront the pervasive antisemitism of his supporters, which had a decisive impact on the fate of the Jews in the Civil War. Many of the statements at the trial and the reactions that followed continued, moreover, to disclose a stubbornly antisemitic cast of mind. Reflecting back on the trial, Shulhyn, for example, informed Margolin: "The greatest misfortune for the Jewry is that Schwartzbard is acquitted." The result was to lodge "the sentiment of hatred . . . even in the hearts of those Ukrainians who were absolutely foreign to any antisemitism." Members of the defense committee, he complained, in accusing Petlyura of creating the turmoil that spawned the violence, had failed to recognize the devastation inflicted upon Ukraine itself by outside forces. They had failed to mention "our great pogrom—the pogrom of Ukraine." The trial, he warned, was "a catastrophe . . . for Jewish-Ukrainian relations," a catastrophe created by the "racial fanaticism" of Schwarzbard's defense.[150] From Shulhyn's perspective, the Ukrainians were the victims, not only of Soviet aggression—"our pogrom"—but of Jewish ill will. It was the Jews (in their role as Communists and in their international organizations) who hated the Ukrainians, not the reverse. If Ukrainians became antisemites, it was for good cause.

Where did responsibility in fact lie? From the Ukrainian perspective, the Jews had made choices that put their own people at risk. Ukrainian leaders had not been able to protect them from the consequences of their own actions. The chaos and violence of the Civil War, unleashed by the downfall of the monarchy and deepened by the Bolshevik campaign of violent class warfare, provided the context in which vulnerable masses could be manipulated by outsiders pursuing a political agenda. The strategy was successful, spokesmen for the UNR argued, because the UNR had not exercised the kind of power necessary to translate noble sentiments into political authority, not because its leaders lacked the will, but because the conditions of civil war frustrated their intentions.

Despite its tortured logic, the Ukrainian argument was not merely self-serving. Civil war, by definition, entails the breakdown of authority. It unleashes popular passions, encourages the demonization of real and imagined enemies, and provides a field day for demagogic appeals, antisemitic and otherwise. In fact, Bolshevik and Ukrainian leaders faced many of the same challenges and contradictions. Neither Lenin nor Petlyura was antisemitic by conviction; both denounced antisemitism as incompatible with the political goals and values of their respective movements, but neither leader was in control of his armed forces and both were faced with pogroms committed by men fighting on their behalf.

It was a fact largely unmentioned in Soviet-era accounts, but troops directly under Red Army command, as well as brigades loosely attached to Red forces, were themselves guilty of pogrom violence, as Bolshevik leaders at the time were well aware. Outfits associated with the Red Army were responsible for a series of pogroms in spring 1918, including a serious massacre at Glukhov (Glukhiv) in the Chernigov region on March 7–9, 1918.[151] The Red Cavalry under Semyon Budenny (1883–1973) was the most serious offender.[152] Like the Directory, the

Bolsheviks made various attempts to stop the pogroms, also with limited success, although the overall number of Red pogroms was considerably smaller.

Despite differences in scale, the form and intractability of pogrom violence emerged from structural features shared by both movements. An analogue to the *atamanshchina* existed on the Red side. Leon Trotsky (1879–1940), as commissar of war, denounced partisan tactics (*partizanshchina*), but the Red Army nevertheless enlisted the services of various self-generated brigades operating under their own leadership. Indeed, none of the proto-armies in the Civil War had firm command structures or disciplined units, whether under direct authority or under self-appointed chiefs. They all, moreover, drew on the same largely peasant population for their foot soldiers, and the men frequently changed sides. As the Red Army developed, Trotsky began to impose a conventional structure and dispense with delegated violence, but he met with serious resistance and did not entirely succeed.[153]

The problem of Red antisemitism thus emerged from the same conditions that produced the antisemitism associated with the UNR. In ballooning from under ten thousand to almost fifty thousand men by February 1919, the Red Army, now concentrated in Ukraine, absorbed many of the peasant militias that had recently fought against it. Some of them maintained their own leadership. The fifteen thousand men under the Ukrainian ataman Matvy Hryhoriïv, while fighting for the Soviet cause were responsible for some of the most intensely murderous pogroms of that terrible year—under the Red flag—and for more of the same when they turned against the Reds. The commander of Soviet forces in Ukraine, Vladimir Antonov-Ovseenko (1883–1938), was unable to stop the pogroms, but nor could he afford to relinquish the support of these volatile outfits, inspired in their demonic energy by the antisemitic rallying cry. Other brigades were incorporated directly into Red Army units, which themselves engaged in pogroms and—though still defending Soviet power—demanded an end to the "Yid-Commissars." The "Yid" was an all-purpose pejorative, with often fatal consequences for actual Jews. And the problem was not limited to detached or semi-detached paramilitaries. Even inside the apparatus, some local soviets were eager to rid themselves of Jews.[154]

Soviet officials sent by Moscow to run the Ukraine were often resented. It is hard to tell where the animus originated. Local Jews might be taking the brunt for the behavior of the Communists, or Communist officials might be hated primarily because they were Jews, or seemed to be.[155] Moscow was aware that the presence of officials perceived as Jews antagonized the Ukrainian population. In a draft decree of November 1919, the Central Committee directed explicitly that Jews and "city people" not be appointed to positions in the Ukrainian apparatus. In its published form, the decree did not mention Jews, but the meaning of "city people" was nevertheless clear.[156] Cohorts sent to Ukraine in December 1919 and spring 1920 were vetted to exclude Jewish comrades.[157] The exclusion was not in itself a symptom of covert antisemitism, but the overlap of categories was an ominous sign.

Endeavoring to avoid the pejorative association of Soviet power with Jewish rule, the Sovnarkom nevertheless maintained its official opposition to antisemitism. In mid-April 1918, it formulated a decree, signed by Lenin, "On the Struggle Against Antisemitism and the Jewish Pogroms."[158] Published on July 27, 1918, a good three months after Glukhov, the decree tried to reframe both problems in class terms. The autocracy, it explained, had used antisemitism to deflect the people's anger away from their true oppressors—their political overlords and economic exploiters. Now it was the "bourgeois counterrevolution," inheriting the imperial mantle, that induced the most backward elements among the tired and hungry masses, still poisoned by the propaganda of the old regime, to commit "occasional excesses against the Jewish laboring population."

Like Petlyura, Lenin thus blamed the impulse behind the pogroms on outsiders or enemies (here the "counterrevolutionary bourgeoisie") who exploited resentments harbored by some still unenlightened followers. The "mistreatment of any nation," the decree warned, was "unacceptable, criminal, and shameful." Not all Jews, however, deserved sympathy or protection. Only Jewish workers were brothers; the "Jewish bourgeoisie," the "Jewish moneybags" (*evreiskie bogachi*), must be treated as enemies, though "not," the decree warned, "as Jews but as bourgeois." The decree did not confront the question of how this distinction was to be maintained, or whether naming even some Jews as legitimate targets of aggression did not reinforce, rather than counter, antisemitic myths. The decree merely ended by exhorting Soviet officials to "nip the antisemitic movement in the bud, treating *pogromshchiki* and pogrom agitators as outside the law."

In late March 1919, Lenin made a speech again denouncing antisemitism as a tool of reactionary forces, "a cabal of landowners and capitalists," exploiting popular ignorance to keep themselves in power, by deflecting popular anger toward the Jews. Repeating the terms of the earlier decree, he tried to separate the righteous anger against capitalist exploitation from the disreputable anger directed at Jews. "Among the Jews there are kulaks, exploiters, capitalists: as there are among Russians and in all nations," setting the laboring masses against each other. "Shame on those who spread hatred toward the Jews, on those who spread hatred toward other nations." The speech was recorded, but apparently not widely heard.[159] It was published only in early spring 1924, shortly after Lenin's death.[160]

This speech and the July 1918 decree were, in any case, ill-suited to calming the anger directed at Jews, who were easily equated with the social roles the Bolsheviks tried to define in purely class terms. During the Civil War and early Soviet years, small-town Jews were often involved in petty trade, smuggling, and deals that were by definition shady, given the rules imposed by the new regime (as illustrated by the case of Morris Greenfield and the occupants of David Bergelson's fictitious shtetl). The invective against "bourgeois and petty bourgeois speculators" was just as dangerous to Jewish traders and merchants as overtly antisemitic rants.[161] These ambiguities complicated the impact of the party's official position. In this sense, the call to class war, though designed as prophylaxis, replicated the contours of the antisemitic imagination. Nor was antisemitism in its direct form alien to numerous Soviet officials, a fact that is hardly surprising, given precisely the entanglement of ideologically opposite social codes.[162]

Soviet pronouncements were intended precisely to disentangle these associations. It was difficult, however, for socialists of any stripe to accept the ideological adaptability of antisemitism. Even the Jewish Bund, a fierce socialist critic of Communist power, defended the essential integrity of the revolutionary masses, blaming the outrages committed by the Red Army on "the presence of benighted elements who have attached themselves to the Bolshevik movement."[163] Having exonerated the foot soldiers of the revolution, the Bund nevertheless attacked the Bolshevik leadership for "creating particularly favorable conditions for the appearance of anti-Jewish pogroms and the growth of pogromist sentiment. . . . Bolshevik power deepens the economic breakdown of the country, deepens the civil war, and its politics and terror create an atmosphere of anarchy and impunity."[164]

Despite their rejection of antisemitism, the Bolsheviks were thus seen as a menace to the Jews in a broader, more dangerous sense. Similar views were expressed by Jacques Delesvky (Yakov Yudelevsky, 1868–1957), a former Socialist Revolutionary writing in the *Jewish Tribune* in April 1920. "Wherever," he warned, "the government, though not itself antisemite, lives by excesses and creates among the uncultured people the idea of hounding certain sections of the population, excesses, especially against the Jews, inevitably occur amongst other such outrages. The orgy of demoralisation, anarchy and loose living which Bolshevism fosters, and is in turn fostered by it, constitutes a favourable soil in which pogroms may spontaneously thrive. Such pogroms do happen, indeed, under Bolshevist rule, and the Bolsheviks do not deny them." The Communists might discourage "*special* pogroms against the Jews," Delesvky observed, but "the political psychology of Bolshevism" always demands an "object of demagogic violence." The Bolsheviks had "opened a new era of general massacre," and when all other targets had been exhausted, the turn of the Jews as Jews would come again.[165]

The Bolsheviks' aggressive class-war rhetoric and their ruthless assault on their enemies, including the arrest and execution of erstwhile comrades on the left, tempted their opponents to blame them exclusively for the violent character of the Civil War. The Bolsheviks were clearly not the only ones, however, who had contributed to the collapse of political authority, the implosion of imperial society, and the economic catastrophe that both caused and followed the revolution. Nor were they alone in using terror as a political instrument. Sergey Gusev-Orenburgsky, a veteran of *Shchit*, explained these atrocities more evenhandedly as a result of "the contempt for human life and other people's property instilled in the masses in the course of many years of external, then civil war, with its Red and White terrors, extorted tributes, requisitions, searches, raids, hostage-taking."[166]

Indeed, it did not take much for the Jews to end up in everyone's cross hairs. In this "atmosphere of anarchy and impunity," it was particularly difficult for any of the contestants to define their enemies precisely. The Jews were particularly vulnerable targets. Throughout the Great War they were castigated as devious and disloyal, and they continued to be distrusted. For anti-Communists, the equation of Soviet power with the Jews was a given. The UNR might formally denounce the pogroms, but it nevertheless often used rhetoric that hinged on that very equation. The Bolsheviks fell into a similar trap. Denunciations of the "Jewish bourgeoisie," intended to emphasize its economic function and downplay its ethnic profile, invoked social categories that in many minds overlapped with the category of "the Jew." Drawing on the same population that supplied Petlyura with his foot soldiers, the Red Army absorbed the habits and myths they brought with them. Bolshevik rhetoric relabeled an existing map.

Bolshevik internationalism of course led the party to condemn ethnic or racial scapegoating, but it also proved an obstacle to dealing with the problem of Jews as special targets of violence. This was a matter of organization, as well as exhortation. With some reluctance, in early 1918 the Sovnarkom created a Jewish department (Evreiskii komissariat, or Evkom) within the Commissariat of Nationalities and a Jewish section (Evsektsiia) within the party.[167] The Evsektsiia was staffed mainly by members of the Left Poale Zion, Marxists who tried to reconcile their Zionism with support for the Soviet regime and opted to work within the apparatus.[168]

Advocating for Jewish concerns as Communist insiders, the section's Moscow bureau initiated measures to combat antisemitism even before the July 27, 1918, decree. Responding to the Red Army pogroms in Glukhov and Eastern Galicia, the bureau tried to rouse the Sovnarkom to action. Applying the standard formula, it described the incidents as the work of "dark forces," in this case "the Polish bourgeoisie and Romanian landowners, supported by the Austro-Hungarian army." Whatever their origin, the pogroms gave the Soviets a bad name. "The Mensheviks and Right SRs, traitors to the revolution," were exploiting the opportunity; "the entire bourgeois press tries to show the pogroms are the work of the Bolsheviks." The Moscow bureau demanded the Sovnarkom "once and for all put an end to this provocation and in its powerful voice issue a decisive protest against the pogroms and against the handful of traitors to the revolution, who use them for political ends."[169] As socialist opposition to the Bolshevik government ramped up in summer 1918 and repression intensified, however, the Poale Zion activists were expelled from the Jewish Section, which lost its relative independence.[170] In 1919, with fighting concentrated in Ukraine, local Bolsheviks took the initiative in condemning and trying to stop pogroms from erupting in the Red Army. Official pronouncements were intermittent, however, and warnings were hard to enforce.[171]

The pogroms became an issue at the 1919 Paris Peace Conference, as we have noted. All forces active in the Civil War hastened to present themselves as suitably enlightened on the Jewish question and worthy of compensation for destruction caused by the opposing side. The Soviets prepared testimony, in addition, for the Genoa Conference in 1922, documenting damage inflicted by Polish forces on Soviet territory, including the consequences of pogroms.[172] This occasion was the context for an English-language account complied by Elias Heifetz (Elye Kheyfets, 1885/1890–1960?), published in New York in 1921 under the aegis of the Jewish People's Relief Committee of America.[173] A long-standing member of the Jewish Bund, Heifetz had joined the pro-Bolshevik faction that split in 1919. Appointed by Moscow to chair the committee for aid to pogrom victims sponsored by the Russian Red Cross, he collaborated with Jewish organizations in Kiev to compile documents and testimony, some of which he included in the volume destined for an international readership.[174]

Heifetz's presentation illustrates the standard Soviet line on the Civil War pogroms. Focusing on the activities of the Directory, the independent Ukrainian brigade chieftains, and Denikin's army, he accused "the reaction" of using "the massacre of the Jews as a method for political warfare."[175] Unable to deny that some "anti-Jewish excesses and pogroms" were committed by Red Army soldiers in Ukraine,[176] he explained them as the work of "Ukrainian freebooters" temporarily attached to the Red Army.[177] These independent operators, known for their "antipathy to strangers, especially Jews," were "therefore easily accessible to antisemitic agitation, especially in moments of doubt when they were not clear what attitude they should assume toward the Soviet power."[178] Unstable in their allegiances, their loyalties were always in question, but they were always "against the power of the Jews."[179] Even when fighting under the red flag, they sometimes shouted: "Down with the Jewish commissars!"[180]

Comparisons with Ukraine were unavoidable. When it came to Red pogroms, Heifetz took the onus off the Soviet leadership; when it came to pogroms committed by UNR forces, he held Petlyura and the Directory to account.[181] While viewing pogroms as a blot on the Soviet record, he considered them intrinsic to the Ukrainian agenda. "The lamentations and pharisaic attempts at justification, to the effect that the Directory could not control the bands or the crowds, that the latter had gone further than the Directory had intended, can not exculpate it in any way, not even legally, not to say morally and politically. It is not merely that it *could* have foreseen the consequences of its doings, it did foresee them, it desired them, counted on them and took advantage of them."[182]

Soviet spokesmen and Ukrainian nationalists thus took aim at each other, yet with respect to the Jews their positions had a number of features in common, as we have tried to show. Neither the Sovnarkom nor the Directory, at the top levels, propagated antisemitic slogans. In both cases their positions were nevertheless vulnerable to abuse. The Ukrainian nationalists were devoted to destroying the power of "outsiders," among whom the Jews occupied a prominent place, and second-tier leaders did not hesitate to identify them as such. The Communists directed their venom at class enemies easily recognizable as Jewish stereotypes. Both regimes attracted the support of some Jewish activists and the opposition of others. Pogroms were far from the only issue defining the spectrum of Jewish politics during the Civil War.

Among the contestants in that struggle, the Communists were alone in welcoming Jews into their ranks on an equal basis and in positions of power. Joining the Communists was a way for many Jews to escape the threat of violence inflicted on a scale that resisted any form of improvised self-defense. Casting their lot with the rising power, they embraced the ideology that rejected nationalism, though claimed to respect nations. It seemed an alternative to demagogic nationalist appeals that established solidarity at the expense of the Jews, considered always in some sense alien. Some young Jewish men, enraged at the pogroms, joined the Red Army, which allowed them to enlist and provided an instrument with which to restore their dignity and exact revenge. Trotsky disapproved of their "nationalist" motives.[183] Here in a nutshell was the Soviet contradiction.

In a brief convergence of interests, while the Civil War was still underway, the campaign mounted by the diaspora Jewish organizations to bring the world's attention to the disgrace of the pogroms coincided with early Soviet efforts to seek restitution in the international arena and present the Communist regime as a morally upstanding member of the community of nations, a victim of the same forces that ravaged the Jews.[184] Hence the delegation of Heifetz to present the Soviet case, as Margolin did for the Directory. Seven or eight years later, when the Schwarzbard trial hit the front pages, Soviet representatives were not part of the discussion, but well-entrenched positions emerged yet again on the international stage.

Jews and Ukrainians were not the only parties to the 1927 trial. The Ukrainians were not the only ones to insist they were not antisemites. The French participants took the opportunity of the trial to demonstrate that antisemitism was antithetical to the founding principles of the French Republic. The outspoken antisemitism preceding and surrounding the Dreyfus Affair had not vanished, but the Great War marked a change, and the 1920s represented something of a lull. Jews were recognized for their service in the French army and immigrants were needed to take the place of the men who had not returned. In 1927 residency requirements for naturalization were reduced from ten to three years. It was only with the Great Depression, which hit France in 1931, and the election of Léon Blum (1872–1950) as prime minister in 1936, that politically aggressive antisemitism made a comeback. Charles Maurras (1868–1952), leader of the fascist Action française, called for Blum's assassination. A group of businessmen warned the chief rabbi of France: "Beware that the crimes of Léon Blum and his band not redound upon your entire race."[185]

The year of the Schwarzbard trial was therefore a positive moment. Yet there was a sense of unease. The republican legacy was not secure. As historian Vicki Caron puts it, "the Jewish question came to epitomize the very values that the republic stood for."[186] All the principal actors in the trial positioned themselves on the left and therefore had a political stake in its outcome. Among them, Schwarzbard's probono attorney, Henry Torrès (1891–1966), was the dominant figure. Born in Normandy to assimilated Jewish parents, Torrès inherited the mantle of progressive French republicanism. His grandfather, a former minister of the interior, was among the founders of the Ligue des droits de l'Homme, established in 1898 for the defense of Dreyfus.[187] Wounded and decorated during the war, Torrès joined the SFIO (Section française de l'Internationale ouvrière), but in 1920 switched to the French Communist Party. He was expelled a few years later, after making a name for himself in a number of anarchist trials, and in 1927 rejoined the SFIO.[188]

On the Ukrainian side, attorney César Campinchi (1882–1941), representing Petlyura's family, was also a socialist; ten years later he served in Léon Blum's second cabinet. Jacques Biélinky (1881–1943), a Jewish journalist reporting on the trial, praised Campinchi's speeches as "moderate, proper, and delivered without hatred" by "a loyal adversary . . . not at all antisemitic," who did not seem to be wholeheartedly behind his own case.[189] Campinchi insisted he had indeed done his best on Petlyura's behalf, "firmly persuaded that Petlyura's memory should not be tarnished by responsibility for these massacres." He pronounced himself nevertheless "a friend and admirer of the Jewish race."[190] Albert Willm had socialist credentials, as well, though they did not prevent him from making the tasteless comments about the Jews' "messianic dream of universal domination," cited above, which offended the Jewish press. Petlyura, for his part, had originally considered himself a Social Democrat, though his nationalism had later come to define him. Schwarzbard described himself as an anarchist.[191]

The lawyers and intellectuals who testified on Schwarzbard's behalf defended the honor of France as a bastion of political enlightenment. Torrès declared himself a republican: "the instinct of the French people," he asserted, "has always been to grant liberty, justice, courage, dignity to man, to all men and in consequence also to Jews."[192] He admonished the jury: "Today, Gentlemen, you are responsible for the prestige of our Nation and for the thousands of human lives that depend on the verdict of France."[193] The historian Alphonse Aulard (1849–1928) pronounced in the same spirit: "As the historian and disciple of this French Revolution which emancipated the Jews, which gave the world the example of treating them as men, as citizens, I take this occasion to protest against antisemitism and its crimes, which offend the spirit of France."[194] Another witness was Bernard Lecache (1895–1968), the son of Jewish immigrants from Ukraine. Now, in connection with the Schwarzbard trial, Lecache founded the Ligue internationale contre les pogromes (today, La Ligue internationale contre le racisme et l'antisémitisme).[195] Like the Ligue des droits de l'Homme, the Ligue internationale contre les pogromes inserted the specifically Jewish cause in a universal civil rights and humanitarian framework.

The testimony of the writer Joseph Kessel (1898–1979) cut close to home. Like Schwarzbard, a Russian-born naturalized French citizen (with better command of French), he too had volunteered for the French army. As a French officer he had been stationed in Russia. "There have been massacres and horrible massacres," Kessel asserted, "in which Petlyura's troops have played a large role. Their leader—whether he wanted it or not—is accountable."[196] The writer had come forward, he explained, because this was for him "a personal cause, as it is the cause of all Jews who have a drop of blood in their arteries. Like Schwarzbard, I am Jewish and like him of Russian origin. . . . Like him, I have had the chance to be affected by the incomparable spirit of France, the spirit of liberty, courage, and justice."[197] In Russia the Jews did not defend themselves, but Schwarzbard had imbibed the spirit of France ("*la génie de France*"). His former passivity was unacceptable to "a man who has rubbed shoulders with the free Parisian crowds."[198]

Advocates of Jewish rights in France had long seen the Jewish cause as an aspect of their French patriotism,[199] but the "spirit of France" was not unambiguous. The climate had changed for the better after the Great War, but the war itself created tensions, especially for foreign nationals. After August 1914 resident citizens of Allied countries were obligated either to volunteer for the French army or return home to fight. Schwarzbard and Kessel had faced this choice. The "volunteers" were concentrated in the French Foreign Legion, where they endured the contempt and abuse of their officers. As Gabriel Séailles (1852–1922), a leader of the Ligue des droits de l'Homme, remarked: "The Jews who went off to war in the pure spirit of sacrifice had the right to be treated as honorable men. They encountered derision, curses, vulgar offenses, they were insulted, abused, treated as criminals."[200] On June 20, 1915, a group of these foreign legionnaires, including three Russian Jews, staged a revolt. After the mutiny, the remaining Jews were integrated into the regular French army, but Jewish men now avoided the draft; many left the country.[201] The Paris municipal authorities demanded measures against shirkers; the antisemitic press attacked the immigrants as an "outrage to the alliance with Russia"; the left-wing press, by contrast, deplored the treatment of Jews in Russia and praised the courage of the Jewish volunteers.[202]

In January 1916 the Paris police formed a committee to examine the military status of resident foreigners. The sociologist Émile Durkheim (1858–1917) was assigned the Russian case. Active in Jewish community organizations, Durkheim was obviously concerned with the impact on Jews, but his report also stressed the consequences for France: it was not good to appear antisemitic. He was sensitive to foreign opinion. "In order to send a few hundred extra soldiers to the front, we are giving the Germans in America an excuse to accuse France of intolerance. Their treatment is compared to the persecutions the Jews have suffered in Russia; France's good name is compromised." The president of the committee feared France might acquire the reputation of having "gone over to pogrom politics."[203]

The number of Jewish immigrants from Russia and Poland had

increased dramatically between 1900 and 1914 and continued to grow after the start of the Russian Civil War in 1918. At the moment of the Schwarzbard trial, immigrant Russian and Polish Jews constituted over half the Jewish population of Paris.[204] The Austrian writer Joseph Roth, who had ended up in Paris himself, reflected, in 1927, that France should have been relatively easy for these newcomers from the East. "Their faces do not give them away. Their vivacity does not attract notice. Their sense of humor meets that of the French part way. Paris is a real metropolis." Prejudice existed, but it was still an improvement on what the immigrants had left behind. "Eastern Jews, accustomed to a far stronger, cruder, more brutal anti-Semitism, are perfectly happy with the French version of it," Roth concluded wryly.[205]

Their situation was not in fact quite so benign. France needed fresh manpower after the war, but the French model of citizenship did not accommodate cultural differences. The numbers and habits of newcomers from the East provoked a hostile reaction not only among committed antisemites but also among acculturated French Jews. The Consistory of Paris, representing the established Jewish community, called them "an invasion and a menacing evil."[206] The conservative Jewish newspaper, *L'Univers israélite*, once edited by Torrès's grandfather, deplored the notices and posters in Yiddish appearing on the walls of heavily immigrant neighborhoods.[207] French-speaking Jews had acquired civilization; the Easterners stood out as uncouth. French Jews shared the basic attitudes of the culture they had adopted.

The tension between assimilated (respectable) French Jews and the "uncivilized" newcomers was a sore point for the Jewish community. The influx brought anti-Jewish feelings to the surface. In October 1926, in the wake of Petlyura's murder, *L'Univers israélite* sent reporter Jacques Biélinky to the Belleville district, where Jews had on occasion been attacked by working-class mobs.[208] Born in Vitebsk in 1881, the year of the great pogroms, Biélinky was later injured in the Kishinev pogrom of 1903. He participated as a Menshevik in the 1905 Revolution, was arrested in 1906, and spent three years in prison. Escaping a term of Siberian exile, he arrived in France in 1909 as a political refugee. In Paris, he wrote for various Jewish newspapers in three languages—French, Russian, and Yiddish. In 1927, he was naturalized. Deported on March 23, 1943, he died in Sobibor.[209] Despite the sojourn in France, his life had run the gamut of East European Jewish travails.

Now, in 1926, Biélinky made the rounds of Belleville, interviewing the locals. An official told him, "there's no difference between French Jews and foreign Jews; they are all Jews and will never be French. . . . I find them all deeply unappealing."[210] A resident, more circumspect, remarked: "You ask what I think of the Jewish immigrants? Well, I think they would do better to stay at home. All the same, I am not an antisemite, nor a reactionary. . . . If they want to become good citizens they have to live like us and speak our language. No double nationality, no camouflage: either they belong to the Jewish nation or to the French nation. I condemn the attacks on the Jews . . . but these poor people must adapt to our life and our mentality."[211] Two types: the proud antisemite and the "I'm not an antisemite."

The not-yet-naturalized journalist also recorded anxiety on the part of the Jews themselves. A Jewish shopkeeper insisted relations were fine until the newcomers had come along. The idle youth who spent their days lounging in the cafés, spilling onto the sidewalks, conversing loudly in Yiddish, provoked the justified resentment of hard-working neighbors.[212] Biélinky himself agreed that the bad behavior of the Eastern Jews cast a shadow over the whole community; the youth must be helped to adapt.

The fate of foreign Jews in the context of the Russian-Ukrainian-Polish wars had been largely ignored even by the French-language Jewish press.[213] The trial, by contrast, attracted a lot of attention. Three hundred Jewish journalists were in attendance. Their reports emphasized Schwarzbard's distance from his origins, depicting him as a respectable member of the French community, ignoring his shaky command of French, his youthful anarchism, stressing his military service (wounded and decorated in the war), and his occupation as an upstanding tradesman.[214] Schwarzbard's defense also stressed his respectability, his devotion to his new country. The jury were impressed. As one member later explained, they were moved by the horror of the pogroms, "which shocked me to the depths of my conscience as the good Catholic that I am." They were also swayed by Schwarzbard's identification with France: "During the war Schwartzbard bravely fought for France, whereas the civil party furnished no evidence that Petlioura had ever done anything for our country. Quite the contrary, Petlioura's negotiations with Germany, revealed by the defense, did not please us, as you can imagine!"[215] The reference must have been to the peace treaty concluded by Ukrainian representatives in early 1918 in the attempt to establish the country's sovereignty and secure its independence from Soviet Russia.

In the end, Schwarzbard was acquitted. The Ukrainian emigration, still incensed at being labeled antisemitic, were fortified in their belief that Jewish organizations from across the world had served as agents, witting or unwitting, of a conspiracy launched by Moscow to destroy what was left of the leadership of the Ukrainian nation. They predicted (or threatened) retaliation. The French, for their part, might conclude that the ghost of Dreyfus had been put to rest. In 1936, ten years after Petlyura's murder, Léon Blum became prime minister. Antisemitism in France, for that and other reasons, experienced a resurgence. In June 1940, with the fall of France, Marshal Philippe Pétain (1856–1951) established the antisemitic, collaborationist Vichy regime, of which Biélinky was one of many victims.[216] Over the span of the Great War, the Russian Revolution, and the Russian Civil War, the efforts of the transnational Jewish leadership, in response to the plight of East European Jews, to demonstrate the humanitarian dangers of antisemitism as a political tool had succeeded, for a time, in shifting the tenor of public discourse, at least in nations professing to belong to the enlightened West. Yet no prohibition was ever established. Even after the destruction of the European Jews during the Second World War, antisemitism remained in circulation.

CHAPTER THREE

"How to Convince Them You're Not"

The Enigma of Andrzej Bobkowski

JACQUES BIÉLINKY, the naturalized Russian-born Jewish journalist, a native of Vitebsk, who had covered the Schwarzbard trial for the Parisian Jewish press, kept a diary from 1940 to 1942. During that time, in July 1941, the Germans occupied Vitebsk and three months later massacred what remained of its considerable prewar Jewish population. In occupied Paris, Biélinky scrawled his impressions of daily life, written in French, on ordinary copybook paper. Interlarded with newspaper clippings of events and public notices, his notes ended up in the YIVO archives in New York City. They were published—unrevised—almost fifty years after his death in 1943 in Sobibor in Poland.[1]

Andrzej Bobkowski, another writer from Eastern Europe with an outsider's perspective on occupied France, also recorded his experiences in the form of a personal journal. Unlike Biélinky, Bobkowski had literary aspirations, he did not write in French, and he was not Jewish. Unlike Biélinky, he survived the war and lived long enough to see his journal in print. The two inhabitants of occupied Paris walked the same streets and read many of the same newspapers, no doubt listening to the same radio broadcasts from London, but their perspectives diverged sharply. Biélinky was concerned with the fate of the Jews in France and back where he had come from. Bobkowski, by contrast, was preoccupied by news of the sufferings of Nazi-occupied Poland and by the grim forebodings of its postwar future.

Bobkowski's journal entries stop on August 25, 1944, with the liberation of Paris. He spent the next decade revising the text for publication. *Szkice piórkiem* (Pen Sketches) appeared finally in 1957, under the imprint of the Instytut Literacki in Maisons-Laffitte, attached to the Polish émigré group Kultura. Kultura had been founded after the war as a center for the cultivation of liberal values and a politically independent Polish culture.[2] The book elicited little immediate response. Until recently, few Polish-speakers anywhere had heard of Bobkowski. None of his work had been translated and the international literary public was unaware of his existence. It was only the discovery of *Szkice piórkiem* in post-Communist Poland that made him something of a cult figure for the younger generation—an object of admiration and controversy.

Debate revolved around the discovery that Bobkowski had adjusted the language of the journals in their published form to reflect postwar expectations in relation to a number of political issues. Like such notable European intellectuals as Paul de Man (1919–1983), Günter Grass (1927–2015), and Alfred Fabre-Luce (1899–1983),[3] who later concealed or distorted positions they had held during the war, Bobkowski executed a retrospective cleansing of expressions and opinions he later did not wish to see in print. He did not apparently see this as a deception. Recognizing the voice of the journals as a narrative creation, he nevertheless insisted he was true to himself all along. Yet, after the war, off the page, Bobkowski felt the urgent need, as he put it, of "creating myself over again from scratch [*stworzenia sobie na nowo*]."[4] The published journals reflect this postwar reconstruction.

The saga of the notebooks' publication is itself as convoluted as its reception and Bobkowski's posthumous reputation have been. Preparation of the final edition of the journals (two volumes, running to 740 pages) was a long process, as Bobkowski negotiated the divided world of Communist and émigré Polish culture. In December 1948 he concluded a contract with the nonparty Czytelnik publishing house in Poland, hoping his widowed mother, who was still there, would benefit from the proceeds.[5] When this option failed, he agreed to give the manuscript to Kultura.[6] Meanwhile, several passages appeared in homeland Polish and émigré journals and attracted the attention of critics.[7]

Recognition of *Szkice piórkiem* as the work of literature Bobkowski intended it to be was long in coming. Its editor, Jerzy Giedroyc (1906–2000), Kultura's founder and guiding spirit, spoke of "a conspiracy of silence" (*spisek milczenia*); one critic describes the émigré press as having been "laconic."[8] Bobkowski's death in 1961 provided a brief occasion for reflection and literary polemic.[9] An underground (*drugi obieg*—samizdat) version of the text appeared in 1987 in Cracow.[10] A Polish edition was published in London in 1985 and a French translation in Switzerland in 1991.[11] In 1995 a Polish edition appeared in Warsaw, reissued in 2003 and in 2007, fifty years after the original. Polish readers then discovered a hitherto unknown master of modern Polish prose.[12] The writer Paweł Huelle (b. 1957) has called the notebooks an "absolute revelation."[13] Readers seemed also to have discovered a paragon of moral rectitude.

The conceit of the journal was authenticity. Presented in diary form, with dated segments, the 1957 edition conveys the impression of immediacy. A few scholars ventured, however, to compare the earlier published excerpts with the complete text, wondering what the author might have altered. They wondered, in particular, if some of Bobkowski's political observations had been adjusted or added post facto to endow him with more historical foresight than he could have mustered at the time. After the death of Bobkowski's wife Barbara (née Birtus, 1913–1982), the original copybooks ended up in the Polish Institute of Arts and Sciences of America (PIASA) in New York City (fifteen blocks from Biélinky's archive at YIVO).[14] When scholars began to compare them to the 1957 text, the discrepancies emerged.[15] "Our reading of Bobkowski is entering a new, fascinating stage," culture critic Andrzej Horubała (b. 1962) observed. "The fact of the discovery of the wartime manuscripts should mark an end to the naive reception of his work that has persisted over the last few decades."[16]

The subject of the Jews was the center of controversy. The passages Bobkowski had later removed or altered in view to publication contained routine antisemitic clichés and aggressively hostile attitudes, even when he was clearly aware of what was happening to the Jews, not only on Polish soil but all around him in Paris. Yet the text he prepared for Kultura, though inattentive to the plight of the Jews, presented antisemitism as an outmoded prewar affliction that its author had managed to avoid. How important were his youthful views? Had he ever in fact overcome them or did he think they would now, after the war, damage his reputation? These were subjects of anguished debate. Giedroyc had demanded certain alterations.[17] Might these perhaps have been among them? At the moment when *Szkice piórkiem* appeared in print, Kultura was confronting the issue of antisemitism in Poland.[18] Forms of expression once routine had changed their meanings since the war and would sound quite different in retrospect than they had at the time. Change of image? Change of heart? Bobkowski never said.

Bobkowski's life was all along what critics have characterized as a project in auto-creation (*obszar działań autokreacynych*) or self-mythologizing (*autolegendotworzenie*).[19] His exemplar was fellow countryman Joseph Conrad (1857–1924). Józef Teodor Konrad Korzeniowski, as is well known, was born to Polish parents in Berdichev (Berdyczów Berdychiv), a town originally situated in the Polish-Lithuanian Commonwealth, but then located in one of the Ukrainian provinces of the Russian Empire; it is now in Ukraine. In 1867 the boy's father took him to Cracow, then in Austria; in 1874, after the death of his parents, his uncle sent him to Marseilles, where he entered the merchant marine. In 1886 the future writer acquired British citizenship; in 1889 he was formally divested of his Russian passport. His first novel, written in English, was published in 1895 under the pen name Joseph Conrad.

Bobkowski, like Conrad, was born outside what was at the time still fractured Poland, in his case on October 27, 1913, in Wiener Neustadt, Austria. His father, Henryk (1879–1945), descended from the nobility of northeastern Poland, was a general in the Austrian army, in 1913 attached to the Theresianische Akademie (Theresian Academy). His mother, Stanisława, née Malinowska, was connected by family ties and artistic inclination to the leading theatrical circles of Warsaw.[20] The son's upbringing reflected the duality: "I was an only child," Bobkowski recalled in 1958, "born into the most improbable marriage, between Pani Malinowska, . . . delicate, cultivated, surrounded constantly by the company of writers, . . . playing, singing—and a soldier in the Austrian army."[21] Marked by both sides, he struggled equally against cultural elitism and patriotic posturing. After graduating from Gymnasium, he signaled his determination to find his own path by attending the Warsaw School of Economics (Szkoła Główna Handlowa). He dubbed himself a "hooligan of freedom" (*chuligan wolności*), [22]seeking freedom from convention, from constraint, from community, from his own origins. Like Joseph Conrad, he adopted an entirely new language, although in this case, it was still Polish.

Polish though he decidedly remained, Bobkowski wanted to escape a narrow Polishness: he coined the word "Kosmopolak" to describe both Conrad and himself. The cosmopolitanism that liberated him from a narrow Polishness was, however, the product of a Polish upbringing that endowed him with fluency in both German and French and a broad acquaintance with European culture. Theater was in the family's bloodstream. His own freedom-loving pose was a theatricalized self-presentation. On the page, it produced the portrait of a character wanting to escape preconceptions, prescriptions, and external controls. The character, of course, sets itself up for debunking—and along with it, the author.

In life, Bobkowski kept trying to demonstrate his ability to set his own course. The dramatic gesture remained his hallmark. In March 1939 he and his new wife, Barbara (called Basia in the diary), left Poland for France. Their goal was to continue on to Buenos Aires, where he hoped to work for the commercial section of the Polish embassy.[23] When war broke out in September 1939, the couple were stopped in their tracks. Bobkowski attempted to enroll in the French army but was rejected. In February 1940 he took a position at a French munitions factory in Châtillon, on the outskirts of Paris, which employed Polish workers.[24] Four days before the Germans took Paris on June 14, 1940, the workers were ordered to evacuate to the Vichy-ruled so-called *zone libre* in the south of France.[25] Leaving Basia to mind their apartment, on June 12, 1940, Bobkowski joined the men in the great exodus of cars, trucks, carts, and people heading south. About a hundred miles from Paris, in Sully-sur-Loire, he and a companion left the others, who continued on by truck, and set off on bicycles for the remaining five hundred miles. They reached their destination, Carcassonne, on July 3.

On August 28, Bobkowski decided to make his way back, also on bicycle. If, in leaving Paris he was part of the crowd, the return was unexpected, almost a dare, moving literally "against the current." This was his second dramatic gesture: the young man in shorts, spending the golden days of September 1940 pedaling from Carcassonne, by circuitous routes via Nice, along the Riviera, through the Alps, back to Paris, then under German occupation. He is accompanied by one of the Polish workers: the Warsaw taxi driver Tadeusz Wylot, familiarly Tadzio.[26] They carry their food, equipment, tent, and clothing in their packs. They sleep in the tent, picnic on the grass, bathe in the rivers and the sea. They glory in the weather and the beauty of southern France. When stopping to eat and in the evenings and off-moments, Bobkowski opens an ordinary lined copybook, in which he records, in a steady, legible hand, the sights and sensations of life on the road, his observations of nature, of people, of everyday life. He reflects on history, on the human condition. The notes will emerge as an improvised version of the well-known genre of the philosophical travelogue, here inscribed under emergency conditions, in which the philosopher sometimes encounters a French gendarme or a German border patrol and a diverse array of natives, with opinions galore, recounted from the perspective of two footloose Polish guys, appraising it all from their peculiar, displaced angle of vision.

The hardy bikers reach Paris on September 29, 1940. From then on, the notebooks cover life in and around Paris up to the Liberation. Still attached to the factory in Châtillon, Bobkowski apparently engaged in some conspiratorial activity involving the provision of false papers, but he spoke little about it.[27] After the war, together with the writer Andrzej Chciuk (1920–1978), he co-edited a journal for young people.[28] Defining himself politically as "a liberal reactionary of a realistic anti-intellectual coloration, with strong anti-Communist accents and a visceral hatred for Russia,"[29] he was associated for a time with a group founded in London in February 1945 to protest the decisions taken at Yalta concerning Poland, which it hoped would emerge as a democratic state within a Central European confederation.[30] In Paris, he worked for a bookstore, for the Polish YMCA, and as an editorial assistant for Kultura. He also published a few small pieces in literary journals in Poland and in the émigré press.[31]

Crucial for his literary future and for the context of his postwar political views was his association with the circle around Kultura, centered on its creator, Jerzy Giedroyc. Born in the Byelorussian city of Minsk, to Polish-speaking Lithuanian parents, Giedroyc—another hybrid product of the old empire—spent his childhood years in Russia. After completing his studies at Warsaw University, he obtained a position in the Polish Ministry of Trade. In the 1930s he also worked as a journalist, but in 1939, after the German invasion of Poland on September 1, he was evacuated along with the Polish government to Romania. Bobkowski's uncle, Aleksander Bobkowski (1885–1966), who had served in the cabinet, was part of the evacuation.[32] After 1941 Giedroyc fought in the Second Polish Army Corps, a force composed of Polish refugees and deportees released from the Soviet Union, under the command of General Władisław Anders (1892–1970). From 1943–1944 he belonged to its propaganda office. In 1945 he held a leading position in the information department of the Polish government in exile (Rzeczpospolita Polska na uchodźstwie), which had formed after the German invasion. Based first in France and as of June 1940 in London, it was recognized by the Allies as the country's legitimate successor regime.[33]

It was General Anders, a fierce anti-Communist, who provided the seed money for the establishment of Kultura and its press, the Instytut Literacki, established in Rome in 1946 under Giedroyc's direction. In 1947 Kultura moved to Paris, settling in Maisons-Laffitte. When the general tried to repress the publication of a travel report on Communist Poland, Giedroyc repaid his debt and established his financial independence.[34] Kultura published books and a journal, *Kultura,* modeled on the Free Russian Press (*Vol'naia russkaia tipografiia*) of the 1860s, edited by the exiled Alexander Herzen (1812–1870) in London, an outpost of free thinking beyond the reach of autocrats and official ideologues.[35] *Kultura*'s editors and contributors were anti-fascist and anti-Communist. They were cosmopolitan patriots of an extra-territorial Polish culture and modern Polish literature.

Giedroyc was determined, through the medium of culture and free discussion, to create the basis for a future democratic Poland. Kultura published the émigré writers Czesław Miłosz (1911–2004), Witold Gombrowicz (1904–1969), Józef Czapski (1896–1993), and Gustaw Herling-Grudziński (1919–2000), and a host of other writers and thinkers, some from inside the country, who challenged the available political options. This was the milieu in which Bobkowski spent the first postwar years. He shared Kultura's commitment to finding a Polish voice beyond the polarities of conservative nationalism and pro-Soviet Communism, but he nevertheless soon made another break.

As his third and final grand gesture, Bobkowski resumed the voyage interrupted in September 1939. The urge he had felt before the war to escape not only from Poland but from Europe itself now acquired greater urgency. In June 1948 he and Basia took ship from Cannes, bound for Guatemala.[36] Without a word of Spanish, with nary a penny to his name, Bobkowski embarked for the New World, like Joseph Conrad setting sail. From this remote outpost, which he chose as the primitive alternative to overly refined European civilization and dehumanized North American modernity, Bobkowski corresponded energetically with family, friends, and colleagues. Facing the hardship of starting a new life by his own unaided efforts, he opened a model airplane shop, based on his life-long hobby, and eked out a living. He sent his pieces to Giedroyc for publication in *Kultura*. Not all ties were broken; the project of Polish letters crossed the ocean. Bobkowski, still in Guatemala, died of brain cancer on June 26, 1961, at the age of forty-eight.

The writer's death was commemorated in a special double issue of the London-based émigré literary journal, *Wiadomości*, in August 1962.[37] *Szkice piórkiem* had barely had time to make an impression. It was at first valued, as the earlier published excerpts had been, by a small handful of Polish writers and critics, for the originality of its style and the strenuous attempt to break with literary and political expectations. Further recognition came slowly. In 1983, twenty-five years after the book's publication, the respected literary critic Roman Zimand (1926–1992) dubbed it an "unknown masterpiece" (*arcydzieło nieznane*).[38]

Zimand had also spent the war outside Poland. In 1940, the fourteen-year-old and his parents, along with other Polish citizens, were evacuated eastward into the Soviet interior. They remained in Kazakhstan until 1944, thus escaping the extermination of the Jews. Returning home, Zimand at first embraced the Communist regime, but after 1956 joined the democratic opposition and was expelled from the party. Marginalized in his academic career, he wrote for the underground press and for *Kultura* under a pseudonym. In 1981, he was interned under marshal law. He is buried in the Jewish cemetery in Warsaw.[39] A decade later, in 1995, another literary critic, attached to the same institute in Warsaw where Zimand had made his career, but thirty years Zimand's junior, lamented that Bobkowski's titles were out of print, his letters unpublished, his moral and philosophical vision lost to a generation of postwar Poles.[40] Since then, however, the texts and correspondence have appeared in the bookstores and a new cohort is assessing the man and the message.

What was that message? What had *Szkice piórkiem* accomplished? Who was the hero of Bobkowski's own story? From the literary standpoint, what makes this journal compelling is the quality of the prose at its best. The vivid, ironic, understated art of the tale reflects the perspective that Bobkowski, only twenty-six when he began, brought to his experience of the crisis unfolding around him. If the style embodied the spirit, the spirit represented a philosophical stance shaped by the political and cultural environment in which he was immersed. Bobkowski shared the "catastrophic" view of European culture not uncommon at the time, but, as Zimand comments, he "was a catastrophist of an anti-metaphysical turn, savoring the beauty of the moment, the taste of every detail, the joy of physical exertion."[41]

This posture is important not only to the charm of the narrative, at its most charming, but also to its intellectual contours and its moral dark side. Bobkowski was an absolute individualist, most at home on the seat of a bicycle, in a foreign country, far from parties, proprieties, and ideologies. He was a philosophical writer who rejected abstractions and melodrama. He evoked the particulars—human, natural, historical—that came his way. He loved the bicycle as a means of locomotion. It put the breeze in his hair; it allowed him to explore the roads and byways, then to throw down his tent, stretch out on the grass, and steal some fresh-plucked grapes to nibble with his strenuously assembled supply of cheese and wine, and have a good smoke. The bicycle was mechanical, but handcrafted: a piece of work. The exhilaration of the road belongs particularly to the first part of the journal, when Bobkowski is riding through the French provinces, and the language shares the momentum and joy of movement. The tone changes when he is confined to Paris, food supplies dwindle, and the war grinds on.

The ride through France was also a journey of reflection, of literary, political, and philosophical free association—an openness to cultural influences from all sides and on all levels of sophistication: a declaration of anti-elitism. Translating for Tadzio—peddling at his side, sharing his tent and his smokes—the wonders and paradoxes of European culture: the Greeks, the Nazis, the French. Citing the Russian romantic poet Mikhail Lermontov (1814–1841), as well as the Polish bard Adam Mickiewicz (1798–1855); *Gone with the Wind* (the film, which appeared in 1939), together with smutty drinking ditties. Glimpsing after-images of Austrian painter Egon Schiele (1890–1918) in the indolent life of a French prostitute; cursing the cobblestones in provincial French towns that threatened his bicycle tires and his backside. The anti-intellectual intellectual instructed his working-class sidekick with more than a dose of condescension, of course.

An amateur saturated with European culture, Bobkowski savored its treasures—literary, culinary, scenic—while he nurtured his independence. A Pole adrift in wartime Europe. A young man living in the present, writing in the present, immersed physically in the present. As Zimand comments on Bobkowski's gift for the description of nature, there is nothing contemplative about it: "Whether it's the Mediterranean Sea or some other pond, Bobkowski will have swum in it. Whether it's the Alps or Paris, it's seen from his bicycle seat. That means, it's first observed on the fly, then mulled over, then constructed."[42]

Preoccupied with what he considered the dual moral crisis of Nazism and Bolshevism, Bobkowski was a moral absolutist who did not look for absolutes to fill the void. The story of the bicycle ride through Vichy France was an assertion of this refusal of abstractions; one might call it a principled refusal of principles. Bobkowski liked contrast, disjuncture, surprise. He was religious in an implicit mode, not confessional. Though sometimes sentimental, his basic stance was ironic. His highest value was personal independence, the freedom of the individual person. Hence, his leap from what he saw as the moral collapse of European culture and politics, into the unknown of Guatemala, a place with no claim to the "civilization" that had let him down—at least from his point of view, a relief. What connected the young man on the bicycle with the older man in the model airplane shop was the fascination with how things work, with the solving of real problems, the modesty of everyday details, the deliberate descent from the intellectual summits. Fixing his bike, pitching his tent, filling his copybooks, getting his fingers stuck in the glue.

Despite his ferocious political opinions—anti-Communist, anti-Nazi, and vociferously hostile to puffed-up Polish patriotism—Bobkowski insisted on his refusal of politics. The journal was relentlessly anti-ideological, a challenge to myth making in all its forms, and therefore difficult for both the emigration and the Communists. One thinks by analogy of the account of the canonically heroic Warsaw Uprising by the poet Miron Białoszewski (1922–1983), which de-dramatizes, by meticulously describing in concrete detail, the experience of being caught inside, the unheroic character of fear, desperation, and survival; the unheroic character of heroism.[43] Like Białoszewski, Bobkowski eschews any kind of posturing or generalization, except only to take it apart. His account of the war is not about death; it embodies precisely the feeling of being alive, set adrift on an open road, a new course opened by the catastrophe, free to choose his own path. Unlike Białoszewski, however, Bobkowski does not reduce the drama of the war in order to emphasize the horror, as hyperbole cannot do. Bobkowski avoids the horror altogether. He avoided it philosophically, stylistically, and physically—neither his existence nor his dignity was ever seriously in danger.

The notebooks constitute Bobkowski's conversation with European culture through the filtered consciousness of the war, from its relatively sheltered margins. "To write about the war in Poland in this way just wasn't done," comments Zimand, explaining the book's failure, still in 1983, to "be readable" to Polish readers. "*Szkice piórkiem* violates a taboo so deeply rooted that it is entirely internalized," he notes.[44] "Every second critic is on intimate terms with Gombrowicz, but no one mentions Bobkowski."[45] It is naturally ironic that Bobkowski himself should later have become the object of a myth, and one moreover of his own creation: the free spirit, the free mind. And as naturally, that iconoclasts should arrive to unmask him.

Bobkowski is not a thinker (on principle and by nature): "Intellect?—life, not intellect."[46] Nor is he an originator of literary forms. His originality resides in the vitality of his prose, the deployment of a Polish idiom that both echoes and departs from the canon. The published journal exudes spontaneity. Of course, there were literary models. *Jacques le fataliste* (the gentleman and the sidekick) by Denis Diderot (1713–1784),[47] the stories of Ivan Bunin (1870–1953) or Katherine Mansfield (1888–1923) ("in which nothing happens, and yet so much has occurred"[48]), not to speak of Joseph Conrad. Bobkowski admired Oscar Wilde (1854–1900) ("But perhaps being natural is itself but a pose?"[49]). For his views on politics, for his philosophical posture, Bobkowski also relied on models. A good part of the journal consists of reflections on society and culture that echo the commonplaces of his day.

The champion of originality was a man of his time. His guiding ideas were acquired from a series of popular philosophizers, among whom he singled out Hermann Alexander Graf Keyserling (1880–1946) for special attention. Keyserling was in the air at the time. The writer and art critic Léon Werth (1878–1955), for example, mentions the "philosopher journalist" in his own memoir of the exodus from Paris in 1940.[50] A Baltic German married to Bismarck's granddaughter, Keyserling was born in Livonia, then part of the Russian empire, today divided between Latvia and Estonia, and studied in Dorpat (now Tartu), Heidelberg, and Vienna, before becoming a popular travel writer and culture critic. *Encyclopedia Britannica* describes his ideas as "often platitudinous or obscure."[51] He had his fans, but also critics and scoffers. Pro or con, he attracted notice.

Bobkowski was a fan. On the occasion of Keyserling's death in April

1946, he composed an appreciation, hoping to acquaint Polish readers with the philosopher's views. The terms in which he praised Keyserling's work could easily apply to his own. The "pronounced aversion to everything abstract" was a feature they shared. *Das Reisetagebuch eines Philosophen* (*Travel Diary of a Philosopher*), which Bobkowski praised as "a splendid analysis of the countries he visited and their national character," was notable for its "digressions and remarks, unexpected insights and descriptions, in which the ideas move progressively from the field of fine observation towards the solution of always relevant problems."[52] In a volume on the spirit of Europe, Keyserling again surveyed the distinctive cultural personalities of the individual nations, in all their splendid diversity. Such a cosmopolitan outlook was music to the Kosmopolak's ears. Individualism, in his view, was the core European value, which extended also to countries.

For the same reason, the Baltic nobleman was a resolute opponent of internationalism, the merging, blending, or transcending of differences. His brand of locally rooted conservatism reflected the same regard for the particular that animated Bobkowski's observations and reflections, and indeed his literary style, at its best when evoking details and sensuous impressions. The devil of abstraction in Bobkowski's view took the form of political ideology—red and brown. Nazism and Communism were equally objectionable forms of collective tyranny. In a passage missing from the published version, he excuses the violence perpetrated by the "Russian peasant disemboweling the Volga squire and the first Hitlerites abusing the jews [*sic*]" as an expression of spontaneous emotion: "they had simply 'had enough.'" The real criminals, by contrast, were Stalin and Lenin, who had never themselves killed a man, but had turned this "blind and righteous murder into a system."[53] In some contexts, he included the United States as yet another version of what he deplored about political and social modernity: mechanized, soul destroying, homogenizing.

And, of course, Keyserling did not avoid the question of the Jews. In a survey of European cultures organized by nation, the Jews, as a people without a nation, did not merit a section of their own. They do, however, deserve a warning. Jews were acceptable, in Keyserling's eyes, only as long as they remained faithful to their religion, otherwise, as he put it, "they so easily degenerate . . . morally . . . and physically."[54] In a language that later became toxic in a literal sense, he declared: "The Jews are, for the other nations, more or less beneficial parasites;

either they further the interchange of material, as middlemen, or else they destroy."[55] When they cease to adhere to their laws and customs, which have guaranteed their identity over the centuries, they become the carriers of a destructive internationalism. "*It is for Europe's sake that the internationalist idea must not conquer Europe.* . . . Nations are nothing else than raw material for the self-realization of what is individual and unique."[56] His italics. Jewish-style internationalism was not the cosmopolitanism he or Bobkowski took as their guide.

Reflecting on Keyserling after the war, Bobkowski seems to be defending the philosopher's reputation. He notes that Keyserling was drawn to the ideas of Houston Stewart Chamberlain (1855–1927), but had rejected Chamberlain's racism. He praises him for defending Albert Einstein's place in German culture. He reports that Keyserling was harassed by the Nazis (he was forbidden to publish once Hitler came to power, though he approved of much of what the Nazis had to offer), but managed to leave the country in 1942.[57] Bobkowski does not mention the comments on the Jews that pepper Keyserling's volume on Europe, although he took note of these passages as he was reading along.[58]

Bobkowski imagined himself, like Keyserling, surveying the European landscape with the critical distance provided in his case by physical displacement and cultural detachment. If his banner is "freedom" and "authenticity"—a striving for simplicity and immediacy—it is a potential created, he realizes, by his sudden thrust into liminal space. Against these requirements, the young man judges Europe and finds it wanting. The core European values of freedom and individualism, he complains, are not reflected in the everyday habits and political behavior of the Europeans around him. The natives conform, rather, to the demands of respectability; they imitate their neighbors, follow their leaders, or succumb to the panacea of ideology.

Bobkowski, for his part, strives to free himself from the bonds of convention and the power of intellectual authority. It is precisely his high-minded posture, as a man of unmediated reactions, disdaining compromise and hypocrisy, challenging the norm, that provoked his readers' distrust, well before the later revelations. The first issue was "authenticity." Had this allegedly spontaneous record of direct experience been altered for publication? In 1958, during the post-1956 Polish "thaw" (*odwilż*), the journal *Nowa kultura* (The New Culture) published a critique of *Szkice piórkiem* that accused Bobkowski of having introduced changes that endowed him with uncanny political foresight.[59] *Nowa kultura* was the organ of the Union of Polish Writers, but in these years it demonstrated a certain independence. Doubts were expressed also in the émigré press concerning various predictions of a political nature.[60]

Bobkowski rejected these accusations. In a letter of February 20, 1958, to the literary critic Tymon Terlecki (1905–2000), he wrote: "As for the predictions that give the impression of having been added ex post, I must assure you that I discarded many of those predictions. Too many have no doubt remained. But I did not add anything. It's hard to explain, but when I revised the text for publication I was often surprised. The explanation is nevertheless simple. Paris was at the time an excellent observation post. The perfect armchair."[61] Bobkowski thus again confirmed the image of himself as truth teller: a keen and honest observer; yet while insisting he "did not add anything," he confessed to editorial meddling ("revising the text for publication"). The ambiguity was already there. Writing in 1983, Zimand defended the "authenticity" of the 1957 edition. Bobkowski, he said, in editing the text for publication had introduced a few words not earlier used in Polish, such as "helicopter" and "mass culture." Nevertheless, Zimand warned, until the original manuscript became available no final conclusions could be drawn.[62] It turns out, in fact, that "helicopter" and "mass culture" had already entered the Polish vocabulary during the war,[63] but other features of the published text were decidedly retroactive.

Decades later, once the original manuscripts were examined, scholars were able to pursue the question Zimand had left in suspense. They did not, however, confirm his assumptions. It was already clear that Bobkowski was not averse to revision. Not all published versions were identical. The excerpts Bobkowski had released soon after the war differed to some degree from the corresponding passages in the 1957 Paris edition. He may have altered the early pieces to increase their chances of appearing in Poland, where his mother would have benefited from the proceeds. He called them "fragments," he explained, to signal their incompleteness. In this connection, he spoke of a pact with the reader: "What I care about is a certain honesty with respect to the reader (to oneself)."[64] The phrase suggests he had in mind a deeper truthfulness, unaffected by textual alterations. Terlecki in 1962 described his writing as: "absolute truth-telling."[65]

Fast forward three decades, when this assertion would be challenged. In 1993, the critic Maciej Urbanowski at Jagiellonian University in Cracow concluded: "*Szkice piórkiem* after the end of the occupation of Paris in 1944 was not a finished work and over the years was subject to a certain reworking."[66] The suspicion of "retouching" is troubling for readers, Urbanowski explains, because of the "pact" of documentary accuracy implicit in the diary form, which postulates the identity of the book's author, narrator, and hero.[67] In fact, Urbanowski reminds us, diaries are not exempt from the ambiguities of fiction; and what Bobkowski produced was not even a diary, but merely "sketches" or notes. Bobkowski himself conceded: "even what you write on the spur of the moment is already a bit of a lie, a deformed thought, a true sound warped in transmission."[68] On a less philosophical plane, in 1947 the writer informed Giedroyc that he was busy revising the first part of the journal, which "needed a rather great deal of reworking and weeding out with respect to many things of a personal nature unfit for publication."[69]

The debate over the status of the journal heated up in 2011, the fiftieth anniversary of Bobkowski's death, when Łukasz Mikołajewski (b. 1982), while completing his doctoral dissertation at the European University Institute in Florence, published an essay called "Fictionalized Memory" in a volume devoted to the various aspects of Bobkowski's personality—"Rebel, Cyclist, Cosmo-Pole."[70] Mikołajewski had been investigating the attitudes toward "Europe" or "the West" expressed before and after the war by Bobkowski and another Polish writer, both of whom remained in emigration.[71] With access to the copybooks deposited in PIASA, Mikołajewski set out to learn whether, between 1944 and 1957, Bobkowski had altered his opinions on the topics of Communism, the United States, and popular mass culture. The version published by Kultura, he concluded, consisted almost entirely of text from the original notebooks, but some passages had been reworded, many excluded, and some new ones inserted.[72]

Whatever Bobkowski himself might later have implied, the published version departed in certain crucial respects from the notes he took at the time. Consistently anti-Communist and critical of bourgeois capitalist culture, before, during, and after the war, by 1957 Bobkowski had become more stridently anti-Soviet and less ambivalently pro-American. The key elements of his former attitude toward Europe and European culture nevertheless remained. He continued to believe the core values of individualism and freedom retained their luster, but the French and German cases showed him how far that culture had sunk. His later views, Mikołajewski argues, reflected the starker juxtapositions of the Cold War. He concludes, as would be expected, that Bobkowski's opinions shifted with the times, and shifted in rather predictable directions, though the essential orientation endured. Mikołajewski's most troubling discovery was, of course, the writer's youthful hostility toward the Jews and indifference to their fate, attitudes that clashed with the humanistic perspective Bobkowski consistently championed.

Mikołajewski was not the first to probe the issue of Bobkowski's attitude toward the Jews. The question emerged soon after the writer's death, in the memorial issue of *Wiadomości* published in 1962, which included reminiscences by the writer Andrzej Chciuk, with whom Bobkowski had collaborated in Paris right after the war. Chciuk had arrived in France in 1940, joined the Resistance, been interned, and escaped. Like Bobkowski, he later abandoned Europe, in his case leaving for Australia in 1951, but he remained active in the intellectual world of the emigration. To his credit, Chciuk testified, Bobkowski had provided various people with false papers during the Occupation and had saved "a number" of Jews. He did so, Chciuk asserted, "although he found them personally rather distasteful. In contrast to those who did much less, but talked about it a lot, he did not try to turn the fact to his own advantage."[73]

Chciuk mentions Bobkowski's dislike of the Jews in order to praise him for alleged good deeds that transcended his personal feelings. Why mention these feelings at all, unless they already needed explaining? Twenty years later, Zimand, also in a defensive mode, corrected Chciuk's impression. "Chciuk was a well-known philosemite," Zimand writes, "while Bobkowski's relationship to the Jews was normal. Considering his temperament and his 'foul-mouth,' he may well have said something in Chciuk's presence that struck the philosemite as tactless, if not blasphemous."[74] Yet the "philosemite" did not love Bobkowski any the less for his off-color remarks. Either Bobkowski had expressed himself with a certain restraint, or "tactlessness" was still, right after the war, not as taboo as it later became. Bobkowski's aversion may well have fallen within the spectrum of feelings about the Jews that did not at the time qualify as "antisemitic."

Chciuk was responding, after all, to the tone of Bobkowski's conversation, not to the comments buried in the unpublished version of his wartime notes. Yet Chciuk was not wrong. Bobkowski did find the Jews distasteful, at least in the years Chciuk knew him. The original manuscript contains expressions of hostility and disgust, recycles numerous antisemitic clichés, and shows little empathy for the Jews' suffering or regret for their fate. The absence of concern is evident even in the amended, published version. Zimand, for example, felt called upon to explain certain omissions. If Bobkowski had worked for the Resistance, or if he had helped the Jews, Zimand suggested, he would not have said so. Not only did one not mention such things, but, Zimand explains, "[t]he poetics of *Szkice* is programmatically, demonstratively civilian and anti-heroic."[75] If Bobkowski had been a hero in real life, the role would not have suited his literary persona.

Bobkowski's silences are nevertheless telling. He did not, in fact, omit all reference to his record of service during the war. He describes his part in aiding and assisting the remaining Polish workers in Châtillon, helping them avoid deportation to forced labor. He records various times when he ran personal risks in the discharge of his duties.[76] He also notes the occasion on which he tried to help one of Basia's former classmates, a Jewish woman whose husband had been deported.[77] Overall, however, his voluminous descriptions of life in occupied Paris include very little about its Jewish inhabitants. Yet, on the eve of the war, fully half the Jews in France were immigrants and of these many were Polish.[78] For such a keen observer, for such an omnivorous consumer of impressions and types, one so sensitive to the moral atmosphere around him, his scope was rather limited when it came to the Jews.[79]

For obvious reasons, Bobkowski would have had a very different perspective on the Jewish experience of the Occupation than that of the Jews themselves. To understand what he did not notice or failed to mention, it is instructive to compare his observations with those recorded by Jacques Biélinky at the same time. The month of September 1941, for example, began with the opening of a well-publicized antisemitic exhibition in the second arrondissement. Bobkowski mentions all sorts of performances, films, concerts—but this item passes him by. Biélinky takes note and goes on to report the internment of Jews and the execution of hostages, as featured in the newspapers. Bobkowski comments on none of this, until September 19 to 22, 1941, when both diarists mention the imposition of a curfew and the shooting of twelve hostages.[80]

A dramatic moment that would have been hard to ignore was the bombing on October 5, 1941, of seven Paris synagogues. Biélinky describes the destruction in detail.[81] Entries in Bobkowski's published notebooks for that date and the days following mention nothing. One of the buildings was located on rue Pavée, near the Saint-Paul metro in the heavily Jewish district that Bobkowski occasionally visited to see a friend.[82] Though otherwise attentive to the appearance of people in the metro, cafés, train stations, shops, and theaters, he never mentions the area's Jews. He knows they are there; a Polish acquaintance takes his suppers at "Yitsek's place near the Hôtel de Ville."[83] A few Jewish figures appear in passing: a Jew from Antwerp, encountered during the exodus from Paris, with an uncle in Cracow; a busy black marketeer with a laughable name; a "Monsieur Joseph," described as "a small, swarthy little Jew, somewhat dirty, somewhat elegant," a shady wheeler-dealer who helped Bobkowski sell dollars under the counter; Basia's classmate, who remains unnamed.[84] For all his interest in the texture of everyday life, Jews did not capture his attention.[85]

Perhaps there's no reason they should have. In this regard, Bobkowski's indifference probably did not distinguish him from the average Parisian and, of course, he and Biélinky inhabited different worlds, which overlapped very little, despite the occasional visit to Saint-Paul. Biélinky was part of a communications network among Jews that obviously did not include Bobkowski. They nevertheless did share the same physical and public terrain—posters on the walls, information in the newspapers. Signs on phone booths proclaimed: "*Accès interdit aux juifs.*" Signs in café windows warned: "*Entrée interdite aux Israélites.*"[86] Much of this knowledge indeed could not be avoided and Bobkowski was interested in events, both large and small. He eagerly followed news of the war and commented on the doings of the Pétain regime. He reports hearing radio broadcasts from the Polish government in London, which in 1942 and 1943 reported on the fate of the Jews, as did the Free French program on the BBC, which he also heard.[87] His clippings from the collaborationist *Paris soir*, now in his archive, include comments on the dangers posed by foreign, especially Polish Jews. Biélinky also saved clippings—reporting events, arrests, anti-Jewish regulations, and roundups—from various sources, including the German-run *Petit Parisien*. In short, both diarists scanned the press for the information they cared about and then chose what to mention in their notes.[88]

Among the mundane differences that nevertheless separated the experience of the two men was the issue of bicycles, a seemingly minor theme that looms large in Bobkowski's story. He spends much of his time either riding them—through southern France or all over Paris when he returns—or looking to buy them or trying to repair them, and he describes this preoccupation in great detail, emphasizing its significance, both practical and symbolic, for life under the Occupation. "The bicycle is the basic means of locomotion," he records on October 3, 1940.[89] By July 3, 1944, more urgently: "the bicycle is becoming the only means of locomotion."[90] In May 1942, however, as Biélinky complains, the Paris police had confiscated all bicycles belonging to Jews, who were no longer permitted to use them, with the obvious consequences for their chances of survival.[91] Perhaps this order was not well known to the people it did not affect. Whether Bobkowski was thus simply unaware of the privilege he enjoyed, or knew of the prohibition but didn't bother to note it, in either case this particular disability imposed on the Jews in occupied Paris was clearly not a subject that touched him.

Bobkowski's response to his immediate surroundings and to the fate of the Jews, near and far, was informed not only by personal likes and dislikes but by his awareness of the larger political context, and particularly the fate of Poland, as shaped by the war and its aftermath. In the original notebooks, politics and prejudice went hand in hand. Militantly anti-Nazi and militantly anti-Communist, Bobkowski was also anti-German and anti-Russian, positions he combined with standard-issue antisemitic clichés. From this perspective, the war presented him with a number of equally unappealing possible outcomes: either the Germans, who had betrayed their roots in European culture, would win and rule the world; or the Anglo-Americans would win and the Jews would run it; or the Soviet Union, known to be in Jewish hands, would overrun Eastern Europe and impose its tyranny on Poland. These basic fears, for the future of Europe and, in particular, the future of Poland, emerge clearly in the Kultura edition, but the terms in which they are presented are no longer what they were during the war, when he recorded his immediate reactions and reflections.

The contrast between the wartime notes and the postwar edition illustrates the degree to which Bobkowski felt in retrospect, for whatever reason, that he had to adjust his narrative voice. The manuscript entry for September 21, 1941, for example, contains a passage entirely absent from the Kultura version. It concerns a radio broadcast by General Władysław Sikorski (1881–1943), prime minister of the London-based government in exile, in which he wished the Jews a good Jewish New Year.[92] Bobkowski is disgusted. "If he intends to do that in the future Poland," he comments, "better not to have him around . . . I would give a lot to know what Polish society feels about the jews [*sic*] at this moment. Jews are indeed the biggest 'BUT' in the event of England and America winning the war. They will be taking over again."[93] In the same manuscript entry, he confesses: "If the Germans were not Germans, who knows whether I would not assert that they are right and should win the war. There's something refreshing in their idea. . . . Perhaps the jews [*sic*] have simply deprived me of the ability to think broadly and are putting me in a pro-German mood?"[94]

In relation to local events, the decree imposing the yellow Stars of David announced on June 1, 1942, aroused mixed feelings. Noting that the Jews were obliged to purchase the insignia with two points from their textile coupons, Bobkowski originally said the two points reminded him of "crushing lice with your thumbnail."[95] The phrase was no doubt meant to convey the German point of view, as well as his own disapproval, but it was ambiguous enough to be removed in the published version. An expression likening Jews to lice might not be read as ironic. The Kultura entry instead signals an unambiguous shock: the two points, he now asserts, "have driven me almost insane." The decree, he adds, had offended French sensibilities and was "tragic, repugnant, and hopeless."[96]

Clearly, he felt a correction was needed. The comments on the Stars of David were amplified in the Kultura entry for June 9, 1942,[97] which contains a passage that does not exist in the manuscript. "Starting today, the Jews are wearing yellow stars with the word 'JEW' in black characters, formed to look like Hebrew letters. I try not to notice them because I'm ashamed. How few people realize what savages we, WHITE PEOPLE, have become. I'm ashamed for the entire race, the marvelous race that built the modern world, created technology, conquered nature, mastered so many diseases — for what? In order, in 1942, to compel their brothers, perhaps their most valuable element, their leaven, to wear a humiliating badge, like medieval lepers. If I were a colored man, I would lose all respect for the whites. There may come a time when the highest price will have to be paid for the amusements of madmen. The price of our existence. Our technology and our savagery will be used to destroy us."[98] Us, that is, "white people." As the language suggests, the passage may have been composed when Bobkowski was already in Guatemala, where his position of superiority would not have been asserted with respect to the Jews but to "the colored men" who owed him a respect he imagines he might forfeit.[99] Overall, Bobkowski's attitude toward black people in the Kultura edition is condescending, but not hostile.[100]

Like the imposition of the Stars of David, certain catastrophes befalling the Jews could not be ignored by anyone in Paris. From July 15 to 16, 1942, 13,500 Jews from all over the city were rounded up and interned in the Vélodrome d'hiver sports stadium, from which they were first deported to the nearby camp at Drancy and then to Auschwitz. Biélinky, not surprisingly, expressed his horror at the roundup, noting on July 17 that "everyone is talking about it."[101] This "everyone" might have included only the Jews of his acquaintance, but Biélinky insists the French show open concern for the Jewish fate. On July 24, he writes: "From various sides one learns that the Parisian population grows increasingly sympathetic to the Jews."[102]

Bobkowski did not immediately respond to this event. During the month of July 1942, visits from friends distracted him from his writing, leaving an unusual silence.[103] It was only on August 4, 1942, almost three weeks after it occurred, that he mentions the roundup. The entry in the copybook calls it "a Saint Bartholomew's Night, or rather a Saint Adolf's Night." It notes that "on the territory of the entire occupied zone all foreign Jews have been interned in camps. This has made an enormous impression on the French. The separation of children over three years old from their mothers has aroused particularly vitriolic comments."[104]

Where he heard these comments he does not say, but the Vélodrome d'hiver roundup indeed marked a turning point in French opinion, at least as represented in the underground press, which for the first time, and only for a brief moment, expressed a sense of moral outrage at the fate of the Jews and the complicity of Vichy officials. Its reports focused particularly on the fate of children and women, amplifying the cause for indignation and suggesting that no limits were sacred and the French themselves might be the next target, if only to be dragooned into forced labor. The Resistance in general took pains to avoid the impression it was fighting on behalf of the Jews or even cared what was happening to them.[105] Free French broadcasts on the BBC from London also downplayed the specificity of the Jewish fate.[106]

Bobkowski was clearly not the only Parisian for whom the plight of the Jews was not a moral priority, but his notes at the time begin by suggesting he did in fact care. The indignant references to St. Bartholomew's Night and the women and children in the original entry are followed in a different spirit, however, by the confession that he is "curious to see whether after the war there will really be fewer of them in Europe."[107] His attention then shifts to "a rumor, most probably from Jewish quarters," that "the Poles are next in line and everyone" — that is, the Poles — "believes it." Panic ensues. This rumor, he notes, had been "spread with typical Jewish malice."[108] The same entry — in both versions — ends with a scene in which Bobkowski and a friend are standing in line and conversing in Polish. A Jewish woman next to them "regarded us with hatred and said: 'It's true, isn't it, that things are good here in OUR France? But Poland, sir, will not exist anymore.' . . . Perhaps she was right? But even France didn't help her."[109] The original entry then concludes: "Now she has her France and they will transport her to the Poland that will 'exist,' but without them. There they will be taught a lesson."[110] It is clear that in August 1942 Bobkowski had a good idea of what was happening to the Jews when they reached Poland.

The Kultura entry for August 4, 1942 departs from the original in small but crucial details that alter the tone considerably. It, too, begins with Saint Bartholomew's Night and the reference to women and children. The sentence wondering how many Jews will survive the war is replaced, however, by an expression of horror and dismay: "I can only note it down," he says of the Vélodrome d'hiver roundup. "I have no strength to comment. Only an internal scream and the feeling of everything ripping apart."[111] The rumor about the Poles' impending fate is described now as "probably" Jewish and "quite understandable, started out of despair." And, on a note of apparent self-reflection: "Are they supposed to love us?"[112] The mention of Jews being transported and "taught a lesson" is gone.

A different kind of self-reflection characterized sections in the manuscript notebooks that concerned the fate awaiting Poland, and Europe itself, after the war. Bobkowski was well aware of trading in antisemitic commonplaces. A passage from the original notebooks dated August 8, 1942, missing from the Kultura text, observed: "despite all the differences, America is nothing but the overseas affiliate of European jews, and moreover Eastern European—from Bełz, Rzeszów, and Tarnopol. It's horrible—and dangerous. When you read about those Morgenthaus, Borahs [*sic*], Lippomans [*sic*] and dozens of others surrounding Roosevelt, your blood runs cold."[113] A passage in the original entry for August 11, 1942, also missing in 1957, confesses: "I'm writing like some kind of Goebbels, but, what's worse, I am ever more convinced that 'der internatzionale Jude' [*sic*], this Anglo-American jew, is just as deadly as the Aryan who is now trampling us under foot. That's why, although I yearn for the end of the war, I also fear it."[114]

These fears do not abate. The manuscript entry for May 30, 1943, predicts that after the war "50 or 100 jews together with masonic goys will again be plotting new business deals, deciding to whom to sell their stockpiles—especially of ammunition and arms."[115] Two and a half years of war had done nothing to change the attitude expressed in September 1940 that English victory would mean the triumph of "Jewish-Masonic capitalism," against which Hitler was fighting, though unfortunately only in the interests of German domination.[116] The same May 30, 1943, entry in the Kultura version eliminates all the sentences that make Bobkowski sound like Goebbels, even to himself, while retaining the basic underlying meaning. Now, he merely predicts that shortages and hunger will follow the war, "all Europe will be ravaged and hungry," but "help will come," in the guise of humanitarian aid. At the same time, "Germany will be rebuilt—on the sly," and "they" (unidentified) will be "pulling the strings."[117]

A similar thought appears in unpublished notes taken from Bobkowski's reading during the war: "It often occurs to me to wonder, whether despite everything Hitler will not one day become a prophet. If Bolshevism inundates Europe, if after winning the war the Jew appears to the world in all his insolent pride and takes the reins, then who knows if Hitler will not acquire the aura of a freedom-fighter. Paradoxical, but an entirely possible paradox, entirely acceptable."[118] The prospect of Jewish world domination haunts him, as it did every bona fide antisemite. Notes on the *Protocols of the Elders of Zion* can be found among his papers.[119]

The same menace threatened Poland and even France. The original entry for August 11, 1942, includes the passage (absent in 1957): "In Poland the words 'jewry' and 'masonry' were greeted with laughter. It was considered good style among cultured people to make fun of 'Endek nonsense.'" The reference is to Roman Dmowski's antisemitic Endecja (National Democratic Party), a force in Polish politics even before the Great War, now represented both in the government in exile and its affiliates inside Poland.[120] "Mocked, because not understood, not understood, because not seen. The Jewish question in Poland boiled down to a hundred thousand Jewish shops, large and small, to jewified pubs and spas, to *Wiadomości Literackie* [The Literary News] and in general to the 'small jew.' Rare was the person who SAW what in fact jewry and that laughable 'masonry' could amount to. Was it known that in free and free-thinking France teachers, clerks, policemen, soldiers, practically everyone whose career depended on the opinion of powerful superiors 'at the top,' all of them, were afraid of going to church for Sunday mass, that they concealed their religious beliefs in order to advance, in order not to destroy their careers? Because there 'at the top' sat the jew, sat the gentlemen from the masonic lodge, sat the bacillus of destruction [*bakcyl destruktu*]. People did not know and did not fully realize who the jew was in the lands of the great democracies and what power he had achieved."[121]

This suppressed passage may possibly help explain Bobkowski's fulminations about the Jews. He liked being naughty. He liked bucking the current, whatever it was, particularly if it was considered righteous. He scorned the formulaic Marxism he encountered among his friends at school.[122] Antisemitism was widespread, even dominant, in interwar Poland, but it was not universal. Here Bobkowski takes pleasure in rejecting what we would call the "politically correct" repudiation of antisemitism in certain intellectual circles. He probably thought of himself as speaking the truth about the place of the Jews in Polish society and the world. In general, he distanced himself from what he considered knee-jerk Polish patriotism. Yet, in redeeming what others mocked as "Endek nonsense," he was endorsing the official position of the party that dominated the early years of the post-1918 Polish Republic and whose views returned to popularity at the end of the 1930s.[123] The Szkoła Główna Handlowa had been the site of riots organized by Endek sympathizers in the years that Bobkowski was enrolled,[124] but his cohort seems to have preferred Marx to Dmowski. By resisting the pressure of his left-wing friends, Bobkowski, the contrarian, was succumbing to a more powerful current. He was also giving in to powerful emotions. When, in September 1942, Polish radio in London broadcast the voice of a Polish rabbi, Bobkowski and his wife cringed at his Jewish accent. "We both felt sad," he recorded in his notebook (a sentence removed from the final text). "Exactly as if a giant bird shaped like a jew in a black gabardine had momentarily blocked out the sun."[125]

The Endecja, for its part, was unapologetic. Dmowski never pretended that antisemitism was not at the core of his party's appeal. In 1916 he told the European public: "The Jews in Poland . . . in their mass do not belong to the Polish nationality: their language is Yiddish, a German dialect, and they are organised as a separate Jewish nationality against the Poles. In these conditions the struggle against the Jews is a national struggle."[126] The Russian Civil War and the fight for independence forced representatives of the new-born Republic of Poland nevertheless to go on the defensive. Extensive reporting in the American press on the murder of Jews by Polish forces inspired large demonstrations and protests by Jewish leaders, demanding international action.[127] News of pogroms in Lemberg (Lwów, Lviv) in November 1918 and in Pińsk and Wilno (Vilna, Vilnius) in April 1919 undermined Poland's image as the long-suffering victim of aggression and increased international concern with the issue of minority rights. The U.S. State Department warned the Polish National Committee that if stories of the pogroms were true, "the sympathy of the American people for Poland's national aspirations will undoubtedly be affected."[128] In return, Jan Paderewski (1860–1941), Polish president and foreign minister, insisted that "there have been no pogroms in Poland to justify these reports or these charges against the Polish people." The Bolsheviks, Paderewski insisted, echoing a familiar refrain, had created a state of anarchy, in which both Jews and Christians fell victim. If Polish troops had shot any Jews, it was in response to crimes committed by Bolsheviks who "happened to be Jews."[129]

The Polish government bitterly resented the Minority Rights Treaty imposed on Poland by the Paris Peace Conference in 1919, partly as a result of the campaign mounted by an alliance of Jewish organizations.[130] The success of that effort had, of course, been facilitated by the publicity given to pogroms committed by Polish forces. This resentment was not confined to the political Right. A left-leaning Polish politician accused the Jewish representatives in Paris in 1919 of having unleashed "a great wave of calumnies and hatreds," which he called a "constant barrage of lies and baseless accusations," responsible for "eroding the foundations of the Polish state."[131] The nationalists deplored what they thought of as Jewish interference, whether foreign or domestic, in the affairs of an exclusively Polish nation. The first president of the Second Polish Republic, the politically moderate engineer, Gabriel Narutowicz (1865–1922), was not himself Jewish. His election had been supported, however, by the bloc of minority parties, leading the Endek press to denounce him as a tool of the Jews. When, in an atmosphere of heated antisemitic agitation and street violence, Narutowicz was shot to death by a lone assassin, the Right at first disowned the deed, but soon began to laud the perpetrator, who was tried and executed, as a national hero.[132]

Endek antisemitic nationalism dominated Polish politics, but it nevertheless did not monopolize the field. Piłsudski's party had promoted a more inclusive, though not more democratic, vision of the Polish nation. In 1920, Piłsudski appointed the distinguished Jewish historian Szymon Askenazy (1865–1935) as Poland's first delegate to the League of Nations.[133] When that same year the Warsaw University Senate refused to approve Askenazy's professorial appointment, a long list of literary and academic figures issued a public protest. Among them was the internationally renowned legal sociologist Leon Petrażycki (1867–1931). Like Biélinky a native of Vitebsk, Petrażycki had built a career in Russia. Along with Maxim Vinaver, he had represented St. Petersburg for the Kadet Party in the First Duma. He returned to Poland in 1919, when hopes for a democratic Russia had been defeated.[134] Both advocates of secular liberalism were hybrid sons of the old empire, which they had both opposed. Their cosmopolitanism derived from an intermingling of cultures within the imperial frame that did not undermine, but reinforced their sense of civic obligation and shielded them from nationalist extremes.

As Polish society struggled between competing political identities, exclusivist nationalism gained the upper hand. In 1926 Piłsudski staged a coup that established him as the country's authoritarian leader, but upon his death in May 1935, the government continued its move to the right, promoting new restrictive legislation aimed at the Jews.[135] In 1934, Poland formally renounced the Minority Rights Treaty.[136] Józef Beck (1894–1944), foreign minister from 1932 to 1939, believed the Jews did not belong in Poland. He had urged the Western Powers to help solve Poland's "Jewish problem" by providing a place to which they could be relocated.[137] The call for mass emigration was supported by leading politicians, who continued to see the Jews as an alien force, detrimental to the Polish nation.[138] By this time, as historian Paul Brykczynski remarks, antisemitism and the discourse of "the Polish Majority" had transcended party lines.[139]

Against the antisemitism omnipresent in interwar Polish society, its rejection was therefore a cultural and political marker. Bobkowski feelings on this subject conflicted with the position flaunted by many of his acquaintances. They were also at odds with the humanistic values he himself professed, a tension he was loath to acknowledge. When faced with a real Jewish person, with whom at least Basia had a personal bond, he nevertheless felt obliged to help.[140] On April 14, 1943, five days before the beginning of the Warsaw Ghetto Uprising, he noted the appearance of his wife's former classmate, endangered by the arrest and deportation of her husband.[141] At the time, he confessed to his notebook: "I was not particularly delighted by this encounter, because despite everything I have come to hate the Jews more and more."[142] On July 1 he reported that he had been "making the rounds" on her behalf, then added: "I would never have imagined that loving the Jews as I do I would ever be helping someone from this cursed tribe of Judas. But there's no way around it. . . . At least, when the Great Democracies win the war, I'll be rewarded. . . . I'm covering my tail. Too bad I don't have any jews or jewesses in the family. It would make my career after the war. . . . I'm clever, no?" These lines do not appear in the published version.[143]

Meanwhile, the Jews in the Warsaw ghetto had not been asking for help, but defending their dignity, if not their lives, against hopeless odds. In the published entry for May 5, 1943, Bobkowski calls the uprising, which was still in progress, "extraordinary and impressive" (*niesamowite i imponujące*).[144] The original response, which he later omitted, has, by contrast, a mocking undertone that he clearly needed to expunge: "Well, the jews have stood up for themselves. Extraordinary." Here the same word (*niesamowite*) sounds more like "amazing —who would have thought? who would believe it?" And he goes on: "What's sad in all this is only that the destruction of the small jew does not solve the problem. The problem remains forever the same so long as the great jew remains at the helm of the world economy. Each U.S. banknote bears Morgenthau's signature. In the course of the war the struggle of the great jew for continuing supremacy over the world has become increasingly obvious."[145]

Andrzej Chciuk was clearly not mistaken in thinking his friend disliked the Jews, but he may not have realized how deep the antipathy went. The notebooks show that even during the war, when he knew what the Nazis were up to, Bobkowski continued to feel and express a strong aversion to what he thought the Jews stood for, dismay at what he considered their historic role, and a visceral distaste for how they looked, sounded, and behaved. Yet, on March 2, 1949, less than a year after the writer had arrived in Guatemala, he sent a letter to Giedroyc in Paris, with a seemingly urgent plea: "Do you know a way to convince the Jews that one is not an antisemite?"[146] It sounded as if he might already have begun to rethink his wartime opinions.

The question was not, however, a mea culpa, but a grievance. It appears in the midst of a passage describing the conditions Bobkowski had encountered in Guatemala, including the relationship between the non-Jewish Poles and the Polish Jews who had all ended up there after the war. In general, he complained, the Jewish survivors regarded the gentile Poles as nothing short of Gestapo agents. Jewish jewelers refused to buy the diamonds offered by impoverished Polish ladies, imagining they had been torn from the severed fingers of murdered Jews. A Jewish group had asked the refugee aid organization on which Bobkowski himself relied to stop offering assistance to the Poles. This, "even though," Bobkowski informs Giedroyc, "for three years during the war I helped a Jewess out of my own pocket. I ran all over the place, hustling up other kinds of help and I hustled well. And now they're paying me back. Sheer stupidity. It's a cursed problem."[147] In 1943, he had privately joked that his act of reluctant charity would stand him in good stead after the war; he now seemed to be calling in his moral chips.

The charge that accusations of antisemitism were a Jewish strategy for discrediting well-meaning or justly aggrieved gentiles was a move favored by confessed antisemites, as we have seen.[148] Yet, Giedroyc's reply is something of a puzzle. "There's no remedy or recourse against the Jews," he wrote. "Did you know that [Arthur] Koestler, when he renounced his British citizenship and left for Palestine was hounded by the Jewish wiseacres [*Żydowina*] as an antisemite and fascist?"[149] If the charges against the Jewish Koestler (1905–1983) represent the reductio ad absurdum of Jewish fastidiousness, Giedroyc implies, Bobkowski need not worry on this account. In any case, the editor seems to have accepted his correspondent's quirky sense of humor. Bobkowski was a talented writer, with a notoriously off-color voice, whom Kultura wished to publish. His personal discomfort with the Jews, well known to his friends, was not out of place in the intimacy of private correspondence.

Bobkowski, for his part, met the challenge of establishing his postwar reputation by inserting a number of passages into the final text that advertised his good credentials.[150] Thus, the published entry for September 1, 1940, describes a visit to two French sisters and their elderly mother. The mother at one point blurts out: "*Eh bien, vous savez, je n'aime pas les Juifs.*" When the daughters chide her, she falls silent. Bobkowski comments: "This antisemitism of hers was like tobacco, which her daughters were constantly forbidding her to sniff. It's curious, but with antisemitism this often happens. Some people need it, like cigarettes, black coffee, or alcohol. In Poland, especially among the older generation, it above all worked as a stimulant. Alas, among the young it often took the form of a narcotic."[151] Bobkowski himself never stopped smoking, one might want to observe, and drinking—as in his youthful glory days—always figured as a gesture of freedom, not dependence. But that's taking a metaphor too far.

Other inserted passages, presumed to belong to the original time of writing, made it seem as though the young Bobkowski had himself been enlightened all along. Outsiders treat Poles with benevolent condescension, he complains, but this, he comments ruefully, was "exactly the way 'cultured' antisemites treat the Jews," which is to say, dislike them, avoid them, but: "'When it comes down to it, one shouldn't behave swinishly.'" Poles, he observes, often display "a horrifying lack of tact. The same lack of tact with which we so often reproach the Jews. We are very much like them and that is doubtless the source of our antisemitism."[152] Another post hoc passage affirms Bobkowski's respect for cultural differences: "I very likely detest nationalism even more than communism, and if I were very rich I would endow a department of cosmopolitanism and critical judgment at one of our universities."[153] In defense of people like himself, who refuse to stay home or return home, but "prefer to roam the world" and are therefore derided as "cosmopolitans," he adds, with a wink: "which is to say, almost—Jews. And what can be worse—between you and me—than a Jew?"[154] Irony, at the expense of antisemites, perhaps; a gesture of solidarity, maybe; but only in retrospect. Or another cover-up moment.

Bobkowski thought of himself as an iconoclast, a cultural and political nonconformist. Yet when it came to the Jews, his outlook during the war conformed in essential ways to the attitudes that dominated Polish opinion, across "broad swaths of the political spectrum," as prevalent in the London government in exile and the underground in Poland, as in the Polish public at large.[155] It was possible, of course, for a person of similar background to have understood the moral implications of antisemitism, even at the time. The memoirs of the painter and writer Józef Czapski, a close associate of Giedroyc at Kultura, offer a striking contrast to Bobkowski's notebooks in tone, temperament, and sensibility. As an officer in the Polish army, Czapski spent two years in Soviet captivity. His account of the suffering of fellow deportees and prisoners goes out of its way to portray Polish Jews as loyal members of the Polish nation. A number of passages, clearly designed to refute harmful stereotypes and invidious assumptions, depict individual figures with empathy and even affection.[156] Bobkowski did not, under much less strenuous circumstances, evidence a similar compassion or independence of mind. On the question of the Jews, his critical faculties seemed to fail him.

The London government, for its part, presented a mixed picture. The National Council (Rada Narodowa Rzeczypospolitej Polskiej) had two Jewish members and a few relatively tolerant socialists, but also representatives of the antisemitic Endecja.[157] The cabinet also included overtly antisemitic figures. Prime Minister Sikorski's own past was not unmarred. As premier in early 1923 he had impugned the loyalty of Poland's Jewish citizens and asserted that the "Aryan Christian majority" should rule Poland. His personal secretary, Józef Retinger (1888–1960), in 1941 announced that Poland "desires to develop normally but is hindered from doing so by the high percentage of Jews in its demographic organism."[158]

Sikorski nevertheless needed Allied support, particularly with a view to anticipated demands for the postwar settlement. Convinced the Allies were "uncompromising in their attitude towards antisemitism," he felt obliged, at least rhetorically, to demonstrate his adherence to principles of ethnic toleration, including equal rights for the Jews.[159] Given the U.S. reluctance to accept Jewish refugees during the war and the prevalence of antisemitism in Britain, this conviction is surprising.[160] The Endeks, for their part, persisted in opposing any concession to Jewish demands, which they understood to emanate from a powerful global lobby that imposed its will on the Western powers. Inside Poland, the London government was represented by underground organs: a civilian administration (the Delegatura) and the Home Army (Armia Krajowa), in which ethnic minorities were not represented. The Delegatura warned that pronouncements seemingly sympathetic to the Jews would alienate the domestic population.[161] It looked forward to a postwar Poland without Jews.[162] Hostility only increased after September 17, 1939, once the Soviet Union had taken possession of eastern Poland, since the Jewish Commissar equation was firmly implanted. Indeed, many Jews at first welcomed the Red Army as a protection against the Nazi invaders.[163]

In February 1940, Jan Karski (1914–2000), the courier who in 1942 was to inform the West about the Nazi camps, reported on the mood in Poland after the Soviet invasion. The locals, Karski observed, perceived the Jews as favoring the Russians and eager to join the occupation regime. Many Poles, he said, sympathized with Nazi policies, which they felt would "teach the Jews a lesson." This was the expression Bobkowski himself would use in August 1942. "The Poles," Karski said, "wait for the moment when they will be able . . . to take revenge upon the Jews . . . ; the overwhelming majority . . . literally look forward to an opportunity for 'repayment in blood.'"[164] It was important, Karski felt, for Sikorski's government to take a strong stand in support of the Jews, but he warned that such a move would be unwelcome.

Sikorski thus faced pressure on the international front to abandon aggressively anti-Jewish policies, while risking a backlash at home, should he seem too greatly under Western influence. His official pronouncements therefore attempted to maintain a posture of neutrality.[165] Jewish organizations abroad, particularly the American Jewish Committee and the World Jewish Congress, continued to urge him to make a statement in support of Jewish rights in the future Poland, but he refused. When news arrived of the mistreatment of Jewish soldiers in Polish uniform, MP Josiah Wedgwood (1872–1943), not himself Jewish, commented in the House of Commons: "the feelings of Poles toward Jews can only be paralleled by the feelings of Germans toward Jews."[166] Sikorski ordered the abuses to stop, but his cabinet insisted the Jews were merely trying to avoid military service and spoil Poland's image into the bargain.[167]

Charges of antisemitism were interpreted as a Jewish tactic to damage Poland's image. Minister of Information Stanilsaw Stroński

(1882–1955) expostulated: "Our conscience with regard to the Jews is completely clear, and anyone who assails us for antisemitism is a provocateur." He blamed "certain Jewish circles" (the classic phrase) for using England "as the proper ground for settling accounts with Polish nationalists."[168] A propaganda pamphlet aimed at English readers insisted that the Polish population, despite its own suffering, was demonstrating "Christian compassion towards their Jewish fellow-countrymen, who are suffering even more terribly."[169] Despite such protestations, Sikorski's cabinet continued to view the Jews as harmful to Polish state interests and clung to the idea of getting rid of them (while leaving their property behind).[170] Jewish property was widely considered to have been purloined from the Polish nation, to which it was thought rightfully to belong.[171]

It was only in early November 1940, with the appearance of Polish Jewish refugees testifying to the plight of Jews in Poland and demanding an official commitment to future Jewish rights, that Sikorski finally issued a declaration denouncing Nazi racism and promising civic equality for the Jews after the war.[172] Because the Jewish lobby was particularly strong in both the United States and Britain, the London government explained, "[t]he more and the better these two democracies appreciate and understand Poland's position, the better our chances for full victory." Therefore, "it ought to be one of the aims of Polish policy to obtain the unqualified support and sympathy of these Jewish communities."[173]

This concession was a strategy for neutralizing Jewish antipathy toward Poland. It was not an expression of sympathy for the Jews. Back in occupied Poland, most Poles welcomed the disappearance of the majority of Jews and feared the return of survivors in the role of Communists should Germany lose the war.[174] No political party in Poland during the war envisioned a postwar society that included Jewish citizens.[175] People could be heard to remark that "Hitler is doing at least one good thing for Poland—he is freeing it from the Jews."[176] The nationalist sector of the anti-Nazi underground press applauded the disappearance of "millions of parasites" and thanked the Germans for having "rendered us most valuable assistance in this matter."[177] Endecja activists sometimes recoiled at German methods, but they applauded the results. "Finally justice has been done," one wrote. The Jews deserved their fate. The "power of our Jewry will be broken," another rejoiced. Poland was at last getting rid of the "internal occupier."[178] As historians Daniel Blatman and Renée Poznanski have put it: "It was legitimate to fight against the Nazi enemy, the Soviet enemy and the Jewish enemy—the three traditional foes of Poland—all at the same time."[179] There was no need for cognitive dissonance.

The German invasion of the Soviet Union on June 22, 1941, did not mitigate Polish hostility toward the Jews or render the Soviet Union more sympathetic, but it shifted the political options. Poland was in the uncomfortable position of having to ally with the power with which it had fought a bitter war in 1920–1921, by which it had been invaded in 1939, and which blocked its territorial aspirations in the east. Under British pressure, on July 30, 1941, Sikorski signed an agreement with Soviet ambassador Ivan Maisky (1884–1975, born Jan Lachowiecki to a Russified Polish family), which restored diplomatic relations and provided for the formation of a Polish army inside the Soviet Union, but it did not obtain Soviet recognition of the borders established by the Treaty of Riga in 1921.[180] Still looking for allies, Sikorski's minister for nationalities met with Chaim Weizmann (1874–1952), president of the World Zionist Organization, in September 1941, to discuss the role of Polish Jews in building Palestine after the war. Władysław Raczkiewicz (1885–1947), president of the London government, explored the option of British support for postwar Jewish resettlement. The goal was still to get rid of them.[181]

It was in this context, in September 1941, that Sikorski got on the radio and offered his greetings on the Jewish New Year. The prime minister nevertheless needed also to placate the Endecja and other right-wing Polish leaders in the cabinet as reformed after the July 1941 pact with the Soviet Union. Early in 1942 he warned the British that Poland could not "continue to maintain 3.5 million Jews after the war. Room must be found for them elsewhere."[182] In May 1942 Endecja spokesmen in England expressed support for the Zionist project of settlement in Palestine. This was again, on the surface, a friendly gesture toward the Jews, but transparently a reiteration of the long-standing desire of the Polish Right to be rid of the Jews altogether. The statement was understood in this sense by the American Jewish Council, which denounced it.[183] The Endeks nevertheless continued to resent what they thought of as Jewish power and prevented Sikorski from going too far in appeasing the Jews.[184]

Similar views were expressed by the underground organizations operating inside Poland. In addition to the Delegatura and Home

Army, answerable to London, the underground included an array of organizations spanning the range of prewar ideologies, from reactionary antisemites to pro-Soviet Communists, all, except for the extreme Left, aggressively anti-Jewish.[185] The Home Army press, for example, generally depicted the slaughter of the Jews less as a human tragedy in its own right, than as a warning to the Poles that they too would be subject to "the Jewish method."[186] The Poles, however, would "not be intimidated," Home Army spokesmen warned. They would avoid the "errors made by the Jews," whom it accused of cooperating with the enemy, quarreling among themselves, and despite feeble attempts at self-defense proving by and large to be cowardly and passive.[187] Unlike the Home Army, in 1942–1943 the Communist Polish People's Guard (Gwardia Ludowa) accepted some Jewish units. Its record was nevertheless not unambiguous. The Guard at times sheltered Jews in the forests, but sometimes murdered them.[188]

The general consensus thus allowed for some variation.[189] The Home Army on occasion condemned the betrayal of Jews as an act of treason and encouraged Poles to help them escape.[190] Its widely circulated official organ, the *Biuletyn Informacyjny* (Information Bulletin), was edited by one Aleksander Kamiński (1903–1978), a prewar leader of the Polish scouts, with ties to Jewish scouting circles and contacts inside the Warsaw ghetto. The *Biuletyn* printed continuous reports on the expanding assault on the Jewish population, including detailed descriptions of conditions in the ghettos and murder in the camps. These reports, while not always featured on the front page, often included expressions of moral outrage.[191] Yet some Home Army and Delegatura pronouncements condemned Jewish self-defense brigades as bandits and some Home Army units attacked Jews hiding in the forests.[192] The underground Catholic press showed a similar ambivalence. Collaboration in the murder of the Jews was unacceptable, some Catholic writers warned, even though there was reason to resent them and regard their departure with relief. At the same time they reproached the Jews for their alleged passivity in the face of their own threatened extinction.[193]

Beginning in late 1942, once the scope of the disaster had begun to emerge, the London government started to alter its tone.[194] Yet even then, if its propaganda took note of the fate of the Jews, it did so in the belief that news of Jewish suffering would generate sympathy for the plight of the Polish nation.[195] In October the Delegatura nevertheless sponsored the Council for Aid to the Jews (Rada Pomocy Żydom, or

Żegota).[196] This was a collaborative effort, funded by Jewish organizations abroad, involving the Home Army, Polish members of the Democratic and Socialist parties, and Jewish underground leaders. It also included representatives of the militantly anti-Nazi Catholic Front for the Rebirth of Poland (Front Odrodzenia Polski), which at the same time also disseminated what one historian describes as "violent anti-Jewish propaganda."[197] Reluctance was the norm. When it became known in November that Jews were being gassed in Auschwitz, Polish reports minimized the fact, to preserve the image of the camp as the site of Polish death and suffering, which indeed it also was.[198] It was only in May 1943, after the Warsaw Ghetto Uprising, that Sikorski began broadcasting appeals that urged the Polish population to help the Jews.[199]

The Soviet Union was, of course, a much more consequential threat to Poland's national interests than the Jews, who were dependent on both these nations for their chances of survival. The Soviet invasion of Poland was followed by the deportation of over a million Polish citizens, a third of them Jewish, into the Soviet interior.[200] In the complex negotiations surrounding the fate of the deportees after the July 1941 Sikorski-Maisky pact, Moscow pressured the territory's former inhabitants to abandon Polish for Soviet citizenship, in order to be able to substantiate its claim after the war to the territory it had occupied in 1939. Soviet dispositions in regard to the Jewish inhabitants of that territory and to Jews from western Poland who had fled east to escape the Nazi invasion were particularly convoluted. The stakes involved Jewish access to Polish-sponsored (and heavily Jewish-funded) relief efforts, as well as to the right to leave the Soviet Union for other destinations.[201]

In this complicated situation, Sikorski's London government and the Polish embassy in Moscow acted with the Polish national interest in mind: to be able to reclaim the eastern territory after the war. Sometimes this goal coincided with Jewish interests, since Jews were numerous among the Polish internees and Poland therefore had a stake in counting them. Sikorski's good intentions were doubted, however, by the committee representing the future interests of Jews in postwar Poland (Reprezentacja Żydostwa Polskiego), constituted by Jewish organizations in Palestine. The Reprezentacja seems to have believed the prime minister wielded more influence with the Soviet authorities in facilitating Jewish access to relief and their release from detention than he actually possessed. Both sides felt aggrieved and mutual hostility persisted.[202]

For the Jews who had been deported, the Soviet option was not straightforward. The eastward deportation of Polish citizens was a by-product of Soviet aggression against Poland that nevertheless proved the salvation of many Jews.[203] Of the 10 percent of Polish Jews who survived the Holocaust, almost three-quarters did so by spending the war within Soviet borders. Among them was Roman Zimand, then in his teens. Some had fled east of their own accord, others were transported and interned. But despite their reputation as Communist enthusiasts, few of the Jewish internees in the Soviet Union embraced the opportunity to stay there. Many had endured brutal conditions and met with antisemitism from Soviet personnel. Two leaders of the Jewish Bund, Henryk Ehrlich (1882–1942, married to the daughter of historian Simon Dubnow) and Wiktor Alter (1890–1942), were arrested and murdered by the NKVD.[204]

The Polish option was complicated for different reasons. The Polish Army in the Soviet Union, constituted in August 1941 after the Sikorski-Maisky pact, manifested the kind of crass antisemitism that reinforced Jewish distrust of Polish authorities, whatever their temporary convergence of interest in resolving issues of citizenship and repatriation. Józef Czapski, who worked for the army's educational department, resisted pressure to dismiss its Jewish members. He recalled Father Kamil Kantak (1881–1976) as "quoting *The Protocols of the Elders of Zion* as if it were the holy gospel" and deplored what he called "our own native anti-Semitism, with its innate mindlessness."[205]

This army also provides a striking example of the need felt by antisemites, for political reasons, to hide their true colors. Commanded by General Władisław Anders, who had been released after twenty months in Soviet prison, it drew its ranks from Polish soldiers in the Red Army and from the Polish deportees.[206] Anders was a courageous figure, responsible for the salvation of many lives and for the impressive performance of his men when they reached Europe. While assembling his army, however, he was dismayed when a large percentage of volunteers turned out to be Polish Jews. He viewed the Jews as traitors, who had welcomed the Soviet invasion in 1939, and referred to them as "malcontents and malingerers, cowards and thieves."[207] He did everything he could to keep them out of the ranks, expel as many as possible, and mistreat those that remained. This was the same General Anders who employed Giedroyc and Czapski in his propaganda office and funded the establishment of Kultura, but with whom Giedroyc soon parted ways.

Stanisław Kot (1885–1975), the Polish ambassador in Moscow, was more circumspect. Noting that the Polish Army had a "systematic antisemitic policy,"[208] he suggested that having Jews in the army might benefit the Polish cause after the war. In the short run, he warned, Anders's conduct was damaging Poland's image in the West. Under pressure from Kot, Anders ordered the army to treat the Jews on a par with what he called "genuine Poles."[209] The purpose, he explained in an order of November 14, 1941, was "to put an end to all of the malicious insinuations and gossip being generated behind our backs — which in all likelihood emanate from sources hostile to us — about alleged antisemitism in our forces."[210]

Anders admitted to his officers that the allegations were in fact not mistaken, but, he assured them, the soldiers' "antisemitic outbursts are a response to the disloyal and often hostile behavior of Polish Jews from the eastern territories during the years of our ordeal 1939–40."[211] Pressure from the English was forcing him "to relate positively to the Jewish question," because Jewish "influence in the Anglo-Saxon world is considerable." His men must understand "that our raison d'état requires that we do not annoy the Jews, for at present antisemitism can bring the most disastrous and incalculable effects upon the Polish cause." Later, he promised, "When we are masters in our own home after our victorious campaign, we shall dispose of the Jewish question as the greatness and sovereignty of our homeland and ordinary human justice demand."[212] Sikorski, for his part, told Stalin on December 3, 1941, barely three months after he had wished the Jews a happy New Year, that he didn't want them in the Polish Army, because they were bad soldiers and black marketeers.[213]

Representatives of Sikorski's government continued to believe the Jews were conspiring against Polish interests. In spring and summer 1942, the Polish Army and a certain number of affiliated civilians were evacuated from the Soviet Union in the direction of Palestine, with a way station in Iran.[214] In April 1942 Anders visited London, where he seems to have realized that "the Jewish lies . . . could have a fatal effect upon the next evacuation."[215] Polish diplomats feared the influence of "international Jewish circles" on Poland's standing with the Allies.[216]

Their impact had to be neutralized, not discounted. The proportion of Jews in the Polish ranks, as of Jewish civilians evacuated along with them, was vastly lower than their share of the deportees eager to leave, but they no doubt owed their opportunity to the general's need to have some evidence of his professed good intentions.[217] Ambassador Kot, who had earlier tried to moderate Anders's ill-considered zeal, was part of a Polish mission to Palestine also in spring 1942 to enlist Jewish support for Polish war aims. A member of the National Council on the same mission explained—not very diplomatically—that the Jews needed to atone for having welcomed the Soviet invasion, undermined Polish territorial claims, and damaged Poland's reputation with their complaints. They now had the chance, he suggested, to "rehabilitate themselves in the eyes of the Polish population by speaking out in defense of Polish interests."[218]

As for Bobkowski, he was in a position in Paris to monitor the changing disposition of the London government, whose radio broadcasts he managed not to miss. In May 1943 he and Basia went to the theater and critiqued the performances; he commented briefly on the Warsaw Ghetto Uprising, as we have seen; but no entry, even in the published version, mentions the emerging news of the extent of the Jewish disaster or registers London's apparent change of heart or at least change of tone.

Despite his cultural iconoclasm, the young writer, it turns out, had all the markings of a run-of-the-mill prewar antisemite and he failed, either during the war or in the immediate postwar years, to mobilize the moral indignation he expended on other subjects on behalf of the murdered Jews. It is impossible not to confront the dark side of his persona, especially as its initial concealment and belated revelation seem to follow the arc of public consciousness in post-Communist Poland, including a defensive reaction against the emergence of difficult truths.

The turning point in this coming to consciousness was marked by the publication of *Sąsiedzi* (*Neighbors*), by sociologist Jan Tomasz Gross, which focused on the collective murder of the Jewish inhabitants of the town of Jedwabne by their Polish neighbors in 1941. First published in Polish in 2000, then in English a year later, the exposé, as we have mentioned, issued a call for public accounting and set off a storm of controversy in Poland that has still not died down.[219] Gross has continued to pursue the issue of Polish antisemitism during and after the war.[220] Anna Bikont's investigation of current attitudes, published first in Poland in 2004, uncovered antisemitic feelings and preconceptions that still endure.[221]

It is against this background that the recent debates about the moral standing of the younger and older Bobkowski have unfolded. The essay published by Łukasz Mikołajewski in 2011, which documented the erasure of Bobkowski's original antisemitic remarks, charged the writer with deliberately concealing opinions he once had held but never openly confronted, resorting instead to censorship and camouflage. The incontrovertible evidence and Mikołajewski's accusations sparked a heated debate among Polish literary scholars and journalists. The debate, which began in academia, spread to public venues and the internet. The anguish at the heart of the discussion reflects the injury to an earlier enthusiasm: the embrace of a new hero, someone who seemed to have escaped the traps set by history and culture—a free man and a Pole.

Readers had been eager to set the newly discovered figure on a pedestal. To some extent, reflected culture critic Andrzej Horubała, Bobkowski "was a writer we invented, a writer we read through the prism of our dreams and desires, . . . who had a lot of credit with us." Someone like him was bound to have surfaced, "to set the tone for Polish literature, to redeem it." Precisely such "a sharp-tongued fellow, . . . glass of Canadian Club in his hand," writing in his off-hours, was made to be a hero, "the author of twentieth-century Polish literature."[222] Websites sprang up celebrating his life and spirit,[223] documenting a group that in 2010 retraced his bicycle journey through France,[224] displaying the material (including photos and a video) presented at an exhibit at the Muzeum Literatury in 2013, marking the centenary of his birth.[225] Scholarly considerations of his opus continue to appear.[226] The field has been dubbed, affectionately, "bobkologia."[227]

By the time the centenary had rolled around, however, "demystification" had set in. The image of the "legendary writer, the author of the cultic *Szkice piórkiem*, considered by many lovers of literature a model of intellectual independence, refusal to compromise, and insight," had taken some serious hits.[228] If there was no going back to the old Bobkowski, there was still disagreement on how to balance his various parts, in terms of ethical contrasts and shifting self-presentation. Maciej Nowak, at the Catholic University in Lublin (KUL), who had also seen the original disturbing passages, had his own view of what the revelations meant. "I see it differently," Nowak wrote in response to Mikołajewski's charge of "fictionalized memory." Bobkowski's revisions should not be considered a moral lapse — falsification or camouflage — but a moral evolution.[229]

Overall, Nowak rejects the imposition of ex post moral judgments and concepts of falsification or dishonesty in the study of literary texts. He does not consider the final product a deception, but a work of literature based on a primary text that had naturally undergone revision, a process common to all published diaries.[230] He is thus less inclined than Mikołajewski to condemn Bobkowski's wartime attitudes as personal failings and more willing to credit him for suppressing them at the end. Antisemitism was after all endemic in interwar Poland and pervasive in occupied France. "The young Bobkowski," Nowak remarks, "turns out to have been simply a child of his times."[231] Writers as enlightened on the subject of the Jews as Czesław Miłosz and Maria Dąbrowska (1889–1965), Nowak points out, had been known in those same difficult years to express their dislike of them.[232] In full knowledge of the disaster the Jews had suffered, Dąbrowska was nevertheless annoyed after the war with the way survivors kept harping on the Holocaust. "God, what an obsession!" he quotes her as complaining.[233]

In Bobkowski's case, Nowak maintains, it is unfair to apply our current standards to opinions that before and even during the war were accepted as normal.[234] They should not compromise the writer in ethical terms. The offensive passages in Bobkowski's notebooks must be understood, moreover, in light of the fact, Nowak maintains, that the writer could not at the time have understood the full extent of the destruction of the Jews.[235] The truth, when he later learned it, Nowak believes, must have left Bobkowski deeply shaken (*głęboko nim wstrząsnęło*) and led him to reconsider his earlier views.[236] Nowak at the same time praises the writer for resisting the dictates of political ideology, for sensing the dangers of "political correctness" (*polityczna poprawność*), even then.[237] "This is a person," Nowak comments, "who managed to veto the demands of the entire world on the basis of the feeling of absolutely sovereign freedom."[238] How the writer could simultaneously accept the prejudices of his day, while at the same time demonstrating his absolute freedom of thought, is not entirely clear. Like most people, he was not consistent. In the postwar environment, Bobkowski seems to have relaxed his resistance to "political correctness." His revisions seem to endorse the view—even then, not a consensus—that the language of antisemitism was no longer acceptable in public discourse.

Nowak is not the only commentator to maintain that the views Bobkowski once held but subsequently either abandoned or at the very least decided to conceal and that are now considered objectionable ought not affect his value as a writer or his meaning for Polish culture today. Others recall the attractive option Bobkowski presented in the early post-Communist days, in detaching conservative politics from cultural conservatism and transcending ideological extremes. "Bobkowski," observed writer and literary critic Andrzej Stanisław Kowalczyk (b. 1957), "was proof that one could take a critical position toward socialism, opt for capitalism, the free market, and individualism, while not being a nationalist, chauvinist, or narrow-minded."[239]

It was not merely the fact of suppression, but the nature of what had been suppressed that nevertheless continued to trouble some colleagues. Aleksander Fiut (b. 1945), a literary scholar at Jagiellonian University, felt unable to ignore "the clearly antisemitic accents and ideas" in Bobkowski's work. "Bobkowski manages to question various ideologies and various tendencies," Fuit remarked, "but in this case does not seem to notice his own limitations."[240] Andrzej Horubała similarly concluded that the damage to the writer's self-created myth could not be overlooked. "His tale values life over literature, worships authenticity and truth, but whenever it can—it revises. Revises, deletes. Crosses out, smooths over." How much easier it would have been without the notebooks, the critic sighs, for Polish readers to have lived with their illusions; yet how much more interesting and complicated the reading of Bobkowski had become.[241]

Interesting, but troubling nonetheless. Like Fiut, the participants in a conversation posted by the political website Kultura Liberalna in 2012 did not think the sanitized version of the young author's views should stand unchallenged, even if the writer had later realized, in some fashion or other, that he no longer wished to present himself as he once had been when it came to the subject of the Jews, while never relinquishing the image of a morally continuous persona. Some of the titles in the Kultura Liberalna discussion reflect an ironic skepticism: "Construct Your Own Bobkowski"—"Sketches with an Eraser"—"The Retouched European." More bluntly: Was he an antisemite?

Bobkowski himself had confessed in his original notes that he sounded like "some kind of Goebbels." Was it part of his "bad boy" persona to let the emotions flow? In fact, simple dislike was not the heart of the matter. Many people—liberals, socialists, even Jews—expressed discomfort, repulsion, resentment in relation to the Jews, while at the same time acknowledging the political—and it turned out, mortal—dangers of thinking this way. Bobkowski seems never to have grasped the implications of his private (and, as Chciuk testified, not always private) feelings—in terms of the values he continued to champion—for the disaster that unfolded in real life.

In sum, Bobkowski spent the war in relative security, venting his hostility to the Jews and wishing them to be gone—at least from Poland. He later covered his tracks, thus betraying his reputation as a fearless truth teller and cultural maverick. What would have redeemed him? As *Gazeta Wyborcza* journalist Marek Beylin (b. 1957) has observed, Bobkowski may have cleaned up the text for postwar consumption, removing the offensive language, but the structure of thinking he wanted to repudiate, or at least to disguise, left its mark. Having described the Jews as a "bacillus of destruction," he now described them as the "leaven" of the human race.[242] He thus continued to view them, Beylin objected, as "an alien collectivity. They are not individuals"—Bobkowski's fundamental ethical category—"not ordinary citizens, but something special, specific." Substituting a positive for a negative, but keeping the Jews in a separate category, he showed he hadn't understood what was at stake in the attitudes he had absorbed. However enticing his literary style, Beylin concluded, "Clichés remain clichés."[243]

The myth of Bobkowski as a free thinker was not the only casualty of these revelations, commented Paweł Rodak (b. 1967), recent director of the Institute of Polish Culture at Warsaw University. His wartime record demonstrates that even a critical distance from the militant nationalism associated with antisemitic views is no guarantee against them.[244] Even in the picture of occupied Paris presented in the revised 1957 edition, the Polish Jews of Saint-Paul barely impinge on his universe, and the Polish Jews he encounters in Guatemala remain alien and antagonistic. He does not accept them as part of his social existence. They do not belong to the Polish elites he despises, nor to the Polish workmen he nurtures in Châtillon, nor to the hardy Polish immigrants making their way in France, whose ingenuity he admires. They are not, in that sense, Polish.

To satisfy the requirements of a Literary Hero, from the perspective of the postwar, post-Jedwabne Polish intelligentsia, the young Bobkowski should ideally have rejected the antisemitic worldview to begin with and shown an empathetic sensitivity to the plight of the Eastern European Jews, even if they were not the center of his attention. It is possible, of course, as Nowak speculates, that he did come to recognize the enormity of what had occurred during the war and in the process genuinely overcame his earlier prejudices and dislikes. Such an evolution is suggested by one of the newly inserted passages, a fond portrait of his German teacher, a Miss Dora Vogel, whom he remembers having assigned him *Nathan der Weise* (*Nathan the Wise*), Gotthold Lessing's play about religious toleration, when he was her teenage pupil.[245] This cameo is clearly meant as a programmatic statement, yet elsewhere the Kultura text retains traces of his original feelings. Among the various characters Bobkowski encounters in his Paris dealings, two Jewish figures are portrayed as individuals. Both are engaged in black-market activities, a function to which Jews, as deal makers and finaglers, were supposedly well suited (though Bobkowski's Warsaw pals did rather well in this department, as he did himself in his own modest way). The desperate woman he was compelled to assist because she turned up on his (Parisian) doorstep does not come alive on the page. She is never named.

The various post facto additions suggest, however, that Bobkowski was not being entirely ironic when, in correspondence with Giedroyc, he wondered: "How to convince them you are not an antisemite?" It seems he was trying to do just that. Yet in the same letter, he expressed his annoyance at the Jews for continuing to leverage their victimhood, at the expense of the Poles. Perhaps, as he always had, he simply refused to be censored, even after the war, even in relation to the Jews, if only in private. And Giedroyc seems to have accepted the transgressive side of the writer's character as part of his charm. The notebooks, however, in both manuscript and published versions, are centered on the affirmation of moral absolutes, the value of life, the irreducible importance of the individual person, the reliance on personal authenticity. "Integrity" (in English) is the word Terlecki used to describe their basic feature.[246] It is a characteristic, as various participants in the recent debates have concluded, that is difficult to reconcile with either the original sentiments or with the failure to explain the process that led to their suppression.

What did the Jews want and how did they feel? Bobkowski noticed their hostility during the war (the Jewish woman standing in line) and the resentment that persisted even in postwar emigration. The Jews continue to reproach you, he implies; they insist you love them and are not easily satisfied. This was, of course, not the case. As the Russian Jewish liberal Daniil Pasmanik put it in 1923: "Jews are not asking for love. In the emotional sphere Judeophobia will remain for a long time, but it must disappear from the arena of positive law and political relations."[247] This had been Maklakov's position, as well. Antisemitism was not something that could be wished away; firewalls, in the form of laws and institutions, must be built to contain it.

Sometimes, even laws were not enough. Jacques Biélinky, who shared the experience of occupied Paris with Bobkowski, from a very different corner of the map, can testify to what the Jews might have felt or wanted. Contra Pasmanik, Biélinky wanted to be loved. As a naturalized Jew who had found refuge in the land of civil equality from the injuries he had suffered at home, he had an enormous stake in thinking the French would live up to their principles. When the Jews were obliged to wear the yellow Star of David, when they were rounded up, humiliated, and murdered, he insisted the people of Paris were on their side. In the metro, he noted in his diary, an "Aryan" boy rises to give him a seat; French housewives stand in line for their Jewish neighbors, when Jews are forbidden to shop for more than an hour a day; people greet him on the street, shake his hand; "*la population parisienne*" is shocked by the Vélodrome d'hiver.[248]

What bothered Biélinky were his fellow Jews. He was an immigrant who had become French and thus could walk both sides of the street. Already in the 1920s, he deplored the condescension with which assimilated French Jews regarded the immigrants from Eastern Europe, yet he too insisted the newcomers must learn to fit in. The war had raised the stakes. On June 4, 1942, he noted that Hungarian Jews in France were exempt from wearing the yellow star. "If Jewish solidarity were more than a legend created by antisemites," he complained, "the privileged Jews should of their own free will wear the badge to show their sympathy and solidarity. But they won't. Cowardice, pettiness, and egotism are characteristic of all 'civilized' men, Jews and non-Jews."[249]

On August 8, 1942, he overhears "an old 'French' Jew" who "repeats the insanities about the responsibility of the immigrant Jews for the current persecutions." The old man concludes: "They should not have been allowed to enter France." Biélinky observes ruefully: "The diatribes continue, but a question arises: either Jewish solidarity exists or it does not exist. In the first case, it would be the duty of French Jews to extend a warm welcome to the immigrant Jews fleeing persecution in Eastern Europe.... In the second case, the persecuted Jews would have the right to benefit from the laws of the Republic to arrive in France, without regard for whether or not this pleases the Jews who pretend to be native. In both situations the Jewish antisemites would have to hold their tongues."[250]

Are Jews antisemites, too?[251] It was apparently hard even for Jews to like the Jews of Poland. The consequences of this distinction were serious indeed. These consequences did not, of course, result from the tensions within the Jewish population, but from forces beyond its control. Well-established Jews had extensive networks in French society, which contributed to their chances of survival, but the immigrants had networks and institutions of their own.[252] In the end, as we know, Jews who were French citizens survived at a higher rate (90 percent) than immigrant Jews who did not have French citizenship (60 percent). We know that Vichy went out of its way to protect its own Jews, but showed less reluctance to sacrifice the others.[253] Biélinky, despite his French papers, was deported to Sobibor in 1943.

In Poland, where circumstances were dramatically different, 90 percent of the prewar Jewish population perished. The revelations about Bobkowski seem to confirm the worst aspects of Polish political culture, before and during the war. Even in its immediate aftermath, the antisemitism of the majority of the population and the Catholic Church was unmitigated by the disappearance of almost all Jews, and those who returned or remained were subject to assaults and murder.[254] Bobkowski's duplicity—if that's what it was—nevertheless has an encouraging side. He managed by sleight of hand to get his readers to believe he had not ever been an antisemite, to the joy and relief of many post-Communist Polish intellectuals and the reading public. And those same enthusiastic readers were disappointed by the truth when it emerged, even if they differed in how to understand the evident contrasts in his persona. This is not the same Poland, for all its enduring contradictions, as the Poland of 1939 or 1944. Whether or not the *Wartime Notebooks*, as a finished product, stand up as a work of literature is for critics and readers to determine. The cutting room floor is revelatory, too, however, not just of Bobkowski, the person and the writer, but of the more general problem of the cultural and political meanings of antisemitism across the arc of the Second World War.

A Tale of Two Mobilizations

Some Conclusions

THE CONCEPT OF "antisemitism" has no simple meaning. There is a vast literature on the subject of how to define it. On one level, it constitutes an all-pervasive antipathy to a people labeled "the Jews," in ethnic and religious terms, sometimes in racial terms, as well. On another, it amounts to a system of prejudice that feeds on the ancient antagonism directed by exponents of Christianity at the adherents of the creed from which the new faith emerged.[1] At the same time, it designates a Weltanschauung, a way of seeing the world, in which human societies are prey to hidden forces identified with a power known as "the Jews," which conspires to control them. In the modern period, it has provided the ideological core activated by political leaders seeking to attract a broad-based popular following—a form of demagogic populism that identifies a particularly virulent enemy as the target of hostility and violence, an enemy embodied in "the Jew." Antisemitism, in its modern form, thus has psychological, religious, and political dimensions.

It is the political dimension of antisemitism in the modern period that is highlighted in this book. In each of the three East European cases examined here, antisemitism features as an instrument of mass mobilization, providing a simplistic interpretation of the social world, which is deployed by movements and regimes in the interests of establishing or sustaining their power. In each instance, this mobilization is confronted by a counter-mobilization, a form of Jewish activism operating within and across national borders. The power of the Jews, as a stateless diaspora in the international arena, was not self-sustaining, however. It depended on the backing of states whose interests, for whatever reason, coincided with their goal of obstructing or mitigating the consequences of antisemitism as a political force and a humanitarian disaster. The story told here is thus a tale of two mobilizations.

It is easy to conclude, with the narrative extending to the end of World War II, and with the current resurgence of antisemitic provocations across the globe, that antisemitism has emerged victorious from this confrontation. The cases explored here demonstrate, however, that Jewish efforts managed successfully, within the sphere of Western democratic politics, to discredit antisemitism, as a discourse and political practice, into the start of the twenty-first century. Against this moral shift, Nazi antisemitism was belligerently transgressive, but many antisemitic nationalist ideologues were forced into sheepish hypocrisy or tactical submission by the impact of the Jewish diaspora's organized counter-campaign. This margin of success was possible, of course, only so long as the institutional framework of the Western-model constitutional state maintained its standing. Whatever their domestic deficiencies, the democracies exemplified and promoted a rights-based regime that provided the umbrella of citizenship. Once the platform on which campaign and counter-campaign faced off comes into question, as it has in recent years among the erstwhile Great Powers and their national clients, the outcome of the contest begins to seem less and less secure.

Despite the recent challenges, however, the taboo is still to be reckoned with. In the wake of World War I, as we have seen, outright antisemites were obliged, for largely instrumental reasons, to avoid the label. Even during World War II this inhibition retained its force with regard to the political leaders of dependent nations, whose prospects for the postwar settlement relied on the backing of the anti-Axis powers. The aftermath of the Holocaust reinforced the need for camouflage yet again. Take the example of Poland. The attitudes comprising interwar antisemitism were still the norm decades after the war, despite the catastrophic elimination of almost all Polish Jews, but educated people now felt called upon to disclaim them. Tadeusz Mazowiecki (1927–2013), then the editor of a reform-minded Catholic periodical, wrote in 1960: "There are no antisemites among us. No one, except for one or two fanatics, would own this label today. And in any case, kind and gentle people have always said, 'I am not an antisemite, I condemn this type of attitude . . . but those Jews.'"[2] Forty years later, the sociologist Hanna Świda-Ziemba (1930–2012) used slightly different words for the same thing: "[A] certain form of political correctness took shape after the Holocaust, according to which spectacular, drastic attacks on Jews are evil, but at the same time even authentic antisemites treat the designation 'antisemite' as an affront. This is why Poles are offended when Poland is called an antisemitic country, and why even the most antisemitic statement is prefaced by the declaration: 'I'm not an antisemite, but . . .'"[3] Joanna Beata Michlic, at the UCL Centre for the Study of Collective Violence, dubs this awkward combination "antisemitism without antisemites."[4]

The notion that antisemitism is an affront can have contradictory results. It can inspire efforts at education, produce hypocrisy, or reinforce the determination of true believers to stick to their guns. In 2006, for example, a monument was erected in Warsaw in honor of Roman Dmowski, an unrepentant antisemitic ideologue, but also a founder of the independent nation. Controversy ensued. Protesters cited his politics of hatred and in particular his antisemitism.[5] The monument remains. On the other side of the ledger, Warsaw now has a Museum of the History of the Polish Jews (POLIN Muzeum Historii Żydów Polskich), built with combined public and private support, which opened officially on April 19, 2013, the seventieth anniversary of the start of the Warsaw Ghetto Uprising. An international board of scholars shaped the exhibition, which stresses the long arc of Polish-Jewish cohabitation. The museum is surrounded, however, by monuments attesting to Polish efforts to save the Jews during the war, as though the Poles had done all they could to prevent the tragedy with which that historical symbiosis ended.[6]

On the assumption that charges of antisemitism constitute a stain on the national reputation, Poland continues to struggle with its history in relation to the Jews. Since 2000, when Jan Gross published *Neighbors*, the inheritors of the Endecja mantle have engaged in a campaign to whitewash the history of nationalist antisemitism and of Polish involvement in the persecution of the Jews. In 2005 the regime introduced standards for the writing of history (so-called *polityka historyczna*) designed to counteract "all the lies voiced against the Polish nation" propagated by *Neighbors* and the research and discussions that ensued.[7] This policy endorses the myth that ethnic Poles figured exclusively as the victims of wartime atrocities, but in no way as perpetrators or participants in actions now universally decried.

Gone are the days when Dmowski bragged or Shulgin boasted. Dmowski's nationalist heirs in the current government insist the Polish record is clean. According to the present official version, the "so-called Kielce pogrom" of July 4, 1946, in which forty-two Jews were murdered, was actually a Communist provocation.[8] This notion echoes the position taken immediately after the war by the remnants of the organized underground still active in Poland, with respect to anti-Jewish violence, in general, and Kielce, in particular, which they viewed as a Jewish-Communist scheme "to arouse the worst opinion of Poland abroad" and justify the presence of Soviet forces in the country. This same defeated but persistent underground disseminated propaganda combining Endek-style antisemitism with anti-Communist animus, while at the same time realizing that it was not "at the present moment . . . in our interest to fan the flames of antisemitism."[9]

Jews are thus blamed, yet again, for provoking the anger directed against them: by joining the Communists who victimized the Poles; by blaming the Poles for responding to the harm they—as Communists and simply as Jews—had caused them. The official government line today perpetuates this defensively accusatory posture. Thus, the government-backed Institute of National Remembrance (Instytut pamięci narodowej—IPN), which enjoys a large budget and pursues an energetic campaign of education and propaganda, insists that Poland has no need to apologize for supposed crimes against the Jews. "Other nations and people also suffered tragedies," a spokesman declared; "the Holocaust was one of the slaughters of the modern era, and not even the greatest one."[10] Poles went out of their way to help the Jews, the IPN affirms, despite the "lack of support on the part of the Jews for Poles who were deported and arrested between 1939 and 1941 by the Bolsheviks."[11]

In today's Poland, it is now a criminal offense to imply that Poles in any way approved or abetted the operation of the Final Solution.[12] The statute penalizing the act of "publically insulting the Polish Nation or Republic" has been used against Professor Gross to prosecute the expression of such views.[13] The Polish League Against Defamation (Reduta dobrego imienia), created in 2013, uses the courts to promote its goal of "correcting false information on Poland's history, in particular World War 2, the role of Poles in the war, [and] Polish people's attitude to Jews."[14] In 2017 the league targeted Professor Jan Grabowski, at the University of Ottawa, author of a book on Polish-Jewish relations during the war, in which, it contended, "he falsifies the history of Poland."[15] It found the award bestowed on the work by Yad Vashem in 2014 particularly "disturbing."[16] A letter sent to all the institutions with which Grabowski was affiliated declared: "The attempts to ascribe part of the responsibility for the crimes of the World War II and the Holocaust to the Poles are evidently actions damaging Poland."[17] Historians from the Polish Center for Holocaust Research came to Grabowski's defense.[18] He himself sued the league for libel and won his case.

The nationalist Right nevertheless keeps alive the sense of injury, both at the harm allegedly inflicted on Poland by the Jews and at the opprobrium now attached to defending oneself—or the nation—against them. One Catholic website, for example, described the left-liberal *Gazeta Wyborcza*, edited by Adam Michnik (b. 1946), as a "kosher newspaper" (*gazeta koszerna*), which it accused of publishing "lies that have affected Poland's image in the world."[19] Unapologetic antisemitism has also proliferated in the Polish media, but the guiding thread is the assertion that Jews worldwide are on a campaign to damage Poland's reputation, precisely by blaming Poland for the fate of the Jews and minimizing the crimes they have themselves perpetrated against the Polish people.[20]

The phenomenon in which denial demonstrates what it purports to deny is by no means limited in time and place to the aftermath of the war or to the Polish example. The power and the stigma of antisemitism were joined at the hip from the moment at the end of the nineteenth century when it became a political weapon. In Eastern Europe, in the first half of the twentieth century, antisemitism intensified its effects, both as an instrument of popular mobilization and as a widely accepted template for understanding the world. Yet, as these three essays have shown, the paradigm did not go unchallenged; there were times when antisemitism became a moral and political disadvantage.

In the first case, imperial Russian liberals adopted Jewish rights as part of their overall political vision: a neutral public sphere and the rule of law; not minority rights, but full legal integration, leaving the Jews to create community and define themselves culturally under conditions of civil equality. This is the emancipationist, liberal posture that Shulamit Volkov counterpoises to the antisemitic "cultural code." The position is recognizable in the Russian example, though for some of the gentile players, notably Vasily Maklakov and Count Ivan Tolstoy, this code clashed with their cultural background. Under circumstances of revolution and civil war, in which political choices narrowed, liberals made compromising alliances, however; they maintained their core values, but lacked a viable alternative to the authoritarian challenges with which they were faced.

The case of Symon Petlyura also raises the issue of what conditions are needed to resist the force of antisemitic mobilization. It poses the question of what counts as antisemitic at any given point in time. Petlyura did not adopt antisemitism as an explicit political posture. His official pronouncements opposed it and evidence suggests they reflected his personal views. Yet the Ukrainian National Government and its supporters employed the marked language of the antisemitic repertoire: invoking the power of world Jewry, the Jews' alleged responsibility for the violence directed against their own communities, Jewish money, Jewish messianism. The government's mixed messages reflect the collision of opposing pressures: from the mobilized Jewish diaspora and Western opinion, on the one hand; from the popular following and local leaders, on the other. The rhetoric surrounding Petlyura contradicted the leader's avowed intentions.

In testing the relative weight of ideology and cultural pressure, the case of the early Soviet regime provides a useful comparison. Caught in the same conjuncture (weak state, endemic political conflict, social upheaval), it was also unable to prevent outbreaks of anti-Jewish violence among its own forces. Antisemitism in the ranks nevertheless clearly contradicted the socialist message, which favored class conflict over ethnic animosity as an animating principle. Ukrainian nationalism, by contrast, had targeted Poles and Jews as hostile to Ukraine's ethnically defined national aspirations. Petlyura was himself a socialist. As leader of the nation, he had to reconcile the tension between his two ideological commitments. To act decisively against antisemitism and antisemitic violence would have been to alienate his lieutenants and lose his base. Yet, on equally pragmatic grounds—and perhaps also from conviction—he indulged in certain "gestures" (Maklakov's cynical term) designed to mitigate the consequences. These gestures may have been sincere, not calculating, but their failure was guaranteed and they were therefore relatively painless.

Neither Petlyura nor the principal Bolshevik leaders were ideological antisemites. They nevertheless propagated or tolerated scenarios, though not necessarily aimed at Jews, that accommodated Jews as suitable objects. Socialist categories were disturbingly adaptable; invidious labels were mutable. Behind the abstraction of world capitalism the face of the Jew could easily be discerned by anyone used to antisemitic invective. More generally, a view of the world conceived as controlled by global conspiracies—of capitalists, or Communists, or "enemies of Ukrainian statehood"—encouraged people so inclined (for whatever reason) to include the imagined conspiracy of Jewish moneybags or Jewish commissars among them.

The Soviet and Ukrainian camps, both non-antisemitic at the highest levels, each suffered from this pattern of conflation. Bolshevik propaganda during the Civil War, when overt antisemitism was rampant on the anti-Bolshevik side, offered a set of terms and an image of the social and ideological enemy that overlapped considerably with the antisemitic scheme; indeed, some of the categories were interchangeable. The "Jewish exploiter" and the "capitalist exploiter" were virtually synonymous. Antisemitic motives on the part of an aggrieved populace might well energize the positive response to Bolshevik rhetoric, without complicity from on top, just as antisemitic motives might energize popular anger against the Bolshevik regime. Similarly, in the Ukrainian case, Petlyura rejected antisemitism as a rallying cry, but his exhortations against the enemies of Ukrainian nationhood could easily be misunderstood. Given the demography of the Ukrainian lands and the history of explicit antisemitism in the evolution of nineteenth-century Ukrainian nationalism, it was not surprising that such invocations should be interpreted by followers as directed against the Jews, especially since some of Petlyura's acolytes made this connection explicit.

The culture in which their apparatus was embedded and the mentality on which it drew made it hard for leaders to control the impact of slogans and policies. Neither Lenin nor Petlyura, to repeat, adopted an antisemitic program, but their cohorts, entourages, lieutenants, operatives, army officers, and middle-tier administrators were free to maintain and propagate antisemitic prejudices of their own, particularly since these prejudices fit nicely within the contours of the movement's basic appeal. In both cases, moreover, such prejudices tended to echo feelings harbored by the men directly engaged in armed combat. Hence, the proliferation of pogrom violence, more intense among Ukrainian forces, but present when the occasion arose within the Red Army as well.

It was also possible, of course, as I have tried to show, to reject antisemitism in antisemitic terms. Let's call it the "apology paradigm," corresponding to the "pogrom paradigm," which is to say, a standard pattern of accusation and self-exculpation. Every pogrom was explained by its perpetrators as a response to aggression coming from the Jewish side. This aggression could take the form of financial and economic domination; it could take the form of treason in warfare—signaling to the enemy, poisoning the wells; it could take the form of direct attack—throwing rocks, shooting from rooftops or windows, lobbing grenades. And when the Jews complained of having been assaulted, their assailants accused them of trying to besmirch the honor of the honest soldiers, aggrieved peasants, or upstanding nation that had in the first place merely been responding to the Jews' original devious designs. Thus, Petlyura complained that "Jewish circles" were unfairly damaging the Ukrainian cause. His champions at the Paris trial complained that in becoming Communists, the Jews had made themselves into targets for the justified anger of the populace, reduced to starvation and political subjugation by the Soviet behemoth. They depicted Schwarzbard as a witting or unwitting Communist agent. They complained that the Jewish organizations arguing in his defense had ganged up to blacken the Ukrainian leader's name.

Antisemites like to imagine the Jews are engaged in a worldwide conspiracy—one for all and all for one. Yet in an array of political contexts, Jews have differed widely on how to defend themselves against hostility and aggression. Jews have also entered political life in the service of goals and values, such as liberalism, socialism, and communism, that transcend the fate of the Jews. The essays in this book highlight the path associated with the platform of liberal democracy, in which the diasporic communities mobilized their resources on the international stage to press the Jewish case through testimony and advocacy. Their efforts had limited results. But how to take the measure of success or failure? Diaspora activism did not stop the violence against the Jews in Eastern Europe; it did not prevent the rise of Nazism. Neither did the Western Powers. The Soviet regime, for its part, failed in the objective of creating socialism; it failed to avoid antisemitism, indeed it lent its weight to the recodification of antisemitism as anti-Zionism in the Cold War global landscape. The Zionist solution created problems of its own, which have only grown more pressing with the passage of time. The campaign waged by transnational Jewish organizations and their allies nevertheless succeeded in shifting the moral equation.

Some antisemites rushed to proclaim they were not—with some important results but also, of course, some fatal exceptions.

As Daniil Pasmanik remarked in 1923, aversion to the Jews may never go away, but love is precisely not the necessary condition. This was always Maklakov's point and the thrust of Polish linguist Baudouin de Courtenay's answer to the "Jewish Question." Society in its formal organizations, the state in its laws and institutions, must accord the Jews the same status as everyone else. They must have the rights of citizens, whether they are loved or not, and precisely when they are not loved. Wartime conditions create different pressures and demands, of course: the Russian Civil War placed the Jews between armed camps and also on both sides of the battle. All the contending forces deployed violence on their own behalf; none was able to control its character and direction. The situation confronted liberals with choices their principles did not prepare them to make. In terms of subjective emotions (hatred, aversion, attraction, mixed feelings), few were pure. Ambivalence reigned, even among Jews with regard to each other. But the opponents of antisemitism promoted a model that defined a public stage independent of private emotion, in which minorities (not only Jews) have rights, among them the right to be different. They established a discourse that compelled nonliberals striving to establish themselves in the international arena to bend to its pressure, or at least appear to obey its rules. This itself was a major achievement.

The antisemitism demonstrated in the three cases examined here was political at its core. In all three—the Russian Empire and the Russia-centric White movement in the Civil War, and the Ukrainian and the Polish national movements—it was used by elites as an ideology of mass mobilization to further concrete political aims. For the imperial administration in its last decades and for the military opposition to Soviet rule, the goal was to counter the appeal of radical left-wing agitation and to ground state power, whether failing or in hopes of resurrection, in a Russian ethno-political identity. The goal of the breakaway nationalists, by contrast, was to escape from Russian domination, with the help of anti-imperial ethnocentric appeals.

In every case, leaders built on endemic tensions already exacerbated by the transition from traditional to modern societies and economies. The conditions under which this transition occurred in this part of the world were shaped, however, by the policies of the tsarist autocracy.

Most obvious was the segregation of Jews geographically and in social function, restrictions that exaggerated the features that distinguished the Jews as a cultural community from the society around them. On this bounded terrain, the Jews were an important presence in commerce, manufacturing, and urban life, creating social networks and institutions peculiar to themselves, however diverse their economic and cultural profile. As Maklakov put it in 1911, when arguing for the abolition of the Pale: "This policy has managed to unite the Jews into a separate nation [*natsiia*]."[21] It concentrated them, moreover, at the geopolitically contentious intersection of three ethno-linguistic domains. Jews would have been and wanted to be distinctive—by religion, customs, language, sometimes by dress—but the reproach leveled at them by their detractors, that they were a stubborn enclave refusing to join the larger community and pay their dues, was not a separation the Jews had chosen. It was thrust upon them.

Other policies of the tsarist regime that contributed to making the Jews a political problem were not directed at the Jews themselves, but were designed to crush the aspirations of the professional classes of Poland and the Ukrainian provinces, which were striving for cultural and civic autonomy. These frustrated regional elites in the centers of Jewish habitation faced off against an expanding Jewish urban class, no longer confined to the small towns but dominating the growing cities, where industry and commerce—the power of the future—seemed to be in Jewish hands, where Jews seemed to be tied—despite their impaired status—to the imperial center, in both economic and cultural terms. Blocked from access to the broader societies, the Jews began by demanding autonomy within these circumscribed limits, but many, while still embedded in the hybrid cultures to which they were bound, soon dreamed of a state and society of their own.

These developments unfolded in the final decades of the nineteenth century, when antisemitism as a political force had begun to emerge on the European stage. Its growing salience was fed in part by ideologues from Russia, sponsored by an increasingly besieged imperial regime hoping to cut the ground from under burgeoning mass movements by means of a mass mobilization device of its own. There was nothing specifically "Polish" or "Ukrainian" or "Russian" about this sinister modern device. It was employed by outgoing elites—tsarist officials and White Army officers, for example—as well as their nationalist challengers. Antisemitism was as transnational as the Jews, even in nationalist hands.

Nineteenth-century ideologues of rising Ukrainian nationalism did not hesitate to stimulate nativist resentment of groups seen as hostile to their goals—the Poles, with whom Ukrainians were in geographic competition; the Germans and Jews, posing an economic threat—as a way of building a popular following. Polish nationalists, for their part, disparaged the Ukrainians and demonized the Jews. The key leaders of the post-1917 Ukrainian national movement, by contrast, did not hoist the antisemitic banner, but their entourage, collaborators, and enablers had internalized this conception of the political and social map. No government emerged on Ukrainian soil during the Civil War that was strong enough to impose its authority one way or the other, let along curb the use of terror as an adjunct to the battle for its own existence. Clinging to the vestiges of respectability even after its demise, that unsuccessful national government, its remnants now in exile, continued to insist: it had not been antisemitic.

The case of Poland was both similar and different. The amalgam of Polish nationalism and antisemitism in the program of the National Democratic Party antedated the outbreak of the Great War.[22] The xenophobic propaganda launched by all sides in that conflict, and also within the Romanov empire against its own domestic minorities, with particular animus against the Jews—a population shared by Russia and Poland, thus seeming now all the more unreliable than it already had seemed—intensified the antagonism rooted in Endek ideology. Polish socialists and sections of the academic and artistic intelligentsia resisted this pull, but public discourse in Poland had, by 1939, when the real test came, long been saturated with the antisemitic vision of the country's problems and its future.

A self-professed critic of nationalism, Andrzej Bobkowski nevertheless absorbed the pervasive "cultural code" of the interwar years. During the war, he objected when the London government seemed to strike a conciliatory note with regard to the Jews, although it did so only for politically opportunistic reasons, barely masking its underlying convictions. For all the predictability of his commonplace views, Bobkowski remains an ambiguous figure. He cannot be reduced to his antisemitic pronouncements of the war years, nor can he be absolved of having made them. He managed, however, to become part of the postwar project sustained by Kultura of creating an alternative to the Polish default mode. The spirit of Kultura has been strong in post-Communist Poland, and it still animates progressive forces in the academic and creative intelligentsia. Scholars and thinkers have continued to ponder the tenaciousness of antisemitic attitudes in Polish public life.[23] Historians and social scientists continue to ask difficult questions: "Are the Poles antisemites?"[24] Concerning the roots of antisemitism in Poland: "Is the Jew-enemy eternal?"[25] Is it futile to imagine its disappearance?[26]

Some scholars have decided that antisemitism is too vague and value-laden a concept to have retained any usefulness as an analytic term. Historians David Engel and Norman Davies object that it often functions as little more than a term of opprobrium.[27] "Petlyura was an antisemite." "The Poles are antisemitic." "The Ukrainians are antisemitic." The answer is: "He's not." "No, we're not!" "We're not," because the label cannot shuck off its ethical implications. Vasily Shulgin's gleeful display of unrepentant antisemitism in 1927, already—and purposefully—out of sync with the times, would have sounded quite different in 1942 or 1943. It had been dangerous enough in 1919, when "torture by fear" could no longer serve as a metaphor. Shulgin, however, was consistent. Why would someone who saw the world this way apologize or deny it altogether?

Partly, denial was a response to the international environment. In the wake of World War I, the Allies had an interest in stabilizing the map of Europe.[28] The problem of ethnic minorities had caused domestic turmoil, armed conflict, and an outpouring of refugees from the East, which raised the level of already existing racism and antisemitism at their destinations. News of anti-Jewish violence committed by Polish and Ukrainian forces in the wake of the war impeded their leaders' ability to achieve diplomatic aims dependent on outside backing. The role of Jewish organizations in promoting minority rights fueled the antisemitic assumption that within the community of nations, supposedly so solicitous of Jewish interests, the international mafia of Jewish money and Jewish power was plotting behind the scenes. But given the political imperatives faced by aspiring Polish or Ukrainian leaders, or by anti-Bolsheviks trying to motivate the Western world to oppose Soviet power, antisemitism became a liability. It was an instrument they could not easily dispense with, however, since it was deeply rooted in their respective strategies of survival as political movements with actual or aspirational mass appeal. In the Polish case, antisemitism was embedded in the ideology of the nationalist founding party.

To repeat: the context for the emergence or obfuscation of what were considered antisemitic views and policies was not simply moral or intellectual but fundamentally political. When thinking about this period it is difficult in fact to dispense with the concept of antisemitism, since it was so meaningful and explosive to the participants at the time. The "Jewish Question," itself an antisemitic formulation, insofar as it posited the Jews as the problem that needed to be "solved," was smack center on the table. It was an issue that of course demanded the attention of Jewish organizations across the world. Jewish communities used their economic and political muscle to protect their vulnerable members, to protect themselves, even in conditions when those efforts were obviously futile. And, of course, they were reproached by antisemites (proud ones and sheepish ones) both for their alleged passivity and for rallying whatever forces they had at their disposal.

In a period of uncertain statehood, the Great Powers, for a variety of reasons, made the repudiation of antisemitism, at least on the level of official policy, a precondition for national legitimacy. In 1919 they were responding in part to pressure exerted by the transnational Jewish diaspora, itself energized by the fate of the Jews in Eastern Europe during and after the war. This fate caught everyone's attention, not merely as the object of special pleading, but as the most dramatic and shocking result of the politicization of ethnic conflict throughout the region. The exterminationist policies and racist ideology of National Socialism later amplified the murderous consequences of antisemitism under cover of war and deepened the opprobrium attached to antisemitism in all its registers.

As a consequence, patriotic nationalists have gone out of their way to establish their political good standing. In the wake of the Holocaust, notes historian Per A. Rudling, "[d]enial of the fascist and anti-Semitic nature of the OUN [Orhanizatsiia Ukraïns'kykh Natsionalistiv, Organization of Ukrainian Nationalists], its war crimes, ethnic cleansing, and participation in the Holocaust have become central components of the intellectual history of the Ukrainian diaspora."[29] Into the 1980s, historian Taras Hunczak, an erstwhile member of the OUN, today professor emeritus at Rutgers University, Newark, categorically denied that any wartime Ukrainian organizations promoted antisemitism in any form; rather, he insisted, they "accepted Jews into their ranks and sheltered them from Nazi persecution, despite the popular perception of Jews as promoters of communism."[30] The *Encyclopedia of Ukraine*, published by the Canadian Institute of Ukrainian Studies at the University of Toronto, declares: "there has never . . . been a Ukrainian anti-Semitic organization or political party."[31]

Such respectable proponents of the Ukrainian cause indignantly reject the antisemitic label. Outright antisemites (or their spokesmen or apologists), also on the defensive, have adopted the familiar stratagem of denying their antisemitism in antisemitic terms. A diatribe from 1982 urges the Jews to help "dispel the malicious accusations that Ukrainians are 'anti-Semites.'" It accuses them, as commissars and KGB agents, of tormenting the ordinary Ukrainian peasant, in obedience to "the command of your Jehovah." "And yet," its author complains, "when that Ukrainian defended himself, then this was already criminal 'anti-Semitic' [*sic*] and a 'pogrom of the innocent, defenseless Jews.'"[32] A page from an old playbook.

Resurgent post-Soviet nationalism reanimates the old clichés. The case of Symon Petlyura, as the fledgling Ukrainian nation's first political leader, has been a key symbolic moment, as we have seen, in the construction of the Ukrainian national narrative. His role remains a sore point to this day. He is still a nationalist icon. The Symon Petlyura Ukrainian Library in Paris contains a chapel in honor of St. Simon; on May 25, 2016, the ninetieth anniversary of the assassination, Ukrainian television suspended its broadcasts for a minute of silence, filling the screen with the image of a burning candle.[33] In a volume published that same year, with the explicit purpose of reconciling Jewish and Ukrainian interpretations of their intertwined history, Professor Paul Robert Magocsi of the University of Toronto insisted: "Petlyura was hardly responsible for the pogroms, regardless what subsequent Soviet propaganda and post-Soviet chauvinistic-minded historians have claimed."[34] The Jews were, of course, the ones to accuse Petlyura of responsibility at the time and his defenders in 1927 accused them of acting on behalf of Soviet interests. It's an association Magocsi does not make, but he does once again use politics to deflect from the difficult issues presented by Petlyura's record.

Some scholars in Ukraine have attempted to move the discussion to a different plane. In 2008, the distinguished Ukrainian philosopher, Myroslav Popovych (1930–2018), a supporter of the Maidan and of democratic reform, together with the Ukrainian-born Moscow-based historian, Viktor Mironenko (b. 1953), a specialist in Russian-Ukrainian relations, authored a volume on Petlyura's record as a political leader. The volume presents the texts of documents issued by Petlyura's regime on the subject of the Jews, along with material on a range of other matters. Popovych makes clear in the introduction that Petlyura must be acknowledged as head of state of the original Ukrainian National Republic, but the policies he adopted at the time need not be accepted uncritically.[35]

Popovych does not point fingers. Regarding the Schwarzbard trial, he writes: "The judgment of a court is serious. One cannot simply wave it away by casting aspersions on the integrity of the judges. This was the reaction of European public opinion, and if it was mistaken, that must be demonstrated."[36] Insisting that Petlyura "absolutely was not an antisemite," Popovych, like the leader's many posthumous defenders, recognizes that the ataman in chief could not control the various partisan units nominally under his command, could not contain the violence they perpetrated, and could not afford to acknowledge his lack of power.[37] Petlyura thus continues to symbolize something he apparently did not stand for, but from which his reputation as a political figure cannot be detached. There is no trace of soft-core antisemitic reasoning in Popovych's approach to one of Ukraine's hot-button historical issues. There is no vestigial hidden transcript.[38] Indeed, Popovych was among a number of respected historians who were sued by antisemitic ideologues for protesting against the active promotion of antisemitism in Ukrainian academia.[39]

The target of this protest was an officially endorsed institution called the Interregional Academy of Personnel Management (Mizhrehional'na Akademiia upravlinnia personalom, MAUP) that between 1991 and 2010 was the moving force behind the antisemitic resurgence.[40] With ties to the Ukrainian Conservative Party and funding from Saudi Arabia, Iran, and Libya, it had affiliates and branches all over Ukraine, enrolling over 50,000 students, and a vast network for the publication and distribution of antisemitic literature.[41] Its many scurrilous titles included *The Protocols of the Elders of Zion*, in a revised, centenary edition. Together, its publications and website revealed an undisguised antisemitic agenda, replete with hoary clichés. The contemporary element was its anti-Zionism and hostility to Israel.[42]

No apologies or disavowals here. In 2005, MAUP called for an investigation into the "criminal activities of organized Jewry in Ukraine," presented as a petition allegedly signed by a hundred leading public figures. In the same year, it organized a conference on the topic of "Zionism as the biggest threat to modern civilization." The guest of honor was Ku Klux Klan leader David Duke, to whom it awarded an honorary doctorate in history. Another conference was held on the "Jewish-Bolshevik Revolution of 1917." The famine of 1932–1933, the Stalinist terror, indeed the entire Soviet regime, were blamed on the Jews. At the same time, MAUP denounced the Jewish-run media for spreading the myth of Ukrainian antisemitism.[43] It was only toward the end of 2005 that President Viktor Yushchenko (b. 1954), feeling the brunt of international displeasure, first condemned the institution and began to retract his support. By 2007 the wind had gone out of its sails, but in 2010, when Yushchenko decided to rehabilitate the ONU, MAUP joined the revisionist campaign.[44] In this environment, according to John-Paul Himka, professor emeritus at the University of Alberta, it has been difficult for scholars in Ukraine to pursue a nonideological, honestly empirical approach to these dangerous topics.[45]

In post-Soviet Russia, the nationalist Right has also reverted to the old formulas, while rejecting the charge of antisemitism as an expression of "Russophobia" on the part of international Jewish interests. The militantly antisemitic Union of the Russian People, founded after 1905, was revived in 2005. Its publishing house, "The Russian Idea" (Russkaia ideia), had been created in 1996 by a certain Mikhail Nazarov (b. 1948), described by noted scholar John Klier as "a veteran judeophobe writer."[46] Its titles include a reconsideration of the Beilis Case, "from the Russian side," presenting what the editor claims are the true transcripts of the trial, in order to rescue this "taboo topic" from the "dictatorship of liberal opinion," a tyranny exercised mostly by Jewish writers, who are bent on "unmasking" supposedly antisemitic Russia.[47] The entire affair is depicted as a prelude to the final offensive of the "Russian" (in quotation marks) revolution, which "must be recognized above all as the victory of anti-Christian forces, long conspiring to destroy Christian Europe."[48] The Russian Idea website proclaims its duty to expose the nefarious activities of "the enemies of the Orthodox Fatherland" and mount a defense against them. These enemies are the descendants of the "Yid-Bolsheviks" who orchestrated the "anti-Russian revolution of 1917."

Old-style antisemitic rhetoric, already circulating in the 1990s, obtained a new lease on life. In 2002 a law was introduced penalizing ill-defined "extremist activity." In 2005 Nazarov petitioned the chief procurator of the Russian Federation, demanding that Jewish organizations be repressed under this statute, on the grounds that they engaged in conspiracies against the non-Jewish world, for which they harbor an "existential hatred."[49] In support of this demand, Nazarov first gathered a list of 500 signatures, which swelled to 5,000, eventually to 15,000, including many Orthodox priests and some Duma deputies.[50] The letter campaign prompted the formation of a movement with the slogan, "To live without fear of the Hebrews" (*Zhit' bez strakha iudeiska!*), dedicated to the defense of "Russian patriots accused by Jewish activists of so-called 'antisemitism' and the 'instigation of national hatred.'"[51] The "instigation of national hatred," as penalized by a statute in the criminal code, clearly applies to Nazarov's own campaign, but the prosecutor's office declined to take action against him. Nazarov insists that criticism of the Jews does not constitute slander, but merely describes reality. The Jews, he claims, are the agents of "a covert genocide in relation to the Russian people and its traditional culture." Supporters brandish signs: "Judaism is the religion of hatred."[52] This is an "international conflict," Nazarov insists. One side is the aggressor and the other acts simply in self-defense.[53]

A survey of antisemitism in Russia in 2005, conducted by the independent SOVA Center for Research on Nationalism and Xenophobia in Moscow, concluded that "antisemitism is an organic part of the national-radical movement."[54] The "Letter of the 500," SOVA observed, reactivated antisemitism as a public discourse and the reborn Union of the Russian People created a rallying point for various Orthodox-monarchist groups. The center concluded that the "Letter of the 500" brought antisemitism into the limelight and weakened the taboo against it. The SOVA Center, the Levada Center for Public Opinion, and the Human Rights Center "Memorial" uphold the spirit of opposition to the spread of xenophobia in general and antisemitism, in particular, in post-Soviet Russian society.[55] They have all been under pressure from the authorities for their links to "undesirable" foreign sponsors.[56]

Why in 2005, with so many other, more immediate political threats on the horizon, the reactivated "Old Right" needed antisemitism at all is not entirely clear, except for its enduring value as a cultural marker. Perhaps its adherents were encouraged by the example of the

Nobel Prize-winning novelist Alexander Solzhenitsyn (1918–2008), not in their brazenness, but in their adoption of postures obscured by the intervening years of Soviet history.[57] During Soviet times, Solzhenitsyn courageously spoke out against the regime, but after being expelled from the country in 1974, he reverted to nostalgia for its predecessor. In 1994 he returned to Russia, but was disappointed in what he found and in his reception. His role of prophet and moral beacon had outlived its day. Three years before his return, he had published a study of the place of the Jews in Russian history: *Dvesti let vmeste (1795–1995)* (Two Hundred Years Together).[58] His goal, he explained, was to "search for every point of common understanding" between the Russian and Jewish peoples, "cleansed of the bitterness of the past." Rejecting "the excessive vehemence of the two sides," he preferred what he considered a balanced approach, hoping "to engage each other with tolerant mutual understanding and in recognition that each [side] has its share of sin."[59] An example of nationalist apologetics in the guise of even-handedness.

Solzhenitsyn feared a heated response and indeed the two-volume opus gave rise to animated discussion. In Russia, historians complained of incoherence, unprofessionalism, reliance on antiquated sources, and reversion to antisemitic clichés. Viktor Kelner (b. 1945), an authority on Russian Jewish history based in St. Petersburg, dismissed it as "antisemitic journalism."[60] Mikhail Nazarov, by contrast, felt the master had not gone far enough in indicting the Jews.[61] The work's embarrassing status for Western admirers of Solzhenitsyn's Soviet-era profile is marked by the continuing absence of a complete English translation. Reviewers considering the first volume hesitated to condemn him. The late Professor Richard Pipes supposed it was intended to rebut what he considered well-deserved charges of antisemitism stemming from the writer's earlier work. Despite errors, exaggerations, and oversights, Pipes concluded, Solzhenitsyn "absolves himself of the taint of anti-Semitism."[62] Historian John Klier also seemed to take Solzhenitsyn off the hook, declaring, with respect to his treatment of the pogroms, that charges of antisemitism would be "inevitable, if misguided." Yet, Klier nevertheless complained, the novelist "is more concerned at the use of the pogroms by foreign propagandists to discredit Russia than any impact they might have had on the Jews."[63]

Overall, Solzhenitsyn's attempt to refute the charges of antisemitism, which were said to have "rankled" him, offers a compendium of clichés and routine assumptions.[64] When it comes to the Soviet period, he does not escape the paradigm of Judeo-Bolshevism central to twentieth-century antisemitism.[65] "Every nation must answer morally for its past — and for what is shameful about it," he lectures the Jewish people. "And in this spirit the Jewish nation [*evreiskii narod*] should answer for its revolutionary executioners [*golovorezy*] and for the legions who rushed eagerly to serve them. They are not answerable to other nations, but to themselves, to their own conscience, and to God."[66] In particular, "the Jews are the first who must answer for the Jewish-Bolsheviks, not the Russians. This slice of history must concern the Jews very powerfully to this very day."[67]

Who were these Jews? The Bolsheviks of 1917, the writer points out, included: "Uritsky, Larin, Kharitonov, Dimanshtein, Zalkind, Kogan-Semkov, Girshfeld-Stashevskii, Fishman, Volin-Eikhenbaum" — and so on.[68] Liberals were equally to blame — those who hid in the second ranks of the Provisional Government, so as not to stand out: the infamous Vinaver, of course; and "Bliumenfeld, Gruzenberg, Gurevich, Lurye, Shvarts, Ginzburg-Naumov, Rutenberg, Galpern" — and so on.[69] The Jewish Bolsheviks may have been "renegades" (*otshchepentsy*), Solzhenitsyn concedes, acting not as Jews but as ideologues, yet, he insists, as Jews they were alien to the Russian spirit and not only alien but hostile. Even if they did not always act as a bloc, but sometimes disagreed among themselves, they promoted the destruction of Russia.[70] Trotsky in the lead. Some of Solzhenitsyn's claims are supported by recent scholarship — as in the absence of high-level support for tsarist-era pogroms or the Red Army's involvement in anti-Jewish violence — but his purpose is not so much to set the record straight, as to engage in polemics. His antisemitism is a component of his Russian retro-nationalism.

Where does this leave us, in 2019 — a century since the end of the Great War, the onset of Soviet power, the birth of the Second Polish Republic, and the failure of Ukrainians back then to establish an independent nation? The Soviet Union has come and gone, Poland has joined the European Union, and post-Communist Ukraine is still fighting to secure its borders and achieve international respect. The Holocaust and the establishment of Israel have forced the Western world, at least, to acknowledge the magnitude of Jewish suffering and come to terms with state power exercised in the name of the Jews. The existence of Israel, the emergence of postcolonial nations, and the Great Power rivalries of the Cold War reconfigured the uses of antisemitism, now flying the anti-Zionist flag. It is a banner more recently shouldered by transnational terrorists in the name of a politicized Islam.

Perhaps most important, in 2019 we face an internal crisis of Western liberal democracy and a resurgence of demagogic right-wing populism. The crisis is magnified by the impact of Israeli policies promoting an inflammatory, ethno-nationalism of their own. The anti-Zionism of the sort promulgated by MAUP does not, however, constitute a critique of Israeli policy. It provides a vehicle for old-style antisemitic emotion and provocation. In contrast to the 1930s and 1940s, however, Jews have not so far become the primary target of symbolic and physical aggression at the hands of a movement capable of appropriating the powers of a state. Yet, with the icons and rhetoric of twentieth-century racism and xenophobia released from quarantine, Jews again have something to fear. As in the past, the relative safety of the far-flung diaspora cannot be guaranteed by its own isolated efforts, but depends on the continuing vitality of the enlightened forces and political institutions of the societies of which it is part.

In the current international environment, the inhibition against overt antisemitism still dominates Western discourse, but the constraints are progressively wearing away. If "antisemitism without antisemites" is always in apologetic mode, some political figures no longer bother to conceal the structures of Jew-hatred that underlie their demagogic appeals. Hungarian prime minister Viktor Orbán (b. 1963), for example, attacks the Hungarian-born Holocaust survivor and financier George Soros (b. 1930), certain that no translation is needed. Indeed, Hungary today provides a perfect laboratory for the interaction of overt and coded antisemitism. After assuming office in 2010, Orbán made a concerted effort to appear as a supporter of the Jews, funding the renovation of the main Budapest synagogue and the Jewish cemetery, among other gestures. As one Hungarian commentator explained: "During Orbán's first term, the international press criticized him for having alliances with anti-Semitic parties. He understood that the label of anti-Semitism can be deadly for a politician in the European Union."[71]

Even in Orbán's early, pragmatic phase, not-so-subtle subtexts abounded. All along, the prime minister had celebrated the pro-Nazi regime of Miklós Horthy (1868–1957). In 2014, a state-sponsored monument to Hungarian suffering in World War II failed to mention the half-million Hungarian Jews murdered by the Nazis. A separate, privately funded monument was erected nearby as a counter-statement. In 2015, Orbán launched the campaign against Soros, whom he has accused of sponsoring the waves of immigrants flooding Europe.[72] The financier, who has spent billions of dollars promoting "open societies" on the ashes of Soviet communism, is now denounced as "the extreme left" by authoritarian demagogues repudiating liberal democracy.

In the Hungarian context, Soros has appeared as more than an ideological opponent. In the words of Anshel Pfeffer, Budapest correspondent for *Haaretz*: "the terms used to describe him could have been lifted directly from the 'Protocols of the Elders of Zion.'" Posters with images of the financier "as a vulture-beaked predator" prompted complaints from the Budapest Jewish community. Its objections were endorsed by the Israeli ambassador, but the endorsement was retracted by Israeli Prime Minister Benjamin Netanyahu (b. 1949), who complained that Soros "continuously undermines Israel's democratically elected governments by funding organizations that defame the Jewish state and seek to deny it the right to defend itself."[73] A leader of the Hungarian Jewish community remarked: "By shaking the hand of the man who orchestrated the anti-Soros poster, which was a perfect anti-Semitic cliché, Netanyahu is making all the Jews here shiver."[74]

The Hungarian government defends its record in acknowledging the Holocaust and insists the campaign against Soros has nothing to do with the Jews. "It's not a personal campaign against Soros," a spokesman declared. "It's against what he represents—global capitalism in its worst fashion. This is not anti-Semitism, it's pure politics." The code "global capitalism," of course, contradicts his statement. The Orthodox Jewish community in Hungary nevertheless accepts this view, because of its own support for Netanyahu. One Jewish-identified online commentator agreed: "Orbán . . . protects Jews, and keeps out Muslims. So what are we complaining about?" Another chimed in: "the real enmity to Jews and Israel are [*sic*] now found within the unholy alliance between the EU Left and forces of Islam." In the emerging global landscape, the Israeli government and its uncritical supporters are willing to identify with anti-Muslim antisemites in defense of the Jewish state.[75]

Liberal Jews do not equate Israeli politics with the outlook of Jews worldwide. They understand the dangers of coded antisemitism and the dangers of authoritarian rule, even—or especially—with the imprimatur of Israeli leaders. András Léderer (b. 1984), advocacy officer for the Hungarian Helsinki Committee NGO, concedes that overt antisemitism in Hungary and attacks on Jewish targets are nowadays rare, but he describes the anti-Soros campaign as "an anti-Semitic tool. This is the tool that was used against Jews for so many years here in Hungary. It is so effective and powerful because it was used so much over our history."[76] Orbán can keep the lid on violence, while promoting the idiom that keeps the potential for violence alive.

Eastern Europe is not the only staging ground, however, for resurgent antisemitism; it does not have a monopoly on right-wing movements with dubious pedigrees. Antisemitism has found a place, as well, on the radical Right in Western Europe and the United States and has been creeping resolutely toward the political center. In the mainstream Left, antisemitism is associated not with anti-Muslim sentiments, as in the anti-immigrant posture of Viktor Orbán, but with pro-Palestinian critiques of Israel. British Labour Party leader Jeremy Corbyn, for example, has criticized Israel in terms that caused outrage, but he insists he is not antisemitic. In answer to the question, "Is Jeremy Corbyn an anti-Semite?" Josh Glancy, the New York correspondent for the Sunday *Times of London*, reported in August 2018: "the nasty comment from Mr. Corbyn on 'Zionists' not getting 'English irony' has finally snapped the benefit of the doubt extended by many Jewish progressives." Glancy calls this "classic anti-Semitism. Here were a group of Jews with whom Mr. Corbyn has a political disagreement. And he smeared them not on the basis of that disagreement but on the basis of their ethnicity. He accused them of failing to assimilate English values, of not fitting in, of still being a bit foreign."[77] In a defensive move, the Labour Party belatedly resolved to adopt the definition of antisemitism supplied by the International Holocaust Remembrance Alliance, but qualified its terms enough to get previous statements by Labour leaders off the definitional hook.[78] In the U.S. Congress, representative from Minnesota Ilhan Omar (b. 1981) has come under fire for remarks critical of Israel that have been considered antisemitic.[79]

Finally, to put the extreme case of Orbán's Hungary in perspective, consider the way George Soros, a naturalized American citizen, has featured in American electoral politics since the radical Right has taken control of the Republican Party.[80] In 2010 Fox News used Soros as a symbolic whipping boy, accusing him at the same time of "helping send the Jews to the death camps" and plotting a coup against the United States. Recently, Donald Trump Jr. (b. 1977) ("retweeting" the disgraced comedian Roseanne Barr) has spread the claim that Soros is a Nazi; former New York mayor Rudolph W. Giuliani (b. 1944), currently a personal lawyer for President Donald Trump (b. 1946), has promoted the idea that Soros is the Antichrist. A U.S. government-funded radio network called him a "multimillionaire Jew" of "flexible morals" and blamed him for the 2008 financial crisis. Trump's 2016 campaign spotlighted Soros, along with other identifiably Jewish financial figures, to illustrate "global special interests." In 2018 the National Republican Congressional Committee sponsored an advertisement that depicted Soros behind a pile of cash and described him as "bankrolling" the "left-wing mobs paid to riot in the streets." Back in Hungary, Orbán's party has sponsored an advertisement showing Mr. Soros with a smile on his face and the caption: "Let's not let George Soros have the last laugh." The phrase was recognized as an invocation of the "Laughing Jew," an antisemitic cliché.

Let Mr. Soros, the object of so much vitriol, have the last word. After the assault on the Tree of Life synagogue in Pittsburgh on October 27, 2018, in which eleven worshippers were murdered, he commented: "I came to this country to find refuge. I am deeply distressed that in America in 2018 Jews are being massacred just because they are Jewish." A *New York Times* follow-up on the synagogue attack was titled: "How Vilification of George Soros Moved From the Fringes to the Mainstream."[81] The taboo on antisemitism in the public sphere, in force in Western democracies since the Second World War, in acknowledgment of the enormity of the Holocaust, has once again slackened. It is a taboo or inhibition that demands constant vigilance. The underlying impulse never goes away, and not just in Eastern Europe.

Yet antisemitism has varied in time and place, shifting its contours, waxing and waning in political importance. The real danger, on a global scale, lies in the weakening of the institutional structures and political culture that managed to survive the twentieth century in the major Western nations, promoting civil rights, democratic values, and the rule of law. This is what Vasily Maklakov and Maxim Vinaver stood for; it's what Soros stands for; it's what authoritarians of all kinds do not like. The United States has experienced waves of intense anti-immigrant sentiment, one of which — the restriction on quotas in 1924—affected Morris Greenfield directly. It has never come to terms with its own history of racism and violence. Nevertheless, for all their domestic faults, the failure to live up to their own promises, and their hypocrisy on the subject of the Jews, the imperfect Western democracies have provided the Jewish diaspora with the validation and resources with which to conduct international campaigns of advocacy and self-defense. They have provided the institutional platform on which to fight for their own rights and for the principle of rights, in general. This platform is in need of reinforcement.

NOTES

Introduction: Morris Greenfield Encounters Some "Very Fine People"

1. Today Copanca has a population of 5,000, none Jewish. http://localitati.casata.md/index.php?action=viewlocalitate&id=7616 (accessed 3/16/18).

2. Tiraspol is today the capital of the unrecognized breakaway region of Moldova known as Transnistria. The memoir and translation are on deposit at YIVO (Yidisher visnshaftlekher institut, Institute for Jewish Research), in New York: RS 102.349.

3. Historian Salo Baron rejected what he called in a 1928 essay "the lachrymose conception of Jewish history," for its exaggerated focus on moments of crisis and persecution: cited, Benjamin Nathans, *Beyond the Pale: The Jewish Encounter with Late Imperial Russia* (Berkeley: University of California Press, 2002), 8.

4. Iokhanan Petrovskii-Shtern, *Evrei v russkoi armii: 1827–1914* (Moscow: Novoe literaturnoe obozrenie, 2003), 349–53. See the recent (but mostly too late for this book): Semen Gol'din, *Russkaia armiia i evrei, 1914–1917* (Moscow-Jerusalem: Mosty kul'tury, 2018).

5. In fact, Jews served in proportion to their percentage of the population. The military statute of 1912 included a provision that Jewish men returning from emigration would be considered draft evaders. The idea of excluding Jews from the army altogether had been raised, but rejected. The statute nevertheless confirmed all the anti-Jewish regulations. See Petrovskii-Shtern, *Evrei v russkoi armii*, 346, 349, 351–53.

6. Joseph Roth, *The Wandering Jews*, trans. Michael Hofmann (1927; New York: Norton, 2001), 93.

7. David Wolff, *To the Harbin Station: The Liberal Alternative in Russian Manchuria, 1898–1914* (Stanford: Stanford University Press, 1999), 2–6, 9–10.

8. Yoshihisa Tak Matsusaka, "Imagining Manmō: Mapping the Russo-Japanese Boundary Agreements in Manchuria and Inner Mongolia, 1907–1915," *Cross-Currents: East Asian History and Culture Review* (e-journal no. 2, March 2012), online at: http://cross-currents.Berkeley.edu/e-journal/issue-2 (accessed 11/25/18); Matsusaka, *The Making of Japanese Manchuria, 1904–1932* (Cambridge, MA: Harvard University Asia Center, 2001); Ernest Batson Price, *The Russo-Japanese Treaties of 1907–1916 Concerning Manchuria and Mongolia* (Baltimore: Johns Hopkins Press, 1933).

9. Tobias Brinkmann, "Permanent Transit: Jewish Migration during the Interwar Period," in *1929: Mapping the Jewish World*, ed. Hasia R. Diner and Gennady Estraikh (New York: New York University Press, 2013), 67; Marcia Reynders Ristaino, *Port of Last Resort: The Diaspora Communities of Shanghai* (Stanford: Stanford University Press, 2001).

10. Rebecca Kobrin, "The 1905 Revolution Abroad: Mass Migration, Russian

Jewish Liberalism, and American Jewry, 1903–1914," in *The Revolution of 1905 and Russia's Jews*, ed. Stefani Hoffman and Ezra Mendelsohn (Philadelphia: University of Pennsylvania Press, 2008), 228.

11. Perhaps these were examples of I. J. Singer's "wastrel Hasidic youths . . . [who] ceased studying the Torah and played cards in study houses." Quoted, Irving Howe, "Introduction," in I. J. Singer, *The Brothers Ashkenazi*, intro. Irving Howe, trans. Joseph Singer (1937; New York: Penguin, 1993), xiv.

12. Petrovskii-Shtern, *Evrei v russkoi armii*, 216.

13. The island he mentions was probably Russkii ostrov (Russian Island), one of twenty-one islands around the city, this one with an important military base.

14. The location was Ussuriysk, fifty miles north of Vladivostok.

15. Petrovskii-Shtern, *Evrei v russkoi armii*, 213, 215.

16. Ibid., 175 (prejudice), 197, 201–3 (statistical refutation).

17. "Gasiotin" in the English transcription could be Koziatyn/Kozyatyn in the Vinnitsa district of western Ukraine, southwest of Kiev.

18. Mihály Kálmán, "A Forgotten Jewish Army and/or Soviet Proxies? Jewish Self-Defense and Counterinsurgent Paramilitarism in Civil War Ukraine, 1920–1924." CEU lecture, 2016, see Central European University, National Studies Program, online at: http://nationalism.ceu.edu/events/2016-10-18/js-lecture-series-mihaly-kalman-forgotten-jewish-army-andor-soviet-proxies-jewish (accessed 11/25/18).

19. Andrei Cusco, *A Contested Borderland: Competing Russian and Romanian Visions of Bessarabia in the Late Nineteenth and Early Twentieth Century* (Budapest: CEU Press, 2017), 292–93. M. I. Mel'tiukhov, *Bessarabskii vopros mezhdu mirovymi voinami, 1917–1940* (Moscow: Veche, 2010), 25–29.

20. As part of an argument against the Pale of Settlement in the Third Duma, Kadet deputy Vasily Maklakov explained that evasion and bribery were natural responses to unjust laws and restrictions: *Gosudarstvennaia Duma: Stenograficheskie otchety*. Tretii sozyv. 1911 g. Sessiia chetvertaia. Chast' II. Zasedaniia 39–73 (s 17 ianvaria po 5 marta 1911 g.) (St. Petersburg: Gosudarstvennaia tipografiia, 1911), col. 1552 (Zasedanie 54, February 9, 1911).

21. The "Petlyurovtsy" were the followers of Ukrainian leader Symon Petlyura; see below.

22. David Bergelson, *Judgment*, trans. Harriet Murav and Sasha Senderovich (Evanston: Northwestern University Press, 2017); originally as *Mides-hadin* (Vilna, 1929). See Senderovich and Murav, "Introduction," ibid., and Kenneth B. Moss, *Jewish Renaissance in the Russian Revolution* (Cambridge, MA: Harvard University Press, 2009), 5–7, 9.

23. Katherine Sorrels, "Police Harassment and the Politicization of Jewish Youth in Interwar Bessarabia," *East European Jewish Affairs* 47:1 (2017): 62–84. On antisemitism in interwar Romania, see Paul Hanebrink, *A Specter Haunting Europe: The Myth of Judeo-Bolshevism* (Cambridge, MA: Harvard University Press, 2018), 53–54, 75. See also Dmitry Tartakovsky, "Parallel Ruptures: Jews of Bessarabia and Transnistria Between Romanian Nationalism and Soviet Communism, 1918–1940" (Ph.D. Dissertation, University of Illinois, 2009).

24. Moss, *Jewish Renaissance*, 221, 263.

25. "Yiddish also became the lingua franca, the wireless international network linking Jews of distant places, when they met in trade or wandering and resettlement." Benjamin Harshav, *The Meaning of Yiddish* (Stanford: Stanford University Press, 1990), 21.

26. In Bessarabia, it was centered in Kapreshty (Capresti), 112 miles north of Kopanka. Jeffrey Veidlinger, *Jewish Public Culture in the Late Russian Empire* (Bloomington: Indiana University Press, 2009), 287, 59 (libraries).

27. Eli Lederhandler, "Democracy and Assimilation: The Jews, America, and the Russian Crisis from Kishinev to the End of World War I," in *The Revolution of 1905 and Russia's Jews*, ed. Hoffman and Mendelsohn, 248.

28. Simon Rabinovitch, *Jewish Rights, National Rites: Nationalism and Autonomy in Late Imperial and Revolutionary Russia* (Stanford: Stanford University Press, 2014), 4–6, and throughout.

29. See Carole Fink, *Defending the Rights of Others: The Great Powers, the Jews, and International Minority Protection, 1878–1938* (Cambridge: Cambridge University Press, 2004); James Loeffler, *Rooted Cosmopolitans: Jews and Human Rights in the Twentieth Century* (New Haven: Yale University Press, 2018). Also, Mark Mazower, *No Enchanted Palace: The End of Empire and the Ideological Origins of the United Nations* (Princeton: Princeton University Press, 2009), 107.

30. Hanebrink, *A Specter Haunting Europe*, ch. 2.

31. Isaak Babel', *Konarmiia* (Moscow: Gosudarstvennoe izdatel'stvo, 1926); Isaac Babel, *1920 Diary*, trans. H. T. Willetts, ed. Carol J. Avins (New Haven: Yale University Press, 1995).

32. For these discrepancies, see Łukasz Mikołajewski, *Disenchanted Europeans: Polish Émigré Writers from* Kultura *and Postwar Reformulations of the West* (Bern: Peter Lang, 2018). First revealed in: Mikołajewski, "Pamięć fabularyzowana. Powojenne poprawki w *Szkicach piórkiem* Andrzeja Bobkowskiego," in *Buntownik, Cyklista, Kosmopolak: O Andrzeju Bobkowskim i jego twórczości*, ed. Jarosław Klejnoski and Andrzej St. Kowalczyk (Warsaw: Biblioteka "Więzi," 2011); and Mikołajewski, "Disenchanted Europeans: Polish Émigré Writers from *Kultura* and the Postwar Reformulations of the West" (Ph.D. diss., European University Institute, 2012), ch. 3.

33. Rafał Pankowski, "The Resurgence of Antisemitic Discourse in Poland," *Israel Journal of Foreign Affairs* (2018): 1–17, online at: http://www.nigdywiecej.org/docstation/com_docstation/20/r._pankowski_the_resurgence_of_antisemitic_discourse_in_poland._israel_journa.pdf (accessed 2/10/19).

34. Jan T. Gross, *Neighbors: The Destruction of the Jewish Community in Jedwabne, Poland* (Princeton: Princeton University Press, 2001), published first as Jan Tomasz Gross, *Sąsiedzi: Historia zagłady żydowskiego miasteczka* (Sejny: Pogranicze, 2000).

35. Anna Bikont, *My z Jedwabnego* (Warsaw: Prószyński, 2004; Czarne, 2010); *The Crime and the Silence: Confronting the Massacre of Jews in Wartime Jedwabne*, trans. Alissa Valles (New York: Farrar, Straus and Giroux, 2015), 98.

36. Some nineteenth-century Jewish leaders had feared the creation of transnational Jewish organizations would stoke the myth of a worldwide Jewish conspiracy: Jonathan Frankel, "Jewish Politics and the Press: The 'Reception' of

the Alliance Israélite Universelle (1860)," in Jonathan Frankel, *Crisis, Revolution, and Russian Jews* (New York: Cambridge University Press, 2009), 49.

1. Against the Grain: Russians in Defense of the Jews

1. See Jeffrey Veidlinger, *Jewish Public Culture in the Late Russian Empire* (Bloomington: Indiana University Press, 2009), title page verso. Also: Benjamin Nathans, *Beyond the Pale: The Jewish Encounter with Late Imperial Russia* (Berkeley: University of California Press, 2002), 30 (map), 4 (population). "Introduction," in *Warsaw the Jewish Metropolis: Essays in Honor of the 75th Birthday of Professor Antony Polonsky*, ed. Glenn Dynner and François Guesnet (Leiden: Brill, 2015), 11. Density of Jewish population in the Pale and Russian Poland: Nancy Green, *The Pletzl of Paris: Jewish Immigrant Workers in the "Belle Epoque"* (New York: Holmes & Meier, 1986), 16.

2. Quoted, Herman Rosenthal, "Introduction," in Prince Serge Dmitriyevich Urussov, *Memoirs of a Russian Governor*, trans. and ed. Herman Rosenthal (London, New York: Harper & Brothers, 1908), vii.

3. On the importance of "civic emancipation and social integration": Nathans, *Beyond the Pale*, 10, characterizing the overall argument of the book, which focuses on three venues in which Jews played a significant role: St. Petersburg, the universities, and the courts.

4. Kenneth B. Moss, *Jewish Renaissance in the Russian Revolution* (Cambridge, MA: Harvard University Press, 2009).

5. These points are key to Christoph Gassenschmidt, *Jewish Liberal Politics in Tsarist Russia, 1900–1914* (New York: New York University Press, 1995).

6. "Predislovie," in *Pravye partii: Dokumenty i materialy, 1905–1917*, ed. Iu. I. Kir'ianov, 2 vols. (Moscow: ROSSPEN, 1998), 1:14–15. The term "Black Hundreds" derived from the name for armed units formed during the political turmoil of the early seventeenth century, allegedly to defend Orthodox Russia against foreign enemies; it was adopted in a positive sense by the post-1905 Right, in a pejorative sense by their opponents.

7. The "Jewish Question" was a term that went into circulation in the mid-nineteenth century; the term "antisemitism" entered the lexicon in 1879, although the status of the Jews as a social and political problem was already articulated a century before: Jonathan Judaken, "Antisemitism and the Jewish Question," in *The Cambridge History of Judaism*, vol. 8: *The Modern Period, c. 1815–c. 2000*, ed. Mitchell Hart and Tony Michels (New York: Cambridge University Press, 2017), 559–88.

8. Avrahm Yarmolinsky, *Road to Revolution: A Century of Russian Radicalism* (New York: Macmillan, 1959), 247–49; Erich Haberer, *Jews and Revolution in Nineteenth-Century Russia* (Cambridge: Cambridge University Press, 1995).

9. Franco Venturi, *Roots of Revolution: A History of the Populist and Socialist Movements in Ninetenth-Century Russia*, intro. Isaiah Berlin, trans. Francis Haskell (New York: Grosset & Dunlap, 1960), 708; Yarmolinsky, *Road*, 287 (details of her fate vary). On the association of Jews with political radicalism, both in Russia and Poland, see Semion Goldin, "Jews as Cosmopolitans, Foreigners, Revolutionaries: Three Images of the Jew in Polish and Russian

Nationalist Ideology at the End of the Nineteenth and Early Twentieth Centuries," *European Review of History—Revue Européenne d'histoire* 17:3 (2010): 431–44.

10. Gassenschmidt, *Jewish Liberal Politics*, 10.

11. Point made by M. A. Krol', *Stranitsy moei zhizni*, ed. N. A. Zhukovskaia (Moscow: Mosty kul'tury; Jerusalem: Gesharim, 2008), 310–11; Gassenschmidt, *Jewish Liberal Politics*, 7–9.

12. John Klier, "Gintsburg Family" (2010), YIVO Encyclopedia of Jews in Eastern Europe, online at: http://www.yivoencyclopedia.org/article.aspx/Gintsburg_Family (accessed 7/31/18); Gassenschmidt, *Jewish Liberal Politics*, 7–9.

13. David Engel, "Introduction," in *The Assassination of Symon Petliura and the Trial of Scholem Schwarzbard 1926–1927: A Selection of Documents*, ed. David Engel (Göttingen: Vandenhoeck & Ruprecht, 2016), 61–62. Henceforth, *Assassination*.

14. On the strategy of transnational action on behalf of Jewish rights directed at international opinion that was pioneered by the diasporic Jewish elite: Jonathan Frankel, "Crisis as a Factor in Modern Jewish Politics, 1840 and 1881–82," in Jonathan Frankel, *Crisis, Revolution, and Russian Jews* (New York: Cambridge University Press, 2009), 15–31. On the origins and development of diaspora Jewish activism, see Abigail Green, "Old Networks, New Connections: The Emergence of the Jewish International," and Jonathan Dekel-Chen, "Activism as Engine: Jewish Internationalism, 1880s–1980s," in *Religious Internationals in the Modern World: Globalization and Faith Communities since 1750*, ed. Abigail Green and Vincent Viaene (Basingstoke: Palgrave Macmillan, 2012), 53–81, 269–91. Dekel-Chen traces the roots of organized Jewish activism to traditions of philanthropy; he notes "the grey area between philanthropy and political advocacy" that finally emerged (ibid., 276).

15. *Gomel'skii protsess: Podrobnyi otchet*, ed. B. A. Krever (St. Petersburg: Obshchestvennaia pol'za, 1907), title page for journal and newspaper sources; *Delo o pogrome v Orshe 21–24 oktiabria 1905 goda: Obvinitel'nyi akt i sudebnoe sledstvie* (St. Petersburg: Tip. Busselia, 1908); *Delo o pogrome v g. Tomske v 1905 g. (Ochet o sudebnom zasedanii Tomskogo okruzhnogo suda)* (Tomsk: Sibirskoe T-vo Pechatnogo Dela, 1909); *Delo o pogrome v Belostoke 1–3 iiunia 1906 g.: Obvinitel'nyi akt, sudebnoe sledstvie, rechi poverennykh* (St. Petersburg: Tip. Busselia, 1909). For overviews, see "Prilozhenie: Khronika oktiabr'skikh dnei. III: Posle Manifesta," *Pravo*, 48–49 (December 4, 1905): cols. 135–206; *Materialy k istorii russkoi kontr-revoliutsii*: Vol. 1: *Pogromy po ofitsial'nym dokumentam* (St. Petersburg: Obshchestvennaia pol'za, 1908); Iu. Lavrinovich, *Kto ustroil pogromy v Rossii?* (Berlin: Ladyschnikow, [1909]).

16. Examples: *Die Judenpogrome in Russland*, ed. A. Linden, 2 vols. (Cologne and Leipzig: Jüdischer Verlag, 1910), sponsored by the Zionist Relief Fund in London; Jakob Jaffe, *Ursachen und Verlauf der Juden-Pogrome in Russland im Oktober 1905* (Bern: Akademische Buchhandlung von Max Drechsel, 1916). Jaffe, from Vilna, wrote this doctoral dissertation at the University of Bern.

17. Gassenschmidt, *Jewish Liberal Politics*, 9; S. V. Pozner, "Bor'ba za ravno-

pravie," in *M. M. Vinaver i russkaia obshchestvennost' nachala XX veka: Sbornik statei* (Paris: Étoile, 1937), 165–68; Krol', *Stranitsy*, 342. Most recently, Viktor Kel'ner, *Shchit': M. M. Vinaver i evreiskii vopros v Rossii v kontse XIX–nachale XX veka* (St. Petersburg: Evropeiskii universitet v Sankt-Peterburge, 2018).

18. Nathans, *Beyond the Pale*, 325–34; Gassenschmidt, *Jewish Liberal Politics*, 8–10.

19. M. Vinaver, "A Veteran of the Russian Jewish Intellectuals," *Jewish Tribune* 3 (April 1, 1920): 1.

20. Nathans, *Beyond the Pale*. On the precedent: Frankel, "Crisis as a Factor," 15–31. On the similar mobilization of German Jews also faced with a rise in antisemitism: David Engel, "Patriotism as a Shield: The Liberal Jewish Defence against Antisemitism in Germany during the First World War," *Leo Baeck Institute Yearbook* 31 (1) (1986): 147–71.

21. Pozner, "Bor'ba," 168–69.

22. Krol', *Stranitsy*, 343.

23. B. A. Krever, "Predislovie," in *Gomel'skii protsess*, i.

24. Ibid., ii.

25. Quoted, ibid., ix.

26. Ibid., x.

27. Established in 1901: Elie Bar-Chen, "Two Communities with a Sense of Mission: The Alliance Israélite Universelle and the Hilfsverein der deutschen Juden," in *Jewish Emancipation Reconsidered: The French and German Models*, ed. Michael Brenner, Vicki Caron, and Uri R. Kaufman (Tübingen: Mohr Siebeck, 2003), 112.

28. Established in 1860, "devoted to the defense of Jews and the promotion of human rights" across national borders. Alliance website, online at: https://www.aiu.org/en/alliance-israelite-universelle (accessed 8/12/18). See Jonathan Dekel-Chen, "A Half-Full Cup? Transnational Responses to the Beilis Affair," in *Ritual Murder in Russia, Eastern Europe, and Beyond: New Histories of an Old Accusation*, ed. Eugene M. Avrutin, Jonathan Dekel-Chen, and Robert Weinberg (Bloomington: Indiana University Press, 2017), 188.

29. Formed in 1878 on the basis of two existing associations, in order "to conduct an Anglo-Jewish foreign policy": Mark Levene, *War, Jews, and the New Europe: The Diplomacy of Lucien Wolf, 1914–1919* (Oxford: Oxford Uuniversity Press, 1992), 2.

30. Gassenschmidt, *Jewish Liberal Politics*, 14.

31. Levene, *War, Jews, and the New Europe*.

32. Jonathan Frankel, *Prophecy and Politics: Socialism, Nationalism, and the Russian Jews, 1862–1917* (Cambridge: Cambridge University Press, 1981), 463, 493. See Naomi W. Cohen, *Not Free to Desist: The American Jewish Committee, 1906–1966* (Philadelphia: Jewish Publication Society of America, 1972).

33. Frankel, "Crisis as a Factor," 140–41; Simon Rabinovitch, *Jewish Rights, National Rites: Nationalism and Autonomy in Late Imperial and Revolutionary Russia* (Stanford: Stanford University Press, 2014), 188; Michael Beizer, *Relief in Time of Need: Russian Jewry and the Joint, 1914–1924* (Bloomington, IN: Slavica, 2015).

34. Edward H. Judge, *Easter in Kishinev: Anatomy of a Pogrom* (New York: New York University Press, 1992), 84–87 (protests). Examples from Baltimore, Brussels, New York: *Kishinevskii pogrom 1903 goda: Sbornik dokumentov i materialov*, ed. Ia. M. Kopanskii (Chişinău: Ruxanda, 2000), 79–80, 84, 85–86. This publication received funding from the American Jewish Joint Distribution Committee, a remarkable continuity with the time of the actual events; it contains documents in Russian, English, German, French, and Yiddish. See also *Kishinevskii pogrom 1903 goda—vzgliad cherez stoletie: Materialy mezhdunarodnoi nauchnoi konferentsii*, ed. Ia. M. Kopanskii (Chişinău: Pontos, 2004). Judge is still the English-language standard. For a recent treatment: Steven J. Zipperstein, *Pogrom: Kishinev and the Tilt of History* (New York: Liveright, 2018).

35. Brian Horowitz, *Empire Jews: Jewish Nationalism and Acculturation in 19th- and Early 20th-Century Russia* (Bloomington, IN: Slavica, 2009), 257–60; Naomi W. Cohen, *Jacob H. Schiff: A Study in American Jewish Leadership*, 5th ed. (Hanover, NH: Brandeis University Press/University Press of New England, 1999), 132; see also Evyatar Friesel, "Jacob H. Schiff and the Leadership of the American Jewish Community," *Jewish Social Studies* 8:2–3 (2002): 61–72.

36. Jonathan Dekel-Chen, "Philanthropy, Diplomacy, and Jewish Internationalism," in *The Cambridge History of Judaism*, 8: 510; Cohen, *Jacob H. Schiff*, 134–35.

37. Eli Lederhendler, "Democracy and Assimilation: The Jews, America, and the Russian Crisis from Kishinev to the End of World War I," in *The Revolution of 1905 and Russia's Jews*, ed. Stefani Hoffman and Ezra Mendelsohn (Philadelphia: University of Pennsylvania Press, 2008), 248–51.

38. Dekel-Chen, "A Half-Full Cup?" 192; Lederhendler, "Democracy and Assimilation," 249; Cohen, *Jacob H. Schiff*, 145–50.

39. "O Iakove Shife," in V. V. Shul'gin, *"Chto nam v nikh ne nravitsia . . ." Ob antisemitizme v Rossii* (Paris: Russia minor, 1929; rpt. Moscow: Russkaia kniga, 1994), 349.

40. S. M. Dubnov, *Kniga zhizni: Materialy dlia istorii moego vremeni: Vospominaniia i razmyshleniia*, ed. V. E. Kel'ner (Moscow: Mosty kul'tury; Jerusalem: Gesharim, 2004), 285, 287. Original edition, 2 vols. (Riga: Jaunātnes Grāmata, 1935); vol. 3 (New York: Soiuz russkikh evreev, 1957). On Dubnow, see also V. E. Kel'ner, *Missioner istorii: Zhizn' i trudy Semena Markovicha Dubnova* (St. Petersburg: Mir, 2008).

41. Gassenschmidt, *Jewish Liberal Politics*, 19–25; Pozner, "Bor'ba," 172–73; Frankel, *Prophecy and Politics*, 162; Krol', *Stranitsy*, 352 (full name).

42. Dubnov, *Kniga zhizni*, 288.

43. Charters Wynn, *Workers, Strikes, and Pogroms: The Donbass-Dniepr Bend in Late Imperial Russia, 1870–1905* (Princeton: Princeton University Press, 1992).

44. Quoted, "Predislovie," in *Pravye partii*, 1:6, 16 (founding date of Union of the Russian People).

45. Quoted, Ulrich Herbeck, *Das Feindbild vom "jüdischen Bolschewiken":*

Zur Geschichte des russischen Antisemitismus vor und während der Russischen Revolution (Berlin: Metropol, 2009), 53, from "Predislovie," in *Pravye partii*, 1:36 (my translation). See also Iu. I. Kir'ianov, *Pravye partii v Rossii, 1911–1917* (Moscow: ROSSPEN, 2001).

46. "Predislovie," in *Pravye partii*, 1:37.

47. "Doklad na s"ezde soedinennoi komissii predstavitelei pravykh partii v g. Kieve po voprosu o zhelatel'nykh izmeneniiakh v zakonakh o vyborakh v Gosudarstvennuiu Dumu i v polozhenii o uchrezhdenii Gosudarstvennoi Dumy" (October 6, 1906), in *Pravye partii*, 1:237.

48. Pozner, "Bor'ba," 172; *The Memoirs of Count Witte*, ed. and trans. Sidney Harcave (Armonk, NY: M. E. Sharpe, 1990), 592–93.

49. "Predislovie," in *Pravye partii*, 1:30.

50. Laura Engelstein, *Russia in Flames: War, Revolution, Civil War, 1914–1921* (New York: Oxford University Press, 2018), 19. See virulent image in Robert Weinberg, "The Russian Right Responds to 1905: Visual Depictions of Jews in Postrevolutionary Russia," in *The Revolution of 1905 and Russia's Jews*, ed. Hoffman and Mendelsohn, 62.

51. I. I. Petrunkevich, in *Rech'*, cited Matvei Fleer, *Mikhail Iakovlevich Gertsenshtein* (St. Petersburg: P. P. Soikin, 1906), 4.

52. "Otkrytoe pis'mo predsedatelia Astrakhanskoi narodno-monarkhicheskoi partii N. N. Tikhanovicha-Savitskogo prem'eru P. A. Stolypinu v gazete *Russkoe znamia*" (April 28, 1911), in *Pravye partii*, 2:39.

53. Pozner, "Bor'ba," 172.

54. Hans Rogger, "Was There a Russian Fascism? The Union of the Russian People," in Hans Rogger, *Jewish Policies and Right-Wing Politics in Imperial Russia* (Berkeley: University of California Press, 1986), 220.

55. "O Gertsenshteine," in Shul'gin, "*Chto nam v nikh ne nravitsia*," 362–63. On Shulgin: Aleksandr Mindlin, *Gosudarstvennye, politicheskie i obshchestvennye deiateli Rossiiskoi imperii v sud'bakh evreev, 1762–1917: Spravochnik personalii* (St. Petersburg: Aleteiia, 2007), 350–55. See also Faith Hillis, *Children of Rus': Right-Bank Ukraine and the Invention of a Russian Nation* (Ithaca: Cornell University Press, 2013), 263–65.

56. "Predislovie," in *Pravye partii*, 1:38.

57. Rebecca Kobrin, "Białystok" (2010), YIVO Encyclopedia of Jews in Eastern Europe, online at: http://www.yivoencyclopedia.org/article.aspx/Białystok (accessed 7/14/18).

58. *Gosudarstvennaia Duma. Stenograficheskie otchety 1906 god.* Sessiia pervaia. Tom II. Zasedaniia 19–38 (s 1 iiunia po 4 iiulia) (St. Petersburg: Gosudarstvennaia tipografiia, 1906): Zasedanie 23 (8 VI 1906 g.), 1125–41; Zasedanie 33 (26 VI 1906 g.), 1723–46. The First Duma met from April 27 to July 9, 1906. See Shmuel Galai, "The Jewish Question as a Russian Problem: The Debates in the First State Duma," *Revolutionary Russia* 17:1 (June 2004): 31–68; Aleksandr Mindlin, *Gosudarstvennaia Duma rossiiskoi imperii i evreiskii vopros* (St. Petersburg: Aleteiia, 2014).

59. *Gosudarstvennaia Duma. Stenograficheskie otchety 1906 god.* Sessiia pervaia. Tom II. Zasedanie 23 (8 VI 1906 g.), 1129–32. Text of speech: S. D.

Urusov, *Zapiski: Tri goda gosudarstvennoi sluzhby*, ed. N. B. Khailova (Moscow: Novoe literaturnoe obozrenie, 2009), 667–71.

60. N. B. Khailova, "Kniaz' Sergei Dmitrievich Urusov: Ot 'obraztsovogo gubernatora' do 'obraztsa sovetskogo rabotnika,'" in Urusov, *Zapiski* (2009), 5 and 9. On Urusov's career: Mindlin, *Gosudarstvennye, politicheskie i obshchestvennye deiateli*, 333–39.

61. Statutes 269, 1490, and 1606, cited in *Delo o pogrome v g. Tomske v 1905 g.*, 4. Also: *Ulozhenie o nakazaniiakh ugolovnykh i ispravitel'nykh 1885 goda*, ed. N. S. Tagantsev, 11th ed. (St. Petersburg: Gosudarstvennaia tipografiia, 1901), 266–67.

62. M. Vinaver, *Konflikty v pervoi Dume* (St. Petersburg: "Tsentr." tipo-lit. M. Ia. Minkova, 1907), 132; also Lavrinovich, *Kto ustroil pogromy*, 226–28, 243 (impact of entire Duma discussion, including Vinaver's statement); Khailova, "Kniaz' Sergei Dmitrievich Urusov," 10 (Russian newspaper coverage; effect of a bomb).

63. Horowitz, *Empire Jews*, 265–66.

64. Prince Sergei Urusov, *Zapiski gubernatora: Kishinev, 1903–1904* (Berlin: Ladyschnikow, 1907); S. D. Urussow, *Memoiren eines russischen Gouverneurs: Kischinew 1903–1904* (Stuttgart; Leipzig: Deutsche Verl.-Anst., 1907); Urussov, *Memoirs of a Russian Governor* (1908); S. D. Ouroussof, *Mémoires d'un Gouverneur*, trans. S. Persky (Paris: Félix Juven, 1908); Urusov, *Zapiski* (2009).

65. Urusov, *Zapiski* (1907), 7–8.

66. Khailova, "Kniaz' Sergei Dmitrievich Urusov," 8. On Pronin's role: Document 45, "Predstavlenie prokurora Kishinevskogo okruzhnogo suda prokuroru Odesskoi sudebnoi palaty o deiatel'nosti G. A. Pronina i A. I. Stepanova po okazaniiu pomoshchi P. A. Krushevanu i arestovannym za uchastie v pogrome" (June 3, 1903), in *Kishinevskii pogrom 1903 goda* (2000), 87–88.

67. von der Ropp, in *Gosudarstvennaia Duma. Stenograficheskie otchety 1906 god.* Sessiia pervaia. Tom II. Zasedanie 33 (26 VI 1906 g.), 1729–33. Eduard Mikhail Iogann fon der Ropp (Baron Eduard von der Ropp), defines himself as "nonparty," for moderate change: *Gosudarstvennaia duma pervogo prizyva: Portrety, kratkie biografii i kharakteristiki deputatov* (Moscow: Vozrozhdenie, 1906), 9. See website "Geschichte der Wolgadeutschen," online at: http://lexikon.wolgadeutsche.net/article/270 (accessed 8/15/18).

68. Document 71, "Stat'ia v gazete 'Novoe vremia' . . . 'Obviniaemye po Kishinevskomu pogromu,' vozlagaiushchaia na evreev vinu za pogrom i trebuiushchaia prodlit' predvaritel'noe sledstvie" (no later than October 16, 1903), in *Kishinevskii pogrom 1903 goda* (2000), 148–49.

69. Note to Document 71, ibid., 149.

70. Krever, "Predislovie," vi.

71. *Forward From Exile: The Autobiography of Shmarya Levin*, trans. and ed. Maurice Samuel (Philadelphia: Jewish Publication Society of America, 1967); Yehuda Slutsky, "Levin, Shmarya," *Encyclopaedia Judaica* (Thomson Gale, 2007), online at: https://www.encyclopedia.com/religion/encyclopedias-almanacs-transcripts-and-maps/levin-shmarya (accessed 8/5/18); *Gosudarstvennaia duma pervogo prizyva*, 10.

72. *Gosudarstvennaia Duma. Stenograficheskie otchety 1906 god*. Sessiia pervaia. Tom II. Zasedanie 33 (26 VI 1906 g.), 1742.

73. Ibid., 1746.

74. Ibid., 1734.

75. Ibid.

76. Ibid., 1739.

77. Excerpt quoted in Pozner, "Bor'ba," 177.

78. Jonathan Dekel-Chen, "Liberal Answers to the 'Jewish Question': Then and Now," in *Church and Society in Modern Russia*, ed. Elise Wirtschafter and Manfred Hildermeier (Wiesbaden: Harrossowitz, 2015), 141.

79. Pozner, "Bor'ba," 171 (citing Dubnow on leadership), 170 (Gomel); Dubnov, *Kniga zhizni*, 285; *Gomel'skii protsess*, 875–86.

80. "Biograficheskii ocherk," in *M. M. Vinaver i russkaia obshchestvennost'*.

81. M. Vinaver, *Nedavnee: Vospominaniia i kharakteristiki*, 2nd ed. (Paris: Imp. d'Art Voltaire, 1926), x.

82. M. M. Vinaver, *Kadety i evreiskii vopros* (St. Petersburg: Tip. Busselia, 1907), 11. [Rpt. as *"Ka-dety" i evreiskii vopros* (Odessa: Iuzhno-Russkoe O-vo Pechatnogo Dela, 1912), 7.]

83. Vinaver identifies the following in particular: Ivan Petrunkevich (1844–1928), Fyodor Rodichev, Prince Pavel Dolgorukov (1866–1927), Pavel Novgorodtsev (1866–1924), Leon Petrażycki (Lev Petrazhitsky, 1867–1931), Sergey Kotliarevsky (1873–1939/41), and Vladimir Nabokov. Note the range in generations, Nabokov (born 1870) being 25 years Petrunkevich's junior. *Kadety i evreiskii vopros* (1907), 7; *"Ka-dety" i evreiskii vopros* (1912), 5.

84. Quoted in Levene, *War, Jews, and the New Europe*, 12.

85. "Proposed Anti-Semitic Triple Alliance: Secret Russian Memorandum, January 3, 1906," quoted, Lucien Wolf, *Notes on the Diplomatic History of the Jewish Question* (London: Jewish Historical Society of England, 1919), 57 and 59.

86. O. V. Budnitskii, ed., "Belye i evrei (Po materialam rossiiskogo posol'stva v Parizhe i lichnogo arkhiva V. A. Maklakova)," in *Evrei i russkaia revoliutsiia: Materialy i issledovaniia*, ed. O. V. Budnitskii (Moscow; Jerusalem: "Gesharim," 1999), 270. On his personal background, see V. A. Maklakov, *Iz vospominanii: Uroki zhizni* (New York: Chekhov, 1954; rpt. Moscow: Moskovskaia shkola politicheskikh issledovanii, 2011). For his career: Mindlin, *Gosudarstvennye, politicheskie i obshchestvennye deiateli*, 204–9.

87. "V. A. Maklakov — V. V. Shul'ginu" (December 23, 1929), in *Spor o Rossii: V. A. Maklakov-V. V. Shul'gin, perepiska 1919–1939*, ed. O. V. Budnitskii (Moscow: ROSSPEN, 2012), 370.

88. V. A. Maklakov, "1905–1906 gody," in *M. M. Vinaver i russkaia obshchestvennost'*, 63–64. On Maklakov, see recently: Stephen F. Williams, *Reformer: How One Liberal Fought to Preempt the Russian Revolution* (New York: Encounter Books, 2017).

89. Khailova, "Kniaz' Sergei Dmitrievich Urusov," 11.

90. Maklakov, *Iz vospominanii*, 245–46.

91. *Delo o pogrome v Belostoke*.

92. *Gosudarstvennaia Duma. Stenograficheskie otchety*. Tretii sozyv. 1911 g.

Sessiia chetvertaia. Chast' II. Zasedaniia 39–73 (s 17 ianvaria po 5 marta 1911 g.) (St. Petersburg: Gosudarstvennaia tipografiia, 1911): Zasedanie 54 (9 II 1911 g.), 1543–1614.

93. Quoted, "Predislovie," in *Pravye partii*, 1:21.

94. *Gosudarstvennaia Duma. Stenograficheskie otchety*. Tretii sozyv. 1911 g. Sessiia chetvertaia. Chast' II. Zasedanie 54 (9 II 1911 g.), 1546. Point about the right to private opinion made also by P. Miliukov, "Evreiskii vopros v Rossii," in *Shchit: Literaturnyi sbornik*, ed. Leonid Andreev, Maksim Gor'kii, and Fedor Sologub, 3rd ed. rev. (Moscow: Mamontov, 1916), 166.

95. *Gosudarstvennaia Duma. Stenograficheskie otchety*. Tretii sozyv. 1911 g. Sessiia chetvertaia. Chast' II. Zasedanie 54 (9 II 1911 g.), 1545. Mark Antokolsky (1843–1902), born in Vilna/Vilnius, was a sculptor whose statue *Christ Before the People* (1878) created controversy. See Olga Litvak, "Rome and Jerusalem: The Figure of Jesus in the Creation of Mark Antokol'skii," in *The Art of Being Jewish in Modern Times*, ed. Barbara Kirschenblatt-Gimlett and Jonathan Karp (Philadelphia: University of Pennsylvania Press, 2008), 228–54. Rubinshtein may refer to Anton Rubinshtein (1829–1894), pianist, composer, conductor; founder of the St. Petersburg Conservatory. His brother Nikolay (1835–1881) founded the Moscow Conservatory.

96. *Gosudarstvennaia Duma. Stenograficheskie otchety*. Tretii sozyv. 1911 g. Sessiia chetvertaia. Chast' II. Zasedanie 54 (9 II 1911 g.), 1547–48. Witte apparently made a quip about drowning the Jews in the Black Sea, in the same ironic spirit, as the solution some might desire but was obviously not in the cards: see Hans Rogger, "Russian Ministers and the Jewish Question, 1881–1917," in Rogger, *Jewish Policies and Right-Wing Politics*, 85.

97. *Gosudarstvennaia Duma. Stenograficheskie otchety*. Tretii sozyv. 1911 g. Sessiia chetvertaia. Chast' II. Zasedanie 54 (9 II 1911 g.), 1549–50.

98. Ibid., 1554.

99. Ibid., 1554–55. Describing the Duma as "*russkoe narodnoe predstavitel'stvo*."

100. On the Kiev context, see Hillis, *Children of Rus'*, 244–48; Natan Meir, "Beilis, Mendel" (2017), YIVO Encyclopedia of Jews in Eastern Europe: online at: http://www.yivoencyclopedia.org/article.aspx/Beilis_Mendel (accessed 7/26/18). See also *The Beilis Transcripts: The Anti-Semitic Trial That Shook the World*, ed. Ezekiel Leikin (Northvale, NJ: Jason Aronson, 1993); Edmund Levin, *A Child of Christian Blood: Murder and Conspiracy in Tsarist Russia: The Beilis Blood Libel* (New York: Schocken, 2014).

101. S. A. Stepanov, "Delo Beilisa i chernaia sotnia," in *Sprava Beilisa: Pohliad iz s'ohodennia*, ed. I. F. Kuras (Kiev: Instytut natsional'nykh vidnosyn i politolohii NAN Ukraïny, 1994), 59.

102. "Grigori Benenson, Noted Financier," *New York Times* (April 6, 1939), 31. His extensive property was confiscated after the revolution, but he went on to a successful business career in New York and England, becoming an American citizen in 1926. On his contributions to Zionism, the Kadet party, and the Beilis defense, see James Loeffler, *Rooted Cosmopolitans: Jews and Human Rights in the Twentieth Century* (New Haven: Yale University Press, 2018), 66, 205, 217–21 (founding of Amnesty International).

103. Hans Rogger, "The Beilis Case: Anti-Semitism and Politics in the Reign of Nicholas II," in Rogger, *Jewish Policies and Right-Wing Politics*, 46. Former prime minister Sergey Witte accused Shcheglovitov of undermining the entire legal system: *"Shcheglovitovskaia iustitsiia" v Rossii: Ministerstvo iustitsii pozdneimperskogo perioda po materialam Chrezvychainoi sledstvennoi komissii Vremennogo pravitel'stva*, ed. K. P. Krakovskii (Moscow: Iurlitinform, 2014), 16; "Predislovie," in *Pravye partii*, 1:19–20 (executions).

104. Alexander B. [*sic*] Tager, *The Decay of Czarism: The Beiliss Trial*, trans. from Russian (Philadelphia: Jewish Publication Society of America, 1935), 214. Originally: A. S. Tager, *Tsarskaia Rossiia i delo Beilisa: Issledovanie po neopublikovannym arkhivnym dokumentam* (Moscow: Sovetskoe zakonodatel'stvo, Ogiz., 1934; rpt. Moscow; Jerusalem: Gesharim, 1995). On the political importance of the timing, see I. M. Pogrebinskaia, "Sotsial'no-politicheskie aspekty dela Beilisa i ego sviaz' s sovremennost'iu," in *Sprava Beilisa* (1994), 50–53.

105. Quoted, S. A. Stepanov, "Delo Beilisa i chernaia sotnia," in *Sprava Beilisa* (1994), 62.

106. Quoted, Zosa Szajkowski, "The Impact of the Beilis Case in Central and Western Europe," *Proceedings of the American Academy for Jewish Research* 31 (1963): 216.

107. Frederick C. Giffin, "American Reactions to the Beilis Case," *Social Science* 55 (Spring 1980): 89–93; Szajkowski, "The Impact of the Beilis Case in Central and Western Europe," 197–218.

108. Quoted, Tager, *Decay of Tsarism*, 160; see Giffin, "American Reactions to the Beilis Case," 92.

109. Szajkowski, "The Impact of the Beilis Case in Central and Western Europe," 200.

110. Quoted, ibid., 205.

111. Ibid., 203–5.

112. Ibid., 206–7.

113. Quoted, ibid., 215

114. G. M. Reznik, "Sud nad M. Beilisom i mif o ritual'nom ubiistve," in *Delo Mendelia Beilisa: Materialy Chrezvychainoi sledstvennoi komissii Vremennogo pravitel'stva o sudebnom protsesse 1913 g. po obvineniiu v ritual'nom ubiistve*, ed. G. M. Reznik et al. (St. Petersburg: Dmitrii Bulanin, 1999), 15–17. Spasovich stood up for Jewish rights on various occasions, but in relation to the legal profession, he defended a move within the bar to limit the number of Jews: Nathans, *Beyond the Pale*, 348–52.

115. O. O. Gruzenberg, "Moia pamiatka o V. D. Nabokove," in Gruzenberg, *Ocherki i rechi* (New York: Grenich Printing Corp., 1944), 162. See Nabokov's account, "Delo Beilisa," in the liberal legal journal, *Pravo* 44 and 45 (1913).

116. Reznik, "Sud nad M. Beilisom i mif o ritual'nom ubiistve," 14. On Rozanov: Laura Engelstein, *The Keys to Happiness: Sex and the Search for Modernity in Fin-de-Siècle Russia* (Ithaca: Cornell University Press, 1992), ch. 8.

117. Testimony of G. G. Zamyslovskii (April 29, 1917), in *Delo Mendelia Beilisa*, 60–63.

118. O. O. Gruzenberg, *Vchera: Vospominaniia* (Paris: Imprimerie VAL, 1938), 111; O. O. Gruzenberg, *Yesterday: Memoirs of a Russian-Jewish Lawyer*, ed. Ron C. Rawson, trans. Ron C. Rawson and Tatiana Tipton (Berkeley: University of California Press, 1981), 111–12, 115.

119. O. O. Gruzenberg, "Rech' po delu Beilisa" (excerpts), in Gruzenberg, *Ocherki i rechi*, 177–92.

120. Gassenschmidt, *Jewish Liberal Politics*, 9. See Krol', *Stranitsy*, 354.

121. Korolenko cited Sh. M. Gartsman, "Zapreshchennye portrety Beilisa," in *Sprava Beilisa* (1994), 30.

122. Pozner, "Bor'ba," 169. For an earlier blood libel trial, also ending in acquittal: Eugene M. Avrutin, *The Velizh Affair: Blood Libel in a Russian Town* (New York: Oxford University Press, 2018).

123. V. A. Maklakov, "Spasitel'noe predosterezhenie: Smysl dela Beilisa," *Russkaia mysl'* 11 (1913): 135–43 (second pagination). See also O. V. Budnitskii, "V. A. Maklakov i 'evreiskii vopros,'" *Vestnik evreiskogo universiteta v Moskve* 1(19) (1999): 42–94; V. A. Maklakov, *Ubiistvo A. Iushchinskogo: Rech' v Kievskom okruzhnom sude 25 oktiabria 1913 g. (po stenograficheskomu otchetu)* (St. Petersburg: Zubkov, 1914).

124. Quoted from police report, Tager, *Decay of Czarism*, 218–19. Quote also cited in Iokhanan Petrovskii-Shtern, *Evrei v russkoi armii: 1827–1914* (Moscow: Novoe literaturnoe obozrenie, 2003), 351.

125. Budnitskii, "V. A. Maklakov i 'evreiskii vopros,'" 50, 53–54 (Maklakov's later reflections on his role and strategic choices).

126. Semen Gol'din, "Russkoe komandovanie i evrei vo vremia pervoi mirovoi voiny: Prichiny formirovaniia negativnogo stereotipa," in *Mirovoi krizis 1914–1920 godov i sud'ba vostochnoevropeiskogo evreistva*, ed. O. V. Budnitskii (Moscow: ROSSPEN, 2005), 29–46; Semion Goldin, "The 'Jewish Question' in the Tsarist Army in the Early Twentieth Century," in *The Revolution of 1905 and Russia's Jews*, ed. Hoffman and Mendelsohn, 70–76.

127. Jonathan Frankel, "The Paradoxical Politics of Marginality: Thoughts on the Jewish Situation during the Years 1914–1921," in Frankel, *Crisis, Revolution, and Russian Jews*, 134–35; V. Kel'ner, "Evreiskii vopros i russkaia obshchestvennaia zhizn' v gody pervoi mirovoi voiny," *Vestnik evreiskogo universiteta v Moskve* 1(14) (1997): 66–93. A picturesque example: postcards for sale in Moscow in 1916 featured an image of Jews carrying sacks of gold and a warning from Empress Elizabeth (1709–1762) that the Jews were the enemy of all Christians: American Jewish Joint Distribution Committee Archives: AR 14/18, no. 146, p. 1 (May 1916 report sent from Copenhagen to New York office).

128. Levene, *War, Jews, and the New Europe*, introduction and ch. 1; also 39.

129. Ibid., 49.

130. Frankel, "The Paradoxical Politics of Marginality," 140–41; *The Jews in the Eastern War Zone* (New York: American Jewish Committee, 1916).

131. American Joint Distribution Committee Archives, "1914–1919: War and Emergency Relief—Establishment of the JDC," Joint archives, online at: http://archives.jdc.org/our-stories/history-of-jdc/1914-1919/ (accessed 7/29/18).

132. Frankel, "The Paradoxical Politics of Marginality," 144–45.

133. Quoted, Levene, *War, Jews, and the New Europe*, 59.

134. Ibid., 66–69.

135. Ibid., 51–54, 63. Pares was knighted in 1919.

136. Ibid., 71.

137. *Sovet ministrov Rossiiskoi imperii v gody pervoi mirovoi voiny: Bumagi A. N. Iakhontova: Zapisi zasedanii i perepiska*, ed. B. D. Gal'perina et al. (St. Petersburg: Dmitrii Bulanin, 1999), 163; see also *Prologue to Revolution: Notes of A. N. Iakhontov on the Secret Meetings of the Council of Ministers, 1915*, ed. Michael Cherniavsky (Englewood Cliffs, NJ: Prentice-Hall, 1967).

138. On the consequences of brutal treatment: Frank M. Schuster, *Zwischen allen Fronten: Osteuropäische Juden wärend des Ersten Weltkrieges (1914–1919)* (Cologne: Böhlau Verlag, 2004); *Mirovoi krizis 1914–1920 godov*; Peter Gatrell, *A Whole Empire Walking: Refugees in Russia during World War I* (Bloomington: Indiana University Press, 1999); Daniel Graf, "Military Rule Behind the Russian Front, 1914–1917: The Political Ramifications," *Jahrbücher für Geschichte Osteuropas* 22:3 (1974): 390–411.

139. Gabriella Safran, "Rapoport, Shloyme Zaynvl" (2010), YIVO Encyclopedia of Jews in Eastern Europe, online at: http://www.yivoencyclopedia.org/article.aspx/Rapoport_Shloyme_Zaynvl; David Engel, "World War I" (2010), ibid., online at: http://www.yivoencyclopedia.org/article.aspx/World_War_I (accessed 1/19/16); Gabriella Safran, *Wandering Soul:* The Dybbuk*'s Creator, S. An-sky* (Cambridge, MA: Harvard University Press, 2010), 232–47; Polly Zavadivker, "Introduction," in S. A. An-sky, *1915 Diary of S. An-Sky: A Russian Jewish Writer at the Eastern Front*, trans. and intro. Polly Zavadivker (Bloomington: Indiana University Press, 2016), 10–11; Polly Zavadivker, "Fighting 'On Our Own Territory': The Relief, Rescue, and Representation of Jews in Russia during World War I," in *Russia's Home Front in War and Revolution, 1914–22*, Bk. 2: *The Experience of War and Revolution*, ed. Adele Lindenmeyr, Christopher Read, and Peter Waldron (Bloomington, IN: Slavica, 2016), 79–106.

140. "Bor'ba s lozh'iu," *Evrei na voine: Dvukhnedel'nyi illiustrirovannyi zhurnal*, ed. D. Kumanov (Moscow: Moskovskoe izdatel'stvo), no. 1 [1915], 8. "Oproverzhenie trevozhnykh slukhov" and "Upreki 'Russkogo Znameni,'" ibid., no. 4 [1915], 2.

141. For example: "Evrei na voine," "Spisok rannenykh evreev," *Novyi voskhod* 1 (January 8, 1915): 34–36, 57–58. In many issues various columns were blanked out by the censor.

142. *Stenograficheskii otchet: Gosudarstvennaia Duma*. Chetvertyi sozyv. Sessiia II. Chast' V. Zasedanie Gosudarstvennoi Dumy, sozvannoi na osnovanii Vysochaishego Ukaza Pravitel'stvuiushchemu Senatu ot 20 Iiulia 1914 g. Subbota, 26 Iiulia 1914 g. (Petrograd: Gosudarstvennaia tipografiia, 1914), 24; Mindlin, *Gosudarstvennaia duma Rossiiskoi imperii*, 372–74.

143. Levene, *War, Jews, and the New Europe*, 48.

144. Stressing the liberals' failure to defend Jewish rights during the war and the increasing dissatisfaction with the party on the part of Jewish activists, see Rabinovitch, *Jewish Rights, National Rites*, 169–70, 175–78.

145. M. M. Vinaver, "Doklad po evreiskomu voprosu Tsentral'nogo Komiteta partii" (June 7, 1915), in *S"ezdy i konferentsii konstitutsionno-demokraticheskoi partii 1905–1920 gg.*, ed. O. V. Volobuev et al., 3 vols. (Moscow: ROSSPEN, 2000), 3.1:52–80.

146. Ibid., 55.

147. Ibid., 63 (quote), 64–65. See also the reflections of another Kadet, Grigorii Landau, *Pol'sko-evreiskie otnosheniia: Stat'i i zametki* (Petrograd: Trud, 1915). On links between Polish nationalism and antisemitism, see Theodore R. Weeks, *From Assimilation to Antisemitism: The "Jewish Question" in Poland, 1850–1914* (DeKalb: University of Northern Illinois Press, 2006).

148. Vinaver, "Doklad po evreiskomu voprosu," 56–57.

149. On the Miasoedov Affair, involving accusations of treason, see William C. Fuller, Jr., *The Foe Within: Fantasies of Treason and the End of Imperial Russia* (Ithaca: Cornell University Press, 2006); on Jewish espionage, see Semen Gol'din, *Russkaia armiia i evrei, 1914–1917* (Moscow: Mosty kul'tury; Jerusalem: Gesharim, 2018), in particular, 427–36.

150. "Proekt rezoliutsii po dokladu TsK," in *S"ezdy i konferentsii konstitutsionno-demokraticheskoi partii*, 3.1:79–80.

151. "Obsuzhdenie doklada i rezoliutsii TsK po evreiskomu voprosu," ibid., 3.1:89–91, 90 (quote).

152. Ibid., 90.

153. Ibid., 90–91.

154. Ibid., 91 (*iazva antisemitizma*).

155. Ibid., 87–88; 87 (*zhidovskaia*).

156. Michael F. Hamm, "Liberalism and the Jewish Question: The Progressive Bloc," *Russian Review* 31:2 (1972): 163–64; R. Ganelin, "Evreiskii vopros vo vnutrennei politike Rossii v 1915 godu," *Vestnik evreiskogo universiteta v Moskve* 1 (14) (1997): 53.

157. Hamm, "Liberalism and the Jewish Question," 164–65. Ganelin, "Evreiskii vopros vo vnutrennei politike Rossii v 1915 godu," 56–57. On Shulgin's career: Mindlin, *Gosudarstvennye, politicheskie i obshchestvennye deiateli*, 350–55.

158. Hillis, *Children of Rus'*, 263.

159. "Predislovie," in *Pravye partii*, 1:20.

160. R. Sh. Ganelin, "Gosudarstvennaia duma i antisemitskie tsirkuliary 1915–1916 gg.," *Vestnik evreiskogo universiteta v Moskve* 3 (10) (1995): 6–7.

161. Ibid., 10–13, 20–21.

162. Ibid., 13. His speeches republished: G. G. Zamyslovskii, *V bor'be s nenavistnikami Rossii* (Moscow: Institut russkoi tsivilizatsii, 2013). On his career: Mindlin, *Gosudarstvennye, politicheskie i obshchestvennye deiateli*, 140–42.

163. Ganelin, "Gosudarstvennaia duma," 14; A. V. Panfilov, "Shingarev," in *Politicheskie deiateli Rossii 1917: Biograficheskii slovar'*, ed. P. V. Volobuev (Moscow: Bol'shaia rossiiskaia entsiklopediia, 1993), 359–61.

164. Leonid Andreev, "Fakty," *Evreiskaia zhizn'*, 2nd ed., no. 68 (March 11, 1916), cited Ganelin, "Gosudarstvennaia duma," 23. See also Hamm, "Liberalism and the Jewish Question," 170–71.

165. Hamm, "Liberalism and the Jewish Question," 171.

166. Budnitskii, "V. A. Maklakov i 'evreiskii vopros,'" 57–59. On the dangers of including Jewish rights in the liberal agenda, when facing the militantly antisemitic Right, see Hillis, *Children of Rus'*.

167. My translation from V. G. Korolenko, "Dom No. 13," Russian text available online at: http://lib.ru/RUSSLIT/KOROLENKO/r_dom13.txt_with-big-pictures.html (accessed 7/27/18). In Russian: *Dom No. 13-yi (Epizod iz Kishinevskogo pogroma)*, 2nd ed. (London: Tipografiia Bunda, 1903); also London—"House No. 13: An Episode in the Massacre of Kishinieff," *The Contemporary Review* (January 1, 1904): 266–80.

168. "Pis'mo L. N. Tolstogo E. G. Linetskomu ob otnoshenii k sobytiiam 6–8 aprelia 1903 g. v Kishineve" (April 27, 1903), in *Kishinevskii pogrom* (2000), 48–49.

169. "Pis'mo L. N. Tolstogo S. N. Rabinovichu (Sholom-Aleikhemu) o soglasii priniat' uchastie v sbornike, kotoryi predpolagalos' izdat' v pol'zu evreev, postradavshikh ot pogroma" (May 6, 1903), ibid., 70 (note mentions *Hilf: A zaml-bukh fir literatur un kunst* [Warsaw: Folks-bildung, 1903]).

170. Vas. Nemirovich-Danchenko, *O chernykh dniakh: O pogromakh* (Odessa: Ia. Kh. Sherman, 1905), 1–4. The pamphlet, rpt. from *Russkoe slovo*, was passed by the censor, December 12, 1905.

171. Ibid., 7 (*zavoevyvaem*).

172. D. Aizman, "Krovavyi razliv," *Sbornik: Tovarishchestva "Znanie" za 1908 god*, bk. 20 (St. Petersburg: Znanie, 1908), 1–116; Maxim D. Shrayer, "Aizman, David Iakovlevich," *YIVO Encyclopedia of Jews in Eastern Europe*, ed. Gershon David Hundert, 2 vols. (New Haven: Yale University Press, 2008): 1:22–23.

173. M. Gor'kii, "*Mat'* (Prodolzhenie)," *Sbornik: Tovarishchestva "Znanie" za 1908 god*, 321–48.

174. Eric Lohr, *Nationalizing the Russian Empire: The Campaign Against Enemy Aliens During World War I* (Cambridge, MA: Harvard University Press, 2003).

175. Eric Lohr, "Patriotic Violence and the State: The Moscow Riots of May 1915," *Kritika* 4:3 (2003): 607–26.

176. Vadim Belov, *Evrei i poliaki na voine: Vpechatleniia ofitsera uchastnika* (Petrograd: "Biblioteka Velikoi voiny," 1915), 21.

177. Ibid., 78, 79, 82, 84, 85.

178. Ibid., 126–46.

179. Ia. Okunev, "Smert' soldata Branfmana," *Evrei na voine* 11 [1915]: 9–10.

180. Iakov Okunev, *Na peredovykh pozitsiiakh: Boevye vpechatleniia* (Petrograd: M. V. Popov, [1915]), 8–14, 45, 153.

181. F. A. Stepun, "Iz pisem praporshchika-artellerista," *Severnye zapiski* 7–9 (1916), published as a book in Moscow in 1918, with censor's cuts restored; full text reprinted: F. A. Stepun [N. Lugin], *Iz pisem praporshchika-artillerista* (Tomsk: "Vodolei," 2000). On Stepun: V. K. Kantor, "F. A. Stepun: Russkii filosof v epokhu bezumiia Razuma," in F. A. Stepun, *Sochineniia*, ed. V. K. Kantor (Moscow: ROSSPEN, 2000), 3–33; Christian Hufen, *Fedor Stepun: Ein politischer Intellektueller aus Rußland in Europa: Die Jahre 1884–1945* (Berlin: Lukas-Verlag, 2001).

182. Stepun, *Iz pisem praporshchika-artillerista* (2000), 31.

183. Ibid., 75–76.

184. Krol', *Stranitsy*, 354.

185. L. Andreev, "Pervaia stupen'," in *Utro Rossii*; reprinted in *Shchit*, 1-8; Safran, *Wandering Soul*, 237.

186. *Shchit* (see n. 94). See Kel'ner, "Evreiskii vopros." Sologub, who contributed to numerous patriotic publications, also published the sketch, "Vechnyi zhid," in *Evrei na voine* 15 [1915?], 6–7. Lucien Wolf tried to get an English translation of *Shchit* published in England: Levene, *War, Jews, and the New Europe*, 70. An English translation eventually appeared in New York: *The Shield*, trans. Avrahm Yarmolinsky (New York: Knopf, 1917).

187. The phrase "*zhidofil'stvuiushchii kadet*" was applied to Count Ivan Tolstoy: cited Mindlin, *Gosudarstvennye, politicheskie i obshchestvennye deiateli*, 329.

188. Biography in V. I. Fedorchenko, *Imperatorskii Dom: Vydaiushchiesia sanovniki: Entsiklopediia biografii*, 2 vols. (Krasnoiarsk: Bonus; Moscow: Olma-Press, 2000), 2:445–46. Online at: http://necropol.org/tolstoy-ivan.html (accessed 8/26/18). Also: Mindlin, *Gosudarstvennye, politicheskie i obshchestvennye deiateli*, 324–25; L. I. Tolstaia and B. V. Anan'ich, "Graf I. I. Tolstoi i ego dnevnik," in I. I. Tolstoi, *Dnevnik, 1906–1916*, ed. L. I. Tolstaia (St. Petersburg: Evropeiskii dom, 1997), vii–xi.

189. Mindlin, *Gosudarstvennye, politicheskie i obshchestvennye deiateli*, 324–25.

190. Graf I. I. Tolstoi, "Antisemitizm v Rossii," in I. I. Tolstoi and Iulii Gessen, *Fakty i mysli: Evreiskii vopros v Rossii* (St. Petersburg: Obshchestvennaia Pol'za, 1907), 139–220; quote, 141.

191. Ibid., 140.

192. I. I. Tolstoi, *Dnevnik*, 573.

193. Klier, "Gintsburg Family" (2010). Baron Günzburg was among the founders in 1880 of the ORT (Obshchestvo remeslennogo truda), designed to train Jewish workers in useful trades. See Brian Horowitz, *Jewish Philanthropy and Enlightenment in Late-Tsarist Russia* (Seattle: University of Washington Press, 2009).

194. On the problem of antisemitism in neo-Orthodox circles, see Laura Engelstein, "The Old Slavophile Steed: Failed Nationalism and the Philosophers' Jewish Problem," in Laura Engelstein, *Slavophile Empire: Imperial Russia's Illiberal Path* (Ithaca: Cornell University Press, 2009), 192–232.

195. de Courtenay, "Svoeobraznaia 'krugovaia poruka,'" in *Shchit*, 143–46; Jan Niecisław Baudouin de Courtenay, *W "kwestji żydowskiej"* (Warsaw: Skład główny w księgarni G. Centnerszwera i S-ki, 1913); Weeks, *From Assimilation to Antisemitism*, 167.

196. Jerzy Jedlicki, "Resisting the Wave: Intellectuals against Antisemitism in the Last Years of the 'Polish Kingdom,'" in *Antisemitism and its Opponents in Modern Poland*, ed. Robert Blobaum (Ithaca: Cornell University Press, 2005), 76–80.

197. Theodore R. Weeks, "Assimilation, Nationalism, Modernization, Antisemitism: Notes on Polish-Jewish Relations, 1855–1905," ibid., 21.

198. Artsybashev, "Evrei: Rasskaz," in *Shchit*, 15–24.

199. Aleksei N. Tolstoi, "Anna Ziserman: Ocherk," in *Shchit*, 226–34.

200. S. Gusev-Orenburgskii, "Evreichik," in *Shchit*, 70–75.

201. Cited, Pozner, "Bor'ba," 184.

202. American Jewish Joint Distribution Committee Archives: AR 14/18, no. 146, p. 7 (May 1916 report sent from Copenhagen to New York office).

203. Levene, *War, Jews, and the New Europe*, 133–35.

204. Ibid.

205. O. V. Budnitskii, *Rossiiskie evrei mezhdu krasnymi i belymi (1917–1920)* (Moscow: ROSSPEN, 2005); Oleg Budnitskii, *Russian Jews Between the Reds and the Whites, 1917–1920*, trans. Timothy J. Portice (Philadelphia: University of Pennsylvania Press, 2012).

206. See Oleg Budnitskii, "Jews, Pogroms, and the White Movement: A Historiographical Critique," *Kritika: Explorations in Russian and Eurasian History* 2:4 (2001): 751–72; Budnitskii, *Rossiiskie evrei mezhdu krasnymi i belymi*. Also, Engelstein, *Russia in Flames*, pt. 5, ch. 8.

207. Sergei Gusev-Orenburgskii, *Kniga o evreiskikh pogromakh na Ukraine v 1919 g.: Sostavlena po ofitsial'nym dokumentam, dokladam s mest i oprosam postradavshikh*, ed. M. Gor'kii (Petersburg-Berlin: Z. I. Grzhebin, 1921; rpt. Tel Aviv: Aticot Antiquarian Booksellers, 1972).

208. S. I. Gusev-Orenburgskii, *"Bagrovaia kniga": Pogromy 1919–20 g.g. na Ukraine* (Harbin: Dal'nevostochnyi Evreiskii Obshchestvennyi Komitet pomoshchi sirotam-zhertvam pogromov, 1922). See David Wolff, *To the Harbin Station: The Liberal Alternative in Russian Manchuria, 1898–1914* (Stanford: Stanford University Press, 1991).

209. "Predislovie," in *Pravye partii*, 1:35.

210. Quoted from article in *Svobodnaia rech'* (Rostov-on-Don, October 9, 1919), paper close to the Volunteer Army, in Ivan Petrounkewitch, "Nationalism and Anti-Semitism," *Jewish Tribune* 3 (March 1, 1920): 5.

211. "More About the Death of the Tsar," *Jewish Tribune* 5 (April 1, 1920): 8; also S. Poliakoff, "Another Calumny," *Jewish Tribune* 3 (March 1, 1920): 6. On Knox: Levene, *War, Jews, and the New Europe*, 51, 54. For an earlier attempt by Jewish notables in England to refute charges of Jewish responsibility for Bolshevism, see Paul Hanebrink, *A Specter Haunting Europe: The Myth of Judeo-Bolshevism* (Cambridge, MA: Harvard University Press, 2018), 18.

212. "'Po evreiskomu voprosu,' Khar'kovskoe soveshchanie Partii Narodnoi Svobody (3–6 noiabria 1919 g.)," in *S"ezdy i konferentsii konstitutsionno-demokraticheskoi partii*, 3.2:147. Example of blaming the Bolsheviks by a Jewish commentator: D. S. Pasmanik, "The Condition of the Russian Jews Before and After the Revolution," in *Ten Years of Bolshevic Domination: A Compilation of Articles*, ed. Joseph Bikermann (Berlin: Patriotic Union of Russian Jews Abroad, 1928), 153.

213. *Evreiskaia tribuna: Ezhenedel'nik posviashchennyi interesam russkikh evreev*.

214. A similar line was followed by Jewish leaders in Germany and Hungary, faced with the outbreak of revolution in Central Europe, who warned their

own Jewish radicals not to "endanger the whole community." Hanebrink, *A Specter Haunting Europe*, 16.

215. M. M. Vinaver, "Russkaia problema," *Evreiskaia tribuna* 1 (February [*sic*] 27, 1920): 3–4.

216. V. D. Nabokov, "Bol'noi vopros," ibid., 6. Similar point that the violent masses can be manipulated in either direction, by Lenin or Shulgin, appealing to their basest instincts: M. L. Gol'dshtein, "Pogromy," ibid., 6.

217. F. I. Rodichev, "Privet 'Evreiskoi Tribune,'" *Evreiskaia tribuna* 5-6 (February 6, 1920): 1.

218. Nabokov, "Bol'noi vopros," 7.

219. Quoted in English, Elias Heifetz, *The Slaughter of the Jews in the Ukraine in 1919*. Published for the Jewish People's Relief Committee of America (New York: Seltzer, 1921), 113–14. My translation from the original Russian text.

220. Budnitskii, "V. A. Maklakov i 'evreiskii vopros,'" 63.

221. Daniil Samoilovich Pasmanik, *Russkaia revoliutsiia i evreistvo: Bol'she-vizm i iudaizm* (Berlin: Franko-russkaia pechat', 1923), 196.

222. Pasmanik, "The Condition of the Russian Jews Before and After the Revolution," 153.

223. Pasmanik, *Russkaia revoliutsiia i evreistvo*, 196–99.

224. Budnitskii, "V. A. Maklakov i 'evreiskii vopros,'" 64–65.

225. V. A. Maklakov to M. V. Bernatskii (Paris, December 2, 1919), in Budnitskii, ed., "Belye i evrei," 274.

226. Budnitskii, "V. A. Maklakov i 'evreiskii vopros,'" 68.

227. V. A. Maklakov to A. V. Krivoshein (October 29, 1920), in Budnitskii, ed., "Belye i evrei," 284.

228. Quoted, Budnitskii, "V. A. Maklakov i 'evreiskii vopros,'" 73–74.

229. By 1920, having taken refuge in the Crimea, Bulgakov had associated himself with pogromist clergy at odds with General Wrangel's attempts to change the image of the White movement. See Budnitskii, *Russian Jews Between the Reds and the Whites*, 212–15. But see defense of Bulgakov against this charge: A. V. Kartashev, "Antisemitizm i russkaia tserkov'," *Evreiskaia tribuna* 49 (December 3, 1920): 1.

230. The argument of Hillis, *Children of Rus'*.

231. The correspondence was first published in *Evrei i russkaia revoliutsiia*, 374–442. With better commentary in: *Spor o Rossii*.

232. Shul'gin, "O Vinavere," in Shul'gin, "*Chto nam v nikh ne nravitsia*," 359–61, 360 (quote).

233. "V. V. Shul'gin — V. A. Maklakovu" (February 3, 1930), in *Spor o Rossii*, 392.

234. "V. V. Shul'gin — V. A. Maklakovu" (February 12, 1929), ibid., 296–97.

235. "V. V. Shul'gin — V. A. Maklakovu" (December 17, 1929), ibid., 363.

236. Hillis, *Children of Rus'*, 263, 266; *Evrei i russkaia revoliutsiia*, 381 (Shulgin's position on Beilis).

237. V. V. Shul'gin, "Po povodu odnoi stat'i" (attached to letter of February 14, 1925), in *Spor o Rossii*, 237.

238. Shul'gin, "*Chto nam v nikh ne nravitsia*," 102.

239. B. Maklakoff, "Vers la Révolution: La Russie de 1900 à 1917: Le Dénouement," *La Revue de Paris* 31:19 (October 1, 1924): 508–34; 31:22 (November 15, 1924): 274–91; 31:23 (December 1, 1924): 609–31.

240. Maklakoff, "Vers la Révolution" (October 1, 1924), 524.

241. Maklakoff, "Vers la Révolution" (November 15, 1924), 272.

242. Maklakoff, "Vers la Révolution" (December 1, 1924), 609: "*Leur* victoire a asséné au socialisme le coup le plus foudroyant qui pouvait lui être porté."

243. Ibid., 624: "Les bolchéviks ont oublié le marxisme; ils s'imaginaient pouvoir tout obtenir par la force."

244. Shul'gin, "Po povodu odnoi stat'i," 224-45.

245. Ibid., 227.

246. Ibid., 237.

247. Ibid., 228.

248. Ibid., 238.

249. "V. A. Maklakov — V. V. Shul'ginu" (March 5, 1925), in *Spor o Rossii*, 249.

250. Ibid.

251. "V. V. Shul'gin — V. A. Maklakovu" (May 28, 1925), ibid., 252.

252. "V. A. Maklakov — V. V. Shul'ginu" (June 5, 1925), ibid., 253.

253. Ibid., 255.

254. Shul'gin, "*Chto nam v nikh ne nravitsia*." Explaining the motive for the book: Letter from Shulgin to Maklakov (February 1, 1929), in *Spor o Rossii*, 291.

255. Shul'gin, "*Chto nam v nikh ne nravitsia*," 7–8.

256. Ibid., 9–10.

257. "V. A. Maklakov — V. V. Shul'ginu" (December 23, 1929), in *Spor o Rossii*, 373.

258. Ibid., 368.

259. Ibid., 370.

260. Ibid., 371.

261. Ibid.

262. Ibid., 374.

263. Shulamit Volkov, "Antisemitism as a Cultural Code: Reflections on the History and Historiography of Antisemitism in Imperial Germany," *Leo Baeck Institute Yearbook* 23 (1978): 25–46.

264. Ibid., 45.

265. Andrew Sloin, "Speculators, Swindlers and Other Jews: Regulating Trade in Revolutionary White Russia," *East European Jewish Affairs* 40:2 (2010): 103–25. With regard to civil war and post-1921 Soviet initiatives, Sloin notes (112): "In theory, policy targeted speculators abstractly; in practice, the policies targeted Jews discursively and concretely."

2. "That Scoundrel Petlyura": The 1927 Schwarzbard Trial

1. The assassination occurred on May 25, 1926, the trial October 18–26, 1927. Moses Waldmann, "Die Pogrome vor Gericht" (Paris, October 18, 1927), *Jüdische Rundschau* 83/84 (October 21, 1927): 587 [first page]. The contrast with Dreyfus and Beilis was noted at the time: L. Motzkin, Chairman of the Comité

des Délégations Juives, "Our Attitude Toward the Schwarzbard Trial," *Di idishe shtime* (Yiddish organ of Lithuanian Jews), (Kaunas, October 28, 1927), in *The Assassination of Symon Petliura and the Trial of Scholem Schwarzbard 1926–1927: A Selection of Documents*, ed. David Engel (Göttingen: Vandenhoeck & Ruprecht, 2016), 417. Henceforth, *Assassination*.

2. S. M. Dubnov, *Kniga zhizni: Materialy dlia istorii moego vremeni: Vospominaniia i razmyshleniia*, ed. V. E. Kel'ner (Moscow: Mosty kul'tury; Jerusalem: Gesharim, 2004), 284.

3. Sometimes translated as Ukrainian People's Republic.

4. "Voilà pour les pogromes! . . . Voilà pour les massacres!" Cited, "L'Assassinat de l'ataman Petlioura," *Revue des Grands Procès Contemporains* 35 (1929): 290.

5. Biography: Guide to the Papers of Shalom Schwarzbard, YIVO Institute for Jewish Research: http://findingaids.cjh.org//ShalomSchwarzbard.html (accessed 11/28/18). Documents from the trial are now available in digitized form on the YIVO website: The Edward Blank YIVO Vilna Online Collections, RG 80: Mizrakh Yidisher Historisher Arkhiv RG 80: Elias Tcherikower Archive, Series II: Trial of Sholom Schwarzbard: https://vilnacollections.yivo.org/?ca=/item.php~id=rg-80-s2%7C%7Ccol=v (accessed 6/10/19).

6. On courts, see Engel, "Introduction," in *Assassination*, 13.

7. Ibid., 12.

8. Jacques Biélinky, "Le Triomphe de la justice," *L'Avenir illustré* (November 4?, 1927): 4 (667). Clipping in Jacques Biélinky files, YIVO, RG 239, Box 2.

9. "Paris Jury Acquits Slayer of Petlura. Crowded Court Receives the Verdict with Cheers for France. Trial Disclosed Pogroms. Atrocities on Ukrainian Jews Were Dramatically Pictured by Defendant's Counsel," *New York Times* (October 27, 1927), 1, 6.

10. *Der Prozeß Talaat Pascha: Stenographischer Bericht über die Verhandlung gegen den des Mordes an Talaat Pascha angeklagten armen Studenten Salomon Teilirian vor dem Schwurgericht des Landgerichts III zu Berlin, Aktenzeichen: C. J. 22/21 am 2. u. 3. Juni 1921*, ed. Armin T. Wegner (Berlin: Deutsche Verlagsgesellschaft f. Politik u. Geschichte, 1921); translated as: *Genotsid Armian pered sudom: Sudebnyi protsess Talaat Pashi: Stenograficheskii otchet*, ed. Stepan Smbatovich Stepanin, trans. Zorik G. Nazikian (Moscow: Feniks, 1992); Frédéric Magler, "Le Procès Talaat Pacha," *Revue des études arméniennes* 2:1 (1922): 139–45; Marian M. MacCurdy, *Sacred Justice: The Voices and Legacy of the Armenian Operation Nemesis* (New Brunswick, NJ: Transaction Publishers, 2015); Jacques Derogy, *Resistance and Revenge: The Armenian Assassination of Turkish Leaders Responsible for the 1915 Massacres and Deportations*, pref. Gérard Chaliand (New Brunswick, NJ: Transaction Publishers, 2016).

11. "L'Assassinat de l'ataman Petlioura," 290.

12. For a different interpretation of the trial, see Anna Schur, "Shades of Justice," *Law and Literature* 19:1 (2007): 15–30. Schur argues that the universal terms of Schwarzbard's defense, which emphasized his Frenchness, deflected attention from the record of specifically Jewish suffering presented at the trial and obscured both Schwarzbard's sense of his own Jewishness and the Jewish

character of the harm he was avenging. In this connection, she cites Hannah Arendt, who uses the Schwarzbard trial to comment on the relationship between universal and particularist harms and the forms of retribution they require: Hannah Arendt, *Eichmann in Jerusalem: A Report on the Banality of Evil*, rev. ed. (New York: Penguin Books, 1964), 265–67.

13. Alexandre Choulguine, *L'Ukraine et le cauchemar rouge: Les massacres en Ukraine* (Paris: Éditions Jules Tallandier, 1927); rpt. as Oleksander Shul'hyn, *Ukraïna i chervonyi zhakh: Pohromy v Ukraïny* (Kiev: Vyd-vo imeni Oleny Telihy, 2001).

14. "V. V. Shul'gin — V. A. Maklakovu" (February 12, 1929), in *Spor o Rossii: V. A. Maklakov-V. V. Shul'gin, perepiska 1919–1939*, ed. O. V. Budnitskii (Moscow: ROSSPEN, 2012), 296–98.

15. V. V. Shul'gin, *"Chto nam v nikh ne nravitsia . . ." Ob antisemitizme v Rossii* (Paris: Russia minor, 1929; rpt. Moscow: Russkaia kniga, 1994).

16. Quoted, "L'Assassinat de l'ataman Petlioura," 290.

17. Choulguine, *L'Ukraine et le cauchemar rouge*, 19.

18. Mark von Hagen, "1917: The Empire's Diverging Revolutions," The Russia File: A Blog of the Kennan Institute (November 7, 2017), 2, online at https://www.wilsoncenter.org/blog-post/1917-the-empires-diverging-revolutions (accessed 12/31/18). On Jewish communal autonomy, see also Henry Abramson, "Jewish Representation in the Independent Ukrainian Governments of 1917–1920," *Slavic Review* 50:3 (1991): 544–45.

19. Paul Hanebrink, *A Specter Haunting Europe: The Myth of Judeo-Bolshevism* (Cambridge, MA: Harvard University Press, 2018), 26–31.

20. *The Jewish Pogroms in Ukraine: Authoritative Statements on the Question of Responsibility for Recent Outbreaks Against the Jews in Ukraine* (Washington, DC: Friends of Ukraine, 1919), 17–20. The Jews were the lawyer Arnold Margolin, the historian Mark Vishnitzer (Wischnitzer), and Israel Zangwill (1864–1926), a British Zionist.

21. On Wischnitzer's membership in the Historical-Ethnographic Commission, see Christoph Gassenschmidt, *Jewish Liberal Politics in Tsarist Russia, 1900–1914* (New York: New York University Press, 1995), 7. Obituary in the Jewish Telegraph Agency, October 18, 1955, online at: http://www.jta.org/1955/10/18/archive/dr-mark-wischnitzer-jewish-historian-dies-was-73 (accessed 11/28/18).

22. "Aeusserungen von Dr. Mark Wischnitzer," in *Die Lage der Juden in der Ukraine: Eine Dokumentensammlung*, ed. Volodymyr Levyts'kyi and Gustav Specht (Berlin: Ukrainischer Pressedienst, 1920), 68.

23. "Einleitung," ibid., 3.

24. "The Bloodthirsty Hetman," *Jewish Tribune* 8 (May 15, 1920): 3–4 (signed Y.).

25. Mykola Soroka, *Faces of Displacement: The Writings of Volodymyr Vynnychenko* (Montreal & Kingston: McGill-Queen's University Press, 2012).

26. Matthias Vetter, *Antisemiten und Bolschewiki: Zum Verhältnis von Sowjetsystem und Judenfeindschaft 1917–1939* (Berlin: Metropol, 1995), 31.

27. Abramson, "Jewish Representation," 544–45. On the Law of National-

Personal Autonomy of January 24, 1918, see also Piotr Wróbel, "The Kaddish Years: Anti-Jewish Violence in East-Central Europe, 1918–1921," *Jahrbuch des Simon-Dubnow-Instituts* 4 (2005): 216.

28. Henry Abramson, *A Prayer for the Government: Ukrainians and Jews in Revolutionary Times, 1917–1920* (Cambridge, MA: Ukrainian Research Institute and Center for Jewish Studies, Harvard University, 1999), 80–81, 89–90. The concept of "national-personal autonomism" applied to the ethnic communities of multiethnic states, granted control over their own corporate affairs, in cultural, administrative, and economic terms. See Jonathan Frankel, "Dilemmas of Jewish National Autonomism: The Case of Ukraine, 1917–1920," in *Ukrainian-Jewish Relations in Historical Perspective*, ed. Peter J. Potichnyj and Howard Aster (Edmonton: Canadian Institute of Ukrainian Studies, University of Alberta, 1988), 263–65. Frankel explains the failure of minority rights as a result of the collapse of the potential for constitutional democracy offered early in the revolution, both in Russia and Ukraine, where it persisted into early 1918, upon which the model depended. The attitudes of Jewish leaders toward the Ukrainian national project varied according to their ideological commitments and evolved in response to unfolding events (including levels of anti-Jewish violence) and the fortunes of the Ukrainian leadership.

29. Victoria Khiterer, "Arnold Davidovich Margolin: Ukrainian-Jewish Jurist, Statesman and Diplomat," *Revolutionary Russia* 18:2 (2005): 152.

30. Abramson, *Prayer*, 100–101; Abramson, "Jewish Representation," 546; Vetter, *Antisemiten*, 32; Wróbel, "Kaddish Years," 217–18.

31. V. F. Soldatenko, *Grazhdanskaia voina v Ukraine, 1917–1920 gg.* (Moscow: Novyi khronograf, 2012), 286.

32. Ibid., 288.

33. Christopher Gilley, "Beyond Petliura: The Ukrainian National Movement and the 1919 Pogroms," *East European Jewish Affairs* 47:1 (2017): 53–54. Gilley cites Serhii Iekel'chyk [Serhy Yekelchyk], "Trahichna storinka Ukraïns'koï revoliutsiï: Symon Petliura ta ievreis'ki pohromy v Ukraïny (1917–1920)," in *Symon Petliura ta ukraïns'ka natsional'na revoliutsiia*, ed. Vasyl Mykhal'chuk (Kiev: Rada, 1995), 165–217. Yekelchyk focuses on the UNR's anti-pogrom proclamations and the mechanisms established for punishing culprits, but Gilley notes that he offers no evidence of successful prosecutions. In more recent publications, Yekelchyk takes the position that Petlyura personally was not antisemitic and his government had enlightened policies on the Jews, but he was unable to control the behavior of "freebooters" or "maurauding bands," sometimes acting in his name: Serhy Yekelchyk, *Ukraine: Birth of a Modern Nation* (New York: Oxford University Press, 2007), 81. See also Serhy Yekelchyk, "Bands of Nation Builders? Insurgency and Ideology in the Ukrainian Civil War," in *War in Peace: Paramilitary Violence after the Great War*, ed. Robert Gerwarth and John Horne (Oxford: Oxford University Press, 2012), 120.

34. Quoted, Gilley, "Beyond Petliura," 53.

35. Jonathan D. Smele, *Historical Dictionary of the Russian Civil Wars, 1916–1926*, 2 vols. (Lanham, MD: Rowman & Littlefield, 2015), 2:857–59; Michael Palij, *The Ukrainian-Polish Defensive Alliance, 1919–1921: An Aspect*

of the Ukrainian Revolution (Edmonton/Toronto: Canadian Institute of Ukrainian Studies Press, 1995), 184–85; Vic Satzewich, *The Ukrainian Diaspora* (London: Routledge, 2002), 62.

36. L. B. Miliakova, "Vvedenie," in *Kniga pogromov: Pogromy na Ukraine, v Belorussii i evropeiskoi chasti Rossii v period Grazhdanskoi voiny 1918–1922 gg.: Sbornik dokumentov*, ed. L. B. Miliakova (Moscow: ROSSPEN, 2007), xviii.

37. Joshua M. Karlip, "Between Martyrology and Historiography: Elias Tcherikower and the Making of a Pogrom Historian," *East European Jewish Affairs* 38:3 (2008): 264–65; Joshua M. Karlip, *The Tragedy of a Generation: The Rise and Fall of Jewish Nationalism in Eastern Europe* (Cambridge, MA: Harvard University Press, 2013), 165; Kenneth B. Moss, "Tsherikover, Elye" (2010), YIVO Encyclopedia of Jews in Eastern Europe, online at: http://www.yivoencyclopedia.org/article.aspx/tsherikover_elye (accessed 11/28/18).

38. Lidia Miliakova and Irina Ziuzina, "Le travail d'enquête des organisations juives sur les pogroms d'Ukraine, de Biélorussie et de Russie soviétique pendant la guerre civile (1918–1922)," *Le Mouvement social* 222 (2008): 66.

39. David Engel, "Being Lawful in a Lawless World: The Trial of Scholem Schwarzbard and the Defense of East European Jews," *Simon Dubnow Institute Yearbook* 5 (2006): 86-87; N. Gergel, "The Pogroms in the Ukraine in 1918–21" (article originally published 1928), *YIVO Annual of Jewish Social Science* 4 (1951): 237; Karlip, *The Tragedy of a Generation*, 167.

40. Karlip, "Between Martyrology and Historiography," 265–66; I. M. Cherikover, *Antisemitizm un pogromen in Ukraine, 1917–1918: Tsu der geshikhte fun ukrainish-yidishe batsiungen* (Berlin: Mizrekh-Yidishn historishn arkhiv, 1923). See also Lisa Moses Leff, *The Archive Thief: The Man Who Salvaged French Jewish History in the Wake of the Holocaust* (Oxford: Oxford University Press, 2015), 39.

41. I. M. Cherikover, *Di ukrainer pogromen in yor 1919* (New York: Yidisher Visnshaftlekher Institut, 1965).

42. Listed in Gergel, "The Pogroms in the Ukraine in 1918–21," 237, n. 2.

43. Miliakova and Ziuzina, "Le travail d'enquête," 67.

44. Mark Wischnitzer, *To Dwell in Safety: The Story of Jewish Migration since 1800* (Philadelphia: Jewish Publication Society of America, 1948), 99–106.

45. Frank Nesemann, "Minderheitendiplomatie—Leo Motzkin zwischen Imperien und Nationen," in *Synchrone Welten: Zeitenräume jüdischer Geschichte*, ed. Dan Diner (Göttingen: Vandenhoeck & Ruprecht, 2005), 150–51. Délegations juives formed March 25, 1919: Engel, "Introduction," 62.

46. Engel, "Introduction," 62. See Oscar I. Janowsky, *The Jews and Minority Rights, 1898–1919* (New York: Columbia University Press, 1933), 309–11; "Jewish Organisations and the League of Nations," *Jewish Tribune* 24 (January 15, 1921): 6–7.

47. Janowsky, *Jews and Minority Rights*, 311. As in the case of Hungary: Hanebrink, *A Specter Haunting Europe*, 50–51, 73.

48. Quoted, Engel, "Being Lawful in a Lawless World," 86; Document 71: Comité des Délégations Juives, Paris, November 1927, German report, in *Assassination*, 427.

49. *Les Pogromes en Ukraine sous les gouvernements ukrainiens (1917–1920): Aperçu historique et documents* (Paris: Comité des Délégations Juives, 1927) [in English as: *The Pogroms in the Ukraine under the Ukrainian Governments (1917–1920): Historical Survey with Documents and Photographs* (London: J. Bale & Danielsson, 1927), identical, but lacking final chapter on responsibility]. Compare to: *Documents sur les pogromes en Ukraine et l'assassinat de Simon Petlura à Paris (1917–1921–1926)* (Paris: Comité commémoratif Simon Petlura, Librairie du Trident, 1927).

50. Gergel, "The Pogroms in the Ukraine in 1918–21," 238.

51. *Jewish Pogroms in South Russia: Report by the Kieff Pogrom Relief Committee* (London: Central Committee of the Zionist Organisation in Russia, 1920), which focuses on pogroms committed under Petlyura and Denikin.

52. Biography, Miliakova, *Kniga pogromov*, 840. Death notice in I. B. Shekhtman, *Istoriia pogromnogo dvizheniia na Ukraine 1917–1921 gg.*, vol. 2: *Pogromy Dobrovol'cheskoi armii na Ukraine* (Berlin: Ostjüdisches Historisches Archiv, 1932), 6.

53. Miliakova, "Vvedenie," xii, xiii. Also, Abramson, *Prayer*, 110; Gilley, "Beyond Petliura," 46 (accepts Gergel's 60,000 maximum, 40 percent by UNR).

54. Document 49: Lowenthal to Wise, March 25, 1927, typewritten in English, in *Assassination*, 287.

55. On the scope and character of undisciplined violence in the wake of the war, see Jochen Böhler, "Enduring Violence: The Postwar Struggles in East-Central Europe, 1917–21," *Journal of Contemporary History* 50:1 (2015): 58–77; 72 (against Jews).

56. Elias Heifetz, *The Slaughter of the Jews in the Ukraine in 1919*. Published for the Jewish People's Relief Committee of America (New York: Seltzer, 1921), 51–52; Gergel, "The Pogroms in the Ukraine in 1918–21," 240.

57. *Les Pogromes en Ukraine sous les gouvernements ukrainiens* (Comité des Délégations Juives), Appendices, 126; Miliakova, "Vvedenie," xiv; Lars Fischer, "Whither *pogromshchina*—Historiographical Synthesis or Deconstruction?" *East European Jewish Affairs* 38:3 (2008): 305, citing Nahum Gergel, *Di lage fun di Yidn in Rusland* (Warsaw: H. Bzshoza, 1929). See Gergel, "The Pogroms in the Ukraine in 1918–21," 237–52.

58. Document 15: "Doklad upolnomochennogo Otdela pomoshchi pogromlennym pri ROKK [Russian Red Cross] na Ukraine A. I. Gillersona o pogromakh, ustroennykh voinskimi chastiami armii UNR v g. Proskurove i m. Fil'shtin Podol'skoi gub. 15 i 16 fevralia 1919 g." (not before June 1919), in Miliakova, *Kniga pogromov*, 51; Gilley, "Beyond Petliura," 47 (accepts maximum of 1,500 dead).

59. "Ordre à la brigade des cosaques de Zaporojie de l'Armée républicaine d'Ukraine, portant le nom de l'ataman en chef Petlioura. Proskourov, 6 février 1919." Signed Semessenko, YIVO, Tcherikower Archive, File 453, #38195.

60. Different versions of the text: *Les Pogromes en Ukraine sous les gouvernements ukrainiens* (Comité des Délégations Juives), 52; Abramson, *Prayer*, 122, 187; Heifetz, *Slaughter*, 42–43.

61. Gilley, "Beyond Petliura," 54–55.

62. M. A. Krol', *Stranitsy moei zhizni*, ed. N. A. Zhukovskaia (Moscow: Mosty kul'tury; Jerusalem: Gesharim, 2008), 349.

63. V. M. Khiterer, "Arnol'd Davidovich Margolin—zashchitnik Beilisa," in *Sprava Beilisa: Pohliad iz s'ohodennia*, ed. I. F. Kuras (Kiev: Instytut natsional'nykh vidnosyn i politolohii NAN Ukraïny, 1994), 63–66; Alexander B. [*sic*] Tager, *The Decay of Czarism: The Beiliss Trial*, trans. from Russian (Philadelphia: Jewish Publication Society of America, 1935), 242–43. Also: Faith Hillis, *Children of Rus': Right-Bank Ukraine and the Invention of a Russian Nation* (Ithaca: Cornell University Press, 2013), 251–52.

64. Khiterer, "Arnold Davidovich Margolin" (2005), 146–47.

65. Text of letter from Margolin to Ukrainian minister of foreign affairs: A. D. Margolin, *The Jews of Eastern Europe* (New York: T. Seltzer, 1926), 143; Khiterer, "Arnold Davidovich Margolin" (2005), 145–67; Arnol'd Davidovich Margolin, *Ukraina i politika Antanty: Zapiski evreia i grazhdanina* (Berlin: S. Efron, 1921), 125–32.

66. Quoted from the London *Jewish Chronicle*, May 15, 1919, in Heifetz, *Slaughter*, 53. See also "The Jews in the Ukraine: Interview appearing in the 'Jewish Chronicle' of London, England, granted by Dr. Arnold Margolin, Representative of the Ukraine at the Paris Peace Conference," in *The Jewish Pogroms in Ukraine* (Friends of Ukraine, 1919), 17–20. The same interview reprinted in *Die Lage der Juden in der Ukraine*, 65. See also Margolin, *Ukraina i politika Antanty*.

67. "The Jews in the Ukraine: Interview," 17–20.

68. Margolin, *Ukraina i politika Antanty*.

69. Margolin, *The Jews of Eastern Europe*, 139.

70. Ibid.

71. Ibid., 141.

72. Quotes: Gilley, "Beyond Petliura," 48; and 49–50, on use of anti-Jewish stereotypes contributing to the outbreak of pogroms, despite official UNR proclamations.

73. Quoted, Margolin, *Ukraina i politika Antanty*, 270.

74. Quoted, ibid., 270–71. Full text in French translation, in "Appel du Directoire sur les pogromes" (Annexe no. 20), *Les Pogromes en Ukraine sous les gouvernements ukrainiens* (Comité des Délégations Juives), 36–37.

75. Abramson, *Prayer*, 144–46; Margolin, *Ukraina i politika Antanty*, 271. The objection was raised at the trial in the testimony by [M. L.] Goldstein, in Henry Torrès, *Le procès des pogromes: Plaidoirie, suivie des témoignages des Mmes la comtesse de Noailles et Séverine, MM. A. Aulard, Pierre Bonardi et al.* (Paris: Éditions de France, 1928), 95–98.

76. Wróbel, "Kaddish Years," 217.

77. Quoted, Abramson, *Prayer*, 132.

78. Abramson, "Jewish Representation," 549.

79. Quoted, Margolin, *Ukraina i politika Antanty*, 272.

80. Bureau ukrainien de presse. Bulletin d'informations, no. 20 (May 19, 1919), YIVO, Tcherikower Archive, File 452, #38123.

81. "Zakon Direktorii UNR o sozdanii Osoboi Sledstvennoi Komissii dlia

rassledovaniia evreiskikh pogromov" (May 27, 1919), in Symon Vasyl'ovych Petliura, *Glavnyi ataman: V plenu nesbytochnykh nadezhd*, ed. Miroslav Popovich and Viktor Mironenko, trans. from Ukrainian G. Lesnaia (Moscow: Letnii sad, 2008), 240–43.

82. Margolin, *Ukraina i politika Antanty*, 273–74; "Biulleten' Ministerstva informatsii UNR o telegramme S. Petliury o reshitel'noi bor'be s bol'shevistskimi provokatorami evreiskikh pogromov" (July 1919), in Petliura, *Glavnyi ataman*, 244–45.

83. Decree of August 18, 1919: Margolin, *Ukraina i politika Antanty*, 274–75; also in *Die Lage der Juden in der Ukraine*, 35–36.

84. Margolin, *Ukraina i politika Antanty*, 274. Full text in French translation: "La première proclamation de Petlioura contre les pogromes: Ordre du jour du Commandant suprême des troupes de la République populaire ukrainienne, no. 131 (26 Août 1919)," in *Les Pogromes en Ukraine sous les gouvernements ukrainiens* (Comité des Délégations Juives), 75–76. The editors note that this decree was issued eight months after the start of the pogrom wave. Full text in Russian translation: "Prikaz glavnogo komandovaniia voisk UNR" (August 26, 1919), in Petliura, *Glavnyi ataman*, 245–47. English wording: "Soldiers of the Ukrainian People's Republic Ordered to Respect and Protect the Jews: Daily Order by the Supreme Commander [Petlura] to the Troops of the Ukrainian People's Republic" (August 26, 1919), in *The Jewish Pogroms in Ukraine* (Friends of Ukraine, 1919), 15–16. See also Heifetz, *Slaughter*, 54–55.

85. "Prikaz glavnogo komandovaniia voisk UNR" (August 26, 1919), 245–46.

86. Ibid., 245 (brave army).

87. Ibid., 246.

88. Ibid.

89. Ibid., 247.

90. Satzewich, *Ukrainian Diaspora*, 63.

91. "Pis'mo Predsedatelia Direktorii UNR S. Petliury Ministru po evreiskim delam P. Krasnomu s pros'boi dat' ras"iasneniia zarubezhnym evreiskim krugam otnositel'no situatsii s pogromami na Ukraine" (December 29, 1920), in Petliura, *Glavnyi ataman*, 304–5.

92. "Obrashchenie S. Petliury k naseleniiu Ukrainy otnositel'no nedopushcheniia evreiskikh pogromov" (March 18, 1921. n.p.), ibid., 314–16.

93. "Pis'mo S. Petliury Ministru evreiskikh del UNR otnositel'no antiukrainskoi pozitsii evreiskikh deiatelei v Parizhe" (December 21, 1921), ibid., 318–19.

94. YIVO, Tcherikower Archive, File 395, #34986: "Das Wüten der Petljura-Banden in Ostgalizien." This quotes the report from the *Weiner Morgenzeitung* (November 7, 1920).

95. "Die Juden flüchten vor Petljura," *Wiener Morgenzeitung* 644 (November 9, 1920): 1. General Mykhailo Omelianovych-Pavlenko (Tblisi, 1878–1952, Paris), supreme commander of the Ukrainian Galician Army and the Army of the Ukrainian National Republic; defense minister in government in exile.

96. B. Mirsky, "The Petlioura régime," *Jewish Tribune* 8 (May 15, 1920): 3.

An expert in international law, born in Kiev, educated in St. Petersburg, Mirsky emigrated to Paris after the revolution.

97. YIVO, Tcherikower Archive, File 395, #34999: "Die Pogrome in Ostgalizien": Jüdische Presszentrale Zürich, 24 September [*sic*] 1920, no. 111.

98. "Pogrome ohne Ende," *Jüdische Rundschau* 67-68 (October 1, 1920): 517. It's not clear which pronouncement they had in mind.

99. Michael Stanislawski, "Jabotinsky, Vladimir" (2010), YIVO Encyclopedia of Jews in Eastern Europe, online at: http://www.yivoencyclopedia.org/article.aspx/Jabotinsky_Vladimir (accessed 6/17/18). YIVO, Tcherikower Archive, File 451, #38095: "Convention du 4 septembre 1921 conclue entre M. Slavinsky et Jabotinsky," signed at Karlsbad; and ibid., #38096; "Vladimir Zhabotinskii," ibid., File 462, #38674. See also "Telegramma v Evsektsiiu pri TsK RKP(b) o podpisanii dogovora o sotrudnichestve mezhdu sionistom V. Zhabotinskim i predstavitelem pravitel'stva UNR M. Slavinskim" (not before December 6, 1921), in *Evreiskii vopros: Dokumenty 1919–1926 gg.*, ed. V. Iu. Vasil'ev (Vinnitsa: Globus-Press, 2003), 111–12.

100. M. Slavinsky to 12th Zionist Congress, August 30, 1921: YIVO, Tcherikower Archive, File 451, #38097-98 (French typescript). On this episode, see Engel, "Introduction," 37–38; Document 11: "Agreement to create a Jewish gendarmerie in Ukraine, Karlsbad, September 4, 1921," in *Jüdische Rundschau* (December 23, 1921); and Document 12: "Report by Maksym Slavynskyi on negotiations with Vladimir Jabotinsky," Prague, September 16, 1921, in *Jüdische Rundschau* (December 23, 1921), in *Assassination*, 142–46. Also: Joseph B. Schechtman, "The Jabotinsky-Slavinsky Agreement: A Chapter in Ukrainian-Jewish Relations," *Jewish Social Studies* 17 (1955): 289–306.

101. Interview reported in "Du Bulletin d'informations *Pour la Russie*," *L'Univers israélite: Journal des Principes Conservateurs du Judaïsme* 76:15 (Paris, December 17, 1920): 352: online at: https://gallica.bnf.fr/ark:/12148/bpt6k6244618s/f16.image (accessed 6/11/19).

102. Soldatenko, *Grazhdanskaia voina*, 286.

103. Choulguine, *L'Ukraine et le cauchemar rouge*, 103.

104. "Vidnyi galitsko-evreiskii deiatel' o Petliure i o dele Shvartsbarda" (n.d.): Letter from Dr. Israel Val'dman, responding to Louis Marshall (n.d., Russian typescript with handwritten edits), YIVO, Tcherikower Archive, File 453, #38198.

105. V. Jabotinsky, "La Colonisation en Crimée," *Jewish Morning Journal* (June 4, 1926), trans. from Yiddish by court-appointed translator, text in *Documents sur les Pogromes* (Comité commémoratif Simon Petlura, 1927), 268–89.

106. Praise for Jabotinsky concludes the argument in Choulguine, *L'Ukraine et le cauchemar rouge*, 137.

107. Oleksander Shul'gin [*sic*], "Odpovid' Zhabotins'komu," *Tryzub* 41 (99) (October 16, 1927): 15–16.

108. Choulguine, *L'Ukraine et le cauchemar rouge*, 55.

109. Ibid., 58.

110. Ibid., 40–41 (his italics).

111. Ibid., 76–77.

112. Ibid., 94–95.

113. Ukrainian Social Democratic Party, "K ukrainskim rabochim i krest'ianam" [in Russian], YIVO, Tcherikower Archive, File 413, #35805. In another formulation, the Ukrainian SDs blamed both the Communists and the counterrevolution for "using the pogroms for political purposes": "Resolution des Zentralkomittees," from Appendix no. 37, "Memorandum der Ukrainischen Sozialdemokratischen Arbeiterpartei an die Minderheitskommission der sozialistischen Arbeiter-Internationale in Brüssel," Die Ausslandsdelegation der Ukrainischen Sozialdemokratischen Arbeiterpartei (Prague, February 10, 1927), YIVO, Tcherikower Archive, File 414, #35980. Charge that the Communists were behind Schwarzbard's act: testimony of Mykola Chapoval, former Ukrainian general, to Peyre, juge d'instruction, July 20, 1926: YIVO, Tcherikower Archive, File 451, #38067.

114. Front-page editorial: *Tryzub* 41 (99) (October 16, 1927): 1.

115. Quoted, "L'Assassinat de l'ataman Petlioura," 290.

116. Quoted, ibid., 295.

117. Quoted, ibid., 292–93.

118. Albert Willm, "Assemblée nationale": Assemblée nationale website, online at: http://www.assemblee-nationale.fr/sycomore/fiche.asp?num_dept=7423 (accessed 11/29/18).

119. Quoted, "L'Assassinat de l'ataman Petlioura," 293.

120. Quoted, ibid., 295.

121. "Der Freispruch Schwarzbarts" (editorial), *Jüdische Rundschau* 86 (October 28, 1927), front page [p. 603].

122. "Vid Uriadu Ukraïns'koï Narodn'oï Respubliky" (From the Government of the Ukrainian National Republic), signed Viacheslav Prokopovych, chair council of ministers, and Volodymyr Sal's'kyi, minister of the army (October 30, 1927), *Tryzub* 42 (100) (November 13, 1927): 1; O. Lotots'kyi, "Spravzhni pruzhyny," ibid., 11.

123. Jury member quoted after the trial, in Biélinky, "Le Triomphe de la justice": "on accusait Schwartzbard d'avoir des complices,—pas de preuves; d'être agent de Moscou,—pas de preuves non plus." The idea that Moscow inspired Schwarzbard's act persists, however, even in scholarly contexts; see Patricia Kennedy Grimsted, "The Odyssey of the Petliura Library and the Records of the Ukrainian National Republic during World War II," *Harvard Ukrainian Studies* 22 (1998): 184, online at: http://www.archives.gov.ua/Eng/Odyssey.php (State Archival Service of Ukraine, accessed 1/5/19).

124. Gilley, "Beyond Petliura," 56: "The pogroms were not a government-steered campaign of ethnic cleansing, but they were a product of anti-Jewish stereotypes apparently held by many members of the Ukrainian national movement. The fixation on Petlyura has, ironically, shifted the focus away from the culpability of the nationally conscious Ukrainians who did perpetrate pogroms."

125. Ibid.

126. Quotes, ibid., 56.

127. Choulguine, *L'Ukraine et le cauchemar rouge*, 103–4.

128. Ibid., 69.

129. Document 44: Leo Motzkin, Paris, to Louis Marshall, New York (January 30, 1927), in *Assassination*, 272.

130. U.S. Secretary of State Robert Lansing tells the American Jewish Congress in 1920: "Until there is a change in the political situation in the Ukraine, we are almost hopeless." Quoted, Engel, "Introduction," 76. See also Hanebrink, *A Specter Haunting Europe*, 77.

131. "Préface," in *Les Pogromes en Ukraine sous les gouvernements ukrainiens* (Comité des Délégations Juives), 8.

132. Document 35: Schwarzbard Defense Committee (Paris, September 13, 1926), in *Assassination*, 227–28. Margolin urging the press to modify its tone: Document 40: Executive Committee, American Jewish Congress, New York (October 17, 1926), ibid., 252; Document 41: Arnold Margolin to Executive Committee, American Jewish Committee, New York (October 17, 1926), ibid., 253, 263–64.

133. Document 20: Menachem Ribalow, New York (June 4, 1926), editorial, *Ha-Doar*, ibid., 170.

134. Document 25: Abraham Liessin, editorial in *Di tsukunft* (July 1926), ibid., 194.

135. On the dangers, from the Jewish point of view, of thinking of the Jews as a nation, see Document 43: Marvin Lowenthal, Paris, to Stephen S. Wise, New York (November 30, 1926), ibid., 270.

136. For both arguments, see Document 22: Moshe Beilinson, Tel Aviv (June 8, 1926), in the Palestine Hebrew newspaper, *Davar*, ibid., 182.

137. Document 43: Marvin Lowenthal, Paris, to Stephen S. Wise, New York (November 30, 1926), ibid., 270.

138. Document 27: Arnold Margolin to Leo Motzkin, New York (July 12, 1926), ibid., 208–9. See also Document 41: Arnold Margolin to Executive Committee, American Jewish Committee, New York (October 17, 1926), ibid., 253–64.

139. Quoted, Engel, "Introduction," 85, from Document 28: Leo Motzkin, Paris, to Arnold Margolin, New York (July 17, 1926), in *Assassination*, 211 (slightly different wording).

140. Document 28: Leo Motzkin, Paris, to Arnold Margolin, New York (July 17, 1926), in *Assassination*, 211.

141. Quoted, Engel, "Introduction," in *Assassination*, 83.

142. Quoted, ibid., 84, statement of Comité about strategy for the trial, from Document 60: Schwarzbard Defense Committee, Paris (October 1927), 336–41.

143. Cited, Engel, "Introduction," 81, from *American Jewish Yearbook* 29 (1927–1928), 427. As Motzkin put it, Marshall wanted "to cordon the Jewish people off from the deed": Document 68: Leo Motzkin, Kaunas (October 28, 1927), "Our Attitude Toward the Schwarzbard Trial," *Di idishe shtime*, in *Assassination*, 417.

144. Document 67: Louis Marshall to Peter Wiernik, New York (October 29, 1927), in *Assassination*, 411.

145. Document 66: Peter Wiernik to Louis Marshall, New York (October 27, 1927), ibid., 409–10. On opposition to Marshall's position, see Document 75: Joseph Barondess to Stephen S. Wise, New York (November 9, 1927), ibid., 440.

146. Document 68: Leo Motzkin, Kaunas (October 28, 1927), "Our Attitude Toward the Schwarzbard Trial," ibid., 420.

147. Document 15: Mykyta Shapoval to Mykola Shapoval, Prague (May 27–28, 1926), ibid., 156.

148. Document 69: Cabinet of the UNR, Paris (October 30, 1927), *Tryzub* 42 (110) (November 13, 1927): 1-2, ibid., 423. On the provocation, see also Document 36: Levko Chykalenko, "Zionists and 'Zionists'" (September 26, 1926), *Tryzub* 2/2:49, 2–6, ibid. 232–33.

149. Document 69, ibid., 424.

150. Document 70: Oleksander Shulhyn to Arnold Margolin, Paris (October 31, 1927), typewritten copy in English prepared by Margolin for circulation to American Jewish Committee, ibid., 425–26.

151. Brendan Francis McGeever, "The Bolshevik Confrontation with Antisemitism in the Russian Revolution, 1917–1919" (Ph.D. Dissertation, University of Glasgow, 2015), 99–110. See Brendan McGeever, *Antisemitism and the Russian Revolution* (Cambridge: Cambridge University Press, 2019).

152. V. L. Genis, "Pervaia Konnaia armiia: Za kulisami slavy," *Voprosy istorii* 12 (1994): 64–77.

153. See Laura Engelstein, *Russia in Flames: War, Revolution, Civil War, 1914–1921* (New York: Oxford University Press, 2018).

154. McGeever, "Bolshevik Confrontation," 150–67. On Grigor'evshchina, see S. I. Gusev-Orenburgskii, *"Bagrovaia kniga": Pogromy 1919–20 g.g. na Ukraine* (Harbin: Dal'nevostochnyi Evreiskii Obshchestvennyi Komitet pomoshchi sirotam-zhertvam pogromov; D. S. Lemberg, 1922), 8–9.

155. See Stephen Velychenko, *State Building in Revolutionary Ukraine: A Comparative Study of Government and Bureaucrats, 1917–22* (Toronto: University of Toronto Press, 2010), 190–93. Velychenko attributes the animosity felt by ordinary Ukrainians toward the Jews to the fact that in 1919 Soviet government offices in Ukraine were disproportionately staffed by Jews, often refugees who had fled south or cadres sent from Moscow. Russian speaking and perceived as alien to the local culture, the commissars were resented by the locals, Velychenko explains, for their arrogance and sense of superiority.

156. Ibid., 189–90; McGeever, "Bolshevik Confrontation," 262–64. In this connection, McGeever cites Zvi Y. Gitelman, *Jewish Nationality and Soviet Politics: The Jewish Sections of the CPSU, 1917–1930* (Princeton: Princeton University Press, 1972).

157. McGeever, "Bolshevik Confrontation," 265, citing Velychenko, *State Building*, 190; Sergei A. Pavliuchenkov, *Voennyi kommunizm v Rossii: Vlast' i massy* (Moscow: RKT-Istoriia, 1997), 261; Jurij Borys, *The Sovietization of Ukraine, 1917–1923: The Communist Doctrine and Practice of National Self-Determination* (Edmonton: Canadian Institute of Ukrainian Studies, 1980),

255. The ninth party conference in September 1920 again explicitly raised the issue of removing Jews: Pavliuchenkov, *Voennyi kommunizm*, 265.

158. "O bor'be s antisemitizmom i evreiskimi pogromami" (April 12, 1918; *Izvestiia* and *Pravda*, July 27, 1918), discussed in McGeever, "Bolshevik Confrontation," 141–42. Translated here from the Russian text online.

159. McGeever, "Bolshevik Confrontation," 186; Richard Pipes, *Russia under the Bolshevik Regime* (New York: Knopf, 1994), 111, mentions it disparagingly.

160. Lenin, "O pogromnoi travle evreev" (gramophone recording, late March 1919; published in *Molodaia gvardiia*, February-March, 1924), V. I. Lenin, *Polnoe sobranie sochinenii*, 5th ed., vol. 38 (Moscow: Politicheskaia literatura, 1969): 242–43. My translation from the Russian text, online at: http://uaio.ru/vil/38.htm (accessed 6/11/19).

161. D. S. Pasmanik, "The Condition of the Russian Jews Before and After the Revolution," in *Ten Years of Bolshevic Domination: A Compilation of Articles*, ed. Joseph Bikermann (Berlin: Patriotic Union of Russian Jews Abroad, 1928), 153–54.

162. McGeever, "Bolshevik Confrontation," 248–49.

163. Statement of May 1919, quoted, ibid., 117 (translation modified from Russian given in text).

164. Quoted, ibid., 118 (translation modified).

165. J[acques] Delesvky, "Bolshevism and Pogroms," *Jewish Tribune* 5 (April 1, 1920): 3.

166. Gusev-Orenburgskii, *"Bagrovaia kniga,"* 16.

167. Oleg Budnitskii, *Russian Jews Between the Reds and the Whites, 1917–1920*, trans. Timothy J. Portice (Philadelphia: University of Pennsylvania Press, 2012), 81; Arkadi Zeltser, "Commissariat for Jewish National Affairs" (2010), YIVO Encyclopedia of Jews in Eastern Europe, online at: http://www.yivoencyclopedia.org/article.aspx/Commissariat_for_Jewish_National_Affairs (accessed 12/1/16). Zvi Gitelman, "Evsektsiia" (2010), ibid., online at: http://www.yivoencyclopedia.org/article.aspx/Evsektsiia (accessed 11/30/16). Jews involved in the early Soviet institutions focused on Jewish concerns were often themselves remote from the Yiddish-speaking world, while Jews close to popular culture and the Yiddish language tended to keep their distance. Semyon (Shimon) Dimanshtein (1886–1938), head of the Evsektsiia, spanned both worlds. See Gitelman, *Jewish Nationality*, 126–27.

168. When the central Evseksiia office moved to Moscow along with the Sovnarkom, it absorbed the Moscow branch, but the Poale Zion activist Zvi (Grigory Samoilovich) Fridland (1897–1937) remained and enlisted Gorky's support in the anti-pogrom campaign. McGeever, "Bolshevik Confrontation," ch. 5.

169. Text of two letters from which these sentences are drawn: "Obrashchenie Komissariata po evreiskim delam g. Moskvy i Moskovskoi oblasti v SNK o merakh po bor'be s pogromami" (April 19, 1918), signed Tsvi Fridliand, in Miliakova, *Kniga pogromov*, 754–55; "Pis'mo zamestitelia komissara po evreiskim delam NKN RSFSR I. G. Dobkovskogo predsedateliu SNK V. I.

Leninu ob obsuzhdenii voprosa bor'by s pogromami" (April 19, 1918), ibid., 755–56. Quoted, McGeever, "Bolshevik Confrontation," 130.

170. Gitelman, *Jewish Nationality*, 139; Frankel, "The Paradoxical Politics of Marginality," 150; Baruch Gurewitz, "Un Cas de communisme national en l'Union soviétique: Le Poale Sion 1918–28," *Cahiers du monde russe et soviétique* 15 (1974): 340.

171. McGeever, "Bolshevik Confrontation," 178–85.

172. Miliakova, "Vvedenie," xiv–xxv.

173. See "Guide to the People's Relief Committee for Jewish War Sufferers Records, 1915–1924," online at: http://findingaids.cjh.org/?pID=365402 (accessed 10/28/18).

174. Komitet pomoshchi postradavshim ot pogromov pri Rossiiskom Obshchestve Krasnogo Kresta. McGeever, "Bolshevik Confrontation," 209–10. On Heifetz, see also Miliakova and Ziuzina, "Le travail d'enquête," 68; Zalmen Reyzen, "Elye Kheyfets (Elias Heifetz)," *Leksikon fun der yidisher literatur*, vol. 1, cols. 1148–49. Yiddish Leksikon, online at: http://yleksikon.blogspot.com/2016/09/elye-kheyfets-elias-heifetz.html (accessed 3/13/18). See also "Ukraina: Evrei Ukrainy 1914–1920 gg.," in Elektronnaia evreiskaia entsiklopediia (1996), online at: http://eleven.co.il/diaspora/regions-and-countries/15410/ (accessed 8/22/18).

175. Heifetz, *Slaughter*, i–iii; Miliakova, "Vvedenie," xxii.

176. Heifetz, *Slaughter*, 91.

177. Ibid., 85.

178. Ibid., 89.

179. Ibid., 90.

180. Ibid., 92. Similar conclusions were drawn by Naum Gergel in his compendium of data about the 1919–1920 pogroms, published in 1929: Gergel', *Di lage fun di Yidn in Rusland*; see Gergel, "The Pogroms in the Ukraine in 1918–21," 246: "detachments of other armies that had gone over to the side of the Soviets. These troops, under the stress of civil war, broke the military discipline and started making pogroms in the same way they had carried on under anti-Soviet leadership."

181. Heifetz, *Slaughter*, 54.

182. Ibid., 81.

183. Gitelman, *Jewish Nationality*, 166.

184. It was the Evsektsiia that organized the collection of data on the pogroms for the Soviet side: Miliakova, "Vvedenie," xiii, xxiii, xxv, xxvii.

185. Vicki Caron, "The Path to Vichy: Antisemitism in France in the 1930s" (J. B. and Maurice C. Shapiro Annual Lecture, April 20, 2005, United States Holocaust Memorial Museum Center for Advanced Holocaust Studies, Washington, DC), 3–8; 8 (quote), online at: https://www.ushmm.org/m/pdfs/Publication_OP_2005-07-02.pdf (accessed 10/29/18).

186. Ibid., 3.

187. Paula Hyman, *The Jews of Modern France* (Berkeley: University of California Press, 1998), 110. On Torrès's Jewish identity, see the report he addressed

to the "Club de la jeunesse juive" in Paris concerning the trial: *La Tribune Juive: Organe indépendant du judaïsme de l'Est de la France* 6 (November 2, 1927): 88–89. Obituary in Jewish Telegraph Agency, January 6, 1966, online at: http://www.jta.org/1966/01/06/archive/henry-torres-dies-in-france-was-defender-in-historic-jewish-cases (accessed 12/10/18).

188. Engel, "Introduction," 20.

189. Biélinky, "Le Triomphe de la justice."

190. "Une mise au point de Me Campinchi," *L'Avenir illustré* (November 30, 1927), no page. Clipping in Jacques Biélinky files, YIVO, RG 239, Box 2.

191. On Petlyura's shift: Satzewich, *Ukrainian Diaspora*, 62–63; Samuel Schwarzbard, *Mémoires d'un anarchiste juif*, ed. Michel Herman (Paris: Éditions Syllepse, Collection Yiddishland, 2010). The French Communist organ, *L'Humanité* (May 26, 1926), called the assassination an "anarchist provocation": Michael G. Esch, *Parallele Gesellschaften und soziale Räume: Osteuropäische Einwanderer in Paris 1880–1940* (Frankfurt: Campus Verlag, 2012), 428.

192. Torrès, *Le procès des pogromes*, 48.

193. Ibid., 54.

194. Ibid., 58.

195. Bernard Lecache, *Au pays des pogromes: Quant Israël meurt* (Paris: Éditions du "Progrès civique," 1927). He was attacked by the liberal Russian Jewish emigration as an apologist for Soviet Communism: J[acques] Delevsky, "Cain Defends Abel," *Jewish Tribune* 26 (February 15, 1921): 5–6.

196. Torrès, *Le procès des pogromes*, 159.

197. Ibid., 160.

198. Ibid., 163.

199. Jonathan Frankel, "Crisis as a Factor in Modern Jewish Politics, 1840 and 1881–82," in Jonathan Frankel, *Crisis, Revolution, and Russian Jews* (New York: Cambridge University Press, 2009), 26. On being a good Jew and a good Frenchman: Jonathan Frankel, "Jewish Politics and the Press: The 'Reception' of the Alliance Israélite Universelle (1860)," ibid., 37.

200. Quoted Philippe-E. Landau, "Les juifs russes à Paris pendant la Grande Guerre, cibles de l'antisémitisme," *Archives juives* 34:2 (2001): 48.

201. Ibid., 49–50.

202. Ibid., 51.

203. Quoted, ibid., 53 (both quotes). On Durkheim's relationship to his Jewish background: Pierre Birnbaum, "In the Academic Sphere: The Cases of Emile Durkheim and Georg Simmel," in *Jewish Emancipation Reconsidered: The French and German Models*, ed. Michael Brenner, Vicki Caron, and Uri R. Kaufmann (Tübingen: J. C. B. Mohr, 2003), 176–85.

204. Catherine Gousseff, "Les juifs russes en France: Profil et évolution d'une collectivité," *Les Belles lettres: Archives juives* 34:2 (2001): 6; Boris Czerny, "Paroles et silences: L'affaire Schwarzbard et la presse juive parisienne (1926–1927)," ibid., 58.

205. Joseph Roth, *The Wandering Jews*, trans. Michael Hofmann (1927; New York: Norton, 2001), 81, 83.

206. Quoted, Czerny, "Paroles et silences," 58. In 1913 Baron Edmond de Rothschild complained to the Consistory that immigrants "do not understand French customs . . . remain among themselves, retain their primitive language, speak and write in jargon." Quoted, Hyman, *The Jews of Modern France*, 122. See Nancy Green, *The Pletzl of Paris: Jewish Immigrant Workers in the "Belle Epoque"* (New York: Holmes & Meier, 1986).

207. Czerny, "Paroles et silences," 59.

208. Jacques Biélinky, "Les émigrants juifs à Belleville," *L'Univers israélite* 6 (October 15, 1926): 167–70. Cited by Czerny, "Paroles et silences," but here the full text.

209. Renée Poznanski, "Introduction," in Jacques Biélinky, *Journal, 1940–1942: Un journaliste juif à Paris sous l'Occupation*, ed. Renée Poznanski (Paris: Cerf, 1992), 12–14.

210. Quoted, Biélinky, "Les émigrants juifs à Belleville," 167.

211. Quoted, ibid., 168.

212. Quoted, ibid., 169.

213. Jacques Biélinky, "L'Affaire Schwartzbard," *L'Avenir illustré* 10 (December 17, 1926), 3–4 (167–68). Clipping in Jacques Biélinky files, YIVO, RG 239, Box 2.

214. Number mentioned: Biélinky, "Le Triomphe de la justice." On the press in general, Czerny, "Paroles et silences," 61. Military service mentioned: "L'Assassinat de l'ataman Petlioura," 290.

215. Quoted, Biélinky, "Le Triomphe de la justice."

216. "The Holocaust: The French Vichy Regime," Jewish Virtual Library, online at: https://www.jewishvirtuallibrary.org/the-french-vichy-regime#6 (accessed 10/31/18); Renée Poznanski, *Jews in France During World War II* (Hanover, NH: Brandeis University Press/University Press of New England, 2001); Renée Poznanski, "Jews and non-Jews in France during WWII: A Daily Life Perspective," in *Lessons and Legacies V: The Holocaust and Justice*, ed. Ronald Smelser (Evanston: Northwestern University Press, 2002), 295–312; Renée Poznanski, *Propagandes et persécutions: La Résistance et le "problème juif," 1940–1944* (Paris: Fayard, 2008).

3. "How to Convince Them You're Not": The Enigma of Andrzej Bobkowski

1. Another diary protected from retroactive alteration by the Jewish author's death in a Nazi concentration camp is Raymond-Raoul Lambert, *Carnet d'un témoin, 1940–1943*, ed. Richard Cohen (Paris: Fayard, 1985); Raymond-Raoul Lambert, *Diary of a Witness, 1940–1943*, trans. Isabel Best; ed. Richard I. Cohen (Chicago: Ivan R. Dee, 2007).

2. Andrzej Bobkowski [henceforth, AB], *Szkice piórkiem (Francja 1940–1944)*, 2 vols. (Paris: Instytut Literacki, 1957).

3. Günter Grass, *Beim Häuten der Zwiebel* (Munich: Deutscher Taschenbuch Verlag, 2006); Evelyn Barish, *The Double Life of Paul de Man* (New York: Norton, 2014); Daniel Knegt, *Fascism, Liberalism and Europeanism in the Political Thought of Bertrand de Jouvenel and Alfred Fabre-Luce* (Amsterdam: Amsterdam University Press, 2017), 100–103. A Polish example is that of

Leopold Tyrmand (1920–1985), who also altered the text of a diary for publication, in order to recalibrate his earlier political opinions: Leopold Tyrmand, *Dziennik 1954: Wersja oryginalna* (Warsaw: Prószyński i S-ka, 1999).

4. Quoted, Katarzyna Plucińska-Smorawska, *Między historią a literaturą: O* Szkicach piórkiem *Andrzeja Bobkowskiego* (Warsaw: Wydawnictwo Neriton, 2005), 11. Comment addressed to the writer Tadeusz Nowakowski (1917–1996), who remained in emigration after the war, returning to Poland only in 1990.

5. On hopes for family, particularly his mother: AB to Jerzy Giedroyc [henceforth, JG] (March 22, 1947); JG to AB (February 17, 1949); AB to JG (March 2, 1949), in JG, AB, *Listy 1946–1961*, ed. Jan Zieliński (Warsaw: Czytelnik, 1997), 25, 69, 73, respectively.

6. On Czytelnik, see its website: http://www.czytelnik.pl/?ID=podstrona &ID2=o_wydawnictwie (accessed 6/2/16). On the contract: *Jerzy Giedroyc: Kultura, polityka, wiek XX: Debaty i rozprawy*, ed. Andrzej Mencwel, Andrzej Stanisław Kowalczyk, Leszek Szaruga, and Zuzanna Grębecka (Warsaw: Wydawnictwo Uniwersytetu Warszawskiego, 2009), 268–69.

7. Maciej Nowak, *Na łuku elektrycznym: O pisaniu Andrzeja Bobkowskiego* (Warsaw: Biblioteka "Więzi," 2014), 20, 23.

8. Michał Kopczyk, "Wprowadzenie," in Michał Kopczyk, *Refleksja nad kulturą w pisarstwie Andrzeja Bobkowskiego: Arkadia i apokalipsa* (Katowice-Warsaw: "Śląsk" Wyd. Naukowe, 2003), 12. This essay provides a good overview of AB's early reception. For early recognition of AB's talent, see Maciej Nowak, "*Szkice piórkiem* w świetle rękopisu dziennika 1940–1946: Wstępne rozpoznanie," in *Andrzej Bobkowski wielokrotnie: W setną rocznicę urodzin pisarza*, ed. Krzysztof Ćwikliński, Andrzej Stanisław Kowalczyk, and Maciej Urbanowski (Warsaw: Biblioteka "Więzi," 2014), 36.

9. Tadeusz J. Żółciński, "Kosmopolak z Gwatemali," *Więź* 7/8 (1963), cited in Roman Zimand, "Posłowie: Wojna i spokój," in AB, *Szkice piórkiem* (Warsaw: CiS, 2007), 558.

10. Note to Zimand, "Posłowie," 557.

11. AB, *Szkice piórkiem* (London: Kontra, 1985). AB, *En guerre et en paix: Journal, 1940–1944*, trans. Laurence Dyèvre (Montricher: Les Éditions noir sur blanc, 1991). See also *Wehmut? Wonach zum Teufel? Tagebücher aus Frankreich, 1940–1941*, vol. 1, trans. Martin Pollack (Hamburg: ROSPO, 2000).

12. AB, *Szkice piórkiem* (Warsaw: Towarzystwo Opieki nad Archiwum Instytutu Literackiego w Paryżu, Wydawnictwo CiS, 1995, 2003); AB, *Szkice piórkiem* (2007); AB, *Wartime Notebooks, France, 1940–1944*, trans. Grażyna Drabik and Laura Engelstein (New Haven: Yale University Press, 2018). On AB, see Maciej Nowak (in English): https://polska.pl/arts/literature/great -cosmopole/ (accessed 9/4/18); and Polish Radio (in Polish), online at: http:// bobkowski.polskieradio.pl/ (accessed 9/4/18).

13. Cited, Marek Beylin, Łukasz Mikołajewski, Joanna Podolska, Paweł Rodak, Piotr Kieżun, "Andrzej Bobkowski—antynacjonalista, apaństwowiec, antysemita?" *Kultura Liberalna* 205 (December 11, 2012), online at: http:// kulturaliberalna.pl/tag/lukasz-mikolajewski/ (accessed 9/21/18).

14. PIASA Archives: Fonds No. 45: Andrzej Bobkowski Papers. Manuscript

material now online at: http://www.piasa.org/archives/fonds-045.html (accessed 6/11/19).

15. Łukasz Mikołajewski [henceforth, ŁM], "Disenchanted Europeans: Polish Émigré Writers from *Kultura* and the Postwar Reformulations of the West" (Ph.D. Dissertation, European University Institute, Department of History and Civilization, 2012), 285; ŁM, *Disenchanted Europeans: Polish Émigré Writers from* Kultura *and Postwar Reformulations of the West* (Bern: Peter Lang, 2018), 331. Full discussion in: ŁM, "Pamięć fabularyzowana. Powojenne poprawki w *Szkicach piórkiem* Andrzeja Bobkowskiego," in *Buntownik, Cyklista, Kosmopolak: O Andrzeju Bobkowskim i jego twórczości*, ed. Jarosław Klejnoski and Andrzej St. Kowalczyk (Warsaw: Biblioteka "Więzi," 2011), 137–73.

16. Andrzej Horubała, in "Aktualność Bobkowskiego," in *Andrzej Bobkowski wielokrotnie*, 382. In June 2018 Horubała resigned from the conservative website *Do Rzeczy* (To the Point), which he had co-edited, to protest its refusal to publish his response to an antisemitic tweet by the science fiction writer and right-wing journalist Rafał Ziemkiewicz (b. 1964). See https://www.wirtualnemedia.pl/artykul/andrzej-horubala-odchodzi-z-do-rzeczy-pawel-lisicki-zabronil-mi-skrytykowania-rasistowskiego-tweeta-rafala-ziemkiewicza (accessed 9/29/18).

17. Krzysztof Ćwikliński, *Helikopter i kultura masowa: Studia i szkice o pisarstwie Andrzeja Bobkowskiego* (Łomianki: LTW, 2016), 249 (in relation to shortening the manuscript).

18. "Ankieta 'Kultury,'" and K. A. Jeleński, "Od endeków do stalinistów," *Kultura* 9/107 (September 1956): 12–20; "Problem antysemityzmu" (Redakcja), *Kultura* 1/111–2/112 (January-February 1957): 56–79. Konstanty A. Jeleński, "From National Democrats to Stalinists," in *Against Anti-Semitism: An Anthology of Twentieth-Century Polish Writing*, ed. Adam Michnik and Agnieszka Marczyk (New York: Oxford University Press, 2018), 151–61. The context was the antisemitic campaign within the Polish Communist Party. See Jerzy Turowicz, "Anti-Semitism," ibid., 162.

19. Plucińska-Smorawska, *Między*, 11; Stanisław Stabro, "Andrzej Bobkowski —'biografia symboliczna,'" *Ruch Literacki* 4 (1993): 375–89; 381 (quote).

20. Entry of May 8, 1943, in AB, *Szkice piórkiem* (1957), 2:258–59; AB, *Wartime Notebooks*, 443. Her brother, Juliusz Osterwa (1885–1947), co-founded the Reduta theater; see http://www.grotowski.net/en/encyclopedia/reduta (accessed 4/2/19).

21. Letter from AB to Terlecki (February 20, 1958), in AB, *Listy do Tymona Terleckiego: 1956–1961*, ed. Nina Taylor-Terlecka (Warsaw: Biblioteka "Więzi," 2006), 97–98; partially quoted, Plucińska-Smorawska, *Między*, 13.

22. Quoted, Plucińska-Smorawska, *Między*, 23; Zimand, "Posłowie," 554, says Terlecki reports this self-description; see Tymon Terlecki, "Andrzej Bobkowski," *Wiadomości* 32–33 (1962), rpt. as Tymon Terlecki, "Andrzej Bobkowski," in AB, *Listy do Tymona Terleckiego*, 12.

23. Plucińska-Smorawska, *Między*, 10; AB, *Notatnik 1947–1960*, ed. Maciej Nowak (Łomianki: LTW, 2013), 68 (March 1939 departure date).

24. Plucińska-Smorawska, *Między*, 20–21; AB and Zbigniew Koziański,

"Sprawozdanie z działalności Biura Polskiego przy Atelier de construction de Châtillon w czasie okupacji niemieckiej," in JG, AB, *Listy*, 696–97.

25. Plucińska-Smorawska, *Między*, 20–21. Also, ŁM, "Disenchanted Europeans," 248–49; ŁM, *Disenchanted Europeans*, 292. On the status of the workers and Bobkowski's role, see Szymon Konarski, *Cztery lata w okupowanym Paryżu, 14 VI. 1940–25. VIII. 1944* (Paris: Skład główny: "Libella," 1963), 31.

26. ŁM, "Disenchanted Europeans," 289; ŁM, *Disenchanted Europeans*, 337: at first there were two, but in the text reduced only to Wylot.

27. Plucińska-Smorawska, *Między*, 21; Zimand, "Posłowie," 546; Andrzej Chciuk, "O Andrzeju Bobkowskim i jego listach," *Wiadomości* 17:32/33 (854/855) (August 12/19, 1962): 3; AB and Koziański, "Sprawozdanie," 698–99.

28. *Razem Młodzi Przyjaciele* (All Together, Young Friends), produced first in Lyons after 1944, then in Paris from February 1945 to May 1947, sponsored by the Polish YMCA. See ŁM, "Disenchanted Europeans," 213; ŁM, *Disenchanted Europeans*, 251. "Razem, młodzi przyjaciele!" is a line from Adam Mickiewicz, "Oda do młodości" (Ode to Youth, 1820), suppressed by the imperial Russian censor as subversive, ensuring its clandestine popularity.

29. AB, "Sinopis życiorysu," in JG, AB, *Listy*, 695.

30. "Independence and Democracy" (Polski Ruch Wolnościowy "Niepodległość i Demokracja"), which he quit in December 1948: Letter from AB to JG (December 25, 1948), in JG, AB, *Listy*, 52, 57. See "Polski Ruch Wolnościowy 'Niepodległość i Demokracja,'" PWN, Encyklopedia, online at: https://encyklopedia.pwn.pl/haslo/Polski-Ruch-Wolnosciowy-Niepodleglosc-i-Demokracja;3959840.html (accessed 9/4/18).

31. AB, "Sinopis życiorysu," 694.

32. JG, AB, *Listy*, 20 (note).

33. Dariusz Stola, "The Polish Government-in-exile: National Unity and Weakness," in *Governments-in-exile and the Jews during the Second World War*, ed. Jan Láníček and James Jordan (Edgeware, UK; Portland, OR: Vallentine Mitchell, 2013), 93. See "Jerzy Giedroyc," Culture.pl: Artists, online at: http://culture.pl/en/artist/jerzy-giedroyc (accessed 9/21/18).

34. Letter from JG to AB (November 15, 1948), in JG, AB, *Listy*, 46.

35. Włodzimierz Bolecki, "Kultura (1946–2000)," in *The Exile and Return of Writers from East Central Europe: A Compendium*, ed. John Neubauer and Borbála Zsuzsanna Török (Berlin; New York: Walter de Gruyter, 2009), 154 (Kolokol).

36. The pain of this departure is described in AB, *Notatnik*, 56–68.

37. *Wiadomości* 17:32/33 (854/855) (August 12/19, 1962), which included the long appreciation by Terlecki.

38. On other early enthusiasts, see Maciej Urbanowski, *Szczęście pod wulkanem. O Andrzeju Bobkowskim* (Łomianki: LTW, 2013), 13. On Zimand's review as a turning point, see Nowak, "*Szkice piórkiem* w świetle rękopisu dziennika," 37.

39. Zimand, "Posłowie," 542. See Michał Głowiński, "Roman Zimand (1926–1992)," *Gazeta Wyborcza* 858 (April 10, 1992): 9; Michał Głowiński, "Roman Zimand (16 listopada 1926–6 kwietnia 1992)," *Pamiętnik literacki:*

Czasopismo kwartalne poświęcone historii i krytyce literatury polskiej 84/1 (1993): 263–65; and "Zimand Roman," Wirtualny sztetl, online at: https://sztetl.org.pl/pl/biogramy/4234-zimand-roman (accessed 10/1/18).

40. Jan Tomkowski, "Testament Keyserlinga (O Andrzeju Bobkowskim)," in *Sporne postaci polskiej literatury współczesnej: Następne pokolenie*, ed. Alina Brodzka and Lidia Burska (Warsaw: IBL, 1995), 97–98. Tomkowski (b. 1954).

41. Zimand, "Posłowie," 544.

42. Ibid., 552.

43. Miron Białowzewski, *Pamiętnik z powstania warszawskiego* (Warsaw: Państwowy Instytut Wydawniczy, 1971); *A Memoir of the Warsaw Uprising*, trans. and annotated Madeline Levine (New York: New York Review of Books, 2014).

44. Zimand, "Posłowie," 557.

45. Ibid., 558.

46. Quoted, Terlecki, "Andrzej Bobkowski" (1962), 24: "Intelekt? życie, nie intelekt."

47. Entry for September 15, 1940, AB, *Szkice piórkiem* (1957), 1:133–39; AB, *Wartime Notebooks*, 109.

48. Entry for September 22, 1940, AB, *Szkice piórkiem* (1957), 1:163–68; AB, *Wartime Notebooks*, 130.

49. Entry for September 10, 1940, AB, *Szkice piórkiem* (1957), 1:104–11; AB, *Wartime Notebooks*, 86.

50. Posthumously published: Léon Werth, *33 Days*, intro. Antoine de Saint-Exupéry, trans. Austin Denis Johnson (Brooklyn/London: Melville House, 2015), 58, citing Lucien Febvre's description of Keyserling as one of "philosophy's journalists."

51. "Hermann Alexander, Graf von Keyserling," Encyclopaedia Britannica, online at: http://www.britannica.com/EBchecked/topic/315968/Hermann-Alexander-Graf-von-Keyserling (accessed 12/10/18). He was known for *Das Reisetagebuch eines Philosophen: Der kürzeste Weg zu sich selbst führt um die Welt* (1919), *Das Spektrum Europas* (1928), and *Südamerikanische Meditationen* (1932).

52. AB, "Keyserling," *Horyzonty* 7 (1946): 1–7; ibid. 8, 8–13; rpt. in AB, *Ikkos i Sotion oraz inne szkice*, ed. Paweł Kądziela (Warsaw: Biblioteka "Więzi," 2009), 28, 30; note on publication, 209–10. Quoted partially, Plucińska-Smorawska, *Między*, 27. See also Tomkowski, "Testament Keyserlinga," 91–98; Michał Kopczyk, "Bobkowski i Keyserling," in *Andrzej Bobkowski wielokrotnie*, 295–311.

53. PIASA entry for August 11, 1943, quoted ŁM, "Disenchanted Europeans," 326 (Polish) (also ŁM, "Pamięć fabularyzowana," 163); ŁM, *Disenchanted Europeans*, 379. Translations from the Polish excerpts cited in the dissertation are mine throughout. The published version of the dissertation (*Disenchanted Europeans*, 2018), does not include the original Polish of the PIASA citations. The failure in interwar Polish texts to capitalize the word "Jew" usually signified a negative attitude: Brian Porter, "Antisemitism and the Search for a Catholic Identity," in *Antisemitism and its Opponents in Modern Poland*, ed. Robert

Blobaum (Ithaca: Cornell University Press, 2005), 105. Sometimes the only difference between AB's manuscript and the published text is capitalization.

54. Hermann Keyserling, *Europe*, trans. Maurice Samuel (London: Cape, 1928), 218.

55. Ibid., 219.

56. Ibid., 344.

57. AB, "Keyserling," in AB, *Ikkos i Sotion*, 29, 44, 46.

58. AB, notes on Keyserling, *Analyse spectrale de l'Europe*: PIASA, File 45.13, sheet 46.

59. Aleksandr Ścibor-Rylski, "O za długiej książce," *Nowa kultura* 11 (1958), cited Zimand, "Posłowie," 543. See also Maciej Urbanowski, "*Szkice piórkiem* — autentyk czy powieść?" *Dekada Literacka* 15 (75) (1993), rpt. in Urbanowski, *Szczęście pod wulkanem*, 21.

60. Urbanowski, "*Szkice piórkiem* — autentyk czy powieść?" 21–22; Ćwikliński, *Helikopter i kultura masowa*, 241–42.

61. Letter from AB to Terlecki (February 20, 1958), in AB, *Listy do Tymona Terleckiego*, 95. Cited, Urbanowski, "*Szkice piórkiem* — autentyk czy powieść?" 22–23. Terlecki went to France in July 1939 for medical treatment. After joining the Polish Army, he edited the Polish Armed Forces newspaper, first in Paris, then in London until 1948. Remaining in emigration, he worked with Kultura and later taught at the University of Chicago (1964–1972). He died in Oxford. See "Tymon Terlecki. Kronika życia i działalności (1905–2000)," *Pamiętnik Teatralny* 60 (2011), in *Central European Journal of Social Sciences and Humanities*; online at: http://cejsh.icm.edu.pl/cejsh/element/bwmeta1.element.cejsh-6d207357-b1ff-4c4c-92c6-75517946bff3 (accessed 12/10/18).

62. Zimand, "Posłowie," 544–45.

63. Ćwikliński, *Helikopter i kultura masowa*, 252.

64. "O to mi chodzi, o pewną uczciwość wobec czytelnika (wobec siebie)." Urbanowski, "*Szkice piórkiem* — autentyk czy powieść?" 26, quoting letters from AB to his mother, Stanisława Bobkowska, unclear whether dated October 15, 1947 or March 21, 1948.

65. Terlecki, "Andrzej Bobkowski" (1962), 28: "*bezwzględna prawdomówność*."

66. Urbanowski, "*Szkice piórkiem* — autentyk czy powieść?" 26.

67. Ibid., 27.

68. Quoted, Terlecki, "Andrzej Bobkowski" (1962), 28–29, from entry for November 25, 1940, AB, *Szkice piórkiem*, 1:206; AB, *Wartime Notebooks*, 165.

69. Letter from AB to JG (March 22, 1947), in JG, AB, *Listy*, 20. AB's acknowledgment cited in Urbanowski, "*Szkice piórkiem* — autentyk czy powieść?" 23.

70. ŁM, "Pamięć fabularyzowana."

71. ŁM, "Disenchanted Europeans." ŁM is currently a scholar at the Instytut Stosowanych Nauk Społecznych, Department of History of Ideas and Cultural Anthropology, Warsaw University.

72. ŁM, "Disenchanted Europeans," 287–89; ŁM, *Disenchanted Europeans*, 334. My own spot checking of the notebooks against the 1957 edition confirms this assessment.

73. Andrzej Chciuk, "O Andrzeju Bobkowskim i jego listach."

74. Zimand, "Posłowie," 546.

75. Ibid.

76. Urbanowski, "*Szkice piórkiem*—autentyk czy powieść?" 23, citing Konarski, *Cztery lata w okupowanym Paryżu*, [31].

77. Entries for April 14, 1943, and July 1, 1943, AB, *Szkice piórkiem* (1957), 2:248, 267; AB, *Wartime Notebooks*, 436, 450.

78. Daniel Blatman and Renée Poznanski, "Jews and Their Social Environment: Perspectives from the Underground Press in Poland and France," in *Facing the Catastrophe: Jews and non-Jews in Europe during World War II*, ed. Beate Kosmala and Georgi Verbeeck (Oxford; New York: Berg, 2011), 166.

79. By contrast, the memoirs of Szymon Konarski (1894–1981), a Polish bank director, who also spent the war years in Paris, include portraits of individual Jewish figures, as well as commentary on the fate of the Jews in general. Konarski, *Cztery lata w okupowanym Paryżu*, 24–25, and elsewhere.

80. Entries for September 19 and 22, 1941, AB, *Szkice piórkiem* (1957), 1:151–55, 163–68; AB, *Wartime Notebooks*, 205–6. Entries for September 7, 9, 17, 19, 21, 1941, Jacques Biélinky, *Journal, 1940–1942: Un journaliste juif à Paris sous l'Occupation*, ed. Renée Poznanski (Paris: Cerf, 1992), 146, 147, 149, 150.

81. Entries for October 4, 5, 7, 10, 1941, Biélinky, *Journal*, 154–55. Mentioned also in Jean Guéhenno, *Diary of the Dark Years, 1940–1944: Collaboration, Resistance, and Daily Life in Occupied Paris*, trans. David Ball (Oxford: Oxford University Press, 2014), 117. Originally: Jean Guéhenno, *Journal des années noires, 1940–1944* (Paris: Gallimard, 1947).

82. Mentions of Saint-Paul: entries for January 19, 1942, and January 27, 1942, AB, *Szkice piórkiem* (1957), 2:38, 45–47; AB, *Wartime Notebooks*, 267, 275.

83. Entry for October 6, 1941, AB, *Szkice piórkiem* (1957), 1:264; AB, *Wartime Notebooks*, 210.

84. Respectively: entry for June 15, 1940, AB, *Szkice piórkiem* (1957), 1:26; AB, *Wartime Notebooks*, 17; entry for December 1, 1941, AB, *Szkice piórkiem*, 1:281; AB, *Wartime Notebooks*, 224, 225; entry for December 21, 1941, AB, *Szkice piórkiem*, 1:292; AB, *Wartime Notebooks*, 234; entry for April 14, 1943, AB, *Szkice piórkiem*, 2:248; AB, *Wartime Notebooks*, 435. All appear in the PIASA manuscript: File 45.9, Notebook VI (Paris, 2.9.1942–31.12.1941).

85. He was not alone in this curious blindness. As Nicholas Stargardt writes: "For non-Jewish Germans and most Europeans living under German occupation, the deportation and murder of the Jews was neither very secret nor very significant." Nicholas Stargardt, *The German War: A Nation Under Arms, 1939–1945: Citizens and Soldiers* (New York: Basic Books, 2015), 158–59.

86. Photos in Biélinky, *Journal*, facing 161.

87. Blatman and Poznanski, "Jews and Their Social Environment," 200, 211; on Radio London broadcasts, see entry for August 7, 1941, AB, *Szkice piórkiem* (1957), 1:248; AB, *Wartime Notebooks*, 197. On what the Free French said about the fate of the Jews, see Renée Poznanski, "'Nobody is Protected from Deportation': The Free French in London on the Persecution of the Jews," in *Governments-in-exile and the Jews*, ed. Láníček and Jordan, 157, 163–65, 170.

88. AB clippings from René Martel, "La Fenêtre sur la vie," *Paris soir* (January 20 and 22, 1944): PIASA, File 45.5, sheets 57–58. Jacques Biélinky, YIVO, RG 239, Box 4, no pagination.

89. AB, *Szkice piórkiem* (1957), 1:199; AB, *Wartime Notebooks*, 159.

90. AB, *Szkice piórkiem* (1957), 2:392; AB, *Wartime Notebooks*, 551.

91. Entry of May 14, 1942, in Biélinky, *Journal*, 208.

92. Stola, "The Polish Government-in-exile," 100.

93. Quoted from PIASA, ŁM, "Disenchanted Europeans," 322 (Polish); ŁM, *Disenchanted Europeans*, 374.

94. Quoted from PIASA, ŁM, "Disenchanted Europeans," 322 (Polish); ŁM, *Disenchanted Europeans*, 374.

95. Entry for June 1, 1942, AB, *Szkice piórkiem* (1957), 2:110; AB, *Wartime Notebooks*, 318. PIASA, quoted, ŁM, "Disenchanted Europeans," 317 (Polish) (also, ŁM, "Pamięć fabularyzowana," 157); ŁM, *Disenchanted Europeans*, 369.

96. Entry for June 1, 1942, AB, *Szkice piórkiem* (1957), 2:99–100; AB, *Wartime Notebooks*, 318. See Jacques Adler, *The Jews of Paris and the Final Solution: Communal Response and Internal Conflicts, 1940–1944* (Oxford: Oxford University Press, 1987), 42.

97. The entry misdated the onset of the decree, which was in fact June 7, perhaps because in the course of editing AB sometimes moved passages to dates on which they were not written. On rearranging sections: Urbanowski, "*Szkice piórkiem*—autentyk czy powieść?" 27–28; ŁM, *Disenchanted Europeans*, 335.

98. Entry for June 9, 1942, AB, *Szkice piórkiem* (1957), 2:101; AB, *Wartime Notebooks*, 319; quoted, ŁM, "Disenchanted Europeans," 330 (Polish) (also ŁM, "Pamięć fabularyzowana," 170); ŁM, *Disenchanted Europeans*, 370.

99. Point made by ŁM, "Disenchanted Europeans," 330; ŁM, *Disenchanted Europeans*, 385.

100. Entry for September 13, 1940, AB, *Szkice piórkiem* (1957), 1:122; AB, *Wartime Notebooks*, 96. The comments concern black soldiers from Madagascar serving in the French army.

101. Entry for July 17, 1942, Biélinky, *Journal*, 233.

102. Entry for July 24, 1942, ibid., 236.

103. Entry for July 26, 1942, AB, *Szkice piórkiem* (1957), 2:111; AB, *Wartime Notebooks*, 327.

104. Entry for August 4, 1942, AB, *Szkice piórkiem* (1957), 2:114; AB, *Wartime Notebooks*, 329–30.

105. Blatman and Poznanski, "Jews and Their Social Environment," 198–201.

106. Poznanski, "Nobody is Protected," 158, 160–61.

107. Quoted from PIASA, ŁM, "Disenchanted Europeans," 319 (Polish) (also ŁM, "Pamięć fabularyzowana," 159); ŁM, *Disenchanted Europeans*, 372. "Ciekaw jestem czy po tej wojnie będzie ich rzeczywiście mniej w Europie."

108. Quoted from PIASA, ŁM, "Disenchanted Europeans," 320 (Polish) (also ŁM, "Pamięć fabularyzowana," 159); ŁM, *Disenchanted Europeans*, 372.

109. This portion retained: AB, *Szkice piórkiem* (1957), 2:114; AB, *Wartime Notebooks*, 330.

110. Quoted from PIASA, ŁM, "Disenchanted Europeans," 320 (Polish) (also ŁM, "Pamięć fabularyzowana," 159); ŁM, *Disenchanted Europeans*, 372.

111. Entry for August 4, 1942, AB, *Szkice piórkiem* (1957), 2:114; AB, *Wartime Notebooks*, 330.

112. AB, *Szkice piórkiem* (1957), 2:114; AB, *Wartime Notebooks*, 330.

113. Quoted from PIASA, ŁM, "Disenchanted Europeans," 312 (Polish) (also ŁM, "Pamięć fabularyzowana," 156); ŁM, *Disenchanted Europeans*, 363. References are to Henry Morgenthau Jr. (1891–1967), secretary of the treasury under Franklin D. Roosevelt; probably financier Bernard Baruch (1870–1965), economic adviser to FDR; and journalist Walter Lippmann (1899–1974).

114. Quoted from PIASA, ŁM, "Disenchanted Europeans," 313 (Polish) (also ŁM, "Pamięć fabularyzowana," 156); ŁM, *Disenchanted Europeans*, 363.

115. Quoted from PIASA, ŁM, "Disenchanted Europeans," 313 (Polish); ŁM, *Disenchanted Europeans*, 364.

116. Quoted from PIASA, ŁM, "Disenchanted Europeans," 316 (Polish: "*żydowsko-masoński kapitalizm*"); ŁM, *Disenchanted Europeans*, 367.

117. Entry for May 30, 1943, AB, *Szkice piórkiem* (1957), 2:263; AB, *Wartime Notebooks*, 447.

118. Notes on reading: PIASA, File 45.13, sheet 98. "Nieraz przywodzi mi na myśl, czy Hitler nie stanie się kiedyś, mimo wszystko, prorokiem. Jeżeli bolszewizm zaleje Europę, gdy Żyd, po wygranej wojnie, objawi się światu w całej swojej bezczelnej pysze i rozpanoszy się, wowczas kto wie, czy Hitler nie ukazie się w aureoli bojownika o wolność. Paradoksale, ale paradoks zupełnie możliwy, zupełnie do przyjęcia."

119. ŁM, *Disenchanted Europeans*, 367.

120. On the nineteenth-century background, see Brian Porter, *When Nationalism Began to Hate: Imagining Modern Politics in Nineteenth-Century Poland* (New York: Oxford University Press, 2000).

121. Quoted from PIASA, ŁM, "Disenchanted Europeans," 324 (Polish) (also ŁM, "Pamięć fabularyzowana," 161); ŁM, *Disenchanted Europeans*, 376–77. *Wiadomości Literackie* was a liberal Warsaw journal, often attacked by the Endeks in the 1930s: Editors' Introduction to Ksawery Pruszyński, "The Przytyk Market Stands," in *Against Anti-Semitism*, ed. Michnik and Marczyk, 34.

122. Entry for September 12, 1940, AB, *Szkice piórkiem* (1957), 1:118; AB, *Wartime Notebooks*, 92.

123. Jan Grabowski, "Rewriting the History of Polish-Jewish Relations from a Nationalist Perspective: The Recent Publications of the Institute of National Remembrance," *Yad Vashem Studies* 36:1 (2008): 256.

124. ŁM, "Disenchanted Europeans," 314; ŁM, *Disenchanted Europeans*, 365.

125. Quoted from PIASA, ŁM, "Disenchanted Europeans," 323 (Polish) (also ŁM, "Pamięć fabularyzowana," 168); ŁM, *Disenchanted Europeans*, 375.

126. Cited, Sam Johnson, *Pogroms, Peasants, Jews: Britain and Eastern Europe's 'Jewish Question,' 1867–1925* (Houndmills, UK: Palgrave Macmillan, 2011), 159, from Roman Dmowski, "Poland, Old and New," in *Russian Realities and Problems*, ed. J. D. Duff (Cambridge: Cambridge University Press, 1916), 115. On antisemitism in Polish nationalist ideology, see Semion Goldin, "Jews

as Cosmopolitans, Foreigners, Revolutionaries: Three Images of the Jew in Polish and Russian Nationalist Ideology at the End of the Nineteenth and Early Twentieth Centuries," *European Review of History—Revue Européenne d'histoire* 17:3 (2010): 431–44; Andreas Kossert, "Founding Father of Modern Poland and Nationalistic Antisemite: Roman Dmowski," in *In the Shadow of Hitler: Personalities of the Right in Central and Eastern Europe*, ed. Rebecca Haynes and Martyn C. Rady (London: I. B. Tauris, 2011), 89–105; Grzegorz Krzywiec, "Between *Realpolitik* and Redemption: Roman Dmowski's Solution to the 'Jewish Question,'" in *Antisemitism in an Era of Transition: Continuities and Impact in Post-Communist Poland and Hungary*, ed. François Guesnet and Gwen Jones (Frankfurt am Main: Peter Lang, 2014), 69–90; Grzegorz Krzywiec, "Eliminationist Anti-Semitism at Home and Abroad: Polish Nationalism, the Jewish Question and Eastern European Right-Wing Mass Politics," in *The New Nationalism and the First World War*, ed. Lawrence Rosenthal and Vesna Rodic (Houndmills, Basingstoke, Hampshire, UK: Palgrave Macmillan, 2015), 65–91; Grzegorz Krzywiec, *Chauvinism, Polish Style: The Case of Roman Dmowski (Beginnings: 1886–1905)* (Frankfurt am Main: Peter Lang, 2016); Grzegorz Krzywiec, *Polska bez Żydów: Studia z dziejów idei, wyobrażeń i praktyk antysemickich na ziemiach polskich początku XX wieku (1905–1914)* (Warsaw: Instytut Historii PAN, 2017).

127. On the scope of anti-Jewish violence on Polish territory in 1918 and 1919, see Piotr Wróbel, "The Kaddish Years: Anti-Jewish Violence in East-Central Europe, 1918–1921," *Jahrbuch des Simon-Dubnow-Instituts* 4 (2005): 220–21, 222 (in November 1918 more than 100 towns and cities experienced anti-Jewish violence in areas controlled by Polish forces); William W. Hagen, *Anti-Jewish Violence in Poland, 1914–1920* (New York: Cambridge University Press, 2018); Jochen Böhler, *Civil War in Central Europe, 1918–1921: The Reconstruction of Poland* (Oxford: Oxford University Press, 2019), ch. 4.

128. Quoted, Carole Fink, "The Paris Peace Conference and the Question of Minority Rights," *Peace and Change* 21:3 (1996): 287.

129. "Lemberg Pogroms Were Not by Poles. Caused, Paderewski Says, by Ukrainians Who Opened Jails and Armed Criminals," *New York Times* (June 2, 1919), 4; Paul Hanebrink, *A Specter Haunting Europe: The Myth of Judeo-Bolshevism* (Cambridge, MA: Harvard University Press, 2018), 57–58, 79–80. Paderewski's views were echoed by representatives of the Polish community in the United States: "Denies that Poland Is Slaying Jews. Spokesmen Here of the Nation Declares Bolsheviki Were Killed at Pinsk. Statement is Disputed. Manager of Jewish Forward Insists That Reports of Pogroms Have Been Well Substantiated," *New York Times* (May 23, 1919), 2. For the series of charges and denials, see *New York Times*: "36 Jewish Youths Shot. Wrongly Accused at Pinsk of Being Reds, Investigators Report" (May 15, 1919), 3; "Call on Nations to Protect Jews. Massacres in Poland Stir Madison Square Garden Meeting to Earnest Protest" (May 22, 1919), 1; "Jews Give Reports of Polish Pogroms. Answer Denials of Information Bureau Here with Press and Other Statements. Reply by Nathan Straus" (May 27, 1919), 6; "No Polish Pogroms, Paderewski Says. Not a Single Occurrence of the Sort Since He Has Been Premier. All

German Propaganda. Disorders in Russia Placed in Poland to Discredit That Country" (May 29, 1919), 3; "Jewish Ill Treatment Denied by Lubomirski. A Formal Statement by the Polish Minister as to Pogroms and Rumors of Them" (July 27, 1920), 2. On Lemberg, see Wróbel, "Kaddish Years," 221–22; William W. Hagen, "The Moral Economy of Ethnic Violence: The Pogrom in Lwów, November 1918," *Geschichte und Gesellschaft* 31:2 (April-June 2005): 203–26.

130. Oscar I. Janowsky, *The Jews and Minority Rights 1898–1919* (New York: Columbia University Press, 1933), 358–60, 388–89; Fink, "The Paris Peace Conference and the Question of Minority Rights"; Wróbel, "Kaddish Years," 223; Eva Reder, "Im Schatten des polnischen Staates: Pogrome 1918–1920 und 1945/46—Auslöser, Bezugspunkte, Verlauf," *Zeitschrift für Ostmitteleuropa-Forschung* 60:4 (2011): 593–94. David Engel, "Minorities Treaties" (2010), YIVO Encyclopedia of Jews in Eastern Europe, online at: http://www.yivoencyclopedia.org/article.aspx/Minorities_Treaties (accessed 6/6/19).

131. Speech by Stanisław Thugutt (1873–1941), in June 1923, quoted, Paul Brykczynski, *Primed for Violence: Murder, Antisemitism, and Democratic Politics in Interwar Poland* (Madison: University of Wisconsin Press, 2016), 147.

132. Ibid., 122–30.

133. On the conflicts within the Polish political leadership, see most recently: Böhler, *Civil War in Central Europe*, introduction. Also, Brykczynski, *Primed for Violence*, 10–11, 23.

134. Petrażycki had studied in Kiev, Berlin, Heidelberg, Paris, London, and St. Petersburg, and held a chair at St. Petersburg University. He now demonstratively resigned his position in protest over Askenazy's exclusion. "Notes and Comments on Current Topics: Anti-Semitism and the Struggle Against It," *Jewish Tribune* 5 (April 1, 1920): 8; M. R., "Petrajitzki, Askinazi and Warsaw University," *Jewish Tribune* 6 (April 15, 1920): 5. On Petrażycki's biography, see Andrzej Walicki, *Legal Philosophies of Russian Liberalism* (Oxford: Clarendon Press, 1987), 217–26.

135. Szymon Rudnicki, "Anti-Jewish Legislation in Interwar Poland," in *Antisemitism and Its Opponents*, ed. Blobaum, 158–59.

136. Fink, "The Paris Peace Conference and the Question of Minority Rights," 284.

137. David Engel, *In the Shadow of Auschwitz: The Polish Government-in-Exile and the Jews, 1939–1942* (Chapel Hill: University of North Carolina Press, 1987), chs. 2 and 4. Among Jewish leaders, only Jabotinsky looked favorably on the idea of mass migration, since it coincided with his desire to assemble the Jewish diaspora in Palestine. Other Zionists rejected this kind of partnership and most Jewish leaders continued to see a future for Jews in Poland and therefore the continuing need to press for civil rights.

138. Rudnicki, "Anti-Jewish Legislation in Interwar Poland," 160–61.

139. Brykczynski, *Primed for Violence*, 152, 155.

140. He would not have been the only Pole consistently hostile to the Jews who offered them some kind of assistance during the war. See Antony Polonsky, "Beyond Condemnation, Apologetics, and Apologies: On the Complexity of

Polish Behavior towards the Jews during the Second World War," *Studies in Contemporary Jewry* 13 (1997): 207.

141. Entry for April 14, 1943, AB, *Szkice piórkiem* (1957), 2:248; AB, *Wartime Notebooks*, 435.

142. Additional sentence in entry for April 14, 1943, PIASA only: "Nie byłem specjalnie zachwycony tym spotkaniem, bo pomimo wszystko, coraz bardziej nienawidzę Żydów." Quoted from PIASA, ŁM, "Disenchanted Europeans," 325 (Polish); ŁM, *Disenchanted Europeans*, 378.

143. Entry for July 1, 1943, AB, *Szkice piórkiem* (1957), 2:267; AB, *Wartime Notebooks*, 450. PIASA entry for July 1, 1943, quoted, ŁM, "Disenchanted Europeans," 325 (Polish); ŁM, *Disenchanted Europeans*, 378.

144. Entry for May 5, 1943, AB, *Szkice piórkiem* (1957), 2:257–58, reporting news that Tadzio brings from Warsaw; quote, 258; AB, *Wartime Notebooks*, 442.

145. Quoted from PIASA, ŁM, "Disenchanted Europeans," 320 (Polish); ŁM, *Disenchanted Europeans*, 373.

146. Letter from AB to JG, March 2, 1949, in JG, AB, *Listy*, 74: "Panie Jerzy, czy zna Pan jakiś sposób przekonania Żydów, że się nie jest antysemitą?" Also quoted, ŁM, "Disenchanted Europeans," 327; ŁM, *Disenchanted Europeans*, 381.

147. Letter from AB to JG (February 6, 1949), in JG, AB, *Listy*, 67.

148. On the universality and persistence of this feature, which she calls "antisemitism without antisemites": Joanna B. Michlic, "Antisemitism in Contemporary Poland. Does It Matter? And for Whom Does It Matter?" in *Rethinking Poles and Jews: Troubled Past, Brighter Future*, ed. Robert Cherry and Annamaria Orla-Bukowska (Lanham, MD: Rowman and Littlefield, 2007), 160–61.

149. Letter from JG to AB (March 8, 1949), in JG, AB, *Listy*, 77. In 1927, when he went to Palestine, Koestler was a follower of Jabotinsky, whom other Zionists considered a fascist: Louis A. Gordon, "Arthur Koestler and His Ties to Zionism and Jabotinsky," *Studies in Zionism* 12:2 (1991): 152.

150. ŁM, "Disenchanted Europeans," 330–31; ŁM, *Disenchanted Europeans*, 385.

151. Entry for September 1, 1940, AB, *Szkice piórkiem* (1957), 1:82–84; AB, *Wartime Notebooks*, 63.

152. Entry for May 24, 1941, AB, *Szkice piórkiem* (1957), 1:235, 236; AB, *Wartime Notebooks*, 186, 187. Both missing from the May 24, 1941 entry in PIASA, File 45.8, Notebook V (Paris, 29.9.1940–31.12.1940; 1.1.1941–1.9.1941), 89–90, archival no. 342–43.

153. Entry for December 26, 1942, AB, *Szkice piórkiem* (1957), 2:172; AB, *Wartime Notebooks*, 377. Passage missing for same date in PIASA, File 45.9, Notebook VIII (Paris, 3.5.1942–31.12.1942), 175.

154. Entry for March 25, 1943, AB, *Szkice piórkiem* (1957), 2:237; AB, *Wartime Notebooks*, 426. Passage missing in the entry for March 25, 1943 in PIASA, File 45.10, Notebook IX (Paris, 1.1.43–2.5.43), 64–67 (306–9).

155. Blatman and Poznanski, "Jews and Their Social Environment," 186; Shmuel Krakowski, "The Attitude of the Polish Underground to the Jewish

Question during the Second World War," in *Contested Memories: Poles and Jews during the Holocaust and Its Aftermath*, ed. Joshua D. Zimmerman (New Brunswick: Rutgers University Press, 2002), 124, 126 (prevalence of antisemitism in home population).

156. Józef Czapski, *Inhuman Land: Searching for the Truth in Soviet Russia, 1941–1942*, trans. Antonia Lloyd-Jones, intro. Timothy Snyder (New York: New York Review of Books, 2018). His memoir of the Soviet prison camp (*Vspomnienia starobielskie*) was first published by Kultura and in French translation in 1945, the longer version (*Na nieludzkiej ziemi*), also by Kultura, in 1949. On Czapski most recently: Eric Karpeles, *Almost Nothing: The 20th-Century Art and Life of Józef Czapski* (New York: New York Review of Books, 2018).

157. Stola, "The Polish Government-in-exile," 93, 96 ("Antisemitism was a key part of the party identity.").

158. Quoted, in Engel, *In the Shadow of Auschwitz*, 53.

159. Quoted, Stola, "The Polish Government-in-exile," 91. See also Engel, *In the Shadow of Auschwitz*, 72.

160. Aaron Goldman, "The Resurgence of Antisemitism in Britain during World War II," *Jewish Social Studies* 46:1 (1984): 37–50.

161. Stola, "The Polish Government-in-exile," 96–100.

162. Krakowski, "The Attitude of the Polish Underground," 99.

163. Adam Puławski, "The Polish Government-in-exile in London, the Delegatura, the Union of Armed Struggle-Home Army and the Extermination of the Jews," in *Governments-in-exile and the Jews*, ed. Láníček and Jordan, 111; Ben Cion Pinchuk, "Facing Hitler and Stalin: On the Subject of Jewish 'Collaboration' in Soviet-Occupied Eastern Poland, 1939–1941," in *Contested Memories*, ed. Zimmerman, 63, 65.

164. Quoted, Engel, *In the Shadow of Auschwitz*, 60–62.

165. Blatman and Poznanski, "Jews and Their Social Environment," 177.

166. Quoted, Engel, *In the Shadow of Auschwitz*, 71.

167. Ibid., 72–73.

168. Ibid., 73 (quotes), 124–25.

169. *The Persecution of Jews in German-Occupied Poland* (London: Free Europe, 1940), 7. *Free Europe*: a fortnightly review of Central and Eastern European Affairs (London, 1939–1946), whose editorial board included many Polish names. The pamphlet was endorsed by the Bishop Auxiliary of Westminister.

170. Engel, *In the Shadow of Auschwitz*, 75–76.

171. Blatman and Poznanski, "Jews and Their Social Environment," 183.

172. Quoted briefly in demonstration of the Sikorski government's good will: Z. H. Wachsman, *Jews in Post War Europe: The Governments in Exile and Their Attitude Towards the Jews* (New York: H. H. Glanz, 1944), 98.

173. Quoted, David Engel, "Reading and Misreadings: A Reply to Dariusz Stola," in *Polin: Studies in Polish Jewry*, vol. 8: *Jews in Independent Poland, 1918–1939*, ed. Antony Polonsky, Ezra Mendelsohn, and Jerzy Tomaszewski (London: The Littman Library of Jewish Civilization, 2004): 356.

174. Blatman and Poznanski, "Jews and Their Social Environment," 183.

175. Anita J. Prażmowska, *Civil War in Poland, 1942–1948* (Basingstoke, Hampshire, UK: Palgrave Macmillan, 2004), 169.

176. Quoted, Blatman and Poznanski, "Jews and Their Social Environment," 189.

177. Quoted, ibid., 183, from *Barykada* (March 3, 1943). Same quote in Polonsky, "Beyond Condemnation," 215.

178. Quotes from diary entries in 1942 and 1943: Grabowski, "Rewriting the History," 259–61.

179. Blatman and Poznanski, "Jews and Their Social Environment," 187.

180. Anna M. Cienciala, "General Sikorski and the Conclusion of the Polish-Soviet Agreement of July 30, 1941: A Reassessment," *The Polish Review* 41:4 (1996): 401–34.

181. Engel, *In the Shadow of Auschwitz*, 119–20.

182. Prażmowska, *Civil War in Poland*, 169 (quote).

183. Engel, *In the Shadow of Auschwitz*, 122–24.

184. Stola, "The Polish Government-in-exile," 96–97.

185. Puławski, "The Polish Government-in-exile in London," 125; Joanna Beata Michlic and Małgorzata Melchior, "The Memory of the Holocaust in Post-1989 Poland: Renewal—Its Accomplishments and Its Powerlessness," in *Bringing the Dark Past to Light in Postcommunist Europe*, ed. John-Paul Himka and Joanna Beata Michlic (Lincoln: University of Nebraska Press, 2013), 409–10 (on the position of the underground government in Poland, which envisioned a postwar Poland without Jews); Krakowski, "The Attitude of the Polish Underground," 97 (range).

186. Puławski, "The Polish Government-in-exile in London," 126.

187. Quoted, ibid., 127, from "Opór i odpór," *Wiadomości polskie* (November 4, 1942).

188. Krakowski, "The Attitude of the Polish Underground," 102; Stola, "The Polish Government-in-exile," 99.

189. Stola, "The Polish Government-in-exile," 99.

190. Krakowski, "The Attitude of the Polish Underground," 99.

191. Joshua D. Zimmerman, "The Polish Underground Press and the Jews: The Holocaust in the Pages of the Home Army's *Biuletyn Informacyjny*, 1940–1943," in *Warsaw, the Jewish Metropolis: Essays in Honor of the 75th Birthday of Professor Antony Polonsky*, ed. Glenn Dynner et al. (Boston: Brill, 2015), 437–66.

192. Krakowski, "The Attitude of the Polish Underground," 103.

193. Blatman and Poznanski, "Jews and Their Social Environment," 185.

194. Puławski, "The Polish Government-in-exile in London," 129.

195. Engel, *In the Shadow of Auschwitz*, 163–73, 183–84; Stola, "The Polish Government-in-exile," 104. Stola was appointed director of the POLIN Museum of the History of Polish Jews in Warsaw in 2014, a year after the museum opened. His reappointment in 2019 was challenged for political reasons, eliciting widespread protests. As of summer 2019, his status was still unclear.

196. On Żegota: https://www.jewishvirtuallibrary.org/the-379-egota (accessed 11/16/18).

197. Krakowski, "The Attitude of the Polish Underground," 99.

198. Engel, *In the Shadow of Auschwitz*, 201–2.

199. Stola, "The Polish Government-in-exile," 104–5.

200. Keith Sword, *Deportation and Exile: Poles in the Soviet Union, 1939–48* (New York: St. Martin's, 1994), 25–26; Pinchuk, "Facing Hitler and Stalin," 67.

201. Engel, *In the Shadow of Auschwitz*, 126.

202. Ibid., 125–231.

203. Sword, *Deportation and Exile*, 25–26.

204. Engel, *In the Shadow of Auschwitz*, 130. On these two figures, see Czapski, *Inhuman Land*, 121–26.

205. Czapski, *Inhuman Land*, 225, 206, 245.

206. Sword, *Deportation and Exile*, 36–37. See "Kresy-Siberia Foundation Virtual Museum": http://kresy-siberia.org/galleries/liberation/polish-2nd-corps/ (accessed 12/11/18).

207. Quoted, Engel, *In the Shadow of Auschwitz*, 133.

208. Ibid., 134, 138–39; quote, 139.

209. Quoted, ibid., 133.

210. Quoted, ibid., 135.

211. Quoted, ibid.

212. Quoted, ibid., 136.

213. Ibid.

214. Sword, *Deportation and Exile*, ch. 3.

215. Quoted, Engel, *In the Shadow of Auschwitz*, 143.

216. Quoted, ibid., 140.

217. Ibid., 142–43.

218. Tadeusz Kiersnowski (1896–1971), quoted, ibid., 149.

219. Jan Tomasz Gross, *Sąsiedzi: Historia zagłady żydowskiego miasteczka* (Sejny: Pogranicze, 2000); Jan T. Gross, *Neighbors: The Destruction of the Jewish Community in Jedwabne, Poland* (Princeton: Princeton University Press, 2001). See *Wokół Jedwabnego*, ed. Paweł Machcewicz and Krzysztof Persak (Warsaw: Instytut Pamięći Narodowej, 2002); *The Neighbors Respond: The Controversy over the Jedwabne Massacre in Poland*, ed. Antony Polonsky and Joanna Beata Michlic (Princeton: Princeton University Press, 2004); Natalia Aleksiun, "Polish Historians Respond to Jedwabne," in *Rethinking Poles and Jews*, ed. Cherry and Orla-Bukowska, 169–87.

220. Jan T. Gross, *Fear: Anti-Semitism in Poland after Auschwitz: An Essay in Historical Interpretation* (New York: Random House, 2006); Jan T. Gross, with Irena Grudzińska Gross, *Golden Harvest: Events at the Periphery of the Holocaust* (New York: Oxford University Press, 2012).

221. Anna Bikont, *My z Jedwabnego* (Warsaw: Prószyński, 2004; Czarne, 2010); Anna Bikont, *The Crime and the Silence: Confronting the Massacre of Jews in Wartime Jedwabne*, trans. Alissa Valles (New York: Farrar, Straus and Giroux, 2015).

222. Horubała, cited, Beylin et al., "Andrzej Bobkowski—antynacjonalista, apaństwowiec, antysemita?" Cited by Horubała from his earlier essay, "Marzenie o chuliganie," in Andrzej Horubała, "Bobkowski wymyślony,"

website *Do Rzeczy*, online at: https://dorzeczy.pl/1763/Bobkowski-wymyslony.html (accessed 9/24/18).

223. Website, "Andrzej Bobkowski," online at: http://www.andrzej-bobkowski.pl/ (accessed 6/12/19).

224. Website, "Bobkowski 2010," online at: http://bobkowski2010.andrzej-bobkowski.pl/etapy.html (accessed 12/11/18).

225. Muzeum Literatury im. Adama Mickiewicza, "Andrzej Bobkowski. Życie zapisane. Wystawa w 100. lecie urodzin," online at: http://muzeumliteratury.pl/andrzej-bobkowski-zycie-zapisane-wystawa-w-100-lecie-urodzin/ (accessed 9/23/18).

226. Important works include: Urbanowski, *Szczęście pod wulkanem*; *Czytanie Bobkowskiego: Studia o twórczości*, ed. Maciej Nowak (Lublin: Wyd. KUL, 2013); Nowak, *Na łuku elektrycznym*; *Andrzej Bobkowski wielokrotnie*; Ćwikliński, *Helikopter i kultura masowa*; ŁM, *Disenchanted Europeans*. For extensive bibliography of scholarship on AB: Nowak, *Na łuku elektrycznym*, 462–82.

227. Maciej Nowak, "Patrzę inaczej," in *Buntownik, Cyklista, Kosmopolak*, 174.

228. "Andrzej Bobkowski — pisarz legenda, autor kultowych *Szkiców piórkiem*, to dla wielu miłośników literatury wzór intelektualnej niepokorności, bezkompromisowości i przenikliwości." "Bobkowski-demistyfikacja," Notice for Nowak, *Na łuku elektrycznym*, online at: http://angelus.com.pl/2015/02/bobkowski-demistyfikacja/ (accessed 9/24/18).

229. Nowak, "Patrzę inaczej." For Nowak's further reflections on AB, see Nowak, *Na łuku elektrycznym*, and Nowak, "*Szkice piórkiem* w świetle rękopisu dziennika," 33–53.

230. Nowak, in "Aktualność Bobkowskiego," 380; Nowak, "*Szkice piórkiem* w świetle rękopisu dziennika," 43; Nowak, *Na łuku elektrycznym*, 32.

231. Nowak, "Patrzę inaczej," 178; Aleksander Fiut, in "Aktualność Bobkowskiego," 387, comments similarly that AB was "simply a product of his class and time."

232. Nowak, "Patrzę inaczej," 183–84; 184 (quote).

233. Quoted, ibid., 183–84.

234. Ibid., 184–85.

235. Ibid., 184.

236. Ibid., 182 (shocked).

237. Ibid., 387.

238. Nowak, in "Aktualność Bobkowskiego," 380.

239. Kowalczyk, in ibid., 374.

240. Fiut, in ibid., 387.

241. Andrzej Horubała, "Bobkowski wymyślony."

242. Entry for June 9, 1942, AB, *Szkice piórkiem* (1957), 2:101; AB, *Wartime Notebooks*, 319.

243. Beylin, in Beylin et al., "Andrzej Bobkowski — antynacjonalista, apaństwowiec, antysemita?" On Beylin, see Michlic and Melchior, "The Memory of the Holocaust in Post-1989 Poland," 403–4.

244. Rodak, in Beylin et al., "Andrzej Bobkowski — antynacjonalista, apaństwowiec, antysemita?"

245. Entry for September 12, 1940: AB, *Szkice piórkiem* (1957), 1:117–18; AB, *Wartime Notebooks*, 92. The entry in question is dated Saint-Raphaël, September 2, 1940 in the 1957 edition, September 12, 1940 in the 2003/2007 Polish reprint (to correspond with the sequence of dates around it; this dating is followed in the French and English translations). In PIASA, the entry under the heading Saint-Raphaël, September 2, 1940 [File 45.8, Notebook V (Paris, 29.9.1940–31.12.1940; 1.1.1941–1.9.1941), 31–33; archival nos. 161–164], beginning in the same way and including much of the material retained in the 1957/2003 entry, was extensively edited and rewritten. It does not include the passage on Miss Dora Vogel.

246. Terlecki, "Andrzej Bobkowski" (1962), 28.

247. Daniil Samoilovich Pasmanik, *Russkaia revoliutsiia i evreistvo: Bol'shevizm i iudaizm* (Berlin: Franko-russkaia pechat', 1923), 199.

248. Entry for July 24, 1942, Biélinky, *Journal*, 236.

249. Entry for June 4, 1942, ibid., 214–15.

250. Entry for August 8, 1942, ibid., 241. Distrust of Ostjuden was not confined to the Jews of France. For an introduction to this theme: "East European Jews in the German-Jewish Imagination," from the Ludwig Rosenberger Library of Judaica, Joseph Regenstein Library, University of Chicago, Special Collections Exhibition (September 1, 2008–June 30, 2009), online at: https://www.lib.uchicago.edu/collex/exhibits/exeej/ (accessed 12/11/18).

251. On the subject of Western Jews, Joseph Roth writes: "Some of them unfortunately gave in to the temptation to blame Jewish immigrants from the East for the expression of anti-Semitic feeling. It is an oft-ignored fact that Jews, too, are capable of anti-Semitism. One does not want to be reminded by some recent arrival from Lodz of one's own grandfather from Posen or Katowice." Joseph Roth, "Preface to The New Edition" (1937), in *The Wandering Jews*, trans. Michael Hofmann (1927; New York: Norton, 2001), 122.

252. Renée Poznanski, *Être juif en France pendant la Second Guerre mondiale* (Paris: Hachette, 1994), 488–89.

253. Ibid., 478–79; Jacques Semelin, *Persécutions et entraides dans la France occupée: Comment 75% des juifs en France ont échappé à la mort* (Paris: Seuil, 2013), 843, 845–48; Adler, *The Jews of Paris and the Final Solution*, 50.

254. Prażmowska, *Civil War in Poland*, 170–72.

A Tale of Two Mobilizations: Some Conclusions

1. See David Nirenberg, *Anti-Judaism: The Western Tradition* (New York: W. W. Norton, 2013).

2. Tadeusz Mazowiecki, "The Anti-Semitism of Kind and Gentle People," *Więź* (1960), in *Against Anti-Semitism: An Anthology of Twentieth-Century Polish Writing*, ed. Adam Michnik and Agnieszka Marczyk (New York: Oxford University Press, 2018), 185.

3. Hanna Świda-Ziemba, "The Shortsightedness of the 'Cultured,'" *Gazeta Wyborcza* (April 6, 2001), in *The Neighbors Respond: The Controversy over the Jedwabne Massacre in Poland*, ed. Antony Polonsky and Joanna Beata Michlic (Princeton: Princeton University Press, 2004), 119 (e-book pagination).

See also her moving essay: "The Disgrace of Indifference," *Gazeta Wyborcza* (August 17, 1998), in *Against Anti-Semitism*, ed. Michnik and Marczyk, 313–26.

4. Joanna B. Michlic, "Antisemitism in Contemporary Poland. Does It Matter? And for Whom Does It Matter?" in *Rethinking Poles and Jews: Troubled Past, Brighter Future*, ed. Robert Cherry and Annamaria Orla-Bukowska (Lanham, MD: Rowman and Littlefield, 2007), 160.

5. Statement signed by Marek Edelman (1919–2009) and others, online at: http://puszka.waw.pl/pomnik_romana_dmowskiego-projekt-pl-776.html (accessed 10/7/18).

6. Museum website, available at: https://www.polin.pl/en/about-museum/public-private-partnership (accessed 1/8/19). Jan Grabowski, review of *Against Anti-Semitism*, ed. Michnik and Marczyk, *Antisemitism Studies* 2:1 (Spring 2018): 155.

7. Quoted, Joanna Beata Michlic, "'At the Crossroads': Jedwabne and Polish Historiography of the Holocaust," *Dapim: Studies on the Holocaust* 31:3 (2017): 299. For the overall context, see Timothy Garton Ash, "Jesus Rex Poloniae," *New York Review of Books* 65:13 (August 16, 2018): 23–25.

8. For a thorough analysis of the conditions of the pogrom and the involvement of the various postwar political parties, see Anita J. Prażmowska, "The Kielce Pogrom 1946 and the Emergence of Communist Power in Poland," *Cold War History* 2:2 (2002): 101–24. For a scrupulous analysis of the overall character of postwar violence against the Jews, see David Engel, "Patterns of Anti-Jewish Violence in Poland, 1944–1946," *Yad Vashem Studies* 26 (1998): 43–85.

9. Engel, "Patterns," 83 (quotes).

10. Quoted, Jan Grabowski, "Rewriting the History of Polish-Jewish Relations from a Nationalist Perspective: The Recent Publications of the Institute of National Remembrance," *Yad Vashem Studies* 36:1 (2008): 256.

11. Quoted, ibid., 265. As mentioned in chapter 3, a third of Polish citizens deported into the Soviet Union were themselves Jewish. See Keith Sword, *Deportation and Exile: Poles in the Soviet Union, 1939–48* (New York: St. Martin's, 1994), 25–26.

12. Isabel Kershner, "Yad Vashem Rebukes Israeli and Polish Governments Over Holocaust Law," *New York Times* (July 5, 2018), reporting Poland's claim "that the wartime Polish government-in-exile tried to stop the systematic murder of Polish Jews in Nazi death camps by trying to raise awareness among the Western allies, and that it 'created a mechanism of systematic help and support to Jewish people.'" Criticizing the statement, which was endorsed by Israeli Prime Minister Benjamin Netanyahu, Yad Vashem stated: "The Polish government-in-exile and its representatives in occupied Poland 'did not act resolutely on behalf of Poland's Jewish citizens at any point during the war.'"

13. Cited in Anna Bikont, "Jan Gross' Order of Merit," *Tablet* (March 15, 2016), online at: https://www.tabletmag.com/jewish-arts-and-culture/books/198490/jan-gross-order-of-merit (accessed 1/9/19).

14. Text from the league's website, online at: http://rdi-plad.org/ (accessed 1/3/19); see also http://www.anti-defamation.pl/plad/ (accessed 1/3/19).

15. Text from the league's website, online at: http://www.anti-defamation.pl/plad/grabowski-case/ (accessed 1/3/19). Jan Grabowski, *Judenjagd: Polowanie na Żydów 1942–1945: Studium dziejów pewnego powiatu* (Warsaw: Stowarzyszenie Centrum Badań nad Zagładą Żydów, 2011); in English, as Jan Grabowski, *Hunt for the Jews: Betrayal and Murder in German-Occupied Poland* (Bloomington: Indiana University Press, 2013).

16. Quoted from: "Historians Defend Prof who wrote of Poles' Holocaust Complicity," *The Times of Israel* (June 13, 2017), online at: https://www.timesofisrael.com/historians-defend-prof-who-wrote-of-poles-holocaust-complicity/ (accessed 1/3/19).

17. Quote and information from: Paul Lungen, "University of Ottawa Holocaust Historian Sues Polish Group for Libel," *The Canadian Jewish News* (November 22, 2018), online at: https://www.cjnews.com/news/canada/university-of-ottawa-holocaust-historian-sues-polish-group-for-libel (accessed 1/3/19).

18. "Historians Defend Prof who wrote of Poles' Holocaust Complicity."

19. Quote from Parezja.pl, online at: http://parezja.pl/powstancy-byli-antysemitami/ (accessed 10/1/18), defending the honor of the leaders of the Warsaw Uprising. At issue was an article by Michał Cichy (b. 1967), "Poles and Jews: Black Pages in the Warsaw Uprising," *Gazeta Wyborcza* (1994), asserting that some members of the Home Army had murdered Jewish survivors. See Joanna Beata Michlic and Małgorzata Melchior, "The Memory of the Holocaust in Post-1989 Poland: Renewal — Its Accomplishments and Its Powerlessness," in *Bringing the Dark Past to Light in Postcommunist Europe*, ed. John-Paul Himka and Joanna Beata Michlic (Lincoln: University of Nebraska Press, 2013), 418. See also Polonia Christiana website, online at: https://www.pch24.pl/-paszkwil-wyborczej--po-latach-,16739,i.html (accessed 10/1/18). Its statement denounces the "anti-Polish campaign with the goal of transferring responsibility for the Holocaust from the German occupiers onto Poland," portraying "our nation as bestial Jew-murderers."

20. Rafał Pankowski, "The Resurgence of Antisemitic Discourse in Poland," *Israel Journal of Foreign Affairs* (2018): 1–17, online at: http://www.nigdywiecej.org/docstation/com_docstation/20/r._pankowski_the_resurgence_of_antisemitic_discourse_in_poland._israel_journa.pdf (accessed 2/10/19).

21. *Gosudarstvennaia Duma. Stenograficheskie otchety*. Tretii sozyv. 1911 g. Sessiia chetvertaia. Chast' II. Zasedanie 54 (9 II 1911 g.), 1549.

22. Grzegorz Krzywiec, "Eliminationist Anti-Semitism at Home and Abroad: Polish Nationalism, the Jewish Question and Eastern European Right-Wing Mass Politics," *The New Nationalism and the First World War*, ed. Lawrence Rosenthal and Vesna Rodic (Houndmills, Basingstoke, Hampshire, UK: Palgrave Macmillan, 2015), 69–70.

23. See essays in: *Against Anti-Semitism*, ed. Michnik and Marczyk, a selection translated from: *Przeciw antysemityzmowi 1936–2009*, ed. Adam Michnik, 3 vols. (Cracow: Tow. Autorów i Wydawców Prac Naukowych Universitas, 2010). A recent example: "Memory, Identity and the Holocaust: New Studies and Methodological Problems: Conference in Honor of Małgorzata Melchior,"

Warsaw, September 2018, held in the POLIN Museum of the History of Polish Jews, sponsored by the museum, the Institute of Philosophy and Sociology of the Polish Academy of Sciences (Instytut Filozofii i Socjologii, IFIS), the Center for Research on the Jewish Holocaust (Centrum Badań nad Zagładą Żydów), the Polish Academy of Sciences, and Warsaw University. See also the international conference, "November Hopes: Jews and the Independence of Poland in 1918," funded by the Ministry of Science and Higher Education, sponsored by the Polish Society for Jewish Studies, at the POLIN Museum of the History of Polish Jews, November 2018.

24. *Czy Polacy są antysemitami? Wyniki badania sondażowego*, ed. Ireneusz Krzemiński (Warsaw: Oficyna Naukowa, 1996).

25. Alina Cała, *Żyd-wróg odwieczny? Antysemityzm w Polsce i jego źródła* (Warsaw: Wyd. Nisza, 2012), sponsored by the Jewish Historical Institute in Warsaw.

26. Jerzy Jedlicki, "Helplessness," *Gazeta Wyborcza* (June 27, 2009), in *Against Anti-Semitism*, ed. Michnik and Marczyk, 347–56. For a pessimistic assessment: Grabowski, review of *Against Anti-Semitism*, ed. Michnik and Marczyk.

27. David Engel, "Reading and Misreadings: A Reply to Dariusz Stola," in *Polin: Studies in Polish Jewry*, vol. 8: *Jews in Independent Poland* (London: The Littman Library of Jewish Civilization, 2004): 347, citing Norman Davies, "Poles and Jews: An Exchange," *New York Review of Books* 34:6 (April 9, 1987): 43.

28. Carole Fink, "The Paris Peace Conference and the Question of Minority Rights," *Peace and Change* 21:3 (1996): 273–88.

29. Per A. Rudling, "The OUN, the UPA, and the Holocaust: A Study in the Manufacturing of Historical Myths," *Carl Beck Papers*, no. 2107 (Pittsburgh: University of Pittsburgh, 2011), 20. On the complicity of Ukrainians in the Holocaust, see John-Paul Himka, "The Reception of the Holocaust in Postcommunist Ukraine," in *Bringing the Dark Past to Light*, ed. Himka and Michlic, 628–32.

30. Quoted, "The OUN, the UPA, and the Holocaust," 20, from Taras Hunczak, "Ukrainian-Jewish Relations during the Soviet and Nazi Occupations," in *Ukraine during World War II: History and Its Aftermath*, ed. Yuri Boshyk (Edmonton: CIUS, 1986).

31. Quoted, Rudling, "The OUN, the UPA, and the Holocaust," 21, from *Encyclopedia of Ukraine*, ed. Volodymyr Kubijovyč, published Canadian Institute of Ukrainian Studies (University of Toronto: CIUS Press, 1984). In 1969 Hunczak published a defense of Petlyura, rejecting the "undocumented accusations" blaming Petlyura for "alleged crimes against the Jewish people," whereas in fact, he asserted, Petlyura had always been "a supporter of the Jews." Reprinted, revised, as Taras Hunczak, *Symon Petliura and the Jews: A Reappraisal*, rev. ed. (Lviv, New York, Toronto: Ukrainian Historical Association, 2008), frontispiece summary. The 1969 article was vigorously critiqued at the time. See Taras Hunczak, "A Reappraisal of Symon Petliura and Ukrainian-Jewish Relations, 1917–1921," *Jewish Social Studies* 31 (1969): 163–83; and Zosia Szajkowski, "A

Reappraisal of Symon Petliura and Ukrainian-Jewish Relations, 1917–1921: A Rebuttal," *Jewish Social Studies* 31 (1969): 184–213.

32. Quoted, Rudling, "The OUN, the UPA, and the Holocaust," 21, from Petro Mirchuk, *My Meetings and Discussions in Israel: Are Ukrainians "traditionally anti-Semites"?* (New York: Ukrainian Survivors of the Holocaust, 1982), 121, 66.

33. In 1930 the Ukrainian Autocephalous Orthodox Church sponsored the publication of a pamphlet on the trial: Andrii Iakovliv, *Pariz'ka trahediia. 25. travnia 1926 roku: Do protsesu Shvartsbarda* (Prague, 1930; Paris: Komitet oborony pam'iat S. Petliury ta Komitet budovy UAPTs khramu sv. Symona v Paryzhi, 1958). See A. Joukovsky, "The Symon Petliura Ukrainian Library in Paris," *Harvard Ukrainian Studies* 14:1/2 (1990): 218–35; "Ukraine Honors Nationalist Blamed for anti-Jewish Pogroms," *Haaretz* (June 1, 2016), online at: https://www.haaretz.com/jewish/ukraine-honors-nationalist-blamed-for-anti-jewish-pogroms-1.5390122 (accessed 1/5/19).

34. Paul Robert Magocsi and Yohanan Petrovsky-Shtern, *Jews and Ukrainians: A Millennium of Co-Existence* (Toronto: University of Toronto Press for the Chair of Ukrainian Studies, University of Toronto, 2016), 56. For a recent version of the complaint about Soviet propaganda that invokes 1927, see Volodymyr Serhiychuk, *Symon Petliura and the Jewry*, trans. Olexandr Terekh (Kiev: Iunivers, 2000), 2 [originally: Volodymyr Serhiichuk, *Symon Petliura i evreistvo* (Kiev: Biblioteka Ukraïntsia, 1999)], which insists that "opponets [*sic*] of Ukrainian statehood still go on belying [*sic*] one of the greatest statesmen of our people . . . accusing him of Jewish pogroms," while in fact he was "a defender of Jewry in their hard times." Serhiichuk goes on to blame a certain "D. Rabinovich and people like him [who] had learned the art of shouldering guilts on Petliura men still earlier from Lev Trotsky." In 1927, the author says, "vast Jewish groups rushed to defend his killer." Serhiichuk is among historians who insist the OUN was a democratic organization, without antisemitic taint. See Rudling, "The OUN, the UPA, and the Holocaust," 24.

35. Miroslav Popovich, "Petliura: Vstupitel'naia stat'ia," in Simon Vasyl'evych Petliura, *Glavnyi ataman: V plenu nesbytochnykh nadezhd*, ed. Miroslav Popovich and Viktor Mironenko, trans. from Ukrainian G. Lesnaia (Moscow, St. Petersburg: Letnii sad, 2008), 5. Popovich's obituary, online at: http://www.ukrweekly.com/uwwp/myroslav-popovych-philosopher-and-public-figure-87/ (accessed 10/6/18).

36. Popovich, "Petliura," 6.

37. Ibid., 22 (quote), 18, 27.

38. A similarly dispassionate approach is taken by Valery Soldatenko (b. 1946), from 2010 to 2014 head of the Ukrainian Institute of National Memory, more recently associated with the Institute of Political and Ethnonational Research of the Ukrainian Academy of Sciences. V. F. Soldatenko, *Grazhdanskaia voina v Ukraine, 1917–1920 gg.* (Moscow: Novyi khronograf, 2012), 279–301 (on "*atamanshchina*").

39. Per A. Rudling, "Anti-Semitism on the Curriculum: MAUP—The Interregional Academy for Personnel Management," in *Doublespeak: The*

Rhetoric of the Far Right since 1945, ed. Matthew Feldman and Paul Jackson (Stuttgart: ibidem-Verlag, 2014), 192.

40. Information on MAUP from ibid., 170–95. See also Nadine Epstein, "The Mysterious Tale of a Ukrainian University's Anti-Semitic Crusade," *Moment Magazine* (October 12, 2011), online at: https://www.momentmag.com/the-mysterious-tale-of-a-ukrainian-universitys-anti-semitic-crusade/ (accessed 10/5/18).

41. Rudling, "Anti-Semitism on the Curriculum," 173.

42. MAUP's activities are mentioned disapprovingly in Magocsi and Petrovsky-Shtern, *Jews and Ukrainians*, 276. The authors note its spreading influence, but also the reactions against it. They stress Russian efforts to use the issue of MAUP's antisemitism to discredit Maidan and progressive Ukrainian aspirations.

43. From a publication sponsored by MAUP: Vasyl' Iaremenko, *Ievrei v Ukraïny s'ohodni: real'nist' bez mifiv* (Kiev: MAUP, 2003), cited in Rudling, "Anti-Semitism on the Curriculum," 177.

44. Rudling, "Anti-Semitism on the Curriculum," 183.

45. Himka, "The Reception of the Holocaust," 640.

46. John Klier, "Sapper in a Minefield: Russians Read Solzhenitsyn's 'Two Hundred Years Together,'" *Jahrbuch des Simon-Dubnow-Instituts* 2 (2003): 509.

47. *Ubienie Andreia Kievskogo: Delo Beilisa — "smotr sil": Stenograficheskii otchet Kievskogo sudebnogo protsessa* (Moscow: Russkaia ideia, 2006), 6, 9, 8. For a defense against charges of "antisemitism": M. V. Nazarov and A. R. Anzimirov, *Disput Nazarova s Katsmanom o "pravoslavnom antisemitizme"* (Moscow: Russkaia ideia, 2011).

48. *Ubienie Andreia Kievskogo*, 8. For a more sophisticated approach to Orthodox antisemitism, see *Iudaizm: Pro et Contra: Konfessional'nye faktory formirovaniia tsennostnoi struktury rossiiskoi tsivilizatsii: Antologiia*, ed. I. S. Kaufman, E. S. Norkin, and R. V. Svetlov (St. Petersburg: Russkaia khristianskaia gumanitarnaia akademiia, 2017).

49. "Obrashchenie k General'nomu prokuroru RF V. V. Ustinovu v sviazi s usilivshimsia primeneniem k russkim patriotam St. 282 UK RF o 'vosbuzhdenii natsional'noi rozni' po otnosheniiu k evreiam," dated March 7/20, 2005, *Russkaia ideia* (September 15, 2017), online at: https://rusidea.org/ (accessed 10/3/18). See Aleksandr Verkhovskii, "Antisemitism v Rossii, 2005 g.: Osnovnye sobytiia i novye tendentsii," in SOVA Informatsionno-analiticheskii tsentr, dated March 15, 2006, online at: https://www.sova-center.ru/racism-xenophobia/publications/antisemitism/articles-reports/2006/03/d7539/ (accessed 10/3/18). The term used by Nazarov is "*chelovekonenavistnicheskii*."

50. On the numbers: Verkhovskii, "Antisemitism v Rossii, 2005 g."

51. Mikhail Nazarov, *Zhit' bez strakha iudeiska! O prichinakh i tseli "Pis'ma 5000"* (Moscow: Russkaia ideia, 2005). The phrase "*zhit' bez strakha iudeiska*" is a Russian idiom derived from John 19:38, in which John of Arimathea asks Pontius Pilate to allow him to remove Christ from the cross. John is described (King James) as "a disciple of Jesus, but secretly for fear of the Jews" (modern Russian version: "*iz strakha ot Iudeev*"). As an idiom, the phrase means to live

without fear of the authorities. In the Gospel context, it is fear of the Jewish clerics, who will punish John for following Christ. As a protest against the Jews sticking up for themselves, in this case invoking the power of the law (the Russian criminal code), it taps into the notion of the Jews as all-powerful, always a threat to true Christians, as they were in Biblical times to Christ himself. Nazarov plays the role of John petitioning Pontius Pilate, but in the open, not in secret, unafraid to defy the Jews. Thanks to Irina Paperno for pointing me to the New Testament origins.

52. Photo on the cover of: Nazarov, *Zhit' bez strakha iudeiska!*

53. Russian Idea website, online at: https://rusidea.org/ (accessed 10/3/18).

54. Verkhovskii, "Antisemitism v Rossii, 2005 g."

55. Levada Center and Memorial websites, online at: http://www.levada.ru/en/; http://old.memo.ru/s/307.html (accessed 10/7/18).

56. Case against SOVA, online at: https://www.sova-center.ru/about-us/nashi-slozhnosti/2017/12/d38562/ (accessed 10/3/18).

57. For example: Viktor Kozlov, *Evrei v Rossii-SSSR: Realii zhizni i mify "antisemitizma"* (Moscow: Russkaia Pravda, 2010), 7ff, praises Solzhenitsyn, along with I. R. Shafarevich (1923–2017), the notoriously antisemitic Soviet-era mathematician: ibid., 11. This confused screed is subtitled "the myth of anti-semitism." Kozlov reproaches the Jews for thinking Stalin was an antisemite, whereas, he insists, Stalin was a Jew-loving Russophobe. The Jews, for their part, first helped destroy tsarism (among them, the partly Jewish Lenin), then helped destroy the Soviet Union (ibid., 302–3).

58. A. I. Solzhenitsyn, *Dvesti let vmeste (1795–1995)*, 2 vols. (Moscow: Russkii put', 2001, 2002). *Russkii put'* (The Russian Way) is a continuation of the Paris "YMCA-Press," which, since 1921, had been publishing Russian émigré authors. With Solzhenitsyn's support, the press was brought back home and established in Moscow. See website, online at:https://www.rp-net.ru/publisher/about/ (accessed 10/3/18).

59. A. Solzhenitsyn, trans. Jamey Gambrell, "Two Hundred Years Together," *Common Knowledge* 9:2 (2003): 205–6. This text is excerpted from the introductions to the first volume and to the section on World War I.

60. Klier, "Sapper in a Minefield," 502. Klier provides an overview of reactions in Russia.

61. Ibid., 509, 503.

62. Richard Pipes, "Solzhenitsyn and the Jews, Revisited: Alone Together," *New Republic* 22 (November 25, 2002): 28. Similarly clean bill of health: Geoffrey A. Hosking, "Love-Hate Relationship," *Times Literary Supplement* (March 1, 2002): 3–4.

63. John Klier, "No Prize for History," *History Today* 52:11 (November 2002): 60. On Solzhenitsyn's antisemitic clichés, see Valentin Oskotskii, *"Evreiskii vopros" po Aleksandru Solzhenitsynu* (Moscow: Academia, 2004), and Semen Gleizer, *Anti-Solzhenitsyn: Dvesti let kak zhizni net* (Moscow: Blue Apple, 2005).

64. Klier, "Sapper in a Minefield," 500 (rankled).

65. Paul Hanebrink, *A Specter Haunting Europe: The Myth of Judeo-Bolshevism* (Cambridge, MA: Harvard University Press, 2018), 4.

66. Quoted, Gleizer, *Anti-Solzhenitsyn*, 59.

67. Quoted, ibid., 60.

68. Solzhenitsyn, *Dvesti let vmeste*, 2:54–55.

69. Ibid., 2:58.

70. Ibid., 2:75–77.

71. Quoted, Anshel Pfeffer, "With Orban and Soros, Hungary's Jews Trapped Between pro-Israel and anti-Semitic Politics," *Haaretz* (Budapest, July 18, 2018), online at: https://www.haaretz.com/world-news/europe/.premium.MAGAZINE-hungary-s-jews-trapped-between-pro-israel-and-anti-semitic-politics-1.6289081 (accessed 10/30/18).

72. Ibid.

73. Ibid. Also Allison Kaplan Sommer, "Why Netanyahu Hates George Soros So Much," *Haaretz* (September 10, 2017), online at: https://www.haaretz.com/us-news/why-netanyahu-hates-george-soros-so-much-1.5493574 (accessed 1/11/19).

74. Pfeffer, "With Orban and Soros."

75. Quotes from ibid. and online responses to the article.

76. Quoted, ibid. On Léderer, online at: https://www.helsinki.hu/en/about_us/our-team/andras-lederer/ (accessed 4/10/19).

77. Josh Glancy, "Getting Off the Fence About Jeremy Corbyn's Anti-Semitism," *New York Times* (August 27, 2018), online at: https://www.nytimes.com/2018/08/27/opinion/jeremy-corbyn-anti-semitism-labour-britain.html?action=click&module=Opinion&pgtype=Homepage (accessed 8/28/18). For historical context, see Anthony Julius, *Trials of the Diaspora: A History of Anti-Semitism in England* (Oxford: Oxford University Press, 2010); see also Bari Weiss, "Europe's Jew Hatred, and Ours," *New York Times* (November 29, 2018), online at: https://www.nytimes.com/2018/11/29/opinion/antisemitism-europe-jews.html (accessed 8/28/18).

78. Robert Peston, "Labour Poised to adopt International Holocaust Remembrance Alliance anti-Semitism definition 'in full'" (August 28, 2018), ITV website, online at: http://www.itv.com/news/2018-08-28/labour-poised-to-adopt-ihra-in-full/ (accessed 8/28/18).

79. Bret Stephens, "Ilhan Omar Knows Exactly What She Is Doing: The Minnesota Democrat is bringing Corbynism to the Democratic Party," *New York Times* (March 7, 2019), online at: https://www.nytimes.com/2019/03/07/opinion/ilhan-omar-anti-semitism.html (accessed 4/10/19).

80. Information in this paragraph from: Kenneth P. Vogel, Scott Shane, and Patrick Kingsley, "How Vilification of George Soros Moved from the Fringes to the Mainstream," *New York Times* (October 31, 2018), online at: https://www.nytimes.com/2018/10/31/us/politics/george-soros-bombs-trump.html (accessed 10/31/18). See shocking video included.

81. Ibid.

INDEX

THE MENAHEM STERN JERUSALEM LECTURES

Sponsored by the HISTORICAL SOCIETY OF ISRAEL
Published by BRANDEIS UNIVERSITY PRESS

Laura Engelstein, *The Resistible Rise of Antisemitism: Exemplary Cases from Russia, Ukraine, and Poland*

Keith Thomas, *In Pursuit of Civility: Manners and Civilization in Early Modern England*

Peter Burke, *Exiles and Expatriates in the History of Knowledge, 1500–2000*

Paul R. Katz, *Religion in China and Its Modern Fate*

Richard J. Evans, *Altered Pasts: Counterfactuals in History*

Patrick J. Geary, *Language and Power in the Early Middle Ages*

G. W. Bowersock, *Empires in Collision in Late Antiquity*

Sanjay Subrahmanyam, *Three Ways to Be Alien: Travails and Encounters in the Early Modern World*

Jürgen Kocka, *Civil Society and Dictatorship in Modern German History*

Heinz Schilling, *Early Modern European Civilization and Its Political and Cultural Dynamism*

Brian Stock, *Ethics through Literature: Ascetic and Aesthetic Reading in Western Culture*

Fergus Millar, *The Roman Republic in Political Thought*

Peter Brown, *Poverty and Leadership in the Later Roman Empire*

Anthony D. Smith, *The Nation in History: Historiographical Debates about Ethnicity and Nationalism*

Carlo Ginzburg, *History, Rhetoric, and Proof*